REVIEWS IN ENGINEERING GEOLOGY
VOLUME VIII

NEOTECTONICS IN EARTHQUAKE EVALUATION

Edited by
Ellis L. Krinitzsky
Geotechnical Laboratory
Waterways Experiment Station
Corps of Engineers
Vicksburg, Mississippi 39180-0631

D. Burton Slemmons*
Center for Neotectonic Studies
Mackay School of Mines
University of Nevada
Reno, Nevada 89557-0047

The Geological Society of America
3300 Penrose Place, P.O. Box 9140
Boulder, Colorado 80301
1990

*Present address: 2905 Autumn Haze Lane, Las Vegas, Nevada 89117.

Published by The Geological Society of America, Inc.
3300 Penrose Place, P.O. Box 9140, Boulder, Colorado 80301

Printed in U.S.A.

GSA Books Science Editor Richard A. Hoppin

Library of Congress Cataloging-in-Publication Data

Neotectonics in earthquake evaluation / edited by Ellis L. Krinitzsky
    and D. Burton Slemmons.
        p.   cm. — (Reviews in engineering geology ; v. 8)
    Includes bibliographical references.
    ISBN 0-8137-4108-4
    1. Neotectonics—United States—Congresses.   2. Earthquake
prediction—United States—Congresses.   3. Engineering geology—
United States—Congresses.   I. Krinitzsky, E. L.   II. Slemmons,
David B.   III. Series.
TA705.R4   vol. 8
[QE511.42]
624.1'51   s—dc20
[551.2'2]   90-3653
                                                     CIP

10   9   8   7   6   5   4   3   2

Contents

Foreword

This symposium brings together a group of papers that provide guidance for geological assessments of earthquake hazards throughout the contiguous United States.

The relevant literature on the geological aspects of earthquake assessment has become so extensive in recent years that it is both timely and desirable to attempt summaries for key areas. The contributors to this volume have addressed recent developments in their respective regions in new and useful syntheses of current knowledge. The Pacific Coast, the western mountain area, the New Madrid area, New England, and southeastern United States, including Charleston, South Carolina, are reviewed. These are the principal seismically active regions of the United States. Among the contributors are researchers who have made notable additions to the art in their own right.

These investigators have compiled a guide to what is, in effect, the state of the art for assessing earthquake sources. In this regard, we anticipate that their efforts will serve a very practical necessity.

We were helped by many fine reviews, for which we wish to express our gratitude, by Charles W. Welby, Christopher C. Mathewson, Robert C. Bucknam, Leon Reiter, Steven Wesnousky, Robert E. Wallace, Antony J. Crone, David P. Schwartz, Michael N. Machette, Roy J. Shlemon, Robert L. Schuster, Richard Meeuwig, Walter W. Hays, and Allen W. Hathaway.

Ellis L. Krinitzsky
D. Burton Slemmons

Geological Society of America
Reviews in Engineering Geology, Volume VIII
1990

Chapter 1

Estimation of earthquake size for seismic hazards

Craig M. dePolo
Nevada Bureau of Mines and Geology, University of Nevada, Reno, Nevada 89557
D. Burton Slemmons
Center for Neotectonic Studies, Mackay School of Mines, University of Nevada, Reno, Nevada 89557

ABSTRACT

This chapter presents a structured organization of the various types of seismic-hazard estimates, approaches, scaling parameters, techniques, and data used in the estimation of potential earthquake sizes. This organization is designed to facilitate the use of multiple techniques, so that a greater amount of data can be incorporated into the size estimate. An earthquake size analysis begins with the determination of the type of seismic hazard to be estimated, such as characteristic, maximum, maximum credible, or floating earthquakes. The characteristic earthquake is defined as one that is characteristic of a particular fault or area. The maximum earthquake generally is defined as the largest to occur during a given time period, whereas the maximum credible earthquake is the largest that is reasonably physically possible, irrespective of the frequency of occurrence. Floating earthquakes occur along unidentified sources, e.g., along smaller faults adjacent to the major fault zones. The various types of estimates can be made at different levels of conservatism and probabilities of occurrence. Five approaches to earthquake size analysis are: historical earthquake, paleoseismic, source characterization, regional, and relative comparison approaches. For each of these, various parameters are used to scale earthquake size, including fault rupture length, fault rupture area, fault displacement, seismic moment calculations, and strain rates. Techniques include the specific correlations and equations used in the analysis. Data include the information collected and its associated uncertainties. The combined use of several approaches, scaling parameters, techniques, and data may reduce the overall uncertainty (or increase the confidence) in the analysis. Logic trees offer a useful format for presenting multiple estimates and uncertainties in an explicit manner. It is important to understand the type of earthquake size estimate made (e.g., local magnitude, surface-wave magnitude, or seismic moment), and to be internally consistent about the type used throughout the analysis, most importantly in the techniques and data. Current research in seismic-hazard analysis includes studies in intraplate regions (e.g., central and eastern United States) and on fold-related, subduction-zone, and volcanic earthquake sources.

INTRODUCTION

Estimating the size of earthquakes that can occur along a fault or within a given region is a fundamental element of any analysis of seismic hazards. Estimating earthquake size, however, is not simple, and many approaches and methods have been used in the last few decades. The intent of this chapter is to summarize these approaches and methods, and to endorse the use of several

estimation techniques together to enhance the understanding and credibility of the final value. Different types of earthquake size estimates are discussed; then an organization of the various techniques is presented, followed by brief descriptions of these techniques. Fold-, subduction-, and volcanic-related earthquake sources are described at the end of the chapter, and different types of earthquake size measurements are described in Appendix A.

The diversification of methodologies is due, in part, to the

dePolo, C. M., and Slemmons, D. B., 1990, Estimation of earthquake size for seismic hazards, *in* Krinitzsky, E. L., and Slemmons, D. B., Neotectonics in earthquake evaluation: Boulder, Colorado, Geological Society of America Reviews in Engineering Geology, v. 8.

variability in the character and expression of seismic sources and in the amount and kinds of data available. A need for different kinds of estimates also arises when dealing with considerations such as designing for high-risk versus low-risk engineering structures.

The appraisal of earthquake size is feasible because historical data show a correlation between earthquake size and such fault parameters as surface rupture length, surface displacement, and fault rupture area. Earthquake size estimates from these correlations can be combined with historical earthquake data and direct-source size calculations to produce a final earthquake size estimate.

ESTIMATING EARTHQUAKE SIZES

An estimation procedure has been organized into five parts to aid in understanding the individual components making up the procedure. These divisions are: the type of seismic-hazard estimate, approaches, scaling parameters, techniques, and data (Fig. 1, Table 1).

Several types of seismic-hazard estimations have been used to accommodate the wide range of risks posed by various engineering structures. These estimates vary in their degree of conservatism and the time frames considered. Some structures, such as a warehouse that is rarely occupied and houses inexpensive items, do not have to be built as seismically resistant as more critical structures, such as nuclear power plants, whose failure would be more hazardous to a greater population. There will be differences in the conservatism of the respective designs of these structures, and different levels of potential earthquake hazards will be considered. This consideration—the level of potential earthquake hazards—is accommodated by having different types of seismic-

TABLE 1. ORGANIZATION OF TYPES OF SEISMIC-HAZARD ESTIMATES, APPROACHES, SCALING PARAMETERS, TECHNIQUES, AND DATA

Types of Seismic-Hazard Estimates
    Characteristic earthquake
    Maximum earthquake
    Maximum credible earthquake
    Floating earthquake

Approaches
    Historical earthquake
    Paleoseismic
    Source characterization
    Regional
    Relative comparison

Scaling Parameters
    Historical seismicity
    Fault rupture length
    Fault rupture area
    Fault displacement
    Seismic moment
    Strain rate

Techniques
    Earthquake-size–fault-parameter correlations
    Fractional fault length
    Segmentation
    Seismic-moment calculations
    Magnitude-frequency relations
    Maximum likelihood statistics
    (and many others)

Data
    Fault-rupture measurements
    Fault geometry
    Slip rate
    Historical seismicity catalog
    Shear modulus
    Depth of the seismogenic zone
    (and many others)

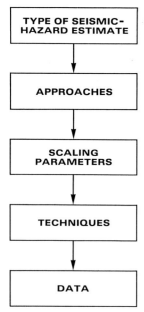

Figure 1. Flow chart showing the major categories developed for the earthquake size estimation procedure.

hazard estimates. Which kind of seismic hazard estimate is needed guides much of the development of a specific seismic-hazard analysis. For example, how the uncertainties in data are considered or weighed in the analysis can be largely a function of the type of seismic-hazard estimate.

Approaches are general ways of estimating earthquake size. Five are presented: the historical-earthquake, paleoseismic, source-characterization, regional, and relative-comparison approaches. These have different relative levels of uncertainty about how the evaluation relates to the seismic source being investigated. For example, if a large earthquake has occurred along a fault and can be adequately characterized, there is a high degree of confidence that the fault is capable of this kind of event. In contrast, estimating the size of a potential event from regional data or comparisons involves considerably more uncertainty.

Scaling parameters are the various parameters or concepts used to scale the earthquake size. Examples of scaling parameters are fault rupture length, surface displacement, rupture area, and seismic moment.

Techniques are the specific empirical and stochastic relations used to estimate earthquake sizes. The data are simply the various input values used for the size estimation. These two categories represent the two largest uncertainties in the estimate. Table 1 is a partial list of common techniques and data.

This organizational scheme can be used as a guideline to aid in conducting a diverse estimation analysis. Flow diagrams and logic trees can be constructed to illustrate an analysis for specific sources and situations using an organizational chart similar to Table 1.

The use of multiple approaches, scaling parameters, techniques, and data is strongly encouraged. Coppersmith (1982) summarized the use of multiple techniques:

> Because each of the magnitude-estimation approaches is subject to some uncertainties, the use of several can result in more reliable estimates of maximum magnitude than the application of any single technique. In this way a wide range of fault behavioral information can be included in the analysis, and the resulting magnitude estimates will be those that are best substantiated by the available data.

Using the multiple approach can lead to an improved understanding of seismic sources, assist in evaluating uncertainties of a size estimation, help gain greater confidence in an estimation value or range, and help flag unusual situations or incompletely expressed fault parameters.

At all steps throughout the estimation process, uncertainties in the techniques and data need to be evaluated and recorded. A complete earthquake size evaluation includes the best value for the type of estimate(s) needed and an evaluation of the uncertainties involved, sometimes expressed as a range in the estimate. A detailed discussion describing the methods and data used, and their associated uncertainties, is important for evaluating the results. These discussions aid future decisions that will be based on the earthquake size estimate.

TYPES OF SEISMIC-HAZARD ESTIMATES

Many types of earthquake size estimates have been named and defined in earthquake-hazard studies to describe or communicate different levels of seismic hazards. At first, the maximum historical earthquake, the largest earthquake recorded in an area, was considered for design purposes. When it was realized that this is not always an adequate procedure because the historical time frame was significantly shorter than the recurrence interval of most large earthquakes, the time frame was extended through statistical and geological techniques. Later, worst-case scenarios were considered for critical structures; these included estimates such as the maximum credible earthquake, which is the largest

earthquake a fault zone can reasonably produce. Recent studies have focused on taking a closer look at the fault data and interpreting the size and frequency of events that have occurred along a fault zone, and synthesizing these data into estimates of the future sizes of earthquakes and their likelihood of occurrence.

A low-risk structure is commonly designed for the maximum earthquake that can be expected during the lifetime of the structure. This may be determined through probabilistic techniques and historical-earthquake data. The seismic-hazard analysis for high-risk structures usually requires a more deterministic input of potentially hazardous seismic sources. A maximum earthquake for a longer time period, or a maximum credible earthquake, might be estimated for these potential sources. A typical seismic-hazard analysis for a high-risk structure consists of characterizing several potential seismic sources. The potential earthquake with the largest impact on the structure or a combination of characteristics from different earthquakes is synthesized into a single earthquake for which the structure is designed. This final earthquake estimate is commonly called the "design earthquake" or the "safety evaluation earthquake." Regulatory agencies often require a specific type of analysis and seismic-hazard estimate for high-risk engineering structures.

A few types of commonly used earthquake estimates are presented in this section; specifically the characteristic, maximum, maximum credible, and floating earthquake.

Characteristic earthquake

"Characteristic earthquake" is a relatively new term proposed by Schwartz and others (1981). It defines earthquakes that are characteristic for a particular area or fault zone. Schwartz and others (1981) and Schwartz and Coppersmith (1984) suggested that segments (sections of a fault or faults that fail during individual earthquakes) of some fault zones fail repeatedly with earthquakes of similar size and in a similar manner. They define these earthquakes of similar size as "characteristic earthquakes." The characteristic earthquake is commonly associated with a recurrence interval that can be determined directly from seismic, paleoseismic, and geological data.

Maximum earthquake

The term "maximum earthquake" has been used since the 1960s and is widely used today (Albee and Smith, 1966; Housner, 1969; Wentworth and others, 1969; Schwartz and others, 1984). A number of definitions and interpretations of the maximum earthquake have been presented, making it especially important to define the term when it is used. A time frame or recurrence interval is commonly associated with the maximum earthquake.

In general, the maximum earthquake can be defined as the largest earthquake expected to occur over a given time interval or exposure time, and is determined using geological and seismological techniques, including fault parameter correlations, source characterization, and historical seismicity. The term "maximum earthquake" is also used for "probabilistic earthquakes," such as the maximum earthquake in a 100-yr time period (sometimes called the "maximum-probable earthquake."). Another, contemporary usage of the term "maximum earthquake" is in reference to the largest earthquake to occur in the magnitude-frequency distribution of a fault.

An example of the use of maximum earthquakes is a review of the proposed liquefied natural gas (LNG) facility at Little Cojo Bay, Santa Barbara County, California, by the LNG seismic review panel (Cluff and others, 1981). The panel presented maximum earthquakes for three different time periods: several hundred years, several thousand years, and several tens of thousands of years. Maximum-earthquake estimates were then made for faults at different distances away from the site (Table 2). The different estimates could then be used for the appropriate time frames and respective risks of different components of the structure.

Maximum credible earthquake

The term "maximum credible earthquake" (MCE) means the largest or maximum earthquake that appears capable of occurring in an area or along a fault (California Division of Mines and Geology, 1975). The maximum credible earthquake is a time-independent earthquake estimate, which distinguishes it from a maximum earthquake.

Common practices of estimating maximum credible earthquakes include maximizing physical characteristics of an earthquake source, using multiple segment failures, or adding an incremental value to historical earthquake data. Maximum credible earthquake estimates are generally used for long-lived, high-risk engineering projects. For example, it is common practice to design large dams to survive maximum credible earthquakes (Federal Emergency Management Agency, 1985; United States Committee on Large Dams, 1985).

Floating earthquakes

Floating earthquakes are earthquakes that occur between the larger seismogenic structures and/or from unidentified sources. They are sometimes referred to as "random earthquakes." This estimate represents the earthquake hazard posed from background seismicity, which is commonly not related to specific faults. The notion of the randomness of floating earthquakes depends on the context; an earthquake is created by some disruptive event—faulting or explosion—but we are limited in our current capabilities to detect all of the sources. Many smaller faults occur between the major faults and can be difficult to identify or characterize with respect to seismic hazard. Many of these faults have no surface expression and/or are difficult to identify as active. In most cases, it is simply not cost effective to try to identify all of the smaller potential earthquake sources, yet these sources can pose significant hazards.

TABLE 2. MAXIMUM EARTHQUAKES PROPOSED BY THE LIQUID NATURAL GAS REVIEW PANEL*

Earthquake Source	Distance From Site (km)	(A) 100s of yrs	(B) 1,000s of yrs	(C) 10s of 1,000s of yrs
F-1 faults	5	4 3/4	5 3/4	6 3/4
Near regional faults	12	5 1/2	6 1/2	7 1/2
Far regional faults	50	7	N/A	N/A
San Andreas fault	100	8 1/4	8 1/4	8 1/2

Notes: Magnitudes 6 1/2 and greater are assumed to be surface-wave magnitudes, M_S. Magnitudes less than 6 1/2 are assumed to be local magnitudes, M_L.

For earthquakes on the F-1 and near regional faults, the magnitudes at the three levels of recurrence are based on a b-value (a parameter in the assumed, standard recurrence curve) of 1.0, and if the rarest event approximates the *maximum credible*, the recurrence curve must truncate sharply at that point. Both assumptions can be debated; the Panel feels that its analysis represents a reasonably prudent and conservative approach to the problem.

N/A = not applicable, because it is judged that earthquakes on faults at about this distance will not control design parameters.

*From Cluff and others, 1981.

The larger floating earthquakes can have magnitudes in the range of 5 to 6.5, depending on seismotectonic settings. Moderate-size floating earthquakes occurring close to urban areas are of major concern. In some areas, especially intraplate areas, seismic zones can be delineated, but the causative seismogenic structures cannot. A floating earthquake can be assigned to these zones. Floating-earthquake values are often determined from historical seismicity and/or by comparing an area to another similar source area for which the seismic hazard is established.

Floating earthquakes are usually small to moderate and can occur anywhere in a region or area. Since the probability of the floating earthquake occurring directly under a specific site is low, the earthquake is sometimes assigned to occur within a prescribed or statistically estimated distance from the site.

APPROACHES

Historical earthquake approach

The historical earthquake approach involves studying historical earthquakes that have occurred on or near a seismic source under consideration. Techniques include the examination of historical records, seismological data, and measurements of surface offsets associated with historical ruptures. Guidelines for evaluating earlier historical earthquakes are presented by Ambraseys (1983).

One of the most attractive features of the historical earthquake approach is that in cases where the data are good, uncertainties associated with the approach can be small. For example, an earthquake of approximately magnitude 8 occurred along the south-central part of the San Andreas fault system in 1857. There is no uncertainty that this section of the San Andreas fault zone is capable of an earthquake the size of the 1857 event.

Historical earthquakes can commonly be used as a lower bound for maximum earthquake estimations. When a historical event is large enough to match its paleoseismic (prehistorical) counterpart, the event can be used as the characteristic or maximum earthquake value directly. However, because maximum earthquakes occur rarely and the historical record is usually short, historical earthquake data provide useful constraints for only a small percentage of potential seismic sources, mostly in more highly active interplate regions.

Paleoseismic approach

The paleoseismic approach is essentially an extension of the historical record and involves the identification and characterization of prehistoric earthquake events. This is usually accomplished by detailed study of the geologic record at locations directly along seismic sources, and indirect studies of adjacent areas that have been affected by paleoseismic events. These studies provide information that can be used to estimate the paleo-earthquake size.

The field of paleoseismology is growing rapidly with new ideas and techniques. These include development of new techniques and strategies for trenching studies, quantitative tectonic geomorphological studies, and new age-determination techniques (Keller and Rockwell, 1984; Pierce, 1986; Allen, 1986, Crone and Omdahl, 1988). These studies are leading to a better understanding of earthquake processes and allow for collection of more data for seismic-hazard analyses.

The paleoseismic approach is similar to the historical earthquake approach in that both usually address an event that is directly attributable to a specific source. A distinction between the two approaches is the added uncertainty associated with the data and interpretation of paleoseismic events, and the different methods and techniques used. A tremendous advantage of paleoseismic studies is that they offer the opportunity to extend the earthquake record beyond the historical record to the actual recurrence time of large earthquake events. Good paleoseismic evidence can become one of the strongest considerations when making decisions about the seismic potential of a source.

The variability in earthquake source characteristics, surficial expression, and locations with evidence of paleoseismic events can make it difficult to gather paleoseismic data, and there can be large uncertainties, especially when data from only one site are used. To counter these problems, several study sites along a fault zone and multiple techniques are commonly required to piece together the paleoseismic history (e.g., multiple trenching studies,

tectonic geomorphic studies, and detailed mapping of surficial geology).

Source-characterization approach

The source-characterization approach is presently the most commonly used approach. The approach involves analyzing the physical characteristics of potential seismic sources, such as the geologic extent of a fault or a potential rupture, and assigning a correlative earthquake size. These parameters are used in empirical earthquake-size versus fault-parameter relations and for direct calculation of estimated earthquake size. The source-characterization approach utilizes nearly all of the scaling parameters and techniques presented on Table 1. The most commonly used scaling parameters include fault rupture length, fault rupture area, fault displacement, and seismic moment calculations.

The source-characterization approach can incorporate more data than the paleoseismic approach, although there is the added interpretation and uncertainty of how this information relates to the potential earthquake source. The source-characterization approach is frequently used because most potential sources have not experienced historical earthquakes, and paleoseismic information is difficult to obtain. In these cases, the source-characterization approach may be the most direct approach available.

When the data are good, seismic source characterization can be accomplished in a relatively quick, routine manner with reasonably small uncertainties.

Regional approach

The regional approach involves looking at the characteristics and data of seismicity and/or the seismotectonics from a region and developing an earthquake size estimate. The approach implies that indirect data are used for the estimate.

The historical seismicity method is one of the most commonly used scaling parameters in regional analyses. Seismicity catalogs of a region are searched and sorted by areas and magnitude; these data are used to compile the sizes, number, and temporal distribution of events. The probabilities for the occurrence of individual earthquake magnitudes for a given time period can then be assessed.

Advantages of the regional approach are that the seismic source does not specifically need to be identified, and that broad areas may be covered. Reservations about using the approach hinge on deficiencies in the input data (e.g., a short record relative to recurrence intervals of large earthquakes). One source of uncertainty is the assumption that the seismic hazard at a particular site is truly represented by a regional analysis.

Regional approaches have been used for assigning seismic hazards to seismic zones that lack identified causative faults. For example, typically in the eastern United States, seismicity is not clearly associated with tectonic structures. In these areas, seismogenic zones are delineated and an earthquake, such as a maximum earthquake for a given time period, can be assigned to this zone.

Relative-comparison approach

The relative-comparison approach involves comparing the source in question with similar seismic sources. A historical earthquake or well-determined seismic-analysis estimate is usually used for comparison. The approach involves establishing a case for the comparison, and reviewing the historical data and/or an estimate for the compared source. Factors that should be similar include tectonic regime, type of displacement, size of the seismogenic zone, and fault parameters such as the length of an earthquake segment. Relative comparisons are commonly used as collaborative evidence to support information derived from other approaches.

The relative-comparison approach can be persuasive, drawing on the precedent of an analogous historical event or a conclusive analysis of a comparable seismic source. In a sense, the relative-comparison approach extends the limited historical and paleoseismological data by spatially expanding the population studied. A source of uncertainty encountered using this approach is the degree of similarity between the sources and/or areas being compared.

SCALING PARAMETERS

The next level in the organization in Table 1 and Figure 1 are the scaling parameters, the parameters used to scale the earthquake size. Several methods have been used to scale earthquake size, including using specific historical earthquake events, instrumental seismicity, and correlations between earthquake size and fault parameters.

Historical-seismicity method

The historical-seismicity method uses historical earthquake data in estimating earthquake size. Background seismicity is compiled and analyzed for a study area. This seismicity may or may not include the size of earthquakes that are of concern, or the time interval being investigated. The historical record may be short relative to the time period of interest (e.g., 50-yr record versus 500-yr event), and the maximum magnitude may not be contained in the record. In these cases, a relation is commonly developed for the existing data, and a value picked from an extrapolation (e.g., Nuttli, 1981).

One of the most common ways to use historical seismicity is to calculate earthquake magnitude-frequency relations (Gutenberg and Richter, 1944; Richter, 1958). Seismological observations indicate that earthquake frequency varies exponentially with earthquake size and that small earthquakes are much more common than larger events. Earthquake frequency for large regions can be represented by the following equation from Richter (1958):

$$\log N = a - b\,M$$

where N is the number of earthquakes of magnitude M or greater per unit time and a and b are constants.

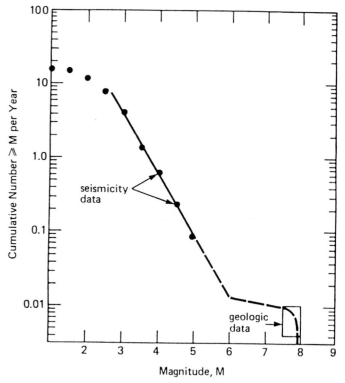

Figure 2. Cumulative frequency-magnitude recurrence relation for an individual fault or fault segment (from Schwartz and Coppersmith, 1984).

Large extrapolations from small, low-magnitude databases can lead to large uncertainties in the magnitude and/or frequency estimation. Further, Wesnousky and others (1983) and Schwartz and Coppersmith (1984) argued that when considering specific sources rather than large regions, the earthquake cumulative frequency-magnitude relation is nonlinear (Fig. 2). A model for this nonlinear form of the cumulative frequency-magnitude relation for an individual fault is presented by Youngs and Coppersmith (1986).

Historical seismicity data are used in earthquake size estimates, in statistical treatments (e.g., extreme-value and maximum-likelihood techniques), for direct use as a minimum estimate of maximum earthquake size, and as a base for the incremental technique. The incremental technique involves adding a set value to the largest historical earthquake size to estimate a larger, less-frequent event (e.g., Basham and others, 1979).

Fault-rupture-length method

The fault-rupture-length method is one of the most frequently used methods for earthquake size estimation. The method involves measuring the potential length of an earthquake rupture, and through empirical relations, estimating the potential earthquake size (Slemmons, 1977; Bonilla and others, 1984).

In the historical record, earthquakes of about magnitude 6 and greater are commonly associated with surface ruptures (Bonilla, 1970; Slemmons, 1977). When historical earthquakes are compiled, the larger earthquakes are generally associated with larger values of parameters, such as surface rupture length, rupture area, and surface displacement (see examples in Table 3). Although there are some important deviations from this generality, this is the premise on which the estimation of earthquake sizes using fault parameters is based. This is consistent with theory; seismic moment scales with the dimensions of earthquake ruptures and the amount of slip (Aki, 1966).

Faults with surface expression and geologic evidence indicating recent activity are found in both interplate and intraplate regions. Where faults can be delineated, potential lengths of earthquake ruptures can be assessed.

There are two main sources of uncertainty in the fault-rupture-length method: the uncertainty in the assignment of a rupture length to a potential event, and uncertainties associated with the empirical relations used for making the size estimates.

Fault-rupture-length estimations. Observed fault rupture lengths associated with historical earthquakes have been estimated in two principal ways: using surface rupture lengths and using aftershock distributions. Surface geologic data appear to scale with earthquake size, and can be used to estimate potential earthquake sizes, even though there is some variability in the completeness of surface expression (Bonilla, 1980). Others have sought "more direct" evidence of earthquake lengths by using aftershock distributions (Acharya, 1979; Wyss, 1979; Darragh and Bolt, 1987). For large earthquakes, the difference between surface-rupture-length and aftershock-length estimates is a small percentage of the overall source and is commonly not significant. Bonilla and others (1984) suggested that, for steeply dipping faults, the difference between the two length estimates is unimportant for earthquakes with surface rupture lengths at least two times the down-dip width.

Darragh and Bolt (1987) pointed out that the difference between the two length estimates is larger and more critical at the moderate earthquake level. Darragh and Bolt suggested that, for moderate earthquakes ($M \leqslant 6.7$), aftershock lengths are better representations of source lengths and are supported by source theory. In practice, however, it is not always an easy task to estimate potential "aftershock lengths" for a seismic-hazard study. Whichever length relation is used for an estimate, it is important to consistently use the same kind of length determination.

It has been observed that larger fault zones commonly do not rupture over their entire lengths during individual earthquake events, but rather some part or percentage of the fault length will rupture (e.g., Fig. 3). After a fault or fault zone has been delineated, some logic or technique needs to be applied to estimate the potential earthquake rupture length. Several techniques have been developed, such as the half-length, fractional-fault-length, and segmentation techniques (Slemmons, 1982a).

Albee and Smith (1966), observing historical events in southern California, concluded that the total length of fault zones is commonly two to five times greater than the segment that

TABLE 3. COMPARISONS OF DIFFERENT EARTHQUAKE SIZES

M_W	M_O* (dynes/cm^2)	Examples[†]	
9.5	2.2×10^{30}	$M_W = 9.5$	800–1,000 km[§] (SZ) 1960 Chile Eq.
9.0	3.9×10^{29}	$M_W = 9$	800 km[§] (SZ) 1952 Kamchatka Eq.
8.5	7.0×10^{28}	$M_W = 8.5$	500 km[§] (SZ) 1929 Chile Eq.
8.0	1.2×10^{28}	$M_S = 7.9$	350 km, 6.6 m (SS) 1958 Fairweather Eq.
7.75	5.3×10^{27}	$M_S = 7.8$	350 km, 3.8 m (SS) 1939 N. Anatolian Eq.
7.5	2.2×20^{27}	$M_S = 7.5$	47 km, 2.7 m (SS) 1970 China Eq.
7.25	9.3×10^{26}	$M_S = 7.2$	50 km, 2 m (SS) 1942 N. Anatolian Eq./
7.0	3.9×10^{26}		
6.75	1.7×10^{26}	$M_S = 6.8$	30 km, 0.3 m (SS) 1966 N. Anatolian Eq.
6.5	7.0×10^{25}	$M_S = 6.4$	25. km, 0.18 m (SS) 1966 Parkfield Eq.
6.25	3.0×10^{25}	$M_S = 6.2$	15 km, 2.5 m (RO) 1969 Peru Eq.
6.0	1.2×10^{25}		
5.75	5.3×10^{24}	$M_S = 5.8$	20 km, 0.2 m (SS) 1977 Iran Eq.
5.5	2.2×10^{24}	$M_S = 5.4$	3.3 km, 0.56 m (R) 1983 Nunez Eq.
5.25	9.3×10^{23}		
5.0	3.9×10^{23}	$M_S = 4.9$	≥ 1.3 km, 0.005 m (N?) 1983 Columbia Eq.

*M_O determined from M_W by the relationship of Hanks and Kanamori (1979), log $M_O = 3/2 (10.7 + M_W)$.
[†]Most of the earthquakes below magnitude 8 are strike-slip events; first number in examples is surface rupture length, second number is maximum surface displacement.
[§]Lengths taken from aftershock areas: SZ - subduction zone, SS - strike slip, RO - reverse oblique, NO - normal oblique, R - reverse slip, N - normal slip.

broke during the historical event. From this observation, Albee and Smith inferred that a potential earthquake rupture would be less than half the length of the fault zone and that a half length could be used for estimating earthquake sizes. Lacking information about what percentage of a fault zone ruptured during an earthquake, many estimates use 50 percent of the total fault length (e.g., Wentworth and others, 1969; Wesson and others, 1975; Freeman and others, 1986).

An indirect way of estimating fault length is the fractional-fault-length technique, developed by Slemmons and Chung (1982) for strike-slip faults in interplate areas. The technique

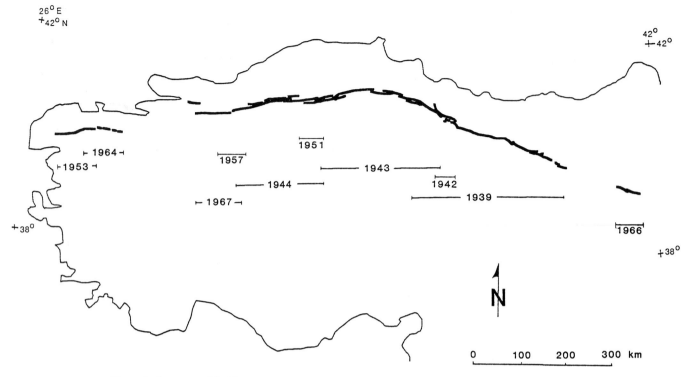

Figure 3. Sequence of faulting along the North Anatolian fault zone (bold lines), Turkey, 1939–1967 (modified from Ambraseys, 1978).

involves estimating the total fault system length (including multiple interconnected faults) and empirically deriving a percentage of the total system length that would rupture during an individual event. The length derived from this percentage estimate is then used in the earthquake size estimations. In both the half- and fractional-fault-length estimates, uncertainties commonly exist regarding the identification of total fault length.

The most direct way for determining fault length is the segmentation technique (discussed in the next section). The segmentation technique utilizes physical information about the fault zone to define rupture zones, and uses earthquake segment lengths to estimate earthquake size. Research on the segmentation technique and concept is ongoing; usefulness of the technique is expected to increase in future seismic-hazard analyses.

Segmentation technique. The segmentation technique investigates the physical characteristics and behavior of fault zones to identify earthquake segments: those parts of fault zones that rupture during an individual earthquake. Earthquakes along the North Anatolian fault system illustrate that large fault systems commonly fail in a segmented fashion (Fig. 3). During the short time period of 1939 to 1967, the North Anatolian fault system ruptured over most of its length, not as a single, throughgoing event but as a series of individual earthquake segments.

The advantage of the segmentation technique is that it offers a more direct, physical way to evaluate fault lengths for a fault system than more arbitrary techniques, such as the half-length technique. The confidence level of an estimate based on a well-documented case of segmentation is usually higher than other length-estimation techniques.

The concept of segmentation has been applied over a large range of scales, from a few tens of meters to hundreds of kilometers (Schwartz and Coppersmith, 1986). Segment lengths corresponding to moderate- and larger-sized earthquakes (≥ 1 km) are the most useful for seismic-hazard analyses. The total extent of the coseismic rupture defines the earthquake segment length.

Complexities of the segmentation concept include earthquake segments that overlap and widely distributed earthquake ruptures. An example of overlapping earthquake segments are the 1940 and 1979 Imperial Valley, California, earthquake segments. DePolo and others (1989) studied historical earthquakes in the Basin and Range Province in the western United States and found that all events greater or equal to magnitude 7 ruptured multiple geometric or structural segments. Further, some of these events involved several faults and were widely distributed (e.g., 1915 Pleasant Valley, Nevada, and 1932 Cedar Mountain, Nevada, earthquakes). The potential for such complexity increases the uncertainty of segmentation scenarios in the Basin and Range Province, as well as elsewhere.

Discontinuities. Individual earthquake segments commonly have different paleoseismic histories and characteristics, and/or are separated from adjacent segments by distinct discontinuities. A discontinuity is the boundary between two segments that can potentially arrest earthquake ruptures. Discontinuities can be generalized into two main categories: geometric and inhomogeneous discontinuities. The characterization and supporting discussion for a segmentation application should address both the characteristics of the segments and their bounding discontinuities.

Geometric discontinuities include fault intersections (e.g., branch faults and cross-fault terminations) and intrinsic fault-zone features (e.g., en echelon steps, fault separations, changes in fault attitude, and fault terminations). Large en echelon steps in fault zones have been identified to be important geometric discontinuities bounding some historical surface ruptures. For example, the southern end of the 1966 Parkfield, California, earthquake rupture ended at a 1-km step in the San Andreas fault system (Eaton and others, 1970). Studies that have investigated the mechanical behavior of en echelon fault steps and examined earthquake behavior near fault steps include those of Segall and Pollard (1980), Bakun and others (1980), Sibson (1985). Bends in fault zones have also been noted to act as discontinuities for some historical ruptures (King and Nabelek, 1985; King, 1986).

King and Yielding (1983) divided geometric features along fault zones into two types: conservative, which transfer slip smoothly; and nonconservative, which require volume changes or subsidiary faulting while transferring slip. Both types are associated with the propagation of a rupture from one fault plane to another of a different orientation. In a conservative geometric feature, the vector of slip lies within both planes (i.e., parallel to the intersection of the two planes). The displacement can transfer smoothly across the change in geometry with little disruption to the slip vector (see Fig. 4). In the nonconservative geometry example, the slip vector is only contained in one plane. Slip along plane A is not conserved; hence, a volume change or subsidiary faulting must occur. The volume change or subsidiary faulting at nonconservative discontinuities tends to disrupt and potentially terminate the rupture.

Inhomogeneous discontinuities include variations in fault width, local stress regimes, and rates and senses of displacement. An example of an inhomogeneous discontinuity is the southern end of the 1906 San Francisco earthquake segment of the San Andreas fault system, near San Juan Bautista, California. There is a distinct change in tectonic behavior across this discontinuity along the San Andreas fault system; north of the discontinuity, displacement occurs during moderate to major earthquakes, while to the south, failure is largely taken up during tectonic creep events (Allen, 1968, 1981). Aki (1979) noted that an abrupt seismic velocity anomaly lies across the San Andreas fault system at this location, and that the anomaly may be related to this change in tectonic behavior.

Use of the segmentation technique. Several factors can make it difficult to delineate fault segments. These factors include variability in the type, amount, and quality of information available, and lack of identifiable or documentable discontinuities along a fault zone.

If discontinuities are large enough, the segmentation of a fault may be intuitively easy (e.g., a 10-km en echelon step is a substantial discontinuity with a high probability of terminating a rupture). Less distinct discontinuities usually require several lines of geologic, seismologic, geometric, structural, and paleoseismic evidence to substantiate their existence. Of these, paleoseismic evidence or an understanding of the earthquake history of a fault can be the most important evidence for segmentation. An example using the estimated ages of faulting to segment the Lost River fault zone is shown in Figure 5. After a particular segment has been delineated, various techniques, such as earthquake size versus fault-length correlations or seismic-moment calculations, can be used to estimate the earthquake size.

Studies are in progress to evaluate and improve the use of the segmentation technique. Knuepfer (1989) reviewed 75 historical earthquake fault ruptures and categorized the types of features found along these ruptures and at the ends. These data are amenable to a statistical treatment for use in future delineation of earthquake segments. Wheeler and Krystinik (1987a, 1987b, 1988) compiled information about the Wasatch fault system in Utah, and used statistical tests of coincidence between a number of parameters to suggest persistence or nonpersistence of segment boundaries. Wheeler and Krystinik examined gravity, seismicity, fault-geometry (e.g., salients in mountain fronts), aeromagnetic,

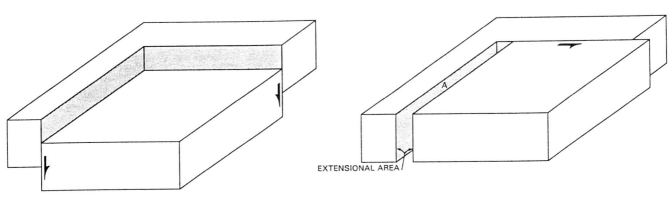

Conservative Displacement — No volume change or new faults created along the two faults with different orientations.

Non conservative Displacement — A volume increase occurs along fault A.

Figure 4. Simple examples of conservative and nonconservative displacements.

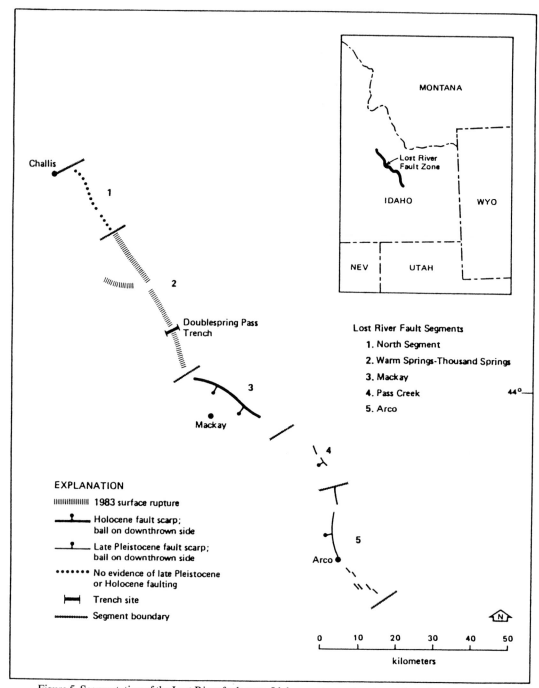

Figure 5. Segmentation of the Lost River fault zone, Idaho; most recent ruptures along the zone are also shown.

topographic, and structural data, and suggested that persistent segment boundaries produce anomalies in most of these kinds of data. Schwartz (1988) summarized progress being made with the segmentation technique, with particular emphasis on fault behavioral data and paleoseismicity. Several papers are also presented in the proceedings of a conference on segmentation and rupture initiation and termination, edited by Schwartz and Sibson (1989).

Empirical earthquake-size–fault-rupture-length relations. After the length of a potential earthquake rupture is as-

sessed, an empirical relation or correlation is used to transform the length parameter into an earthquake size. Most relations assume earthquake size is linearly proportional to the logarithm of length.

Tocher (1958) recognized a relation between earthquake size and surface rupture parameters, such as length of faulting in moderate and large historical earthquakes. Historical earthquake information has been collected and statistically analyzed in many subsequent studies (Iida, 1965; Bonilla, 1967, 1970; Chinnery,

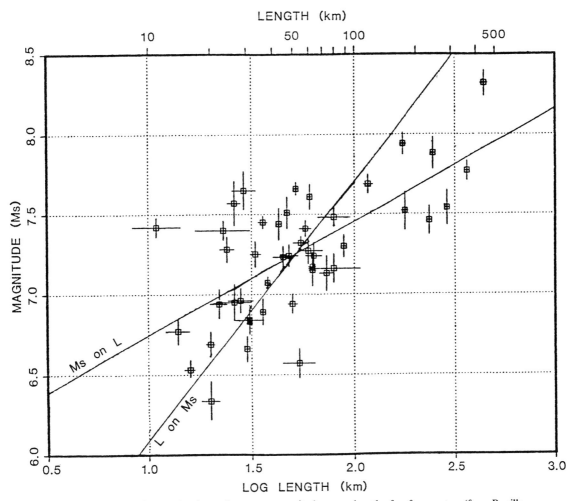

Figure 6. Data and regression for surface-wave magnitude versus length of surface rupture (from Bonilla and others, 1984).

1969; Bonilla and Buchanan, 1970; Mark and Bonilla, 1977; Slemmons, 1977, 1982a; Slemmons and Chung, 1982; Bonilla and others, 1984; Wesnousky, 1986; Wells and others, 1989).

Recent studies, such as Slemmons (1982a) and Bonilla and others (1984), correlated surface-wave magnitudes as a function of fault rupture length. The historical earthquake data were reviewed and reassessed in these studies, and uncertainties in the data are presented in Bonilla and others (1984).

An example of a magnitude–fault length relation is shown in Figure 6. This relation, developed from all historical earthquake events studied by Bonilla and others (1984), is:

$$M_s = 6.04 + 0.704 \, (\log L)$$

where L is the surface rupture length in kilometers. The standard deviation for this relation is 0.3 magnitude units, and the relation is valid over the range of $M_s \sim 5.5$ to 8.

Acharya (1979) emphasized regional variations in rupture length–magnitude relations and suggested that this may account for some of the scatter in regressions using worldwide data. Achar-

ya's database consisted of earthquakes of magnitude 6 or greater. To examine the largest possible data set, he estimated lengths using aftershock distribution lengths, surface rupture lengths, tsunami records, and geodetic information. Acharya's correlation coefficients are high, as are the standard deviations 0.4 to 0.9 units of magnitude. Bonilla and others (1984) and Nowroozi (1985) also found better correlations when they considered regional data. Magnitude versus length relations based on regional data may better characterize sources by distinguishing different tectonic regimes.

Another source of scatter in these regression relations may be the different senses of rupture displacement. Studies by Bonilla and Buchanan (1970), Slemmons (1977, 1982a), and Bonilla and others (1984) suggest systematic differences with sense of displacement, but the data are too few to clearly document this. The scatter in the 10- to 50-km fault length range is the most pronounced, and it is important to attempt to understand because many continental fault zones have lengths or earthquake segment lengths in this range.

Recent studies, such as those of Wesnousky (1986) and

Kanamori and Allen (1986), used seismic moment rather than magnitude in length correlations. Wesnousky (1986) developed a moment versus fault-rupture-length relation using 46 events (Fig. 7). Two regressions are shown in this figure: the solid line for faults with slip rates ⩾1 cm/yr and the dashed line for faults with slip rates <1 cm/yr.

Relations of surface-wave magnitude versus log LD and log LD^2 (where L = length and D = maximum displacement) have been developed (Tocher, 1958; Iida, 1965; King and Knopoff, 1968; Chinnery, 1969; Bonilla and Buchanan, 1970; Slemmons, 1977, 1982a, 1982b; Bonilla and others, 1984; Nowroozi, 1985). Using both length and displacement in a regression relation is thought to incorporate more physical information about an earthquake than one of these parameters individually. The LD versus magnitude relation has a slightly better correlation coefficient than the relations using length alone, but the standard deviation is slightly larger (Bonilla and others, 1984). Slemmons (1982b) found that regressions using log length plus log displacement yielded better correlation coefficients and smaller standard deviations than regressions based solely on length or displacement.

Slemmons and Chung (1982) also developed relations between surface-wave magnitude and the total fault-system length of strike-slip faults. The total fault-system length may include groups of faults, such as the Calaveras, Hayward, Rogers Creek, and Maacama fault zones in California, as well as single fault systems, such as the San Andreas.

Bonilla and others (1984) pointed out that a unique single-value relation between earthquake magnitude and surface-rupture parameters does not exist, due to the many variables that are not taken into account. These variables include stress drop, shape of the rupture surface, and variations in shear modulus. They also compared the variance of measurement errors with the variance of the regression line and determined that the stochastic variance of the regression line was dominant.

Fault-rupture-length relations are widely used in interplate regions to estimate an average or expected earthquake size. These values can be used directly for characteristic and maximum earthquake estimates.

Fault-rupture-area method

The fault-rupture-area method involves using an estimated rupture area to estimate potential earthquake size. The fault-rupture-area parameter is more directly related to the energy released during an earthquake than the simpler fault length (Wyss, 1979; Schwartz and others, 1984). Large differences in fault width (the downdip dimension of a fault within the seismogenic crust) between different faults may result from both different downdip geometry and different thickness of seismogenic crust, and warrants some given consideration in the earthquake size estimate.

Fault-rupture-area estimation. The fault length used in fault-rupture-area estimates may be determined by techniques described in the "Fault-rupture-length method" section. The fault width is usually estimated from the maximum depth of seismicity and information on the dip of the fault. Other techniques, such as regional comparisons (Wyss, 1979) and aspect ratios (length versus width), have been proposed as indirect estimates of fault width (Purcaru and Burckhemer, 1982; Schwartz and others, 1984). The critical notion for fault width studies is the nature and depth extent of the seismogenic zone. How deep will a potential rupture propagate? Aftershock distributions are primarily used for this estimation, although heat-flow studies and theoretical arguments can also be used to approximate this value.

Sibson (1982) examined the distribution of heat flow and the base of seismicity in continental settings and found a consistency between the theoretical and observed seismogenic bases. The fault model used by Sibson and other authors consists of a brittle zone in the upper crust overlying a plastically deforming zone in the lower crust. These two zones are separated by a transitional zone where brittle, plastic, and cataclastic-flow (continuous deformation accommodated by small brittle dislocations) deformation occur (Sibson, 1986; Tullis and Yund, 1987; Scholz, 1988, 1990). The depth of the transition zone is dependent on thermal gradient, rock type, and the type of faulting (i.e., normal versus reverse displacement).

Most of the seismogenic zone is in the brittle zone. However, during the high strain rates associated with earthquake events,

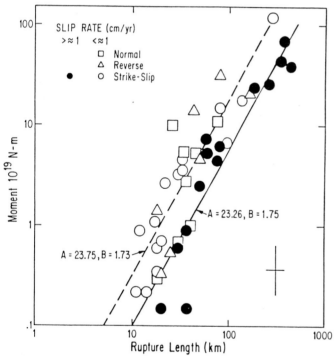

Figure 7. Seismic moment versus earthquake rupture length; data from faults with slip rates above and below 1 cm/yr are distinguished as well as the sense of displacement. Equations for lines are log M$_o$ = A + B log L, the right regression line is for slip rates greater than 1 cm/yr (solid circles); the left line is for slip rates less than 1 cm/yr (from Wesnousky, 1986).

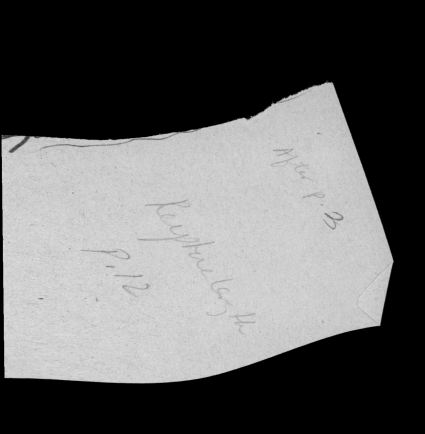

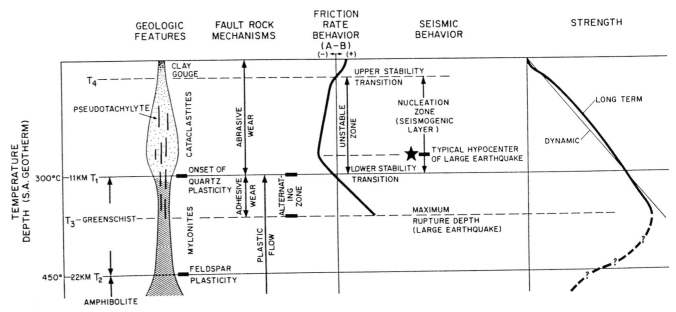

Figure 8. Seismogenic-zone model illustrating geologic, seismologic, and other physical characteristics (from Scholz, 1988).

significant parts of a large earthquake rupture may propagate into the transitional zone (Sibson, 1986). The depth extent of earthquake ruptures and the transitional zone were discussed further by Strehlau (1986) and Hobbs and others (1986). Scholz (1988) suggested that the transitional zone for quartzo-feldspathic rocks in continental fault zones lies between the onset of quartz plasticity at about 300°C and the onset of feldspar plasticity at about 450°C (Fig. 8).

One way to approximate the depth of the maximum-seismic-rupture propagation is to use the maximum depth of the seismicity and add a few kilometers to this value to account for some rupture into the transitional zone. This technique works for deep-driven faults with good seismic data and can be used for many sources in interplate areas.

In intraplate areas, this model may apply to some of the larger, identified tectonic structures. In the eastern U.S., heat-flow rates suggest that seismicity for the deep-driven model should extend downward 20 to 25 km (Chen and Molnar, 1983; Sibson, 1987). However, many historical earthquakes in intraplate regions have had hypocenters at 5 to 10 km depth. A second model has been proposed for these earthquakes. This model involves an earthquake that is shallow and does not necessarily have a lower crustal expression. Sibson (1987) suggested that, "A more appropriate model for this intraplate activity may be to view the upper levels of cratonic crust as a remotely loaded, flawed stress guide where time-dependent failure occurs through processes of stress corrosion." Sibson noted that for this second model, maximum-earthquake sizes will be sensitive to the maximum seismogenic depth.

Empirical earthquake-size–fault-area relations. Empirical relations have been developed between earthquake size and fault area by Wyss (1979), Singh and others (1980), and Bonilla and others (1984). Wyss (1979) compiled 90 area-magnitude estimates to develop the empirical relations shown in Figure 9. Fault areas compiled by Wyss include areas calculated from earthquake moment estimates and aftershock areas. Wyss argued that, based on the theoretical definition of moment and moment magnitude, he expected the slope of the relation between earthquake source area and magnitude to be 1. He then fit a line with the slope of 1 through the data set, and felt that this was the best relation to use. Wyss also calculated a least-squares linear regression of the data for comparison. Wyss's preferred relation is:

$$M = \log A + 4.15$$

for M > 5.6, and his least-squares regression is:

$$M = 0.93 \log A + 4.38$$

for M > 5.6, with a root-mean-square error of 0.3 magnitude units. M is magnitude and A is fault area in square kilometers.

Singh and others (1980) came up with a similar equation. They also calculated quadratic fits to the data and allowed for errors in the data in some regression analyses. They found that the estimates of magnitude were not significantly improved by the inclusion of errors in the regressions.

Bonilla and others (1984) examined regressions on 21 events ($M_s \geq 6$) and estimated fault widths from aftershock and microseismic activity, deformational models, teleseismic models, macroseismic models, depths extrapolated from microearthquakes a considerable distance from the event, and regional

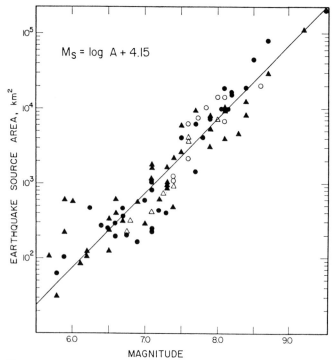

Figure 9. Data and regression for magnitude versus fault-rupture area (from Wyss, 1979).

crustal models. Their results are also similar to Wyss's, with their relation:

$$M = 0.823 \log A + 4.96$$

for M > 6, having a standard deviation of 0.34 magnitude units.

A significant difference between the above studies is that Wyss (1979) and Singh and others (1980) used aftershock lengths in their area calculations, whereas Bonilla and others (1984) solely used surface rupture lengths. This difference in length estimates is small for large earthquakes but becomes important for moderate earthquakes. Length measurements should be similar to the type used in the regression relation, especially for moderate earthquakes.

Using fault-area relations for estimates. Fault-area relations are commonly used in earthquake size estimation. The fault-area method is especially useful in areas with an unusually deep seismogenic zone that could accommodate large potential earthquakes. Fault-area relations can also be used in cases where a fault is blind or buried, such as a blind thrust under an actively deforming anticline. Fault-area relations allow for some uncertainty in the length estimation, without changing the estimate significantly, provided the width estimate is reasonably accurate.

Fault-displacement method

This method involves examination of maximum or average displacement from a paleoseismic event, usually as manifested in surface ruptures or associated deformation. This displacement is then used to scale earthquake size with empirical formulas developed from regressions between historical earthquake sizes and surface displacements.

Surface displacement during earthquakes. There is a high degree of variability in the surface displacements that occur during earthquakes. This variability arises from different characteristics of sources, distribution of tectonic deformation, and the response of near-surface materials. Faults with different senses of displacement can also have different surface expressions. For example, strike-slip displacements may have subdued topographic expressions with little vertical relief, whereas surface displacements with normal-slip components will often create a surface scarp.

Surface displacement is commonly expressed in a distributed fashion in both vertical and horizontal directions. Weak subsurface areas can deform and detach, distorting the transmission of the lower basement offsets to the surface. These distributed fault patterns and detachments can cause rotation and deformation of material near the fault, accommodating tectonic strain. This distributed deformation is missing from distinct offsets along the surface fault, potentially leading to an underestimation of actual displacement (Slemmons, 1977).

The surface is heterogeneous in both materials and processes. This heterogeneity allows surface displacements to be distorted, causing the expression of displacement to be reduced or sometimes exaggerated. Soft materials such as sand and saturated soils may deform diffusely, leaving no distinct displacement evidence. Conversely, backtilting, topographic factors, and compaction can lead to exaggerated fault scarp heights that are larger than tectonic displacements at depth. Deeper soft-surface materials may lurch and, if saturated, liquefy or differentially settle, also causing distortion of the tectonic surface displacement. Another problem of the surface environment is erosion processes. Erosion, particularly of soft materials such as pervasively sheared or highly fractured rock (common along fault zones), can also make it difficult to measure historical and paleoseismic displacements.

Despite the potential variability of surface displacements, they can often be measured or estimated. The best field measurement of displacement is a displacement vector, where two points separated by the fault are matched, and the orientation and absolute displacement are measured. When the piercing points (offset points in the plane of the fault) are too uncertain for an exact match, the orientation of the offsetting fault can be approximated, and the vertical and horizontal offsets, along with their uncertainties, can be measured. Surface scarps are also used to estimate displacement. The ambient slopes around the scarp, the dip of the fault, and the sense of displacement need to be estimated, and techniques such as nomograms (Wallace, 1980) need to be used to estimate net tectonic displacement.

It is useful to compile discrete displacement measurements into displacement curves such as the one shown in Figure 10 for the 1983 Borah Peak, Idaho, earthquake. These allow a visual

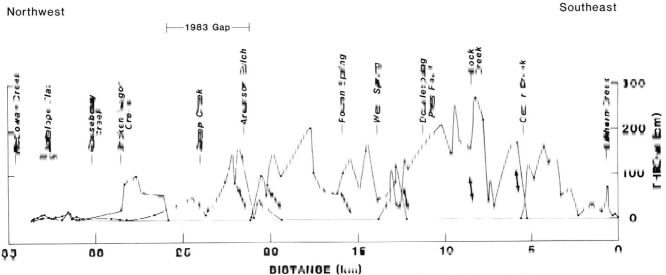

Figure 10. Amount of net throw on surface faults associated with the 1983 Borah Peak, Idaho, earthquake (from Crone and others, 1987). Arrows indicate slip direction.

display of the surface-displacement data and make it easy to ascertain values, such as the maximum displacement, and to view the variability in surface displacement. Such a representation also helps increase confidence that the maximum displacement has been measured.

There are two main types of surface displacements that have been considered in seismic-hazard analyses: maximum displacements and average displacements. The maximum displacement has been used in most compilations and relations to get above the variability of surface expression. Also, maximum displacement values are commonly the only displacement values reported for early historical earthquakes. Even though the maximum displacement is usually distributed along only a small percentage of the total surface rupture, Thatcher and Bonilla (1989) suggested that maximum surface displacements best approximate geodetic estimates of subsurface displacements; hence, the maximum surface displacement may be the best surficial estimate for average displacement in earthquake moment calculations. However, when only a single displacement value is used to characterize an earthquake, potential uncertainties associated with that maximum value become critical.

Average surface displacement has been a difficult parameter to estimate due to the variability of surface rupture displacements and expression. One way to estimate the average surficial displacement is to measure the area under a well-constrained displacement curve, and divide it by the length of the rupture. This can be done easily with a planimeter.

Empirical earthquake-size–fault-displacement relations. Once the displacement is estimated, an empirical relation or correlation is used to convert the displacement into earthquake size. The displacement versus earthquake-size relations and length versus earthquake-size relations have had similar evolutions, and are discussed in many of the same papers (Tocher, 1958; Iida,

1965; Bonilla, 1967; Chinnery, 1969; Bonilla and Buchanan, 1970; Mark and Bonilla, 1977; Slemmons, 1977, 1982a; Slemmons and Chung, 1982; Bonilla and others, 1984; Zhang and others, 1989).

Recent studies, such as Slemmons (1982a) and Bonilla and others (1984), have correlated surface-wave magnitudes with maximum displacement. Standard deviations from these regressions range from 0.3 to 0.4 magnitude units. An example of one of these relations using all earthquakes is shown in Figure 11. An example of a surface-wave magnitude versus maximum displacement regression for strike-slip faults is:

$$M_s = 7.00 + 0.782 \ (\log D_{max})$$

where D_{max} is the maximum surface displacement in meters per earthquake event (Bonilla and others, 1984).

Recent studies of fault displacement have been considering physical processes and models of earthquakes. For example, scientists are attempting to determine if displacement relates to the length of an earthquake rupture (L model; Scholz, 1982) or the vertical, downdip width of a fault (W model; Bodin and others, 1987). Favoring one model over the other would suggest a different, nonlinear shape to earthquake-size versus fault-displacement relations.

Using fault-displacement relations for estimates. Earthquake-size versus maximum-displacement relations estimate the average or expected value of earthquake size for a maximum displacement. Similar to fault length, this value can be used directly in characteristic- and maximum-earthquake estimates.

Field measurements of the displacement are rarely "maximum," due to problems with preservation of offsets and the relative rarity of the occurrence of maximum displacements along a surface rupture. These values, however, are commonly used as

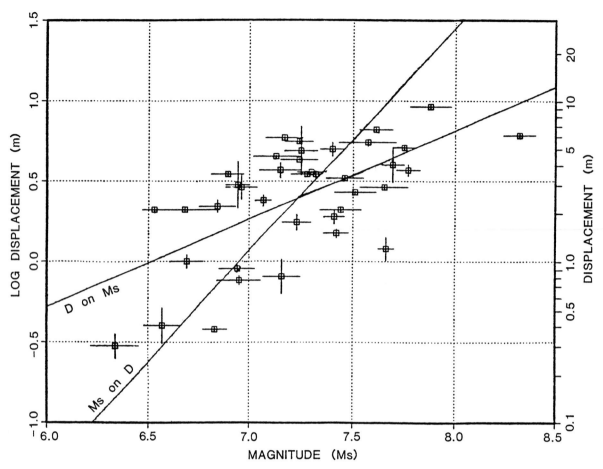

Figure 11. Data and regression for surface-wave magnitude versus maximum surface displacement (from Bonilla and others, 1984).

input into the magnitude–maximum displacement relation, and a magnitude estimate made. Since these relations are developed for the maximum displacement, a slightly smaller magnitude value is calculated when less than maximum values are used. This uncertainty should be evaluated when making earthquake size estimates based on surface displacements. One way to minimize this uncertainty is to take care in identifying the largest displacement along a fault, increasing the likelihood of measuring the maximum displacement.

Seismic-moment method

The seismic-moment method requires the most data for estimating earthquake sizes, but provides an estimate that is best supported by seismic theory and observations. Earthquake size can be represented by seismic moment and/or moment magnitude. The seismic moment can be estimated from seismograms and provides a link between seismologic and geologic information. An equation that relates fault parameters to earthquake moment is:

$$M_o = LWD \, \mu m$$

where M_o = seismic moment, L = fault rupture length, W = fault width, D = average displacement over the rupture surface, and μm = shear rigidity (commonly 3 to 3.5×10^{11} dynes/cm^2 for crustal rocks) (Aki, 1966). These variables, which have been previously discussed, can be estimated fairly confidently; perhaps the most difficult to ascertain is the average displacement. The transformation of seismic moment to moment magnitude is accomplished using empirical relations between the two parameters (see Appendix A).

To a first approximation, earthquake ruptures along a fault become larger with increasing earthquake size until they reach the limits of the seismogenic zone. Commonly, between magnitude 5 and 6, the rupture reaches the surface. At this point, surface displacements are probably fragmentary, and smaller than subsurface maximum or average displacements. As the length versus width aspect ratio of the rupture increases, surface displacements may approach subsurface displacements, and a modal or maximum surface displacement may be a reasonable estimate of the subsurface average displacement.

Seismic-moment estimates will improve as better source models, more accurate fault-parameter measurements, and a better understanding of rock properties are achieved. Direct-moment calculation has the advantage of not having the uncertainties introduced when empirical correlations are used for estimations. Moments and moment magnitudes are anticipated to have a larger, more important role in future seismic-hazard analyses.

Strain-rate method

The strain-rate method involves looking at geological, paleoseismological, geodetic and historical surface displacement, and seismic strain rates and assigning earthquake size values. Strain rates have been used in empirical analyses and directly over a time period to estimate potential earthquake sizes, although the use of strain rates to constrain maximum earthquakes is not common. Strain rates are more commonly used to constrain the timing or interseismic interval of earthquake events (Molnar, 1979; Anderson, 1979; Youngs and Coppersmith, 1986).

Strain-rate data. Strain-rate data are derived from a wide variety of time ranges, including long-range, intermediate-range, and contemporary time frames. Long-term rates, on the scale of millions of years, are derived from geologic information (e.g., offset of a geologic unit along a fault). Long-term data average a large number of earthquake events, but the time periods considered can be so long that seismotectonic regimes can change. Hence, the slip rate determined from long-term data may be significantly above or below the present rate. Strain rates derived over time intervals ranging from tens of thousands to hundreds of thousands of years are prime data for seismotectonic studies. This intermediate time-frame data may be obtained from geologic, paleoseismic, and geomorphic analyses. Contemporary strain rates are available for some faults from historical earthquakes and geodetic measurements. Cumulative earthquake moments can be calculated for areas with high background seismicity or large events to give seismic strain rates. Strain-rate information from all three time frames (long term, intermediate term, and contemporary or short term) is useful for characterizing a seismic source.

Strain-rate relations. Smith (1976) suggested using slip rates along a fault to estimate a maximum earthquake. Smith used Brune's (1968) seismic-moment–fault-slip relation and Gutenberg and Richter's (1944) magnitude-frequency relation to develop a relation that uses present-term geologic slip-rate data to estimate a maximum earthquake over the time interval in which the slip rate is taken.

Woodward-Clyde Consultants (1979) compiled slip-rate and historical earthquake data for strike-slip faults in California. The relation developed by Woodward-Clyde Consultants for strike-slip faults in California is:

$$M_s = 7.223 + 1.263 \log S$$

where S is slip rate in mm/yr (Schwartz and others, 1984). This relation gives reasonable earthquake size estimates for high-slip-rate faults, but is considered misleading for low-slip-rate faults. Earthquakes from low-slip-rate faults do not have a representa-

tive sampling in this relation, due to long interseismic intervals. Further, low-slip-rate faults are considered capable of producing large earthquakes, although they occur less frequently (Schwartz and Coppersmith, 1986; Kanamori and Allen, 1986; Cao and Aki, 1986). Wesnousky (1986) chose to divide the data of seismic moment versus fault rupture length into two groups: (1) from faults with slip rates <1 cm/yr, and (2) from faults with slip rates >1 cm/yr (Fig. 7). Wesnousky identified a difference between these data groups and treated them separately for correlation, noting that the more slowly slipping faults produce a greater amount of slip, and hence, a greater seismic moment.

McGarr (1987) suggested that strain rates might be used in the central and eastern United States as a tool for estimating maximum earthquake sizes. McGarr's method uses strain rates derived from seismicity and moment-frequency distributions.

Knowing the most recent event and the strain accumulation since the occurrence of that event, an estimate of the accumulated earthquake potential along a fault can be made. Jones (1987) noted a slip deficit of 3 to 4.5 m along the Mojave section of the San Andreas fault system since the 1857 Fort Tejon earthquake, and a large slip deficit along the Indio section to the south. Jones speculated that there is the potential for a magnitude 7¼ to 7¾ earthquake to occur along the southern San Andreas fault, based on these historical strain accumulations.

INTRAPLATE REGIONS

There are several types of intraplate tectonic settings. Some provinces are tectonically active and have experienced many historical, large-magnitude earthquakes (e.g., Basin and Range Province, western North America). Other intraplate settings have much lower rates of tectonic activity, such as the central interiors of continents. These are referred to as "mid-plate regions" by Nuttli (1983) or "stable continental interiors" (SCI) by Johnston and others (1987).

Tectonic activity in SCI regions is poorly understood, and there is a significant difference between interplate and SCI regions in traditional seismic source evaluation. Seismic sources in interplate areas are commonly identified and directly evaluated. In SCI regions, which frequently lack identified, specific causative tectonic structures, seismic zones or areas are identified and analyzed. Some seismic zones, such as the New Madrid, Missouri, area (site of three approximately magnitude 8 earthquakes in 1811 and 1812), exhibit narrow zones of seismicity, delineating fault zones (Coffman and von Hake, 1973; Ravat and others, 1987). Other zones are broad areas of seismicity spatially associated with regional tectonic features, such as rifts, uplifts, and thrust belts, but this seismicity is rarely attributable to specific faults.

Studies in the central and eastern United States

The central and eastern United States make up much of the stable continental interior (SCI) of the North American continent. The earthquake potential of this area needs to be better understood and evaluated because of high population, industrial concentration, low attenuation of ground motion, recent recognition of active faults, and occurrence of large and great earthquakes in the historical and paleoseismic records. These factors have contributed to a recent acceleration in research on the seismic hazard of the central and eastern states.

Many seismic analyses compile the historical seismic record for the past few hundred years (commonly as short as 100 yr) and, using magnitude-frequency relations, estimate a maximum magnitude for a given recurrence interval. Unfortunately, the historical record is a small part of the overall earthquake cycle for most faults in this area. A global database from similar SCI regions has been compiled in an attempt to augment the short historical record by substituting space for time (Johnston and others, 1987; Coppersmith, 1987; Coppersmith and others, 1987; Coppersmith and Schneider, 1989). Comparison factors include the types and ages of the geologic units involved, and types and ages of structures or structural belts present.

Until recently, the general consensus was that faults in the central and eastern U.S. did not exhibit Quaternary surface expression. Studies of the Meers fault indicate that, in at least some cases, youthful (Holocene) faults do exist and have identifiable expression (Gilbert, 1983; Luza and others, 1987; Ramelli and others, 1987; Ramelli, 1988; Madole, 1988; and Ramelli and Slemmons, this volume).

Several studies on seismic-hazard methodology have been conducted in this area during recent years by Lawrence Livermore National Laboratory, the Electric Power Research Institute (EPRI), and other agencies. The EPRI approach utilized teams of multiple experts, each team consisting of a geologist, seismologist, and tectonophysicist (Stepp, 1986; Electric Power Research Institute, 1986; Statton and others, 1987). The teams were given the same data sets to avoid uneven knowledge. The teams delineated seismic sources, estimated the sizes and probabilities for occurrence of potential events, and estimated uncertainties for each step of the process. These uncertainties and the variations between teams represent differences in interpretation (since the same data were used) and were ultimately incorporated into the final seismic-hazard analysis.

The regional and relative approaches for earthquake size estimation are commonly used in the central and eastern U.S. In some localized areas where large and great earthquakes have occurred, the historical-earthquake approach can be directly used for maximum earthquake estimates. As future studies unravel the Quaternary faulting and identify other causative tectonic structures in this area, the use of the source-characterization approach should increase (Ramelli and Slemmons, this volume).

FOLD-RELATED EARTHQUAKE SOURCES

Recent earthquakes in California have increased concern about seismic sources related to active folding. The 1983 Coalinga (M_L = 6.7) and 1987 Whittier Narrows (M_L = 5.9) earthquakes are examples of events that occurred in areas where active folding can be documented (Stein and King, 1984; Uhrhammer, 1985; Weber, 1987; Hauksson and others, 1988). Geodetic leveling documented fold structures undergoing significant coseismic deformation during these earthquakes (Stein and King, 1984; Lin and Stein, 1989). The causative structures of these earthquakes do not intersect the surface, and were not identified as seismic hazards prior to these events (Stein and King, 1984; Namson and Davis, 1988; Hauksson and others, 1988).

Discussions of fold-related faults and earthquakes are given by Yeats (1986) and Stein and Yeats (1989). There are a number of second-order faults related to folding, such as flexural-slip faults and bending-moment faults, that may constitute a low hazard because of their limited dimensions and depth (Yeats, 1986). There are also larger, first-order faults at depth that directly relate to tectonic stresses and create the fold structures. These first-order faults can pose a significant seismic hazard (e.g., the 1980 El Asnam earthquake [M_s = 7.3], the 1983 Coalinga earthquake, and the 1988 Armenian earthquake [M_s = 6.9]). Stein and Yeats (1989) noted that historical events as large as M_w = 7.8 have occurred on blind faults associated with folds.

First-order faults may be identified and delineated by investigation of the structure of folds using field, subsurface, and geodetic data, and analytic procedures such as construction of balanced cross sections (Namson and Davis, 1988). Uncertainty estimates should include ranges of the potential dimensions of these first-order structures.

Evidence of Quaternary or contemporary deformation of folds can identify these systems as potentially active and seismogenic. If an underlying structure such as a blind thrust can be deduced, the inferred dimensions of that structure can be appraised for potential earthquake sizes using the source-characterization approach. A fault-area method can be used with the inferred fault dimensions, and the relative-comparison approach is also useful for assessing active fold areas.

SUBDUCTION-ZONE EARTHQUAKE SOURCES

Subduction zones are the locations of the Earth's greatest earthquakes. Subduction zones are megathrusts with slip rates ranging up to about 10 cm/yr. These structures are the boundary between lithospheric plates as they converge and one plate is subducted. Moment magnitude usually is used to scale subduction-zone earthquakes that are large to great in size.

Kanamori (1971, 1977a, 1986) described the behavior of subduction zones as seismic or aseismic, depending on whether the converging plates are strongly or weakly coupled. Large asperities (patches along faults with higher strength) are thought to form where the converging plates are considered strongly coupled. These asperities break during subduction-zone earthquakes, with relatively higher frequency (>1 Hz) energy release than non-asperity areas (Kanamori, 1986). The largest historical earthquakes in the world have occurred along strongly coupled subduction zones. Characteristics of strongly coupled zones are

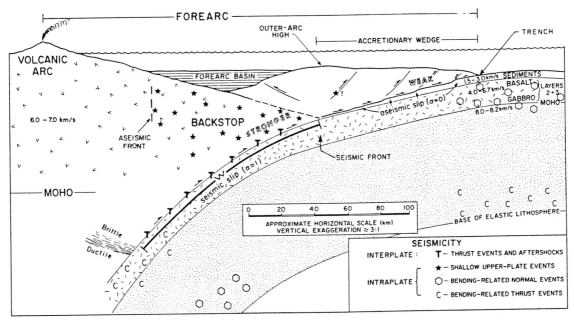

Figure 12. Schematic cross section of the upper part of a subduction zone showing the area of seismic slip (from Byrne and others, 1988).

high convergence rates, young lithosphere being subducted, and a shallow, gently dipping Benioff-Wadati zone.

Two factors that influence the degree of coupling are convergence rate and the age of the lithosphere being subducted (Kanamori, 1977a, 1986; Ruff and Kanamori, 1980). Ruff and Kanamori (1980) developed a relation between maximum observed magnitude, convergence rate, and age of subducted lithosphere. Kanamori (1986) reports this relation as:

$$M_w' = -0.00953T + 0.143V + 8.01$$

where T is the age of the subducted lithosphere in millions of years and V is the convergence rate in cm/yr. M_w' is a value that is close to M_w, but is summed over an earthquake sequence (up to several years in duration) to represent the overall moment release from the sequence (Ruff and Kanamori, 1980; Kanamori, 1986). M_w' can be used to approximate the maximum expected event a subduction zone might produce (Kanamori, personal communication, 1989).

Jarrard (1986) considered different convergent rate values and rates perpendicular to the trench to generate relations similar to Ruff and Kanamori's. Other variables may have a significant, but secondary, influence on earthquake size (Ruff and Kanamori, 1980; Lay and Kanamori, 1981; Jarrard, 1986). An example of these variables is the effect of subducted sediment on earthquake size (Kanamori, 1986; Byrne and others, 1988; Ruff, 1989).

Subduction zones have failed in segments historically, and commonly can be divided into segments a few hundred kilometers long based partly on changes in strike and offsets of trench axes, subducting ocean-floor topography, background seismicity, and various changes in the volcanic arcs (Kelleher and others,

1974; Carr and others, 1974; Kelleher and McCann, 1976; McCann and others, 1979; Lay and Kanamori, 1981; Habermann and others, 1986). Significant variability exists in the size of historical earthquakes, however, between well-documented events and subsequent events rerupturing the same stretch of subduction zone (Lay and Kanamori, 1981; Thatcher, 1990). Lay and Kanamori (1981) proposed that, occasionally, failure of adjacent segments triggers a segment to rupture, increasing the size of the earthquake. Based on historical data, considerable uncertainty exists in defining a characteristic length for subduction-zone events, but maximum rupture lengths may be established with somewhat better confidence.

The width of the zone is defined by an upper boundary, the seismic front, and a lower boundary, the seismic cutoff (Fig. 12). The seismic front is at the base of the accretionary wedge and is represented seismically by the upper limit of the Benioff-Wadati zone (Sykes and others, 1987, Byrne and others, 1988). The seismic cutoff is taken to be near the brittle-plastic transitional zone.

If a rupture area along a subduction zone can be delineated, it can be used to estimate potential earthquake sizes. Both Wyss (1979) and Singh and others (1980) used subduction-zone events as the larger earthquakes in their data sets, and Abe (1975) used moments and rupture areas solely from subduction-zone events. If an average displacement can be postulated in addition to a potential rupture area, a seismic-moment estimate can also be made. For subduction-zone events that propagate into the upper mantle, a slightly higher shear rigidity value of 5×10^{11} dyne/cm^2 is used, as an average of the crustal and upper mantle rocks ruptured (Kanamori, personal communication, 1989).

West and McCrumb (1988) compiled data from 14

subduction-zone earthquakes that caused coseismic deformation along coastlines. From these data they observed an earthquake size threshold for coseismic deformation of about magnitude 7, and above magnitude 8½, the length of the zone of coseismic deformation increases. Hence, coseismic deformation lengths may also become a useful tool to evaluate subduction-zone earthquake potential when evidence of paleoseismic uplift is present.

Other approaches that can be used for appraising subduction zones are the relative-comparison approach and the historical-earthquake approach. The latter is commonly applicable because of the relatively short interseismic intervals associated with subduction-zone events (several tens to hundreds of years).

VOLCANIC EARTHQUAKE SOURCES

Historically, volcanic activity has been preceded and accompanied by earthquake activity; hence, active volcanoes can be considered potential earthquake sources. Because volcanoes are constructional in nature, in many cases, it is difficult to see underlying structural features (e.g., vent controlling faults) due to burial. This makes it hard to conduct a complete seismotectonic assessment of many volcanoes, including a source characterization of associated structures. A general approach to volcanic earthquake potential is to consider all earthquakes related to volcanic activity, no matter what the specific source. This permits many types of sources associated with volcanoes to be included, such as explosive as well as elastic dislocation.

Volcanic earthquakes usually have small magnitudes, but a few have had moderate magnitudes (Shimozuru, 1971; Blong, 1984). Moderate-sized events include the 1914 Sakura-zima earthquake (M = 6.7), which occurred 10½ hr after a volcanic eruption began (Shimozuru, 1971); the 1962 Miyake-zima eruption, with many earthquakes greater than magnitude 5, the largest being magnitude 5.9 (Shimozuru, 1971); and the 1980 Mt. St. Helens earthquake of M_s = 5.2 (Kanamori and Given, 1982).

The 1975 Kalapana, Hawaii, earthquake (M_s = 7.1) appears to have been generated by the seaward movement of a large block of the volcano, as indicated by coastal subsidence and horizontal geodetic measurements (Eissler and Kanamori, 1987). A teleseismic P-wave first-motion mechanism was prepared by Ando (1979), who favors a northeast-striking and shallowly southeast-dipping nodal plane. Eissler and Kanamori (1987) compiled observations from the Kalapana earthquake; they noted the large tsunami and a bilobate Love-wave radiation pattern. Eissler and Kanamori concluded from these and other observations that the earthquake was caused by a massive "landslide" failure of the southeastern flank of the island of Hawaii. Comparable earthquakes may be related to other similar active seamounts, but not necessarily to other types of volcanoes.

Maximum volcanic earthquakes for continental settings are in the range of magnitude 6 to 6¾. The potential for larger earthquakes probably would be indicated by visible faults associated with a volcano. Presently, the relative approach is used for assessing volcanoes.

UNCERTAINTIES OF ESTIMATES

Uncertainties exist in several aspects of the size estimation process, including errors in data measurements, interpretations, correlation uncertainties, and uncertainties in comparing one area to another. To illustrate the importance of acknowledging uncertainties, consider two identical size estimates for a large earthquake: one estimate with multiple reasoning and low uncertainties (e.g., ¼ magnitude unit), and the other estimate with large uncertainties (e.g., >1 magnitude unit). Although the same value is estimated, the two estimates must be viewed with different degrees of confidence and usefulness. Explicit presentation of uncertainties in evaluations aid those who must use earthquake size estimates for design parameters and decisions, and help match earthquake size estimates with the acceptable risks.

Uncertainties can be divided into two groups: those that are essentially irreducible and those that are potentially reducible. This consideration can guide further research in the analysis in an attempt to achieve a more confident estimate. Two types of uncertainty that have been fit into these categories have been termed "inherent" uncertainty and "informational" or "statistical" uncertainty (Kulkarni and others, 1984; Youngs and others, 1985). Toro and McGuire (1987) and Electric Power Research Institute (1986) use the terms "randomness" and "uncertainty" to identify these two ideas. The first idea, inherent uncertainty, represents the natural variability of the phenomenon being studied. The observed natural variability (e.g., scatter in correlation data) is due to characteristics of the physics of the earthquake source that are not considered (or known about) in a specific technique. This uncertainty is dictated naturally and generally cannot be changed or improved with additional data collection or refinement.

The second type, informational or statistical uncertainty, can potentially be reduced with additional data, especially for correlations where the data are sparse.

Uncertainties may be expressed in several ways. An estimate can be reported with a ± range of uncertainty (sometimes the range is skewed about the estimate). Uncertainty may also be expressed by reporting the estimated value as a range. Another technique for modeling uncertainty is to cast uncertainties in terms of probability distributions and use Monte Carlo (random number) simulations to describe the resulting uncertainty in seismic-hazard estimations (Bernreuter and others, 1987; Ross, 1987).

LOGIC TREES

The various components of an analysis can be presented in a format called "logic," "decision," or "probability" trees (Figs. 13 and 14). Logic trees are composed of nodes (points where different values, techniques, or states of input are possible) and branches that represent the individual parameter values (Coppersmith and Youngs, 1986). Logic trees also offer a convenient way to deal with uncertainties in data and techniques, and with multiple interpretations (Coppersmith and Youngs, 1982, 1986;

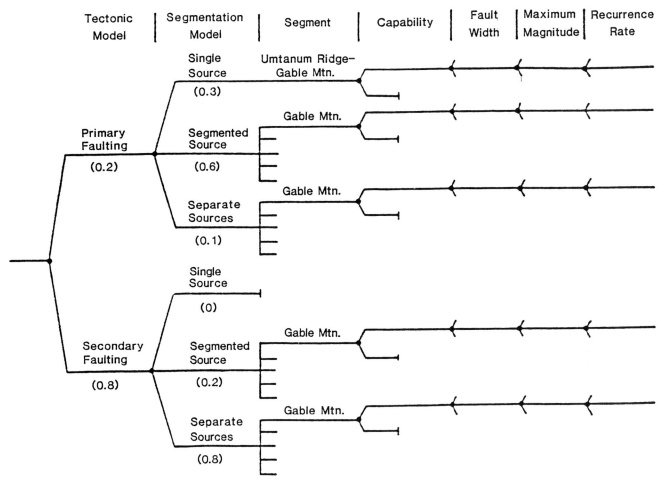

Figure 13. General seismic-hazard logic tree (from Youngs and others, 1985).

Kulkarni and others, 1984). Many estimates, such as for a segment length or a maximum earthquake for a fault, include judgments used to arrive at the final assessment. Logic trees can capture these subjective or intuitive uncertainties, which would otherwise be difficult to quantify. In a logic tree format, the relative confidence or uncertainties of different estimate values can be expressed.

Nodes of a logic tree are arranged to provide for the conditional aspect or dependencies of source parameters and to provide a logical progression of the analysis through to the final value. The branches are each assigned a relative probability, which together add up to one. For example, if a node has two branches, and each branch is equally probable, a value of 0.5 would be assigned to each branch. After the logic tree is complete, the final value is obtained by multiplying the relative probability of each branch by the estimated value of the branch and adding up these products. This format allows an investigator to easily view the overall estimation process and incorporate the maximum amount of information into the estimation.

Logic trees offer an explicit way to handle uncertainties and propagate them through the analysis. A histogram taken from the final branches of the logic tree presents a distribution of the estimated values versus their estimated probability of occurrence (Fig. 14b).

SOME FINAL THOUGHTS

The organization of earthquake-size-estimation procedures presented in this chapter may be used as branches of a logic tree to assist in earthquake size estimations. In a specific application, more nodes and branches will probably be needed to accommodate source-specific and analysis-specific considerations.

A careful evaluation of data and associated uncertainties is essential when assigning an earthquake size estimate to a seismic source. A common uncertainty in fault studies is the "point study problem," in which only one location along a fault zone is studied. Some analyses, such as those using fault displacements, can be very sensitive to the point study problem because of the variability of the data along the fault zone. Multiple techniques and study locations will improve the understanding of a seismotectonic setting and potential, and help flag unusual situations.

Recent research in earthquake size estimation places empha-

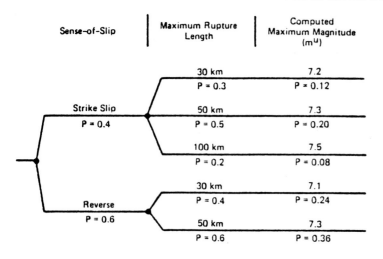

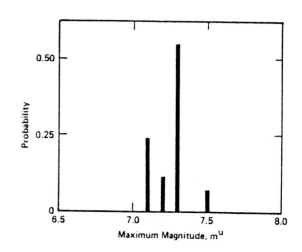

a) Logic Tree of Evaluating Maximum Magnitude   b) Discrete Distribution for Maximum Magnitude

Figure 14. Example of a simple logic tree and graph of the distribution of estimated magnitudes (from Coppersmith and Youngs, 1986).

sis on the use of seismic moment and moment rates, fault segmentation, uncertainties and their practical application in the analysis, and further understanding of the physics of earthquake sources. Seismic-hazard analyses are developing with new emphasis placed on different seismotectonic settings and new potential seismic sources, such as intraplate, fold-related, and subduction-zone settings. One newly proposed potential seismic source is a gigantic landslide (e.g., 1975 Kalapana earthquake [$M_s = 7.1$]; Eissler and Kanamori, 1987).

The estimation process needs to be dynamic, yet logical and verifiable, to facilitate new studies and situations. Probabilistic techniques are gaining importance in seismic-hazard analyses, and earthquake size estimates are increasingly being formated to facilitate this usage. These techniques involve incorporating timing information via earthquake recurrence intervals or slip rates associated with the size estimate. Ultimately, the procedure developed is determined by the type of project being considered and the acceptable risks involved. In future studies, it is anticipated that approaches, scaling parameters, and techniques for estimating earthquake size will be refined to a level approaching that of

the inherent variability in earthquake processes. Based on various uncertainties and our experience, we feel that present procedures, including the use of the multiple approach, can generally allow the estimation of earthquake magnitudes with a precision of about ¼ to ½ magnitude unit.

ACKNOWLEDGMENTS

We thank Robert Akers, A. Wayne Ayers, John Bell, Douglas G. Clark, Diane dePolo, L. Toccoy Dudley, Jeff Howard, Mark McQuilkin, Dick Meeuwig, Lalliana Mualchin, Wil Peak, Alan Ramelli, Leon Reiter, Thomas Sawyer, Nick Varnum, and especially John G. Anderson, Steve Wesnousky, and Kevin Coppersmith for useful reviews and comments. Preparation of this chapter was supported in part by a grant from the Nevada Nuclear Waste Project Office. Many of the studies that contributed to this chapter were done for the U.S. Nuclear Regulatory Commission and the California Division of Safety of Dams. We gratefully acknowledge their support and encouragement.

APPENDIX A: TYPES OF EARTHQUAKE SIZE MEASUREMENTS

Earthquake size is generally gauged by three types of measurements: earthquake intensity, earthquake magnitude, and seismic moment. These measurements are discussed in detail below.

Earthquake intensity

Earthquake intensity is a measure of the degree of physical damage, human perception, and geologic effects of an earthquake at a location or site (Richter, 1958; Steinbrugge, 1982). After an earthquake, the intensity values at many locations are commonly plotted on an isoseismal map, and lines or boundaries between areas with different intensity values are drawn. The first intensity scale developed in 1883 was the Rossi-Forel scale (RF), which had 10 associated values labeled I through X (intensity values are traditionally reported in Roman numerals).

The most commonly used intensity scale in the United States today is the Modified Mercalli scale (MM), which has 12 values, I through XII. Mercalli originated this scale in 1902 and Wood and Neumann (1931) modified it to its present form. The lower part of the scale is based on human perceptions of the earthquakes such as "felt by few at rest." The middle part of the range is a combination of building damage and human reactions. The upper part of the scale incorporates widespread geologic effects of the earthquake, such as landslides and broad fissuring.

Earthquake intensity is a function of many factors, including strong ground-motion characteristics, site conditions, and construction quality. Unfortunately, intensity values have uncertainties due to subjectivity in intensity observations, and structures or situations that do not obviously fit into categories. Some observers assign maximum values, while others assign average values of intensity to a location, causing variability in reports. Intensity values from nighttime earthquakes may be hard to assign due to fewer alert observers. Another problem is that the intensity scale is not linear, due to the various types of observations used for different parts of the scale (Steinbrugge, 1982).

Despite these shortcomings, earthquake intensities have been used worldwide in seismic analyses and examined in some detail by several authors who have developed computer programs to predict intensities for seismic hazards (e.g., Evernden and Thomson, 1985). Several relations have been developed between earthquake magnitude and intensity (Gutenberg and Richter, 1942; Toppozada, 1975; Nuttli and others, 1979; Greenhalgh and others, 1988). These relations allow magnitude values to be assigned to pre-instrumental earthquakes and historical-earthquake databases to be supplemented.

Intensity values are usually the only earthquake size information available for pre-instrumental events, which at times may be critical for seismic-hazard considerations. When considering the seismic hazard of a site, it is useful to review intensity maps of prior earthquakes that affected the site.

Earthquake magnitude

The most commonly used measurement for describing the relative size of earthquakes is magnitude. A number of different magnitude scales have been developed, each based on the measurement of a specific type of seismic wave or phase that has propagated away from the earthquake source (Fig. 15). As a result, several different magnitude values are often assigned to the same earthquake. In practice, the various magnitude scales yield systematically different values of magnitude (Fig. 15). For the analysis of seismic hazards, it is important to recognize the differences between the various magnitude scales, since each is based on the measurement of seismic waves of different frequencies. Excellent reviews of magnitude scales and the quantification of earthquakes have been given by Richter (1958), Bath (1981), and Kanamori (1983).

Local magnitude. Richter (1935) developed the first magnitude scale, now called the local magnitude scale (M_L), using Wood-Anderson seismographs (free period of ~0.8 s). The procedure involves measuring the maximum amplitude of a Wood-Anderson seismogram, measuring the distance from the earthquake source, and comparing the event to a standard or reference earthquake (Richter, 1935, 1958). Richter defined magnitude 0 as an earthquake whose waves create a thousandth of a millimeter amplitude on a seismogram, at a distance of 100 km. Magnitude increases logarithmically with the size of the maximum amplitude, hence, a measured amplitude of 1 mm at 100-km

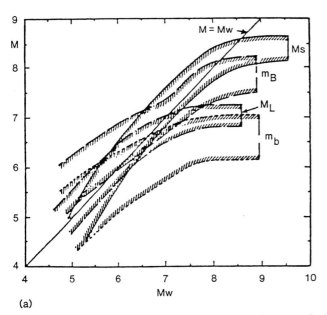

(a)

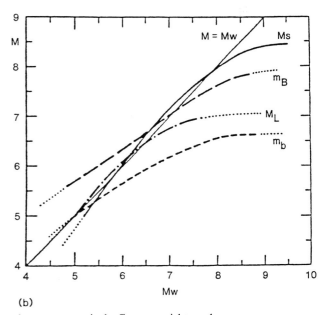

(b)

Figure 15. Relations between various magnitude scales and moment magnitude. Curves on right graph are mid-points of the ranges shown in left graph (from Kanamori, 1983).

distance corresponds to magnitude 3 earthquake. Other studies have used digital seismograms and run them through the response of a Wood-Anderson instrument to estimate local magnitude (e.g., Kanamori and Jennings, 1978).

Most subsequent magnitude scales have been developed to match local magnitude values over various magnitude ranges. Like other magnitude scales (except moment magnitude), M_L "saturates" at some value, in this case about magnitude 7. Saturating means that even though the seismic moment or energy release of the earthquake continues to grow, this magnitude scale becomes a constant, or increases very slowly (Kanamori, 1983).

Because of the high damping of the Wood-Anderson instrument, the maximum amplitude on the seismogram does not necessarily come from waves that have a period near 0.8 sec (John G. Anderson, personal communication, 1989). Nevertheless, engineers have been attracted to the utility of the local magnitude scale, because the free period of a Wood-Anderson instrument is within the period range of common engineering structures (Kanamori and Jennings, 1978).

Surface-wave magnitude. Surface-wave magnitudes (M_s) are determined by measuring the maximum amplitudes of 20-s-period surface waves at regional and teleseismic distances (Gutenberg, 1945a). Since M_s can be measured at teleseismic distances, it is used to assign magnitudes to moderate and larger earthquakes from around the world. Hence, many of the moderate and large earthquakes in the global historical-earthquake record have been assigned surface-wave magnitudes. Consequently, many of the correlations between magnitude and earthquake-rupture parameters (e.g., surface fault length) use surface-wave magnitudes (Slemmons, 1982; Bonilla and others, 1984; Lienkaemper, 1984). Surface-wave magnitudes are "on scale" for earthquakes of magnitudes $\geqslant 5$ and saturate near magnitude 8 (Kanamori, 1983). This range, $5 \leqslant M_s \leqslant \sim 8$, is useful for potentially destructive earthquakes in nonsubduction-zone regions.

Body-wave magnitude. Body-wave magnitudes are computed from the amplitude and period of seismic body waves (i.e., waves that have traveled through the interior of the earth; Gutenberg 1945a, b). In historical catalogs, the long-period body-wave magnitude (m_B) is common and is usually determined from seismic phases such as P, PP, and S, at periods ranging from 0.5 to 12 s (Gutenberg, 1945a, b).

Since the installation of the World Wide Standardized Seismograph Network (WWSSN) in the late 1960s, body-wave magnitudes have been determined using the WWSSN, short-period, vertical-component seismograms at a period of about 1 s (Kanamori, 1983). This is called a short-period body-wave magnitude (m_b). Only the first few seconds of the P-wave arrival are considered for the m_b determination, and despite substantial differences in the phases measured as compared to m_B, the same formula used for m_B is used for m_b (Kanamori, 1983). Kanamori points out many deficiencies of m_b as a magnitude scale, including: (1) there are significantly different amplitudes of P waves from strike-slip versus dip-slip earthquakes caused by the radiation patterns, and (2) the first few seconds only represent a small fraction of the energy of large rupture events.

The short-period body wave scale is commonly used in seismic-hazard analysis in the eastern and central United States, because it is based on the measurement of high-frequency waves that are of direct interest to engineering, and because there exists a data set of body-wave magnitudes for stable continental interiors (Coppersmith and others, 1987).

Nuttli (1973) studied surface waves in eastern North America, and found that he could estimate an equivalent body-wave magnitude by considering the ratio of the amplitude to the period of Love (L_g) waves (surface waves with lateral particle motion). Nuttli used the vertical

components of L_g waves at about a 1 second period (Nuttli and others, 1979; Herrmann and Kijko, 1983, Nuttli, 1983). Using L_g waves to estimate body-wave magnitude is commonly identified by using the symbol m_{bLg} (Coppersmith and others, 1987).

With the various types of measurements of body-wave magnitude, it is important to know how a magnitude was determined for individual earthquakes in a compilation. Body-wave magnitudes are useful for small to large earthquakes; they saturate around magnitude 7.3 (Nuttli, 1981).

Moment magnitude. Moment magnitude (M_w) was developed to represent the energy release of large and great earthquakes (Kanamori, 1977b; Hanks and Kanamori, 1979). The scale is based on the measurement of seismic moment (see next section), which is related to magnitude through energy calculations. The moment magnitude theoretically represents the size of an earthquake at an infinite period, so M_w does not experience the saturation or filtering of energy at particular periods with different earthquake sizes. Subduction-zone hazards include large and great earthquakes whose energy is only accurately represented by moment magnitude.

The moment magnitude can be easily calculated from an earthquake moment value using a relation developed by Hanks and Kanamori (1979) for southern California:

$$M_w = 2/3 \log M_0 - 10.7$$

where M_0 = seismic moment. Table 3 shows how M_w changes with M_0 with different earthquake sizes.

Seismic moment

Seismic moments (M_0) are size estimates that are based on the static displacements associated with an earthquake (Aki, 1966). The use of seismic moments has become preferred in seismotectonic studies because it is a more direct, physical measure of earthquake size than magnitude (Hanks and others, 1975; Wesnousky, 1986). Seismic moment can be determined in a number of ways, including the analysis of seismograms (e.g., considering spectral amplitudes), from field/geologic observations, and from geodetic measurements (Brune, 1968; Kanamori, 1970; Dziewonski and others, 1981; Stein and Barrientos, 1985). This provides a basic link between the geologic data gathered in the analysis of a fault, and the potential earthquake sizes that can be associated with that fault. A seismic-moment rate along a fault can be calculated if information of paleoseismic displacements, or the age of an offset feature, or seismic data are available (Brune, 1968; Wesnousky, 1986). The seismic moment is defined as:

$$M_0 = DA\mu$$

where D is the average displacement across the fault surface, A is the area of the fault surface derived from an estimation of fault length and width, and μ is the average shear rigidity (Aki, 1966; Brune, 1968). For crustal rocks, seismologists typically assume shear modulus values of 3 to 3.5×10^{11} dyne/cm^2 (John G. Anderson, personal communication, 1989).

The moment relation directly facilitates the use of data collected during paleoseismic and geologic studies as input into an earthquake size estimate. Many current seismotectonic studies estimate both moment and magnitude values.

REFERENCES CITED

Abe, K., 1975, Reliable estimation of the seismic moment of large earthquakes: Journal of Physics of the Earth, v. 23, p. 381–390.

Acharya, K. H., 1979, Regional variations in the rupture-length magnitude relationships and their dynamic significance: Bulletin of the Seismological Society of America, v. 69, p. 2063–2084.

Aki, K., 1966, Generation and propagation of G waves from the Niigata earthquake of June 16, 1964; Part 2, Estimation of earthquake moment, released energy, and stress-strain drop from the G wave spectrum: Bulletin of the Earthquake Research Institute, v. 44, p. 73–88.

—— , 1979, Characterization of barriers on an earthquake fault: Journal of Geophysical Research, v. 84, p. 6140–6148.

Albee, A. L., and Smith, J. L., 1966, Earthquake characteristics and fault activity in southern California, *in* Lung, R., and Proctor, eds., Engineering geology in southern California: Los Angeles Section, Association of Engineering Geologists, p. 9–34.

Allen, C. R., 1968, The tectonic environments of seismically active and inactive areas along the San Andreas fault system, *in* Dickinson, W. R., and Grantz, A., Proceedings of the Conference on Geologic Problems of the San Andreas fault system: Stanford, California, Stanford University Publications in the Geological Sciences, v. 11, p. 70–82.

—— , 1981, The modern San Andreas fault, *in* Ernst, W. G., ed., The geotectonic development of California, Rubey volume 1: Englewood Cliffs, New Jersey, Prentice-Hall, Inc., p. 511–534.

—— , 1986, Seismological and paleoseismological techniques of research in active tectonics, *in* Active tectonics: Washington, D.C., National Academy Press Studies in Geophysics, p. 148–154.

Ambraseys, N. N., 1978, Studies in historical seismicity and tectonics, *in* Brice, W. C., ed., The environmental history of the Near and Middle East: New York, Academic Press, p. 185–210.

—— , 1983, Notes on historical seismicity: Bulletin of the Seismological Society of America, v. 73, p. 1917–1920.

Anderson, J. G., 1979, Estimating the seismicity from geological structure for seismic-risk studies: Bulletin of the Seismological Society of America, v. 69, p. 135–158.

Ando, M., 1979, The Hawaii earthquake of November 29, 1975; Lowdip angle faulting due to forceful injection of magma: Journal of Geophysical Research, v. 84, p. 7616–1626.

Bakun, W. H., Stewart, R. M., Bufe, C. G., and Marks, S. M., 1980, Implication of seismicity for failure of a section of the San Andreas fault: Bulletin of the Seismological Society of America, v. 70, p. 185–201.

Basham, P. W., Weichert, D. H., and Berry, M. J., 1979, Regional assessment of seismic risk in eastern Canada: Bulletin of the Seismological Society of America, v. 69, p. 1567–1602.

Bath, M., 1981, Earthquake magnitude; Recent research and current trends: Earth Science Reviews, v. 17, p. 315–398.

Bernreuter, D. L., Savy, J. B., and Mensing, R. W., 1987, Comparison of seismic hazard estimates obtained by using alternative seismic hazard methodologies, *in* Cakmak, A. S., ed., Ground motion and engineering seismology: New York, Elsevier Scientific Publishing Co. Developments in Geotechnical Engineering, v. 44, p. 219–230.

Blong, R. J., 1984, Volcanic hazards; A sourcebook on the effects of eruptions: New York, Academic Press, 424 p.

Bodin, P., Brune, J., Slemmons, D. B., and Zhang, X., 1987, Scaling relations among the source parameters of shallow earthquakes [abs.]: EOS Transactions of the American Geophysical Union, v. 68, p. 1243.

Bonilla, M. G., 1967, Historical surface faulting in continental United States and adjacent parts of Mexico: U.S. Geological Survey Open-File Report, 36 p.

—— , 1970, Surface faulting and related effects, *in* Wiegel, R. L., ed., Earthquake engineering: Englewood Cliffs, New Jersey, Prentice-Hall, p. 47–74.

—— , 1980, Comment and reply on 'Estimating maximum expectable magnitudes of earthquakes from fault dimensions': Geology, v. 8, p. 162–163.

Bonilla, M. G., and Buchanan, J. M., 1970, Interim report on worldwide historic surface faulting: U.S. Geological Survey Open-File Report, 32 p.

Bonilla, M. G., Mark, R. F., and Lienkaemper, J. J., 1984, Statistical relations among earthquake magnitude, surface rupture length, and surface fault displacement: Bulletin of the Seismological Society of America, v. 74, p. 2379–2411.

Brune, J. N., 1968, Seismic movement, seismicity, and rate of slip along major fault zones: Journal of Geophysical Research, v. 73, p. 777–784.

Byrne, D. E., Davis, D. M., and Sykes, L. R., 1988, Loci and maximum size of thrust earthquakes and the mechanics of the shallow region of subduction zones: Tectonics, v. 7, p. 833–857.

California Division of Mines and Geology, 1975, Recommended guidelines for determining the maximum credible earthquake and the maximum probable earthquakes: California Division of Mines and Geology Note 43, 1 p.

Cao, T., and Aki, K., 1986, Effect of slip rate on stress drop: Pure and Applied Geophysics, v. 24, p. 515–529.

Carr, M. J., Stoiber, R. E., and Drake, C. L., 1974, The segmented nature of some continental margins, *in* Burk, C. A., and Drake, C. L., eds., The geology of continental margins: Berlin, Springer-Verlag, p. 105–114.

Chen, W.-P., and Molnar, P., 1983, Focal depths of intracontinental and intraplate earthquakes and their implications for the thermal and mechanical properties of the lithosphere: Journal of Geophysical Research, v. 88, p. 4183–4214.

Chinnery, M. A., 1969, Earthquake magnitude and source parameters: Bulletin of the Seismological Society of America, v. 59, p. 1969–1982.

Cluff, L. S., and 5 others, 1981, Seismic safety review of the proposed liquefied natural gas facility, Little Cojo Bay, Santa Barbara County, California: LNG Seismic Review Panel Report to the California Public Utilities Commission, 33 p.

Coffman, J. L., and von Hake, C. A., 1973, Earthquake history of the United States: U.S. Department of Commerce, National Oceanic and Atmospheric Administration Publication 41-1, 208 p.

Coppersmith, K. J., 1982, Probabilistic evaluations of earthquake hazards, *in* Hart, E. W., Hirschfeld, S. E., and Schulz, S. S., eds., Proceedings of a Conference on Earthquake Hazards in the Eastern San Francisco Bay Area: California Division of Mines and Geology Special Publication 62, p. 125–134.

—— , 1987, Maximum earthquakes, fault slip rates, and earthquake recurrence, *in* Strong ground motion, seismic analysis, design, and code issues short course, April 3–4, 1987, San Francisco, California: Earthquake Engineering Research Institute, chapter 3, 12 p.

Coppersmith, K. J., and Schneider, J. F., 1989, Assessment of maximum earthquake magnitudes within stable continental regions [abs.]: Seismological Society of America Seismological Research Letters, v. 60, p. 12.

Coppersmith, K. J., and Youngs, R. R., 1982, Probabilistic earthquake source definition for seismic exposure analyses [abs.]: Seismological Society of America Earthquake Notes, v. 53, p. 67–68.

—— , 1986, Capturing uncertainty in probabilistic seismic hazard assessments within intraplate tectonic environments, *in* Proceedings of the 3rd U.S. National Conference on Earthquake Engineering Charleston, South Carolina, August 24–28, 1986: Earthquake Engineering Research Institute, v. 1, p. 301–312.

Coppersmith, K. J., Johnston, A. C., Metzger, A. G., and Arabasz, W. J., 1987, Methods for assessing maximum earthquakes in the central and eastern United States: Electric Power Research Institute, Research Project 2556-12 working report, 121 p.

Crone, A. J., and Omdahl, E. M., eds., 1987, Directions in paleoseismology: U.S. Geological Survey Open-File Report 87–673, 456 p.

Crone, A. J., and 6 others, 1987, Surface faulting accompanying the Borah Peak earthquake and segmentation of the Los River fault, central Idaho: Bulletin of the Seismological Society of America, v. 77, p. 739–770.

Darragh, R., and Bold, B. A., 1987, A comment on the statistical regression relation between earthquake magnitude and fault rupture length: Bulletin of the Seismological Society of America, v. 77, p. 1479–1484.

dePolo, C. M., Clark, D. G., Slemmons, D. B., and Aymard, W. H., 1989, Historical Basin and Range Province surface faulting and fault segmentation, *in* Schwartz, D. P., and Sibson, R. H., eds., Workshop on fault segmentation and controls of rupture initiation and termination: U.S. Geological Survey Open-File Report 89-315, p. 131–162.

Dziewonski, A. M., Chou, T.-A., and Woodhouse, J. H., 1981, Determination of earthquake source parameters from waveform data for studies of global and regional seismicity: Journal of Geophysical Research, v. 86, p. 2825–2852.

Eaton, J. P., O'Neill, M. E., and Murdock, J. N., 1970, Aftershocks of the 1966 Parkfield earthquake sequence: Bulletin of the Seismological Eissler, H. K., and Kanamori, H., 1987, A single-force model for the 1975 Kalapana, Hawaii, earthquake: Journal of Geophysical Research, v. 92, p. 4827–4836.

Electric Power Research Institute, 1986, Seismic hazard methodology for the central and eastern United States, v. 1; Methodology: Electric Power Research Institute NP-4726.

Evernden, J. F., and Thomson, J. M., 1985, Predicting seismic intensities, *in* Ziony, J. I., ed., Evaluating earthquake hazards in the Los Angeles region; An earth-science perspective: U.S. Geological Survey Professional Paper 1360, p. 151–202.

Federal Emergency Management Agency, 1985, Federal guidelines for earthquake analyses and design of dams: Federal Emergency Management Agency 65, 45 p.

Freeman, K. J., Fuller, S., and Schell, B. A., 1986, The use of surface faults for estimating design earthquakes; Implications of the 28 October 1983 Idaho earthquake: Bulletin of the Association of Engineering Geologists, v. 23, p. 325–332.

Gilbert, M. C., 1983, The Meers fault of southwestern Oklahoma; Evidence for possible strong Quaternary seismicity in the mid-continent [abs.]: EOS Transactions of the American Geophysical Union, v. 64, p. 313.

Greenhalgh, S. A., Denham, D., McDougall, R., and Rynn, J.M.W., 1988, Magnitude–intensity relations for Australian earthquakes: Bulletin of the Seismological Society of America, v. 78, p. 374–379.

Gutenberg, B., 1945a, Amplitudes of P, PP, and S and magnitude of shallow earthquakes: Bulletin of the Seismological Society of America, v. 35, p. 57–69.

—— , 1945b, Magnitude determination for deep focus earthquakes: Bulletin of the Seismological Society of America, v. 35, p. 117–130.

Gutenberg, B., and Richter, C. F., 1942, Earthquake magnitude, intensity, energy, and acceleration: Bulletin of the Seismological Society of America, v. 32, p. 162–191.

—— , 1944, Frequency of earthquakes in California: Bulletin of the Seismological Society of America, v. 34, p. 185–188.

Habermann, R. E., McCann, W. R., and Perin, B., 1986, Spatial seismicity variations along convergent plate boundaries: Geophysical Journal of the Royal Astronomical Society, v. 85, p. 43–68.

Hanks, T. C., and Kanamori, H., 1979, A moment-magnitude scale: Journal of Geophysical Research, v. 84, p. 2348–2350.

Hanks, T. C., Hileman, J. A., and Thatcher, W., 1975, Seismic moments of the larger earthquakes of the southern California region: Geological Society of America Bulletin, v. 86, p. 1131–1139.

Hasegawa, H. S., and Kanamori, H., 1987, Source mechanism of the magnitude 7.2 Grand Banks earthquake of November 1929; Double couple or submarine landslide?: Bulletin of the Seismological Society of America, v. 77, p. 1984–2004.

Hauksson, E., and 15 others, 1988, The 1987 Whittier Narrows earthquake in the Los Angeles metropolitan area, California: Science, v. 239, p. 1409–1412.

Herrmann, R. B., and Kijko, A., 1983, Short-period L_g magnitudes; Instrument, attenuation, and source effects: Bulletin of the Seismological Society of America, v. 73, p. 1835–1850.

Hobbs, B. E., Ord, A., and Teyssier, C., 1986, Earthquakes in the ductile regime?: Pure and Applied Geophysics, v. 124, p. 309–336.

Housner, G. W., 1969, Engineering estimates of ground shaking and maximum earthquake magnitude, *in* Proceedings of the 4th World Conference on Earthquake Engineering: Chilean Association of Seismology and Earthquake Engineering, v. 1, p. 1–13.

Iida, K., 1965, Earthquake magnitude, earthquake fault, and source dimensions: Nagoya University Journal of Earth Sciences, v. 13, p. 115–132.

Jarrard, R. D., 1986, Relations among subduction parameters: Reviews of Geophysics, v. 24, p. 217–284.

Johnston, A. C., Metzger, A. G., and Coppersmith, K. J., 1987, The seismicity of stable continental interiors [abs.]: Seismological Society of America Seismological Research Letters, v. 58, p. 32.

Jones, L. M., 1987, The size and location of the next great southern California earthquake; Implication of constant stress drops [abs.]: EOS Transactions of the American Geophysical Union, v. 68, p. 1349.

Kanamori, H., 1970, Synthesis of long-period surface waves and its application to earthquake source studies; Kurile Islands earthquake of October 13, 1963: Journal of Geophysical Research, v. 75, p. 5011–5027.

—— , 1971, Great earthquakes at island arcs and the lithosphere: Tectonophysics, v. 12, p. 187–198.

—— , 1977a, Seismic and aseismic slip along subduction zones and their tectonic implications, *in* Talwani, M., and Pitman, W. C., eds., Island arcs, deep sea trenches, and back-arc basins: American Geophysical Union Maurice Ewing Series, v. 1, p. 163–174.

—— , 1977b, The energy release in great earthquakes: Journal of Geophysical Research, v. 82, p. 2981–1987.

—— , 1983, Magnitude scale and quantification of earthquakes: Tectonophysics, v. 93, p. 185–199.

—— , 1986, Rupture process of subduction-zone earthquakes: Annual Review of Earth and Planetary Sciences, v. 14, p. 293–322.

Kanamori, H., and Allen, C. R., 1986, Earthquake repeat time and average stress drop, *in* Das, S., Boatwright, J., and Scholz, C. H., eds., Earthquake source mechanics: American Geophysical Union Maurice Ewing Series, v. 6, p. 227–235.

Kanamori, H., and Given, J. W., 1982, Analysis of long-period seismic waves excited by the May 18, 1980, eruption of Mount St. Helens: A terrestrial monopole?: Journal of Geophysical Research, v. 87, p. 5422–5432.

Kanamori, H., and Jennings, P. C., 1978, Determination of local magnitude, M_1, from strong-motion accelerograms: Bulletin of the Seismological Society of America, v. 68, p. 471–485.

Kelleher, J., and McCann, W., 1976, Buoyant zones, great earthquakes, and unstable boundaries of subduction: Journal of Geophysical Research, v. 81, p. 4885–4896.

Kelleher, J., Savino, J., Rowlett, H., and McCann, W., 1974, Why and where great thrust earthquakes occur along island arcs: Journal of Geophysical Research, v. 79, p. 4889–4899.

Keller, E. A., and Rockwell, T. K., 1984, Tectonic geomorphology, Quaternary chronology, and paleoseismicity, *in* Costa, J. E., and Fleisher, P. J., eds., Developments and applications of geomorphology: New York, Springer-Verlag, p. 203–239.

King, C.-Y., and Knopoff, L., 1968, Stress drop in earthquakes: Bulletin of the Seismological Society of America, v. 58, p. 249–257.

King, G.C.P., 1986, Speculations on the geometry of the initiation and termination processes of earthquake rupture and its relation of morphology and geological structure: Pure and Applied Geophysics, v. 124, p. 567–585.

King, G., and Nabelek, J., 1985, Role of fault bends in the initiation and termination of earthquake rupture: Science, v. 228, p. 984–987.

King, G.C.P., and Yielding, G., 1983, The evolution of a thrust fault system; Processes of rupture initiation, propagation, and termination in the 1980 El Asnam (Algeria) earthquake: Geophysical Journal of the Royal Astronomical Society, v. 77, p. 915–933.

Knuepfer, P.L.K., 1989, Implications of the characteristics of end-points of historical surface ruptures for the nature of fault segmentation, *in* Schwartz, D. P., and Sibson, R. H., eds., Workshop on Fault Segmentation and Controls of Rupture Initiation and Termination: U.S. Geological Survey Open-File report 89-315, p. 193–228.

Kulkarni, R. B., Youngs, R. R., and Coppersmith, K. J., 1984, Assessment of confidence intervals for results of seismic hazard analysis, *in* Proceedings of the 8th World Conference on Earthquake Engineering, San Francisco, California, July 21–28, 1984: Prentice-Hall, v. 1, p. 263–270.

Lay, T., and Kanamori, H., 1981, An asperity model of large earthquake sequences, *in* Simpson, D. W., and Richards, P. G., eds., Earthquake prediction; An international review: American Geophysical Union Maurice Ewing Series, v. 4, p. 579–592.

Lienkaemper, J. J., 1984, Comparison of two surface-wave magnitude scales; M of Gutenberg and Richter (1954) and M_s of "Preliminary determination of epicenters": Bulletin of the Seismological Society of America, v. 74, p. 2357–2378.

Lin, J., and Stein, R., 1989, Coseismic folding, earthquake recurrence, and the 1987 source mechanism at Whittier Narrows, Los Angeles Basin, California: Journal of Geophysical Research, v. 94, p. 9614–9632.

Luza, K. V., Madole, R. F., and Crone, A. J., 1987, Investigations of the Meers fault in southwest Oklahoma: Nuclear Regulatory Commission NUREG CR-4937, 55 p.

Madole, R. F., 1988, Stratigraphic evidence of Holocene faulting in the mid-continent; The Meers fault, southwestern Oklahoma: Geological Society of America Bulletin, v. 100, p. 392–401.

Mark, R. K., and Bonilla, M. G., 1977, Regression analysis of earthquake magnitude and surface fault length using the 1970 data of Bonilla and Buchanan: U.S. Geological Survey Open-File Report 77-614, 8 p.

McCann, W. R., Nishenko, S. P., Sykes, L. R., and Krause, J., 1979, Seismic gaps and plate tectonics; Seismic potential for major boundaries: Pure and Applied Geophysics, v. 117, p. 1082–1147.

McGarr, A., 1987, Contribution to Electric Power Research Institute's Proceedings on Intraplate Maximum Earthquakes, *in* Coppersmith, K. J., Johnson, A. C., Metzger, A. G., and Arabasz, W. J., Methods for assessing maximum earthquakes in the central and eastern United States, working report: Electric Power Research Institute Research Project 2556-12, p. 4-63–4-68.

Molnar, P., 1979, Earthquake recurrence intervals and plate tectonics: Bulletin of the Seismological Society of America, v. 69, p. 115–133.

Namson, J. S., and Davis, T. L., 1988, Seismically active fold and thrust belt in the San Joaquin Valley, central California: Geological Society of America Bulletin, v. 100, p. 257–273.

Nowroozi, A. A., 1985, Empirical relations between magnitudes and fault parameters for earthquakes in Iran: Bulletin of the Seismological Society of America, v. 75, p. 1327–1338.

Nuttli, O. W., 1973, Seismic wave attenuation and magnitude relations for eastern North America: Journal of Geophysical Research, v. 78, p. 876–885.

—— , 1981, On the problem of the maximum magnitude of earthquakes, *in* Hays, W. W., Evaluation of regional seismic hazards and risk: U.S. Geological Survey Open-File Report 81-437.

—— , 1983, Average seismic source-parameter relations for mid-plate earthquakes: Bulletin of the Seismological Society of America, v. 73, p. 519–535.

Nuttli, O. W., Bollinger, G. A., and Griffiths, D. W., 1979, On the relation between modified Mercalli intensity and body-wave magnitude: Bulletin of the Seismological Society of America, v. 69, p. 893–909.

Pierce, K. L., 1986, Dating methods, *in* Active tectonics: Washington, D.C., National Academy Press collection Studies in Geophysics, p. 195–214.

Purcaru, G., and Burckhemer, H., 1982, Quantitative relations of seismic source parameters and a classification of earthquakes: Tectonophysics, v. 84, p. 57–128.

Ramelli, A. R., 1988, Late Quaternary tectonic activity of the Meers fault, southwest Oklahoma [M.S. thesis]: Reno, University of Nevada, 123 p.

Ramelli, A. R., Slemmons, D. B., and Brocoum, S. J., 1987, The Meers fault; Tectonic activity in southwestern Oklahoma: U.S. Nuclear Regulatory Commission NUREG/CR-4852, 25 p.

Ravat, D. N., Braile, L. W., and Hinze, W. J., 1987, Earthquakes and plutons in the midcontinental-evidence from the Bloomfield complex: Seismological Research Letters, v. 58, p. 41.

Richter, C. F., 1935, An instrumental earthquake magnitude scale: Bulletin of the Seismological Society of America, v. 25, p. 1–32.

—— , 1958, Elementary seismology: San Francisco, California, W. H. Freeman, 768 p.

Ross, S. M., 1987, Introduction to probability and statistics for engineers and scientists: New York, John Wiley and Sons, 489 p.

Ruff, L. J., 1989, Do trench sediments affect great earthquake occurrence in subduction zones?: Pure and Applied Geophysics, v. 129, p. 264–279.

Ruff, L. J., and Kanamori, H., 1980, Seismicity and the subduction process: Physics of the Earth and Planetary Interiors, v. 23, p. 240–252.

Scholz, C. H., 1982, Scaling laws for large earthquakes; Consequences for physical models: Bulletin of the Seismological Society of America, v. 72, p. 1–14.

—— , 1988, The brittle-plastic transition and the depth of seismic faulting: Geologische Rundschau, v. 77, p. 319–328.

—— , 1990, The mechanics of earthquakes and faulting: Cambridge, Cambridge University Press, 439 p.

Schwartz, D. P., 1988, Geologic characterization of seismic sources; Moving into the 1990s, *in* von Thun, J. L., ed., Earthquake engineering and soil dynamics; 2, Recent advances in ground-motion evaluation: American Society of Civil Engineers Geotechnical Special Publication 20, p. 1–42.

Schwartz, D. P., and Coppersmith, K. J., 1984, Fault behavior and characteristic earthquakes; Examples from the Wasatch and San Andreas fault zones: Journal of Geophysical Research, v. 89, p. 5681–5698.

—— , 1986, Seismic hazards; New trends in analysis using geologic data, *in* Active tectonics: Washington, D.C., National Academy Press Collection Studies in Geophysics, p. 215–230.

Schwartz, D. P., and Sibson, R. H., eds., 1989, Fault segmentation and controls of rupture initiation and termination: U.S. Geological Survey Open-File Report 89-315, 447 p.

Schwartz, D. P., Coppersmith, K. J., Swan, F. H., III, Somerville, P., and Savage, W. U., 1981, "Characteristic" earthquakes on intraplate normal faults: Seismological Society of America Earthquake Notes, v. 52, p. 71.

Schwartz, D. P., Coppersmith, K. J., and Swan, F. H., III, 1984, Methods for estimating maximum earthquake magnitudes, *in* Proceeding of the 8th World Conference on Earthquake Engineering, July 21–28, San Francisco, California: Englewood Cliffs, New Jersey, Prentice-Hall, Inc., v. 1, p. 279–285.

Segall, P., and Pollard, D. D., 1980, Mechanics of discontinuous faults: Journal of Geophysical Research, v. 85, p. 4337–4350.

Shimozuru, D., 1971, A seismological approach to the prediction of volcanic eruptions, *in* The surveillance and prediction of volcanic activity: Paris, UNESCO, p. 19–45.

Sibson, R. H., 1982, Fault zone models, heat flow, and the depth distribution of earthquakes in the continental crust of the United States: Bulletin of the Seismological Society of America, v. 72, p. 151–163.

—— , 1985, Stopping of earthquake ruptures at dilitational fault jogs: Nature, v. 316, p. 248–251.

—— , 1986, Earthquakes and rock deformation in crustal fault zones: Annual Reviews of Earth and Planetary Sciences, v. 14, p. 149–175.

—— , 1987, Alternative models for continental seismicity and maximum seismogenic depth: Seismological Society of America Seismological Research Notes, v. 58, p. 32.

Singh, S. K., Bazan, E., and Esteva, L., 1980, Expected earthquake magnitude from a fault: Bulletin of the Seismological Society of America, v. 70, p. 903–914.

Slemmons, D. B., 1977, Faults and earthquake magnitude, *in* State of the art for assessing earthquake hazards in the United States, Report 6: U.S. Army Engineers Waterways Experiment Station Miscellaneous Paper S-73-1, 129 p.

—— , 1982a, Determination of design earthquake magnitudes for microzonation, *in* Proceedings of the 3rd International Earthquake Microzonation Conference: Seattle, Washington, v. 1, p. 119–130.

—— , 1982b, Fault capability and earthquake parameters at the Skagit/Hanford site of Puget Sound Power and Light and other utilities, *in* Safety evaluation report related to the construction of Skagit/Hanford Nuclear Project, units 1 and 2: U.S. Nuclear Regulatory Commission NUREG-0309, supplement 3, appendix G, p. G1–G56.

Slemmons, D. B. , and Chung, D. H., 1982, Maximum credible earthquake magnitudes for the Calaveras and Hayward fault zones, California, *in* Hart, E. W., Hirschfeld, S. E., and Schulz, S. S., eds., Proceedings of a Conference on Earthquake Hazards in the Eastern San Francisco Bay Area: California Division of Mines and Geology Special Publication 62, p. 115–124.

Smith, S. W., 1976, Determination of maximum earthquake magnitude: Geophysical Research Letters, v. 3, p. 351–354.

Statton, C. T., Quittmeyer, R. C., Engelder, T., Turcotte, T., and Kelleher, J., 1987, Tectonic framework, seismic source zones, and seismicity parameters for the eastern United States; An application of the EPRI methodology, *in* Cakmak, A. S., ed., Ground motion and engineering seismology: Berlin, Elsevier Science Publishing Co. Developments in Geotechnical Engineering, v. 44, p. 207–218.

Stein, R. S., and Barrientos, S. E., 1985, Planar high-angle faulting in the Basin and Range; Geodetic analysis of the 1983 Borah Peak, Idaho, earthquake: Journal of Geophysical Research, v. 90, p. 11355–11366.

Stein, R. S., and King, G.C.P., 1984, Seismic potential revealed by surface folding; 1983 Coalinga, California earthquake: Science, v. 224, p. 869–872.

Stein, R. S., and Yeats, R. S., 1989, Hidden earthquakes: Scientific American, v. 260, p. 48–57.

Steinbrugge, K. V., 1982, Earthquakes, volcanoes, and tsunamis; An anatomy of hazards: Skandia America Group, 392 p.

Stepp, J. C., 1986, An overview of EPRI's seismic hazard methodology development program, *in* Hays, W. W., ed., Proceedings of Conference 34, A Workshop on "Probabilistic Earthquake Hazards Assessments," San Francisco, California, November 25–27, 1985: U.S. Geological Survey Open-File Report 86-185, p. 353–368.

Strehlau, J., 1986, A discussion of the depth extent of rupture in large continental earthquakes, *in* Das, S., Boatwright, J., and Scholz, C. H., Earthquake source mechanics: American Geophysical Union Geophysical Monograph 37, p. 131–145.

Sykes, L. R., Byrne, D. E., and Davis, D. M., 1987, Seismic and aseismic subduction; Part 2, Aseismic slip at zo nes of massive sediment supply and nature of great asperities at convergent margins: EOS Transactions of the American Geophysical Union, v. 68, p. 1468.

Thatcher, W., 1990, Order and diversity in the modes of circum-Pacific earthquake recurrence: Journal of Geophysical Research, v. 95, p. 2609–2623.

Thatcher, W., and Bonilla, M. G., 1989, Earthquake fault slip estimation from geologic, geodetic, and seismologic observations; Implications for earthquake mechanics and fault segmentation, *in* Schwartz, D. P., and Sibson, R. H., eds., Workshop on Fault Segmentation and Controls of Rupture Initiation and Termination: U.S. Geological Survey Open-File Report 89-315, p. 386–399.

Tocher, D., 1958, Earthquake energy and ground breakage; Bulletin of the Seismological Society of America, v. 48, p. 147–153.

Toppozada, T. R., 1975, Earthquake magnitude as a function of intensity data in California and western Nevada: Bulletin of the Seismological Society of America, v. 65, p. 1223–1238.

Toro, G. R., and McGuire, R. K., 1987, Calculational procedures for seismic hazard analysis and its uncertainty in the eastern United States, *in* Cakmak, A. S., ed., Ground motion and engineering seismology: Berlin, Elsevier Science Publishing Co. Developments in Geotechnical Engineering, v. 44, p. 195–206.

Tullis, J., and Yund, R. A., 1987, The brittle-ductile transition in feldspathic rocks [abs.]: EOS Transactions of the American Geophysical Union, v. 68, p. 1464.

Uhrhammer, R. A., 1985, The May 2, 1983, Coalinga earthquake and seismicity rates and strain energy in the central Coast Ranges, California, *in* Rymer, M. J., and Ellsworth, W. L., Mechanics of the May 2, 1983, Coalinga

earthquake: U.S. Geological Survey Open-File Report 85-44, p. 61–82.

United States Committee on Large Dams, 1985, Guidelines for selecting seismic parameters for dam projects: International Commission on Large Dams, 39 p.

Wallace, R. E., 1980, Discussion, "Nomograms for estimating components of fault displacement from measured height of fault scarp": Bulletin of the Association of Engineering Geologists, v. 17, p. 39–45.

Weber, F. H., Jr., 1987, Whittier Narrows earthquakes, Los Angeles County: California Geology, v. 40, p. 275–281.

Wells, D., Coppersmith, K., Zhang, X., and Slemmons, D. B., 1989, New earthquake magnitude and fault rupture parameters; Part 1, Surface rupture length and rupture area relationships [abs.]: Seismological Society of America Seismological Research Letters, v. 60, p. 27.

Wentworth, C. M., Bonilla, M. G., and Buchanan, J. M., 1969, Seismic environment of the Burro Flats Site, Ventura County, California: U.S. Geological Survey Open-File Report 73-360, 42 p.

Wesnousky, S. G., 1986, Earthquakes, Quaternary faults, and seismic hazard in California: Journal of Geophysical Research, v. 91, p. 2587–12631.

Wesnousky, S. G., Scholz, C. H., Shimazaki, K., and Matsuda, T., 1983, Earthquake frequency distribution and the mechanics of faulting: Journal of Geophysical Research, v. 88, p. 9331–9340.

Wesson, R. L., Helley, E. J., Lajoie, K. R., and Wentworth, C. M., 1975, Faults and future earthquakes, *in* Borcherdt, R. D., ed., Studies for seismic zonation of the San Francisco Bay region: U.S. Geological Survey Professional Paper 941-A, p. 5–30.

West, D. O., and McCrumb, D. R., 1988, Coastline uplift in Oregon and Washington and the nature of Cascadia subduction-zone tectonics: Geology, v. 16, p. 169–172.

Wheeler, R. L., and Krystinik, K. B., 1987a, Persistent segment boundaries on the Wasatch fault zone, central Utah [abs.]: Seismological Society of America Seismological Research Letters, v. 58, p. 31.

—— , 1987b, Evaluating coinciding anomalies along a fault trace or other transverse; Simulations and statistical procedures: U.S. Geological Survey Bulletin 1802, 12 p.

—— , 1988, Segmentation of the Wasatch fault zone, Utah; Summaries, analyses, and interpretations of geological and geophysical data: U.S. Geological Survey Bulletin 1827, 47 p.

Wood, H. O., and Neumann, F., 1931, Modified Mercalli intensity scale of 1931: Seismological Society of America Bulletin, v. 21, p. 277–283.

Woodward-Clyde Consultants, 1979, Report of the evaluation of maximum earthquake and site ground motion parameters associated with the offshore zone of faulting, San Onofre Nuclear Generating Station: Unpublished report for Southern California Edison Company, 241 p.

Wyss, M., 1979, Estimating maximum expectable magnitude of earthquakes from fault dimensions: Geology, v. 7, p. 336–340.

Yeats, R. S., 1986, Active faults related to folding, *in* Active tectonics: Washington, D.C., National Academic Press Studies in Geophysics, p. 63–79.

Youngs, R. R., and Coppersmith, K. J., 1986, Implications of fault slip rates and earthquake recurrence models to probabilistic seismic hazard estimates: Bulletin of the Seismological Society of America, v. 75, p. 939–964.

Youngs, R. R., Coppersmith, K. J., Power, M. S., and Swan, F. H., III, 1985, Seismic hazard assessment of the Hanford region, eastern Washington state, *in* Proceedings of the Department of Energy Natural Phenomena Hazards Mitigation Conference, Las Vegas, Nevada, October 7–11, 1985: U.S. Department of Energy, p. 169–176.

Zhang, X., Slemmons, D. B., Wells, D., and Coppersmith, K., 1989, New earthquake and fault rupture parameters; Part 2, Maximum and average displacement relationships [abs.]: Seismological Society of America Seismological Research Letters, v. 60, p. 27.

MANUSCRIPT ACCEPTED BY THE SOCIETY AUGUST 18, 1989

Geological Society of America
Reviews in Engineering Geology, Volume VIII
1990

Chapter 2

Probabilistic seismic-hazard analysis using expert opinion; An example from the Pacific Northwest

Kevin J. Coppersmith and Robert R. Youngs
Geomatrix Consultants, Inc., One Market Plaza, Spear Street Tower, Suite 717, San Francisco, California 94105

ABSTRACT

To illustrate methods for incorporating uncertainty into seismic-hazard analyses, we describe the characterization of earthquake sources used in a seismic-hazard analysis for a site in western Washington. A simple and effective tool for incorporating uncertainty into seismic-hazard analysis is called a logic tree; one was used in this study to include the range of possible characteristics of the Cascadia subduction zone seismic sources. At present, considerable uncertainty exists regarding the earthquake potential of the Cascadia zone, particularly due to the completely aseismic nature of the interface between the Juan de Fuca and North America plates. A key issue is whether this aseismic behavior is merely a function of our short period of historical observation (i.e., interseismic quiescence) or representative of longer-term behavior (i.e., aseismic subduction). To develop a complete seismic-source characterization spanning the range of interpretations regarding the earthquake potential of Cascadia, a group of 14 experts was selected based on their experience with the Cascadia subduction zone. These experts assessed source characteristics, including subduction-zone geometry, potential seismic sources, probability that each potential source is active, expected locations and dimensions of rupture, maximum earthquake magnitude, earthquake recurrence models, geologic recurrence intervals, plate convergence rate, and seismic coupling.

In general, all of the experts identified two distinct subduction-zone earthquake sources: an "intra-slab" source representing earthquakes within the subducting Juan de Fuca plate, and the plate interface between the Juan de Fuca and North American plates. An analysis of uncertainties given by individual experts, as well as their differences of opinion, shows that some characteristics of subduction-zone sources are relatively agreed upon, while other characteristics are highly uncertain. For example, it was generally believed that the intra-slab source is seismogenic and that the future locations of earthquakes within the slab will follow the spatial pattern represented by historical seismicity. In contrast, a wide range of assessments was given for the probability that the plate interface is seismogenic and for the amount of seismic coupling between the plates. In making these assessments, the experts relied on a wide range of data sets, including analogies to other subduction zones, thermal-mechanical models of subduction, and geophysical imaging of the Cascadia subduction zone.

The study demonstrates the viability of using expert opinion to assess seismic hazards and illustrates one approach to obtaining a realistic estimate of the uncertainty in the seismic hazard.

Coppersmith, K. J., and Youngs, R. R., 1990, Probabilistic seismic-hazard analysis using expert opinion; An example from the Pacific Northwest, *in* Krinitzsky, E. L., and Slemmons, D. B., Neotectonics in earthquake evaluation: Boulder, Colorado, Geological Society of America Reviews in Engineering Geology, v. 8.

INTRODUCTION

Evaluation of earthquake hazards is currently the focus of considerable scientific and engineering research. While progress is being made, many of the questions concerning the location and nature of potential future earthquakes are unlikely to be answered in the near term. Thus, many engineering and regulatory decisions involving seismic safety must be made in the face of considerable uncertainty about the level of seismic hazard at a particular site. Probabilistic seismic-hazard analysis (PSHA) is an effective tool in making such decisions because it provides a quantitative assessment of the hazard that is consistent with quantitative risk analysis, and it can clarify the range and implications of uncertainties in the seismic hazard (National Research Council, 1988). Quantitative risk assessments allow seismic design and safety considerations to be weighed against economic costs/benefits and contributions to risk from non-earthquake-related sources. The ability of PSHA to represent quantitatively the uncertainty in seismic hazard is an important part of assessing the uncertainty in seismic-risk estimates. Explicit representation of the uncertainty in risk assessments has been found to be an important part of collective decision making (Paté-Cornell, 1986) and is part of the guidelines for risk assessment for nuclear power plants in the United States (U.S. Nuclear Regulatory Commission, 1983).

Depending on the tectonic environment, one must often rely on the use of expert opinion to characterize the earthquake potential of seismic sources for PSHA. This is especially true along the Cascadia subduction zone because, by its very nature, a subduction zone is not amenable to fault-specific field evaluations of earthquake potential, such as those that might be made for an active crustal fault. The problem is further exacerbated by the complete seismic quiescence of the North American–Juan de Fuca plate interface during historical time, precluding the use of seismicity to characterize earthquake potential. Although geological and seismological studies of this margin will likely continue for some time, the use of expert opinion to assess seismic hazards provides a vehicle to incorporate the full spectrum of current scientific thinking regarding the earthquake issue at Cascadia. Precedents for the use of expert opinion in seismic-hazard analyses are provided by recent studies in the eastern United States (Lawrence Livermore National Laboratory, 1985; Electric Power Research Institute, 1986), where the uncertainties regarding earthquake potential are considerable and perhaps comparable to those in the Pacific Northwest.

This chapter describes a PSHA carried out for the Washington Public Power Supply System Unit #3 (Satsop) power plant site in western Washington (see Fig. 1). We focus on the characterization of earthquake sources associated with the subducting Juan de Fuca plate in order to illustrate methods for incorporating expert opinion and scientific uncertainties regarding earthquake potential into PSHA. The assessments provided by the experts are summarized and serve to portray the current thinking regarding the Cascadia subduction zone. The results of the hazard analysis are then briefly discussed. Other aspects of the analysis,

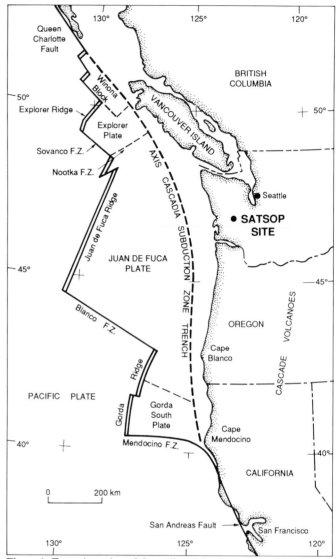

Figure 1. Tectonic setting of Cascadia subduction zone and location of Satsop site (modified from Riddihough, 1984).

including characterization of the shallow crustal earthquake sources, assessment of ground motion attenuation relations, and hazard calculation methodology, are documented in Geomatrix Consultants (1988).

METHODS FOR INCORPORATING UNCERTAINTIES IN SEISMIC-HAZARD ANALYSIS

A PSHA considers various seismic sources that may cause ground motions at a site, the frequency of occurrence of earthquakes of various magnitudes on each source, the maximum magnitude for each source, and the attenuation of the amplitude of ground motions from the sources to the site as a function of magnitude and distance. Each of these characteristics is uncertain and subject to interpretation of available data. We wish to identify explicitly these uncertainties and, more importantly, to incorporate the uncertainties into the analysis. Accordingly, the final results should provide a reasonable representation of what we know and do not know about seismic hazards affecting our site of interest.

Over the past several years, relatively simple techniques have evolved that allow the uncertainties associated with characterizing seismic sources for hazard analyses to be included explicitly and easily. The method used here is a "logic tree," and its value has been proven in many similar studies (e.g., Kulkarni and others, 1984; Youngs and others, 1985; Coppersmith and Youngs, 1986; National Research Council, 1988). A simple example of a logic tree used for assessing maximum magnitude on the basis of fault type and maximum displacement is shown in Figure 2. Logic trees are composed of a series of "nodes," or states, that define the elements of a seismic-hazard analysis (e.g., activity, fault geometry, and length) and, for each node, one or more "branches" define the various values that each element may have. For example, a node of the logic tree may represent "capability," and the branches may be "capable" or "not capable"; or the node may represent "maximum displacement," and the branches may be 2 m, 3 m, and 4 m. The branches represent the possible alternative values for a particular characteristic. Each branch is associated with a probability. The probability is assessed subjectively and reflects the assessor's degree of belief that a particular value is correct. For example, the maximum displacement of 2, 3, and 4 m may be judged from the available data to have relative credibilities of 0.3, 0.5, and 0.2, respectively. Note that the probabilities at a given node sum to 1.0, assuming that the assessor has provided the full range of credible alternatives. An important aspect of logic trees is that the assessments to the right of a node in the tree are dependent on those to the left. For example, from Figure 2a, the assessment of maximum displacement is conditional on the assessment of sense of slip. In this way, the dependencies among various characteristics can be readily accounted for. To complete the example, maximum magnitudes are assessed for each end branch of the logic tree shown in Figure 2a. The resulting values together with their assessed probabilities (the product of all probabilities on the branches leading to the end point) are used to construct a discrete probability distribution for maximum magnitude, as shown in Figure 2b.

SATSOP SEISMIC-HAZARD ANALYSIS

Tectonic setting and uncertainties in earthquake potential

The perception and understanding of subduction in the Pacific Northwest has evolved in the past several years. Past studies of historical seismicity along the Cascadia subduction zone have noted the absence of interface seismicity and have concluded that the interface between the Juan de Fuca and North American plates is either no longer undergoing differential slip (i.e., subduction has ceased) or subduction is occurring aseismically. Im-

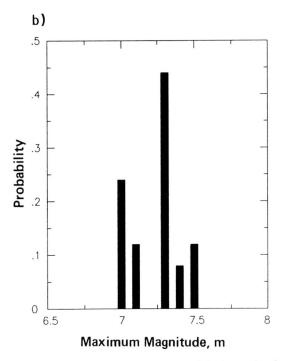

Figure 2. Example use of logic tree. (a) Example logic tree showing two parameters related to maximum magnitude: sense-of-slip and maximum rupture length. The resulting maximum-magnitude values are each associated with a probability that is the product of the conditional probabilities on the branches leading to each magnitude value. (b) Discrete distribution of maximum magnitude resulting from the logic tree assessments.

proved instrumental seismicity coverage in recent years, as well as reexamination of older historical earthquakes, has confirmed a virtual lack of thrust-type earthquakes that might be related to interplate displacement. At the same time, studies of high-resolution seismic reflection data have shown clear evidence of late Quaternary and Holocene deformation in the young, water-saturated sediments of the outer accretionary wedge offshore, suggesting that plate convergence is continuing (Kulm and Peterson, 1984). Empirical studies have hypothesized that the degree of coupling at subduction zones may be a function of the age of the subducting plate and the rate of convergence across the margin (Ruff and Kanamori, 1980). Comparison of the Cascadia zone with other zones on this basis has led to the conclusion by some workers that, despite its historical quiescence, the Cascadia zone may be capable of generating great earthquakes (e.g., Heaton and Kanamori, 1984). Geological studies of estuaries in southwestern Washington suggest that the margin has been subjected to repeated episodes of rapid subsidence, perhaps associated with large, prehistoric interplate earthquakes (Atwater, 1987). Offshore and onshore geophysical studies, including the Lithoprobe project through Vancouver Island (e.g., Clowes and others, 1987), indicate that extremely high sedimentation rates have buried the Juan de Fuca plate, and a thick sequence of sediments has been dragged down the subduction zone to depths of at least 50 km. Thermal-mechanical modeling of the zone (e.g., Sammis and others, 1988) suggests that the combination of the heated nature of the subducted sediments, high fluid pressures, and clay-rich mineralogy serves to prevent the plate interface from accumulating strain energy sufficient to generate earthquakes.

The historical quiescence of the Cascadia subduction-zone plate interface and the variety of approaches being used to understand its behavior, such as those mentioned above, have led to alternative interpretations. The extremes in the interpretations of the potential seismic behavior of the plate interface are: (1) the historical record is characteristic of the long-term behavior of the zone and slippage occurs aseismically, or (2) the historical record represents an interseismic period between the occurrence of large interplate-thrust earthquakes. A variety of behaviors between these two extremes can also be hypothesized. For example, the interface may be weakly coupled such that large events are separated by extremely long recurrence intervals, or the earthquake behavior and rates of activity vary as a function of time.

Given the evolving state of our understanding of the Cascadia subduction zone and its earthquake potential, we have attempted to capture the range of professional opinion and uncertainties by using multiple experts to construct the seismic-hazard model.

Use of expert opinion

Several key tectonic issues (such as the seismogenic capability of the plate interface, the degree of seismic coupling between the plates, earthquake recurrence rates, and the like) are the sub-

ject of ongoing studies but are not likely to be resolved within the near term. Therefore, in order to make engineering decisions at the Satsop site, we attempted to assess the present understanding of the Cascadia zone by questioning experts most familiar with the margin.

In deciding on an appropriate methodology for eliciting expert opinion, we considered the strengths and weaknesses of recent PSHAs involving expert opinion (e.g., LLNL, 1985; EPRI, 1986) because the level of uncertainty and the unlikelihood of short-term resolution of the issues are comparable. By considering these previous studies as well as the specific requirements for a hazard assessment at the Satsop site, a methodology was developed for utilizing expert opinion. The key attributes of the methodology and the purpose for each are summarized in Table 1, and discussed below.

Panel selection. The panel selected for the PSHA was intended to span fields of expertise covering the entire range of the hazard-model components (crustal geometry, seismic capability,

TABLE 1. METHODOLOGY FOR ASSESSING EXPERT OPINION FOR SATSOP SEISMIC HAZARD ANALYSIS

Attribute of Methodology	Purpose
Large number of experts (14)	Encompass spectrum of scientific interpretations; better representation of uncertainty
Experts represent wide variety of disciplines	Incorporate full range of perspectives, data sets, and experience
No single expert required to address all aspects of hazard model	Avoid encouraging expert to go beyond area of expertise
Experts provided with background information and topical reference list	Encourage a uniform basic level data base; provide a focus on key to PSHA
Experts interviewed individually and opinion not associated with expert by name	Allows for free expression of opinion; highly focused discussion
Basis for decisions given and documented	Allows for a technical evaluation of the responses in terms of the scientific issues driving thinking
Interview summaries provided to each expert for review	Ensure accuracy and provide opportunity to change opinion upon reflection
Hazard model developed as components of a logic tree	Model is clearer to experts; allows for sensitivity studies
Full inclusion of uncertainty expressed by experts	Leads to more complete expression of hazard

convergence rate, maximum earthquakes, and earthquake recurrence rate). In addition, a balance of disciplines pertaining to the topic of subduction tectonics and seismicity (e.g., geology, geophysics, seismology, laboratory experimentation, empirical analysis, etc.) was desired. These considerations required that the total number of experts be relatively large (14) for studies of this kind.

A primary consideration in the selection of experts was that they must have had experience with the Cascadia subduction zone or allied experience with other subduction zones having similar characteristics. For example, a suitable expert might be a geologist who has carried out analytical studies of the seismic behavior of subduction zones that are subducting large amounts of sediments *and* who was familiar with the accretionary-wedge characteristics of the Cascadia zone. Because a large part of the uncertainty associated with the Cascadia zone stems from determining its "uniqueness" relative to other subduction zones, it was important that the experts be familiar with *this* zone in order to provide site-specific input to the hazard model. Finally, some of the experts have published interpretations or hypotheses regarding the seismic behavior of the Cascadia subduction zone. As much as possible, we achieved a balanced cross-section of opinion in selecting the panel members.

Consideration was given to individuals in academia, government agencies, and professionals who met the above criteria. The following 14 experts were selected:

John Adams, Canadian Geological Survey
Mark Cloos, University of Texas, Austin
Ronald Clowes, University of British Columbia
Daryl Cowan, University of Washington
Robert Crosson, University of Washington
Gregory Davis, University of Southern California
Thomas Heaton, U.S. Geological Survey
Thomas Hilde, Texas A & M University
Hiroo Kanamori, California Institute of Technology
Vern Kulm, Oregon State University
William McCann, University of Puerto Rico
Thomas Owens, University of Missouri
Robin Riddihough, Canadian Geological Survey
Garry Rogers, Canadian Geological Survey

To guard the privacy of all the experts, particular opinions were not associated with experts by name. Therefore, the experts are indicated by number only (e.g., expert 1) in this chapter. (The expert numbers do not follow the order in the above listing.)

Expert interview process. Eliciting expert opinion for the Satsop hazard analysis occurred through a two-part interview process. The first interview took place in the summer of 1986. The interview was conducted at each expert's office and involved two or three elicitors. A second interview, conducted via telephone, was carried out in the fall of 1987. The second interview was a follow-up to the first and was held in light of feedback from the first interview to gauge any change in opinion over the one-year period. Several weeks prior to the interviews, each expert was sent an introductory letter that contained the following: (1) a summary of the purpose of the study, (2) a review of the methods

to be used to elicit expert opinion in the interview, (3) a list of questions likely to be asked, and (4) a bibliography arranged topically. All of the cited references were made available to the experts at their request. The purpose was to be sure that all of the experts were made aware of any published studies that they might not otherwise have known about. Prior to the second interview the experts were given summaries of all of the expert responses from the first interview.

In the interviews, each expert was asked to provide his assessment of characteristics and probabilities of his logic tree. The basis for each of the assessments was documented to allow for later third-party review.

Elements of the seismic-hazard model

Figure 3 shows the seismic-hazard model logic tree developed for the Cascadia subduction zone. The hazard model logic tree is divided into several components, most of which relate to the tectonic characterization of the potential seismic sources. The 14 experts were responsible for characterizing these components. To help understand the hazard model, each component is discussed below.

Crustal geometry. Each expert was asked to provide his interpretation of the three-dimensional geometry of the Cascadia subduction zone. Each expert provided a cross-sectional sketch of one or more possible geometries showing the location of the Juan de Fuca slab and the North American plate (see examples in Fig. 4). Along-strike variations in geometry (such as changes in slab dip) were also specified. The most common basis for estimating the possible position of the oceanic slab was the distribution of hypocenters of the deeper seismicity beneath Puget Sound, coupled with worldwide analogies to other subduction zones (e.g., expected depth required for magma generation may mark the depth to the slab beneath the Cascades).

Potential seismic sources. The experts were asked to identify all potential seismic sources that could reasonably exist in the western Washington region. It was stated to the experts that shallow crustal potential seismic sources would be considered elsewhere in the study, but they were asked to identify those potential sources that might be present in the shallow crust (upper 20 km) but might not have a surface expression. Potential sources were not necessarily limited to those tectonic features that have been associated with seismicity during the historical period. Areal source zones as well as tectonic feature-specific sources could be identified. In general, all of the experts identified two potential seismic sources: (1) an "intra-slab" source representing earthquakes generated within the subducted oceanic slab, and (2) an "interface" source representing earthquakes generated at the interface between the Juan de Fuca and North American plates. The vertical line in Figure 3 indicates that the contributions from the various identified sources were combined to obtain the total hazard from subduction-zone sources. The characteristics of the various sources were assumed to be independent unless otherwise specified by the experts.

Probability of activity. Each seismic source is associated with an assessment of the probability that it is active or seismogenic. Activity is used here to mean that the source is capable of generating tectonically significant earthquakes. In general, for the subduction-related seismic sources, tectonically significant earthquakes were judged by the experts to be larger than about magnitude 5. The probability of activity is interpreted to be a function of the tectonic role played by a potential source in the present stress regime, and unless that role is expected to change, the probability of activity is independent of time. Thus, "activity" is a binary state (i.e., either yes or no), and the probability of activity expresses the likelihood that the potential source is in an active state or not. Not included here is the likelihood of earthquake recurrence during any specified time period. This is a function of the recurrence rate, which is a separate component of the seismic-hazard model.

The experts considered the probability of activity of the subduction sources (i.e., the intra-slab and interface) to be independent, based largely on observations of subduction zones worldwide.

Location of rupture. To model the seismic sources for the hazard analysis, estimates were made of the three-dimensional location of ruptures for each seismic source. This provides the geometry of the surface over which future ruptures will occur. For example, an intra-slab seismic source might have the following rupture-location characteristics: (1) in cross section, earthquakes will occur in the upper 10 km (brittle portion) of the oceanic slab; (2) the downdip extent will be to depths of about 70 km and updip to the first bend in the slab offshore; (3) the earthquakes larger than magnitude 7 will occur at depths of 50 to 70 km near the downdip bend in the slab (Fig. 4); (4) in map view, the intra-slab seismicity will follow roughly the coastline to

accommodate the "corner" near the Canada–U.S. boundary and will end at the Nootka fault on the north and the Blanco fracture zone on the south (Fig. 1); (5) in map view, the relative frequency of earthquakes in the intra-slab source will spatially match that observed in historical seismicity (i.e., higher concentration beneath the Puget Sound–Georgia Strait region than to south or north, see Fig. 5).

Another aspect of rupture locations that could be specified is that of segmentation of the source. This assessment allows that the maximum dimensions of future earthquake ruptures may be less than the total dimensions of the source. Possible rupture-segment boundaries could be identified, and the probability that they will serve as rupture boundaries could also be assessed (e.g., arch in the downgoing slab at a specified location has a 40 percent change of serving to stop rupture coming from either direction on the plate interface).

As with all components of the seismic-hazard model, alternative hypotheses for the location of ruptures could be given and each associated with a relative weight or credibility.

Maximum earthquake magnitude. Each seismic source was associated with a maximum earthquake magnitude that serves as the upper bound on the recurrence relation for that source. Maximum magnitudes were often directly assessed by the experts based on the largest historically observed magnitudes or by analogy to other subduction zones. For the plate interface source, many experts indicated that the rupture dimensions, specified previously as part of locations of rupture, provided a reasonable basis for estimating maximum magnitudes. In these cases, the magnitudes were calculated using the experts' rupture dimensions and relations between magnitude and rupture area. In general, the magnitudes determined in this manner were greater than or equal to M_w 8. In a few instances, the experts specified developing a

Oceanic Slab Geometry	Sources	State of Activity	Segmentation	Maximum Extent of Rupture	Maximum Magnitude	Recurrence Method	Convergence or Geologic Rate	Seismic Coupling	Magnitude Distribution

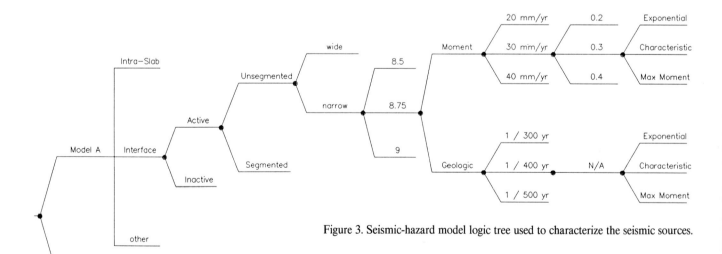

Figure 3. Seismic-hazard model logic tree used to characterize the seismic sources.

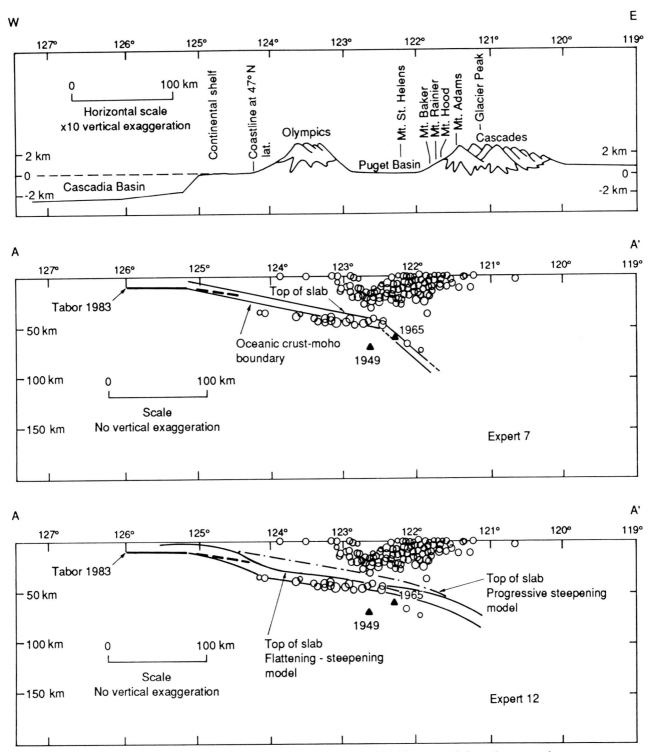

Figure 4. Examples of cross sections prepared by experts 7 and 12. The top panel shows the topography along the east-west section through the site.

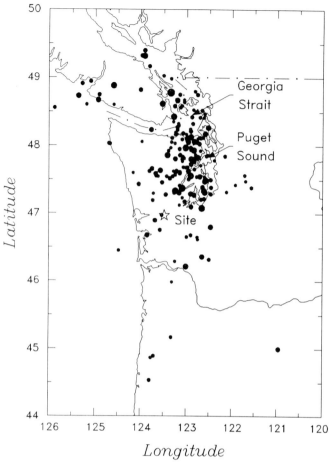

Figure 5. Spatial distribution of intra-slab seismicity inferred to be occurring within the subducting Juan de Fuca plate. Events shown are for the time period January 1970 through March 1987. Symbol size is proportional to magnitude.

energy (i.e., ratio between seismic-moment rate and convergence rate). Coupling could be estimated from the historical record or from an assumed model. For example, the historical record in the Pacific Northwest shows that no thrust earthquakes larger than magnitude 5 have occurred on the plate interface (i.e., the historical seismic-moment rate is very low). If this behavior is judged representative of the longer-term behavior, then α would be close to zero. However, the historical quiescence may be interpreted by some to merely be the result of a short observation period and actually representative of interseismic quiescence. In this case, the seismic coupling might be assessed to be high (i.e., α close to 1.0). A wide variety of approaches were considered in arriving at seismic-coupling estimates, ranging from detailed studies of the mechanical-thermal properties of subducted sediment to analogies to similar subduction zones worldwide.

Earthquake recurrence. Earthquake recurrence or the frequency of occurrence of earthquakes of various magnitudes was assessed for each seismic source. The experts were asked to specify the preferred method(s) for estimating recurrence including the use of: historical seismicity record, seismic-moment rate, or geologic data regarding recurrence intervals. To use the historical seismicity record, the three-dimensional area for gathering recurrence statistics was specified as well as the area over which these recurrence rates were assessed to apply. For example, the deep seismicity zone (>30 km) beneath Puget Sound was used to define a recurrence rate per square kilometer. This rate could, in turn, be judged appropriate for the source at this depth north and south of the seismicity zone.

The seismic-moment rate approach to recurrence estimation was used in many cases to define the recurrence for the plate interface. The convergence rate is multiplied by the seismic coupling (α) to arrive at a seismic-slip rate. To calculate a seismic-moment rate, the slip rate is multiplied by the total area of the seismic source (defined by the assessed source geometry and location of ruptures) and an assumed rigidity (3×10^{11} dyne/cm^2). The use of seismic-moment rate to define recurrence has become standard practice for crustal faults (e.g., Anderson and Luco, 1983; Youngs and Coppersmith, 1985a) and appears to be supported by observations of seismic-moment release observed for several subduction zones (Peterson and Seno, 1984). To use the resulting seismic-moment rate in the seismic-hazard analysis, a recurrence-distribution model was specified that indicates the relative frequency of earthquakes of various magnitudes. The models considered by the experts included: (1) a truncated exponential magnitude distribution based on the familiar form $\log N = a - bM$; (2) a characteristic-earthquake model of the form given by Youngs and Coppersmith (1985b); and (3) a maximum-moment model as described by Wesnousky and others (1983).

Some experts used geologic evidence to define the recurrence intervals between large earthquakes. Typically this type of data does not provide strong constraints on the size of the earthquakes giving rise to the geologic effect. For example, secondary geologic effects such as coastal subsidence or offshore turbidity deposits do not provide direct indications of the magnitude of the

maximum magnitude estimate from the relations between plate age, convergence rate, and observed magnitude (Ruff and Kanamori, 1980), resulting in magnitude estimates of about M_w 8.3.

Uncertainty in the maximum-magnitude estimate was expressed by the experts in terms of a range of values, a preferred value with associated bounds, or discrete values each associated with a relative weight.

Convergence rate. Convergence between the Juan de Fuca and North American plates is considered parallel to the relative plate-motion direction. The convergence rate is the relative rate between the two plates, derived in most cases from the absolute velocities of each plate. Various investigators have shown that the convergence rate at the Cascadia subduction zone has been decreasing over the past few million years (e.g., Riddihough, 1984). Because we are most interested in the present behavior of the plate boundary, the experts were asked to estimate contemporary convergence rates.

Seismic coupling. Seismic coupling (α) is defined as the percentage of the total convergence rate that is released as seismic earthquake with which they were associated. For this study, we assume that the recurrence intervals apply to magnitudes within one-half magnitude of the maximum. The recurrence-distribution model then defines the recurrence rates for smaller magnitudes. Figure 6 illustrates the cumulative form of three recurrence models and compares how they would estimate the frequency of smaller earthquakes when the absolute level of seismicity is fixed by the frequency of the largest events.

Assessments provided by experts

The assessments made by the 14 experts for each component of the hazard model are summarized below. Included here is a summary of individual experts' assessments for each component (Table 2) as well as the distributions of assessments by all experts (termed here "aggregate assessments") for each component. Aggregate assessments are displayed as histograms in Figures 7 through 12.

Crustal geometry. All the experts provided an assessment of the cross-sectional geometry of the subducting Juan de Fuca plate. Most of the experts provided only a single assessment, consisting of the plate dipping at approximately 11° and extending through the zone of deeper earthquakes lying at depths of 30 km or more beneath and to the west of the Puget Basin (Fig. 4). The aggregate weight for this model was 0.6. Two experts provided a slight modification of the 11° dip, consisting of a flat-lying slab with a double bend (see Fig. 4). The aggregate weight on the double-bend model as 0.06. Many of the experts preferred the model recently proposed by Crosson and Owens (1987) that has an arch in the slab along strike. The aggregate weight on the arched-slab model was 0.24.

Seismic sources. All experts identified the Juan de Fuca–North American plate interface and the subducting Juan de Fuca plate as potential sources of thrust and intra-slab normal events, respectively. Some experts also identified potential sources in the overlying North American plate. Evaluation of the hazard from these crustal sources was regarded as a separate part of the study and is not presented here.

Probability of source activity. All the experts made an assessment of the probability that the plate interface and the subducting slab are active or seismogenic. Figure 7 shows the distribution of assessments of activity for the intra-slab and interface sources. The assessments for the intra-slab source are generally at or near unity, based on the past record of seismicity (e.g., the 1946, 1949, and 1965 earthquakes). The assessments for the interface range from near zero to near 1.0, with an average of 0.54. The assessments cluster near zero, near 0.5, and near 1.0. It should be noted that an adjustment was made to the assessments of experts 4 and 13. As indicated in Table 2, column 5, these two experts have probabilities of 0.9 and 0.85 that the maximum magnitudes for the interface are M_w 5 or less. All other experts made the assessment of activity in terms of the probability of the interface being able to generate tectonically significant events ($M_w > 5$). To put the assessments of experts 4 and 13 on a

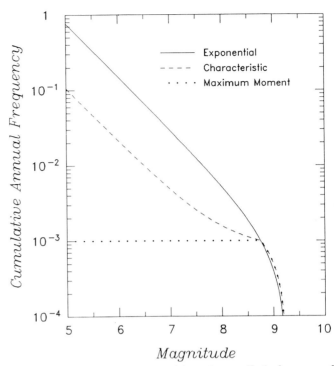

Figure 6. Alternative recurrence models used to specify the frequency of earthquakes of various magnitudes. All three models are fixed at 0.001 events per year of magnitude $\geqslant 8.75$. Note that the characteristic-magnitude and maximum-moment models specify far fewer moderate-to small-magnitude events than the truncated-exponential-magnitude model.

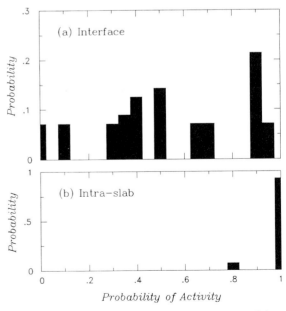

Figure 7. Aggregate distribution of 14 experts' assessments of the probability of activity for (a) the plate interface and (b) the intra-slab source.

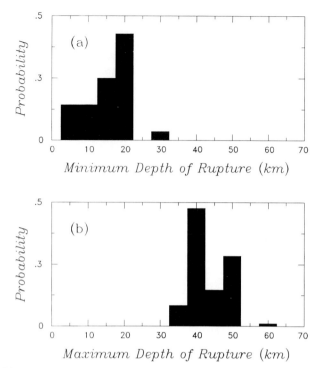

Figure 8. Aggregate distributions that specify the down-dip location of rupture on the plate interface. (a) Aggregate of 14 experts' distributions for minimum depth of rupture on the interface. (b) Aggregate of 12 experts' distributions for maximum depth of rupture on the interface.

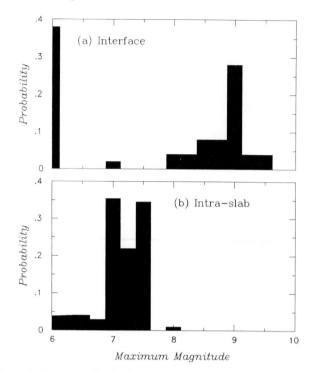

Figure 9. Aggregate distributions for maximum magnitude. (a) Aggregate of five experts' distributions for directly assessed maximum magnitude on the plate interface. (b) Aggregate of 11 experts' distributions for the maximum magnitude on the intra-slab seismic source.

consistent basis, they were adjusted to values of 0.075 for expert 4 (probability 0.75 that the interface is active at any magnitude level times the probability 0.1 that events $M_w > 5$ can occur) and 0.0075 for expert 13 (probability 0.05 that the interface is active at any magnitude level times the probability 0.15 that events $M_w > 5$ can occur). Their maximum-magnitude distributions were then renormalized to include only magnitudes larger than M_w 5. These adjustments were discussed with the experts and they were in agreement.

Location of rupture. The experts estimated the limits of earthquake ruptures, both along the length of the subduction zone as well as the up-dip and down-dip extent. Most experts (aggregate weight 0.64) considered the maximum limits of coherent rupture along the interface to be the boundary with the Explorer plate at the Nootka fault zone on the north, and the Blanco fracture zone on the south (see Fig. 1). Several experts considered further segmentation of the interface to be credible, with a segment boundary generally in the vicinity of 46°N (weight 0.15) or segment boundaries on the northern or southern margins of the arch in the slab proposed by Crosson and Owens (1987) (weight 0.11). An aggregate weight of 0.1 was assigned to no segmentation. The assessments of the minimum depth of rupture along the interface ranged from 5 to 25 km, and the maximum depth of rupture ranged from 35 to 60 km (see Fig. 8).

A majority of the experts (aggregate weight 0.75) stated that

they expect the future distribution of intra-slab events to follow the observed pattern of historical seismicity, with the majority of events occurring generally beneath Puget Sound (see Fig. 5). Alternatives considered included completely uniform seismicity within the down-going slab (weight 0.01) or a concentration of larger events at deeper depths (weight 0.24).

Maximum magnitude. The experts who estimated maximum magnitudes for the plate interface either made a direct assessment or specified that it be calculated from the maximum rupture dimensions using the relation between rupture area (A) and magnitude (M_w) proposed by Abe (1975) and Kanamori (1977). This relation can be written as $M_w = \log_{10}(A) + 3.99$. Regression of published values of M_w and A for recent earthquakes, holding the slope equal to unity, yielded the same relation between magnitude and rupture area. Twelve experts estimated the maximum magnitude for the interface: seven (aggregate weight 0.58) on the basis of their specified maximum-rupture dimensions, and five (aggregate weight 0.42) as a direct assessment based on analogy with other subduction zones or other techniques for magnitude estimation. The aggregate distribution shown in Figure 9a is for those five experts who made a direct assessment, and is thus conditional on the direct assessment procedure being the correct procedure. In general, the maximum-rupture dimensions specified by the experts resulted in maximum magnitudes equal to or greater than M_w 8.

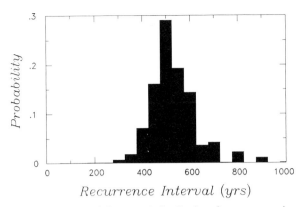

Figure 10. Aggregate of six experts' distributions for recurrence interval of large-interface earthquakes based on paleoseismic data.

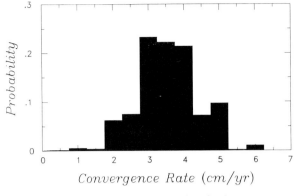

Figure 11. Aggregate of 14 experts' distributions for the convergence rate of the Juan de Fuca and North American plates.

The maximum magnitude for the intra-slab source was assessed by 11 experts on the basis of historical seismicity and analogy with other subduction zones. The aggregated distribution (Fig. 9b) shows a much narrower range than that for the interface source.

Earthquake recurrence method. All experts who assessed earthquake recurrence using historical seismicity data to define the recurrence parameters for intra-slab events. Recurrence estimates for the plate interface were based on either a moment-rate approach or geologic evidence for the frequency of large events. The experts favored the moment-rate approach slightly over the use of the geologic data by a ratio of 0.54 to 0.46.

Geologic recurrence rate. Six of the experts chose to base the recurrence estimates for interface events solely or partially on geologic evidence for possible paleoseismic events, primarily from coastal subsidence (e.g., Atwater, 1987) and offshore turbidite data (Adams, 1985). Figure 10 presents the aggregated distribution for the recurrence interval of large interface events. The aggregate mean value is about 500 years. The distribution of recurrence interval based on seismic-moment rate was much broader, ranging from less than 200 years to several thousand years. This wide range resulted from combining the assessed distributions for convergence rate, plate-interface area, interface maximum magnitude, and seismic coupling.

Convergence rate. All the experts assessed the convergence rate; most based their estimates on the rates published by Riddihough (1984). Nishimura and others (1984), and Verplanck and Duncan (1987). Those experts who made a direct assessment generally gave a wide distribution of values, with a mean value somewhat lower than the published estimates. Figure 11 shows the aggregate distribution for convergence-rate estimates.

Seismic coupling. Figure 12 shows the aggregate distributions for the amount of seismic coupling between the Juan de Fuca and North American plates. Most of the experts gave a wide distribution for the amount of coupling. For example, expert 1 gave a 0:1 bimodal distribution. The bases for estimates of coupling varied greatly, and ranged from analogies with other

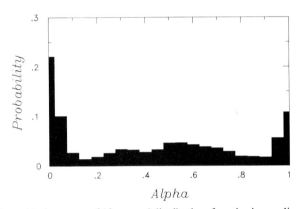

Figure 12. Aggregate of 10 experts' distributions for seismic coupling on the plate interface.

subduction zones to thermal-mechanical modeling of the plate interface.

The product of the plate interface area, convergence rate, and amount of seismic coupling provides the rate of earthquake energy release expressed as seismic moment. For example, with an interface length of 800 km, width of 100 km, convergence rate of 4 cm/yr, and value 0.4 for seismic coupling, the resulting moment rate is 3.84×10^{26} dyne-cm/yr. Assuming all of the moment is released in magnitude M_w 8½ events, a recurrence interval of approximately 200 years would be obtained for these events.

Recurrence model. Three models for the shape of the magnitude distribution were used in the analysis: truncated-exponential-magnitude distribution, characteristic-magnitude distribution, and maximum-moment distribution (see Fig. 6). The aggregate distribution of the experts yielded weights of 0.52, 0.38, and 0.1 for the maximum-moment, characteristic-magnitude, and truncated-exponential-magnitude models, respectively. Most experts preferred the maximum-moment or characteristic-magnitude models for the interface source to account for the historical absence of small- and moderate-magnitude interface

K. J. Coppersmith and R. R. Youngs

TABLE 2. SUMMARY OF EXPERT INTERVIEWS

Expert	Oceanic Slab Gomatry (DIP)	Potential Seismic Sources	Probability of Activity	Maximum Magnitude
1	Top of deep seismicity	Intra-slab [a] Interface [b]	1.0 [a] 0.35 (0.25-0.5) [b]	7.25 (± 0.25) [a] Dimensions [b]
2	Top of deep seismicity	Intra-slab [a] Interface [b]	0.8 [a] 0.4 (0.05-0.2) [b]	>6 - 7 [b]
3	Top of deep seismicity	Intra-slab [a] Interface [b]	1.0 [a] 0.9 [b]	8 [ahallower part of a] $7^{1/2}$ [deeper part of a] 9 (1/2) [b]
4	Top of deep seismicity	Intra-slab [a] Interface [b]	1.0 [a] 0.075 [b]	$7 - 7^{1/2}$ [a] 3 (0.3)⎤ 4 (0.3) 5 (0.3) ⎬— [b] 6 (0.09) 7 (0.01)⎦
5	Top of deep seismicity (0.85-0.9) 10° dip (0.10-0.15)	Intra-slab [a] Interface [b]	1.0 [a] 0.5 (± 0.5) [b]	7 [a]
6	Top of deep seismicity, single bend (0.3) Top of deep seismicity, double bend (0.7)	Intra-slab [a] Interface [b]	1.0 [a] 0.65 (± 0.2) [b]	$6^{3/4} - 7^{1/4}$ [a] Dimensions [b]
7	Top of deep seismicity (0.7)	Intra-slab [a] Interface [b]	0.3 (± 0.2) [b]	Dimensions [b]
8	Top of deep seismicity	Intra-slab [a] Interface [b]	1.0 [a] 0.5 (0.25 - 0.75) [b]	Dimensions [b]
9	Top of deep seismicity	Intra-slab to 50 km depth [a] Intra-slab 50 - 75 km [b] Interface [c] Strike-slip faults in upper plate [d] Accretionary wedge faults [e] Tears in down-going slab [f]	0.9 [a] 1.0 [b] 0.95 ± 0.05 [c] 1.0 [d] 1.0 [e] 1.0 [f]	6.5 (0.1)⎤ 7.0 (0.25) ⎬— [a] 7.5 (0.55) 7.8 (0.1)⎦ 7.0 (0.1)⎤ 7.5 (0.8) ⎬— [b] 7.8 (0.1)⎦ Dimensions [c] $7^{1/2}$ [d] 7.5 (0.8)⎤ ⎬— [e] 8.0 (0.2)⎦

p. 44

P. 40 - 42 Data

Add Conclusions

TABLE 2. SUMMARY OF EXPERT INTERVIEWS (continued)

Expert	Oceanic Slab Gomatry (DIP)	Potential Seismic Sources	Probability of Activity	Maximum Magnitude	
10	Top of deep seismicity	Intra-slab [a]	1.0 [a]	7 1/4 (± 1/4)	[a]
		Interface [b]	0.7 (0.6 - 0.9) [b]	Dimensions	[b]
11	Top of deep seismicity	Intra-slab [a]	1.0 [a]	7 - 7 1/2	[a]
		Interface [c]	0.9 (0.8 - 1.0) [b]		
		Deep crustal source [c]	1.0 [c]	7 1/2 [c]	
12	Top of deep seismicity	Intra-slab [a]	0.95 - 1.0 [a]	~7 1/4	[a]
		Interface [b]	0.9 [b]	9	[b]
13	Top of deep seismicity	Intra-slab [a]	1.0 [a]	6.5 (0.45)	
				7.0 (0.4)	
		Interface [b]	0.0075 [b]	7.5 (0.14) — [a]	
				8.0 (0.01)	
				4 (0.5)	
				5 (0.35) — [b]	
				6 (0.15)	
14	Top of deep seismicity	Intra-slab [a]	1.0 [a]	7.25 - 7.5	[a]
		Interface [b]	0.35 (± 0.25) [b]	8.5 (± 0.5)	[b]
		Accretionary wedge [c]	0.7 (± 0.1) [c]	7 (± 0.25)	[c]
		Tears in slab [d]	0.05 (± 0.05) [d]	5	[d]

Expert	Convergence Rate (mm/yr)		Recurrence Method	Seismic Coupling (α)	Recurrence Model	Geologic Recurrence Large Earthquakes (yr)
1	30 (± 10		Historical seismicity [a]	~0 (0.5 - 0.66)	Expoential [a]	-----
			Moment rate [b]	~1 (0.5 - 0.33)	Max. moment given $\alpha \simeq 1$ [b]	
2	25	(0.1)	Geologic (0.4) [b]	-----	-----	~430 [b]
	30-35	(0.8)				
	40	(0.1)	Moment rate (0.6) [b]			
3	40 (± 19)		Historical seismicity [a]	0.66	Exponential [a]	500 (400 - 1,000) [b]
			Geologic data [b]		Characteristic [b]	
4	10	(0.05)	Historical seismicity [a]	0.05 (0 - 0.15)	Characteristic [b]	-----
	20	(0.5)				
	30	(0.4)	Moment rate [b]			
	40	(0.05)				
5	32	(25 - 40)	Historical seismicity [a]	-----	Exponential [a]	-----
6	0 - 10	(0.04)	Historical seismicity [a]	0.6 (± 0.15)	Exponential [a]	500 - 600 (± 25%) [b]
	10-20	(0.04)				
	20 - 30	(0.4)	Geologic data (0.75) [b]		Exponential (0.2) [b]	
	30 - 40	(0.1)				
	40 - 43	(0.4)	Moment rate (0.25) [b]		Characteristic (0.8) [b]	
7	42 (± 10)		Historical seismicity [a]	1 (1.0)	Exponential [a]	
					Characteristic (0.5) [b]	
					Maximum moment (0.5) [b]	

TABLE 2. SUMMARY OF EXPERT INTERVIEWS (continued)

Expert	Convergence Rate (mm/yr)	Recurrence Method	Seismic Coupling (α)	Recurrence Model	Geologic Recurrence Large Earthquakes (yr)
8	38 (+5, -10)	-----	0.5 (0.2 - 0.7)	-----	-----
9	42 (+ 10)	Historical seismicity [a,b,d,e,f] Geologic data [c]	0.7 - 1.0 (0.54) 0.5 - 0.7 (0.25) 0.0 (0.01)	Exponential [a,b,d,e,f] Characteristic (0.5) [c] Maximum moment (0.5) [c]	500 (± 25%) [c]
10	35 - 50 (± 19)	Historical seismicity [a] Moment rate [b]	0.3 (0 - 0.5)	Exponential [a,b]	-----
11	42 (± 10)	Historical seismicity [a,b] Geologic data [b]	-----	Exponential [a,c] Maximum moment [b]	500 ± 150 [b] ≥150 [c]
12	30 - 35 (25 - 40)	Historical seismicity [a] Moment rate [b]	0.1 (0.05 - 0.5)	Exponential [a] Maximum moment [b]	500 ± 100 [b]
13	43 (± 19)	Historical seismicity [a]	0.05 (± 0.05)	Exponential [a]	-----
14	10 - 20 (0.05) 20 - 30 (0.2) 30 - 40 (0.4) 40 - 50 (0.3) ≥50 (0.05)	Historical seismicity [a,c,d] Moment rate [b]	0.01 (0.2) 0.05 (0.4) 0.10 (0.2) 0.15 (0.15) 0.5 (0.05)	Exponential [a,c,d] Maximum moment [b]	-----

Table 2 summarizes the responses given by the 14 experts. Each of the columns in Table 2 is explained below. Note that blank columns or apparent omissions in the table are the result of the expert declining to characterize these aspects.

Oceanic Slab Geometry. Each of the experts developed a cross-sectional sketch of the geometry of the oceanic slab beneath western Washington. These sketches are described verbally in Table 2. Alternative models are given along with the relative weight assigned to each. expressed as probabilities summing to unity.

Potential Seismic Sources. The subduction-related potential sources of earthquakes are identified and each is assigned a letter, which is shown in brackets (eg., [a]). These letters are used in subsequent columns to specify which seismic source is being described.

Probability of Activity. probabilities of activity are given for each potential seismic source, specified by a letter in prackets. Where expressed by the experts, ranges of estimates are given in parentheses. "Activity" is used here to signify capable of generating tectonically significant earthquakes (usually larger than about M_w 5).

Maximum Magnitude. Direct assessments of the maximum earthquake magnitude are given for the sources specified in brackets. In some cases, a range of values is given, or a best estimate and uncertainty bounds, or discrete values with relative weights assigned to each value. Where the word "Dimensions" appears, the expert indicated that the rupture dimensions that he specified be used to calculate a magnitude (i.e., he did not provide a maximum magnitude extimate directly). See section of text regarding "locations of rupture" to see how the rupture dimensions were estimated.

Convergence Rate. The relative rate of convergence measured parallel to the convergence direction between the North American and Juan de Fuca plates is given in millimeters per year. In some cases, ranges are given or discrete values are given with associated relative weights.

Recurrence Method. The manner in which the experts desired to have the earthquake recurrence rate specified is given in this column. Examples include recurrence based on the historical seismicity record, geologic data for recurrence intervals, or seismic moment rate. The seismic moment rate approach utilizes the extimates of convergence rate and seismic coupling.

Seismic Coupling (α). Seismic coupling is the percentaghe of the total convergence rate that is expressed seismically. Therefore, if the coupling is very high (α = 1.0), then all of the convergence rate will be expressed as earthquakes (i.e., the seismic moment rate from seismicity will be equal to that based on convergence rate). An α = 0 means that convergence is occurring aseismically (i.e., there is no seismic coupling).

Recurrence Model. The recurrence distribution function is specified in this column. Models requested by the experts include an exponential magnitude distribution (i.e., log N = a-bM); a characteristic magnitude distribution (Youngs and Coppersmith, 1985a, b); and a maximum moment model (Wesnousky and others, 1983).

Geologic Recurrence for Large Earthquakes. For those cases where geologic data provided a basis for estimating recurrence, an estimate of recurrence intervals for large earthquakes is given. These recurrence intervals were generally judged appropriate for magnitudes at or near the maximum.

events. All experts used the truncated-exponential-magnitude model exclusively for the intra-slab source.

Hazard results and discussion

Figures 13 and 14 present the assessed seismic hazard at the Satsop site resulting from the Cascadia subduction zone sources. The seismic hazard was computed by constructing a hazard-model logic tree (Fig. 3) for each of the 14 experts using their individual assessments (summarized in Table 2). Where an individual expert declined to assess a particular component of the hazard model, the aggregate distribution of all experts who did assess the component was substituted.

Hazard computations were made using the general approach outlined by Cornell (1968) to develop seismic-hazard curves, which depict the relation between ground-motion level and frequency of exceedance. (The reader is directed to the summary by the National Research Council [1988] for PSHA methodology.) Earthquake ground motions were assessed using attenuation relations specifically developed for subduction-zone earthquakes (Youngs and others, 1988). For each expert, hazard curves were computed using the seismic-source model parameters specified by each end branch of the expert's logic tree. The hazard curves were combined with the weights for each branch of the logic tree to construct distributions of seismic-hazard curves in the same fashion as the example shown in Figure 2. Figure 13 shows the 15th-, 50th-, and 85th-percentile hazard curves developed from each expert's hazard-model logic tree. The percentiles directly reflect the range of uncertainty given by the expert in the various seismic-source characteristics. Note the marked differences in these uncertainties from expert to expert. Also shown in Figure 13 are the 15th-, 50th-, and 85th-percentile hazard curves obtained by aggregating the hazard distributions of all 14 experts. The aggregation was accomplished by computing a compound distribution that assigned equal weight to each expert's hazard distribution. Figure 14 compares the median (50th percentile) hazard curves for each of the 14 experts' hazard models with the aggregate hazard distribution.

Simply stated, the range of uncertainty from the 15th to the 85th percentile curve for each expert (Fig. 13) represents the "within-expert" component of the variability in the final results; the range of differences in the median hazard curves (Fig. 14) represents the "expert-to-expert" component of the total variability. Although considerable emphasis was placed on assessing uncertainty during the expert interviews, many of the experts' assessments led to a fairly narrow range of uncertainty in the hazard compared to the aggregate results (Fig. 14). Studies in other fields show that experts tend to underestimate their uncertainty unless they have been subjected to enough feedback to calibrate the accuracy of their estimates (Capen, 1976; Hofer, 1986; Freudenburg, 1988). In this example, the use of multiple experts with varying backgrounds and approaches to the problem resulted in a wider, and perhaps more realistic estimate of the uncertainty in the hazard. Also, breaking the problem down into the assessment of individual components of the model, as was

done using logic trees, leads to a more realistic assessment of the uncertainties (Capen, 1976).

The results shown in Figure 14 indicate that a large portion of the uncertainty in the computed hazard is due to variability among the experts' assessments. One may then ask what the result would be if a different set of 14 experts were chosen. The stability of the results can be illustrated by examining the variability in the computed hazard if one selects different subsets of the 14 experts. Figure 15 shows the variability in the median hazard for all possible subsets of 4, 7, and 10 experts drawn from the 14 experts used in this study. Each plot shows the minimum and maximum estimate of the median hazard curve and the 5th to 95th percentile range of the median hazard over all possible combinations of experts. (There are 1,001 possible subsets of 4 experts, 3,432 possible subsets of 7 experts, and 1,001 possible subsets of 10 experts.) These comparisons indicate that a new set of experts selected using the same criteria used in this study should lead to a similar estimate of the hazard, provided a large number of experts is used. Therefore, we conclude that the aggregate 50th percentile hazard curve presented in Figure 14 is a good estimate of the median seismic hazard at the Satsop site because a large number of experts were used, and considerable effort was taken to obtain a full spectrum of opinions on the seismic potential of the Cascadia subduction zone.

CONCLUSIONS

The potential earthquake sources of the Cascadia subduction zone were characterized by incorporating a range of expert opinions into the PSHA. The results of the assessments show that some aspects of subduction-zone earthquake characteristics are relatively better known, as indicated by the range of values given by individual experts as well as by the range of expert-to-expert differences. For example, the subducting intra-slab source is believed to be seismogenic, and its geometry down-dip and along strike varies only slightly from expert to expert. Further, the expected future locations of intra-slab earthquakes and their relative frequency of occurrence at different locations within the slab are generally believed to follow the pattern of historical events (i.e., concentrated activity in the slab beneath Puget Sound, but significantly lower levels of activity to the north and south of Puget Sound).

In contrast, many characteristics of the plate-interface source are uncertain, as represented by a wide range of interpretations. For example, the estimates of the probability that the plate is seismogenic showed a nearly uniform distribution between 0 and 1.0; the values for seismic coupling (α) also showed a broad range. Whereas these characteristics typically might be evaluated in other subduction zones on the basis of observed seismicity, the absence of seismicity at Cascadia meant that the interface activity and seismic coupling were evaluated using a variety of scientific methodologies. Some experts relied on analogies to other subduction zones; some called on the results of recent thermal-mechanical modeling; still others drew conclusions based on deep-crustal studies imaging the plate interface.

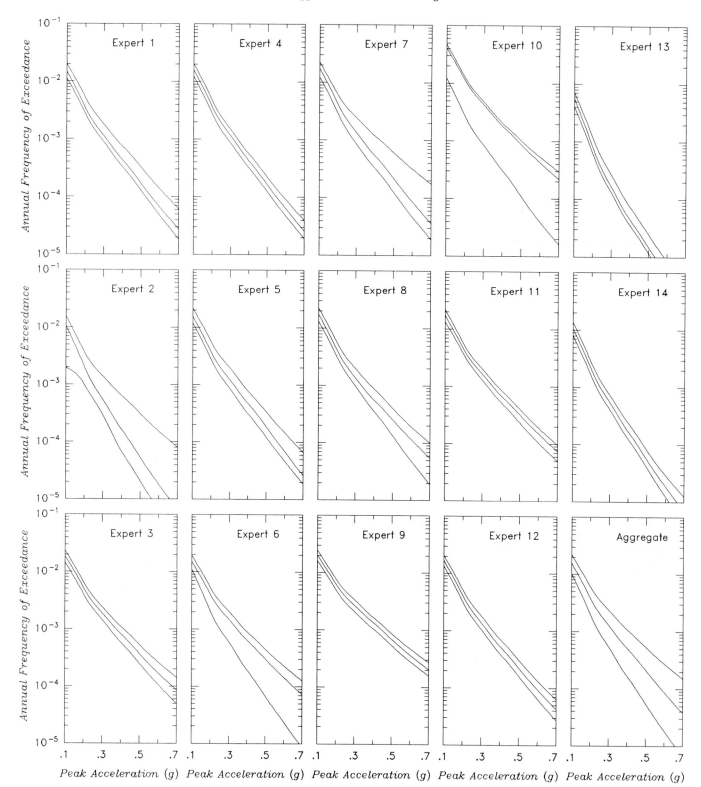

Figure 13. Distribution of seismic hazard based on each expert's seismic-hazard model logic tree. Each plot shows the 15th-, 50th-, and 85th-percentile hazard curves. The lower right-hand plot shows the aggregate of the 14 experts' distributions.

The study demonstrates the viability of expert opinion as as tool for PSHA. Despite the uncertainties in evaluating the seismic potential of the subduction zone, all of the experts readily provided their best judgments using their individually selected data sets. In so doing, each expert acknowledged that assessments of seismic hazard can be made in the face of uncertainty, provided that these uncertainties are properly identified and represented in the hazard analysis. The study also illustrates that some care must be exercised in order to obtain a realistic estimate of the uncertainty in the hazard assessment. This can be achieved by the use of numerous experts with varied approaches to the problem, as was done in the Satsop PSHA. Alternatively, if fewer experts are used, they may need to be tutored in recognizing and properly communicating their uncertainties.

ACKNOWLEDGMENTS

We thank the 14 experts involved in this study for their professional and concerted efforts in making their assessments. Financial support for the study was provided by the Washington Public Power Supply System, whose technical manager was William A. Kiel. We acknowledge his patience and support in this study. We also thank Robert Winkler for his assistance in formulating the expert elicitation process used in this study and Ted Habermann for providing technical guidance during the interviews. Finally, we thank Roy Schlemon, Dick Meeuwig, and Walt Hays for their helpful review comments.

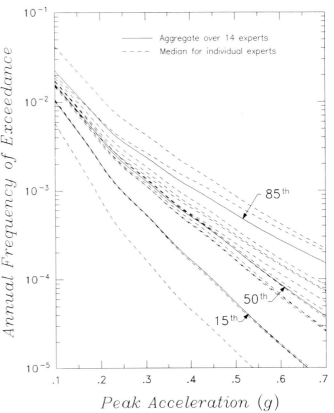

Figure 14. Comparison of 14 experts' median (50th percentile) hazard curves with aggregate distribution of hazard.

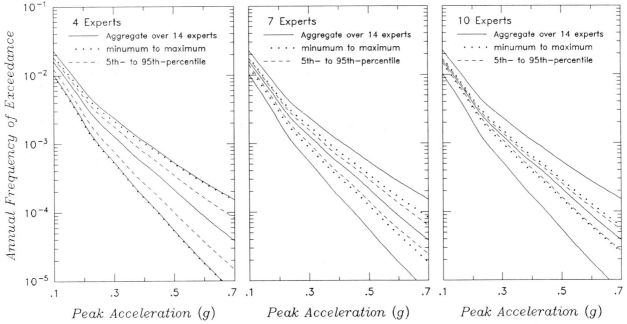

Figure 15. Variability of median hazard estimates for subsets of 14 experts. Solid curves show the 15th-, 50th- (median), and 85th-percentile hazard curves for the aggregate distribution of 14 experts. Dotted curves show the minimum and maximum, median hazard curves obtained over all possible subsets of experts. Dashed curves show the 5th and 95th percentiles of the median hazard curve obtained from all possible estimates for the specified subset of experts. Note the relatively narrow range of median estimates for seven or more experts.

REFERENCES CITED

Abe, K., 1975, Reliable estimation of the seismic moment of large earthquakes: Journal of Physics of the Earth, v. 23, p. 386–390.

Adams, J., 1985, Deformation above the Juan de Fuca subduction zone; Some enigmas with bearing on great earthquake risk [abs.]: EOS Transactions of the American Geophysical Union, v. 66, p. 1071.

Anderson, J. G. and Luco, J. E., 1983, Consequence of slip rate constraints on earthquake recurrence relations: Bulletin of the Seismological Society of America, v. 73, p. 471–496.

Atwater, B. F., 1987, Evidence for great Holocene earthquakes along the outer coast of Washington State: Science, v. 236, p. 1326–1346.

Capen, E. C., 1976, The difficulty of assessing uncertainty: Journal of Petroleum Technology, August, p. 843–850.

Clowes, R. M., and 6 others, 1987, Lithoprobe—southern Vancouver Island; Cenozoic subduction complex imaged by deep seismic reflections: Canadian Journal of Earth Sciences, v. 24, p. 31–51.

Coppersmith, K. J., and Youngs, R. R., 1986, Capturing uncertainty in probabilistic seismic hazard assessment within intraplate tectonic environments, *in* Proceedings 3rd U.S. National Conference on Earthquake Engineering: El Cerrito, California, Earthquake Engineering Research Institute, v. 1, p. 301–312.

Cornell, C. A., 1968, Engineering seismic risk analysis: Bulletin of the Seismological Society of America, v. 58, p. 1583–1606.

Crosson, R. S., and Owens, T. J., 1987, Slab geometry of the Cascadia subduction zone beneath Washington from earthquake hypocenters and teleseismic converted waves: Geophysical Research Letters, v. 14, p. 824–827.

Electric Power Research Institute, 1986, Seismic hazard methodology for the central and eastern United States; Volume 1, Methodology: Palo Alto, California, Electric Power Research Institute Document NP-4726, v. 1, **pages?**

Freudenburg, W. R., 1988, Perceived risk, real risk; Social science and the art of probabilistic risk assessment: Science, v. 242, p. 44–49.

Geomatrix Consultants, Inc., 1988, Seismic hazards assessment for WNP-3, Satsop, Washington, Contract C-20453: Report submitted to Washington Public Power Supply System, Richland, Washington.

Heaton, T. H., and Kanamori, H., 1984, Seismic potential associated with subduction in the northwestern United States: Bulletin of the Seismological Society of America, v. 74, p. 933–941.

Hofer, E., 1986, On surveys of expert opinion: Nuclear Engineering and Design, v. 93, p. 153–160.

Kanamori, H., 1977, The energy release in great earthquakes: Journal of Geophysical Research, v. 82, p. 2981–1987.

Kulkarni, R. B., Youngs, R. R., and Coppersmith, K. J., 1984, Assessment of confidence intervals for results of seismic hazard analysis, *in* Proceedings of the 8th World Conference on Earthquake Engineering: Englewood Cliffs, New Jersey, Prentice Hall, v. 1, p. 263–270.

Kulm, L. D., and Peterson, C., 1984, Western North American continental margin and adjacent ocean floor off Oregon and Washington, Atlas 1, Ocean Margin Drilling Program, Regional Atlas Series: Marine Science International, Woods Hole, Massachusetts, 32 sheets.

Lawrence Livermore National Laboratory, 1985, Seismic hazard characterization of the eastern United States: Livermore, California, Lawrence Livermore National Laboratory Report, v. 1-3, April.

National Research Council, 1988, Probabilistic seismic hazard analysis; Report by the Panel on Seismic Hazard Analysis, Committee on Seismology, National Research Council: Washington, D.C., National Academy Press, 97 p.

Nishimura, C., Wilson, D. S., and Hey, R. N., 1984, Pole of rotation analysis of present-day Juan de Fuca plate motion: Journal of Geophysical Research, v. 89, p. 10283–10290.

Paté-Cornell, E., 1986, Probability and uncertainty in nuclear safety decisions: Nuclear Engineering and Design, v. 93, p. 319–327.

Peterson, E. T., and Seno, T., 1984, Factors affecting seismic moment release rates in subduction zones: Journal of Geophysical Research, v. 89, p. 10233–10248.

Riddihough, R. R., 1984, Recent movements of the Juan de Fuca plate system: Journal of Geophysical Research, v. 89, p. 6980–6994.

Ruff, L., and Kanamori, H., 1980, Seismicity and the subduction process: Physics of the Earth and Planetary Interiors, v. 23, p. 240–252.

Sammis, C., Davis, G. A., and Crosson, R. S., 1988, New perspectives on the geometry and mechanics of the Cascadia subduction zone: Report prepared for the Washington Public Power Supply System, Richland, Washington.

U.S. Nuclear Regulatory Commission, 1983, PRA procedures guide: Washington, D.C., U.S. Nuclear Regulatory Commission NUREG/CR-2300.

Verplanck, E. P., and Duncan, R. A., 1987, Temporal variations in plate convergence and eruption rates in the western Cascades, Oregon: Tectonics, v. 6, p. 197–209.

Wesnousky, S., Scholz, C. H., Shimazaki, K., and Matsuda, T., 1983, Earthquake frequency distribution and mechanics of faulting: Journal of Geophysical Research, v. 88, p. 9331–9340.

Youngs, R. R., and Coppersmith, K. J., 1985a, Implications of fault slip rates and earthquake recurrence models to probabilistic seismic hazard estimates: Bulletin of the Seismological Society of America, v. 75, p. 939–964.

—— , 1985b, Development of a fault-specific earthquake recurrence model [abs.]: Seismological Society of America Earthquake Notes, v. 55, p. 16.

Youngs, R. R., Coppersmith, K. J., Power, M. S., and Swan, F. H., III, 1985, Seismic hazard assessment of the Hanford region, eastern Washington State, *in* Proceedings of the Department of Energy Natural Phenomena Hazards Mitigation Conference, Las Vegas, Nevada, October 7-11: U.S. Government Printing Office, p. 169–176.

Youngs, R. R., Day, S. M., and Stevens, J. P., 1988, Near field ground motions on rock for large subduction zone earthquakes, *in* Proceedings of ASCE Specialty Conference, Earthquake Engineering and Soil Dynamics II, Park City, Utah, June 27-30: New York, American Society of Civil Engineers, p. 445–462.

MANUSCRIPT ACCEPTED BY THE SOCIETY AUGUST 18, 1989

Geological Society of America
Reviews in Engineering Geology, Volume VIII
1990

Chapter 3

Seismic-hazard assessment in the central United States

Arch C. Johnston and Susan J. Nava*
CERI/Memphis State University, Memphis, Tennessee 38152

ABSTRACT

Problems with and approaches to seismic-hazard estimation in the midcontinent of the United States are evaluated by using recent data on stress regime, crustal age and structure, and seismicity of other stable continental regions. Evaluating earthquake hazard in the central U.S. is difficult because of the lack of identifiable seismogenic faults and because of the low rate of seismic activity. Furthermore, the recurrence intervals of large earthquakes are poorly known, in part because of the short historical record that spans only a fraction of the repeat times of these quakes. The seismotectonic regime of the central U.S. is dominated by the Reelfoot rift complex and the associated New Madrid, Missouri, seismic zone. However, there are other major tectonic structures in the region such as the Nemaha ridge, the Midcontinent rift system, and the Wichita-Ouachita orogenic belt; earthquakes generating damaging ground motion (approximately magnitude 5.0 or greater) have occurred in the states of Ohio, Illinois, Oklahoma, Texas, Kansas, Nebraska, Kentucky, Alabama, and Arkansas, as well as Missouri. Opinions vary widely about the best way to delineate seismic source zones in such a diffuse and varied seismotectonic environment. Moreover, detailed paleoseismic or neotectonic data that could improve hazard assessments are extremely sparse in the central United States. The Meers fault scarp in southwestern Oklahoma, with its evidence for Holocene displacement and its lack of background seismicity, highlights a new set of assessment problems. Development of site-specific probabilistic hazard curves are further hampered by the lack of strong ground-motion data and high-resolution attenuation data. We address aspects of the overall seismic-hazard assessment problem for which neotectonic information provides constraints. These include a seismic source zonation for the central U.S. and estimates of maximum possible earthquakes for these zones, especially for the New Madrid region.

INTRODUCTION

There have been numerous attempts to quantify the seismic hazard in the central United States. The three most systematic, comprehensive, and recent were by the U.S. Geological Survey (Algermissen and others, 1982), Lawrence Livermore National Laboratory (Bernreuter and others, 1989), and the Electric Power Research Institute (EPRI, 1986). The USGS study evaluated the whole of the United States while the LLNL and EPRI studies focused on the central and eastern U.S. (east of the Rocky Mountain Cordillera). All these efforts utilized large teams of investigators and required a substantial amount of judgment as to the relative importance of the record of past seismicity versus the seismogenic potential of known geologic and tectonic structures as they are oriented within the regional stress regime. More localized central U.S. seismic-hazard studies have been conducted by Nuttli and Herrmann (1978) and Nuttli (1979).

For this report, the central United States is defined as the region bounded on the north by Canada, the south by Mexico/

*Present address: University of Utah Seismograph Stations, Salt Lake City, Utah 84112.

Johnston, A. C., and Nava, S. J., 1990, Seismic-hazard assessment in the central United States, *in* Krinitzsky, E. L., and Slemmons, D. B., Neotectonics in earthquake evaluation: Boulder, Colorado, Geological Society of America Reviews in Engineering Geology, v. 8.

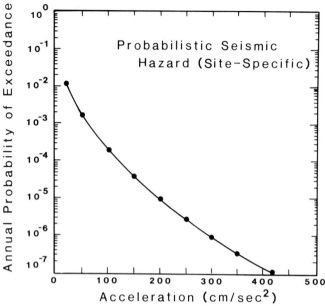

Figure 1. Example of a site-specific seismic-hazard curve showing ground motion (acceleration) plotted against an annual probability of exceedance. This particular curve is for a nuclear power site in Illinois. (After Bernreuter and others, 1989.)

Gulf of Mexico, the west by the Rocky Mountain Cordillera/Rio Grande rift, and the east by the New York–Alabama aeromagnetic lineament as delineated by King and Zietz (1978). It includes the states of North and South Dakota, Nebraska, Kansas, Oklahoma, Minnesota, Iowa, Missouri, Arkansas, Louisiana, Mississippi, Michigan, Wisconisn, Illinois, Indiana, Kentucky, Ohio, and portions of West Virginia, Tennessee, Alabama, Texas, New Mexico, Colorado, Wyoming, and Montana.

Seismic-hazard estimation includes a number of elements. Where active and capable faults are known and mappable, as in the western U.S., the hazard will depend on the seismic potential, i.e., the activity rate and the largest earthquakes that the fault(s) can sustain. In the central and eastern U.S., active faults are rarely identified, and additional, less direct steps are necessary. The "classical" approach to hazard assessment for the central U.S. involves: (1) delineating seismic source zones based on either seismicity, tectonics, or a combination of both; (2) assigning a frequency-magnitude recurrence relation and a maximum possible earthquake for each source zone; (3) developing regional anelastic attenuation relations and applying them to sites within the study area; and (4) producing a hazard curve by incorporating contributions from all source zones at a specific site. For an individual site, the hazard curve presents an estimate of the probability of exceeding a particular ground-motion parameter, usually peak or sustained ground acceleration; an example is given in Figure 1. The usual style of presentation for a region is a contour map showing the level of ground motion that will not be exceeded within a specified time period (e.g. Algermissen and others, 1982).

For this study, as part of a symposium on applying neotectonics to earthquake risk evaluation, we will emphasize the problems of identifiying seismic source zones and assigning source parameters to these zones; this is where neotectonic information is incorporated into the hazard-evaluation process. We do not address the equally important questions of proper probabilistic and statistical modeling of ground motion.

As with seismic hazard, the seismicity and tectonics of the central United States have been the subjects of extensive previous investigations (e.g., Nuttli and Herrmann, 1978; Nuttli, 1979; Van Schmus and others, 1987; Bickford and others, 1986; Hatcher and others, 1987). A detailed and comprehensive reexamination is not included here; rather, our objective is to define the seismicity and large-scale tectonic features in a general sense in order to characterize the problems in seismic-hazard assessments in the region. In our view, the single most difficult problem is estimating the seismic potential of a zone or a crustal structure. Aside from the question of properly delineating the zone, this seismic potential has two components: an estimate of the maximum possible earthquake and an estimate of the frequency of occurrence of moderate-to-large events (magnitude ≥5). Both components are essential for hazard estimation, yet quantitative constraints for these parameters are sparse. For the central U.S. where the historical record of seismicity is short, where the character of the crust at seismogenic depths is obscure, and where the earthquake potential of most of the recognized crustal structures is unknown, assessing the seismic potential is based more on judgment than knowledge. In the following we present a brief overview of the region in terms of its crustal composition, tectonics, stress regime, and seismicity. Finally, we return to the question of seismic "judgement" as part of an exercise of seismic zonation of the central U.S.

CRUST

How can the crust of the central U.S. be usefully characterized for assessing seismic potential? To begin, there is little doubt that earthquakes are generated in the upper crust, above the brittle-ductile transition, 20 to 30 km deep. However, in this region, crystalline basement is concealed beneath a veneer of Paleozoic sedimentary rocks. Virtually all large earthquakes that have sufficient data to closely constrain hypocentral depth occur within the igneous and metamorphic rocks of the upper crust, although some faulting as revealed by aftershocks does extend up into Paleozoic strata. Moreover, there is no documented case of surface fault rupture accompanying any earthquake in the central U.S. (The Meers fault in southwestern Oklahoma is a remarkable exception to this rule for a prehistoric earthquake and will be discussed later in this chapter.)

The crystalline crust of the central U.S. is wholly Precambrian in age, with the possible exception of the southern coastal block (e.g., Hoffman, 1988). Classically, this region is divided into Canadian shield and interior platform, which together comprise a collage of at least five cratonic elements (Fig. 2), the products of major Precambrian orogenic episodes, ranging in age from Superior craton nucleation in the Archean (3.8 to 2.5 Ga) to the middle Proterozoic Grenville orogeny (1.1 Ga) (Sims and Peterman, 1986; Hoffman, 1988). Most age determinations of the crust are from drill-hole samples; the principal outcrops of Precambrian rocks (the Superior craton in Minnesota, the Ozark dome in Missouri, the Llano uplift and Van Horn/Franklin Mountains of Texas, and the Black Hills uplift of South Dakota) are few and isolated.

This representation of a Precambrian central U.S. crust that grew to the south and east via lateral accretion during successively younger orogenies is derived from data only recently available. U-Pb age dating on zircon concentrates from drill cuttings (Van Schmus and others, 1987) is perhaps the most useful technique for applying these data to problems of midcontinent crustal evolution. Reliable dates are obtained from small samples, which (unlike for Rb-Sr or K-Ar dating) can tolerate some minor weathering and/or alteration. A comprehensive evolutionary framework for our study region is developing rapidly.

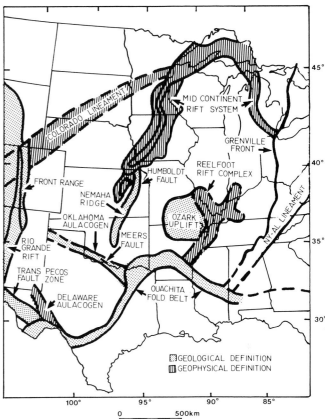

Figure 3. Principal tectonic features of the central U.S. Rift zones and sutures are emphasized over shallow crustal or epeirogenic features. Structures identified primarily by geophysical methods (subsurface) are hatchured; those with clear geological expression (surface) are shaded.

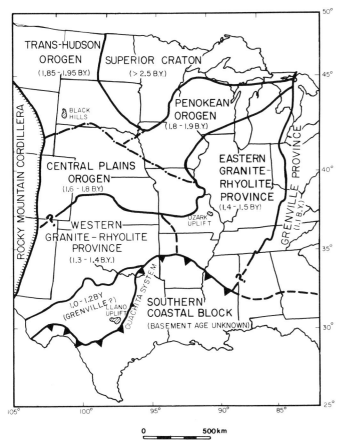

Figure 2. Age subdivisions of the crust of the central U.S. The ages apply to the crystalline basement that is covered by Paleozoic strata over most of the region north of the Ouachita system and are derived mainly from U-Pb zircon dates from drillhole samples.

TECTONICS

North of the Paleozoic Ouachita system, Phanerozoic tectonics had minimal effect on the crust of the central U.S. The interior platform was consolidated into a vast composite craton by about 1,300 Ma. This is not to say, however, that tectonic processes ceased to operate in the region. The most prominent example of this is the Midcontinent rift system (Chase and Gilmer, 1973; Van Schmus and Hinze, 1985; see Fig. 3). It has the strongest gravity signature in the central U.S. consisting of a belt of sharply defined linear positive Bouguer gravity anomalies extending from Michigan to Kansas, with central highs of +60 mgal flanked by lows of –100 mgal. Rocks in the rift system are contemporaneous with those of the Grenville province to the east, raising the possibility that the two are genetically related. Although the origin of the Grenville province is poorly understood, it may represent an ancient continental-collision zone that formed the Midcontinent rift system behind the suture front in response to extensional forces. A present-day analog to this is the Baikal rift zone of central Asia, which lies well north of the India-Asia collision zone.

Figure 3 depicts a number of other primary tectonic features in the central U.S. and categorizes them according to whether they are expressed at the surface (geologically defined) or in the subsurface (geophysically defined). We preferentially emphasized rifts and sutures in this figure because a recent study (Coppersmith and others, 1987; Johnston, 1989) identifies these structures as important features that localize seismicity in the stable interiors of continents.

The Paleozoic Ouachita thrust and fold belt is the major Phanerozoic suture traversing the study area. It is generally interpreted as a continuation of the Appalachian system (Hatcher and others, 1987), but the connections are concealed beneath the Gulf Coastal Plain sediments of Alabama. The Ouachita belt represents the southern boundary of Precambrian North America; it juxtaposes Proterozoic cratonic crust to the north with crust of unknown age and uncertain character (continental or transitional oceanic) to the south (Viele, 1979).

Another possible but less clear continental suture is the New York–Alabama lineament, the eastern boundary of the study area. The crustal structure that produces this aeromagnetic lineament is within Grenville-age crust beneath the Appalachian décollement. It has been interpreted as a major strike-slip fault associated with continental collision (King and Zietz, 1978); al-

ternatively, it may demark the suture between the Grenville crust of North America and an accreted terrane named the Clingman block by Johnston and others (1985) or the Bristol block by Hatcher and others (1987).

Three major failed continental rift complexes or aulacogens intersect the Ouachita belt at high angles: the Delaware aulacogen of west Texas, the southern Oklahoma aulacogen, and the Reelfoot rift complex. All are Eocambrian (575 to 700 Ma) in age (e.g., Gordon, 1988), but at least the Reelfoot rift, and probably the others, experienced additional extension and intrusion during early Mesozoic to Cretaceous time (Braile and others, 1984). The similarity in ages of formation of these rifts suggests that they formed as perhaps failed arms of triple junctions (the Reelfoot rift may represent more than one) during an episode of late Precambrian continental breakup that predated the Ouachita-Appalachian orogeny.

Other smaller crustal features or their geophysical expressions might be included in Figure 3 that perhaps could be relevant to earthquake occurrence in stable continental settings. For example, basement uplifts and basins, gravity and magnetic highs and gradients, mafic and felsic plutons, shallow crustal grabens, and faults with a wide range of dimensions have been considered in the literature. A cause-and-effect relation between these smaller-scale features and seismicity remains tenuous and, therefore, is not promoted here. Local stress concentrations arising from these crustal inhomogeneities may produce moderate-size earthquakes (up to magnitude 5.0 to 5.5), but we contend that the larger, damaging events will be associated with the major crustal features, mainly rifts, shown in Figure 3. In fact, in stable continental regions worldwide, earthquakes exceeding moment magnitude 6.0 are exceedingly rare except in crust that has experienced extensive rifting since the Mesozoic (Coppersmith and others, 1987; Johnston, 1989).

STRESS REGIME

The stress regime—or more accurately, the orientation of the horizontal principal stresses that has the greatest deviation from lithostatic stress—of the contiguous United States has been estimated by Zoback and Zoback (1980, 1989) using earthquake focal mechanisms, in-situ stress measurements, and the orientation of stress-sensitive geologic features. The principal differences between the 1980 and 1989 studies are that, in the more recent study, Zoback and Zoback deleted stress-orientation estimates based on overcoring data or geologic features older than Miocene and included recent wellbore-breakout data. These changes resulted in significant differences in the 1980 and 1989 stress-regime maps in the eastern and western U.S.; however, the stress regime for the central U.S. remained essentially unchanged. This suggests that the stress regime in the central U.S. is remarkably uniform, with the direction of maximum horizontal compression trending from northeast to east-northeast as the region is traversed from northeast to southwest (Fig. 4).

There are some relatively minor exceptions to the simple

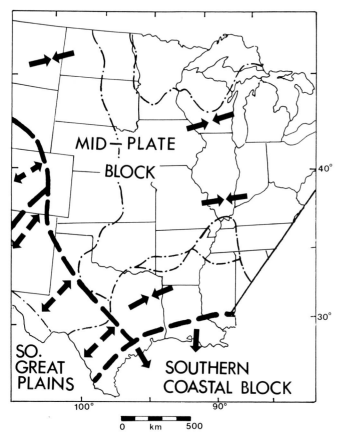

Figure 4. The regional stress regime (horizontal, greatest deviatoric component) for the central U.S. as determined by Zoback and Zoback (1989). Heavy dashed lines separate stress provinces (named); lighter dashed-dotted lines show physiographic boundaries.

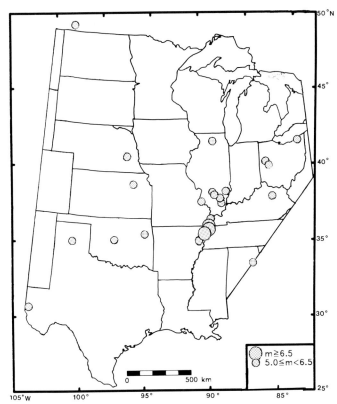

Figure 5. Seismicity of the central U.S. The source is the EPRI (1986) catalog. A plot from the other major catalog for the central U.S. (Nuttli and Brill, 1981) would exhibit a similar pattern but would differ considerably in detail.

standing of stress regime and crustal structure to explain the observed seismicity of the central U.S. and, ultimately, to derive useful estimates of the pattern and severity of future seismic activity.

SEISMICITY

The seismicity of the central U.S. is depicted in Figures 5 and 6. Although the orientation of the horizontal deviatoric component of the stress regime in the central U.S. seems to be very uniform, the distribution of earthquakes decidedly is not. Whether one considers total known seismicity ($m_b \geqslant 3.5$, Fig. 5) or only the larger events ($m_b \geqslant 5.0$, Fig. 6), nonrandomness is obvious. While it is likely that this two to three-century snapshot of seismicity is inadequate to show the complete detailed pattern, we argue that it is sufficient to establish an inherent high degree of clustering. It follows that physical reasons must exist for the observed clustering of seismic-energy release in the central U.S.

The distribution of earthquakes shows little correlation with provinces of similar crustal age (Fig. 2). However, if only larger events are considered (see Table 1), there is a good correlation with primary tectonic structures (Figs. 3 and 6). Thus, it is probable that the type of feature, its geologic age, and its orientation

stress state described above. An extensional stress province is present in the extreme southwestern corner of the study area in Texas and New Mexico, possibly representing a transitional zone between the active extensional tectonics of the Rio Grande rift directly to the west and the stable platform of the central plains. The stress orientation for the basement crust of the southern coastal block (Fig. 2) beneath the thick deposits of coastal plain sediments is unknown. Of course, the magnitude of the horizontal stress deviation from lithostatic conditions at hypocentral depths is not known anywhere in the study region.

This picture of a uniform deviatoric stress state for the central U.S. has several important implications for seismic-hazard estimation. Most, if not all, earthquakes occur in a brittle upper crust, which was assembled and incorporated into continental North America more than 1 b.y. ago. The borders of this region, at all but the northern margin, experienced additional significant tectonism throughout the Paleozoic and into the Cenozoic. Evidence of this Phanerozoic (and the older Proterozoic) activity remains in the form of the primary tectonic features of Figure 3. At present, and probably since the Miocene, this ancient scarred crust is being subjected to a compressive, regionally uniform stress regime that originates from plate-margin interactions remote from the region itself. Our task now is to use this under-

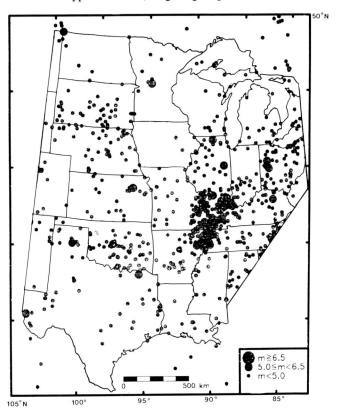

Figure 6. Known earthquakes for the central U.S. of magnitude 5.0 or greater. Compiled from the sources listed in Table 2. Another 13 events, not shown in this figure, would fall between magnitudes 4.7 and 5.1 in some sources but for this study were judged to be less than 5.0 on the m_b or m_{blg} magnitude scales.

TABLE 1. CENTRAL UNITED STATES EARTHQUAKES M ≥5.0

Date	Location lat/long (locale)	Magnitude	MMI_0	Reference
	TWENTIETH CENTURY (1901–1987)			
1987 06 10	38.713/87.954 (SE Illinois)	5.1 m_{bLg}	VI	Taylor and others, 1989
1986 01 31	41.642/81.109 (NE Ohio)	5.0 m_b	VI	Nicholson and others, 1987
1980 07 27	38.18/83.94 (NE Kentucky)	5.2 m_b	VII	Herrmann and others, 1982
1968 11 09	37.96/88.46 (SE Illinois)	5.5 m_{bLg}	VII	Gordon and others, 1970
1952 04 09	35.525/97.850 (Central Oklahoma)	5.5 M_s	Vii	Gordon, 1988
1937 03 09	40.470/84.280 (W. Ohio)	5.0 m_b	VII	Nuttli and Brill, 1981
1931 08 16	30.69/104.57 (SW Texas)	6.3 M_s	VII	Doser, 1987
1925 07 30	35.4/101.3 (N. Texas)	5.2 **M**	VI	Davis and others, 1989
1917 04 09	38.10/90.20 (E. Missouri)	5.0 M_b	VI	Nuttli and Brill, 1981
1916 10 18	33.5/86.2 (N. Alabama)	5.3 M_b	VII	Steigert, 1984
1909 05 26	42.0/89.0 (N. Illinois)	5.0 m_b	VII	Nuttli and Brill, 1981
1909 05 16	50.0/104.0 (U.S.–Canada Border)	5.5 m_b	VI	Horner and Hasegawa, 1978
1905 08 22	36.8/89.6 (SE Missouri)	5.1 m_b	VI-VII	EPRI catalog, 1986
	NINETEENTH CENTURY (1801–1900)			
1895 10 31	37.0/89.4 (SE Missouri)	6.2 m_b	IX	Nuttli and Brill, 1981
1891 09 27	38.25/88.50 (SE Illinois)	5.5 m_{bLg}	VII	Street, 1980
1882 10 22	35.9/95.1 (E. Oklahoma)	5.5 m_b	VIII	Nuttli and Brill, 1981
1877 11 15	41.0/97.0 (E. Nebraska)	5.0 m_b	VII	Nuttli and Brill, 1981
1875 06 18	40.2/84.0 (W. Ohio)	5.2 m_b	VII	EPRI catalog, 1986
1867 04 24	39.17/96.30 (NE Kansas)	5.1 m_b	Vii-Viii	Dubois and Wilson, 1978
1865 08 17	36.5/89.5 (SE Missouri)	5.3 m_b	VII	Nuttli and Brill, 1981
1857 10 08	38.7/89.2 (SW Illinois)	5.1 m_b	Vii	EPRI catalog, 1986
1843 01 05	35.5/90.5 (NE Arkansas)	6.0 m_b	VIII	Nuttli and Brill, 1981
1838 06 09	38.5/89.0 (S. Central Illinois)	5.0 m_{bLg}	VI	EPRI catalog, 1986
1812 02 07	36.5/89.6 (SE Missouri)	7.4 m_b/8.8 M_s	XII	Nuttli, 1983
1812 01 23	36.3/89.6 (SE Missouri)	7.1 m_b8.4 m_s	X-XI	Nuttli, 1983
1811 12 16	36.0/90.0 (NE Arkansas)	70 m_b/8.3 m_s	-----	Street and Nuttli, 1984
1811 12 16	36.0/90.0 (NE Arkansas)	7.2 m_b/8.5 m_s	XI	Nuttli, 1983

within the prevailing contemporary regional stress regime are all important contributing factors to earthquake generation in stable continental interiors.

The most pronounced cluster of activity (Figs. 5 and 6) centers on the confluence of the Mississippi and Ohio Rivers at the head of the Mississippi embayment and is clearly spatially associated with the Reelfoot rift complex of Figure 3. No earthquake exceeding magnitude 6 has occurred in the central U.S. outside of this zone since settlement of the region by Europeans. (The 1931 West Texas event, moment magnitude 6.3 [Doser, 1987], occurred in a zone of active faulting associated with the Rio Grande rift and thus has a closer affinity to western U.S. tectonics than to the stable midcontinent.)

The great New Madrid earthquakes of the winter of 1811–1812, as well as the current seismicity of the zone (Figs. 7 and 8), have been extensively discussed in the literature; we need not repeat those discussions here (see Johnston, 1982, for an overview). Clearly, from Figures 3, 5, and 6, and Table 1, the New Madrid zone, including its probable northward extensions, completely dominates central U.S. seismicity. In fact, it has the highest seismic-moment release rate of any seismic zone in a

stable continent region in the world (Coppersmith and others, 1987; Johnston, 1989). Why is the New Madrid region unique, considering that other continental interiors contain numerous primary tectonic structures and are thought to be subject to fairly uniform regional stress regimes?

The answer to the preceding question is not straightforward and requires a degree of speculation or seismic judgement. One possible answer is that, with a much longer record of seismicity, other crustal structures in the central U.S. or in other stable continental regions might be the loci of large earthquakes, i.e., the assumption of a temporally stochastic pattern of earthquake occurrence is invalid. While we cannot exclude this possibility, we do not favor it and cite the highly stochastic character of the longer seismicity record of China (e.g., McGuire, 1979).

We propose four factors that, combined, make the Reelfoot rift complex especially, perhaps uniquely, susceptible to a high rate of seismicity and the generation of major earthquakes. First, as previously mentioned, it is a major, throughgoing crustal structure. This may be essential to localizing a high strain rate (Anderson, 1986).

Second, the rift is oriented ideally with respect to the re-

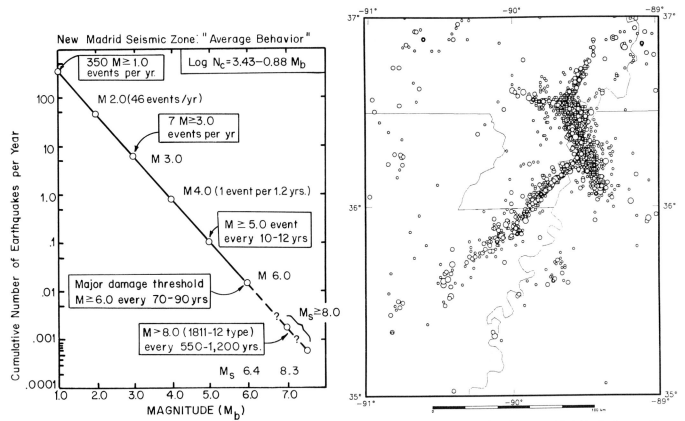

Figure 7. The frequency-magnitude relation for the New Madrid seismic zone (modified from Johnston and Nava, 1985). The data base combines annualized historical seismicity (m_b 3.8 to 6.2) from Nuttli and Brill (1981) and the instrumental seismicity of Fig. 8. Recurrence for events of magnitude exceeding m_b 6.2 is extrapolated.

Figure 8. Instrumental seismicity of the New Madrid seismic zone. Data are from the Central Mississippi Valley Earthquake Bulletin published by Saint Louis University. Magnitudes range from low magnitude 1 to magnitude 5.0; depths range from 23 km to shallow (5.0 km, restricted).

gional stress regime (Fig. 4) for the ratio of shear-to-normal stress to be maximized on preexisting fault systems. (Note that its active west-northwest segment is a good left-lateral strike-slip representation of the auxiliary nodal plane for the right-lateral strike-slip mechanism of the southwest-trending axial zone [Fig. 8].) Other major structures of Figure 3 tend to strike perpendicular or parallel to the regional stress, yielding a less-than-optimum ratio of shear-to-normal stress.

Third, the major Mesozoic-Cenozoic reactivation of the Reelfoot rift is tectonically relatively young, and its crustal disruption has not had time to heal. This may be the factor that explains the aseismicity of the middle Proterozoic midcontinent rift system.

Fourth, and most speculative, is the observation that the Reelfoot rift complex is saturated with water from the largest of the North American drainage systems. It is a wet seismogenic structure, and some evidence suggests that this may be an important contributing factor for intraplate earthquake generation (Nava and Johnston, 1984; Costain and others, 1987).

CHARACTERIZATION OF INTRAPLATE SEISMIC SOURCE ZONES

To provide a seismic-hazard evaluation for the central United States, we must confront the problem of defining seismic source zones in a region virtually devoid of identifiable active faulting. We propose as a useful approach a classification of seismic source zones that includes information on the degree of knowledge available to define the zone.

In regions such as the central U.S. that lack identified active faults, the concept of a seismic source zone is in itself an admission of lack of knowledge. Abundant seismologic evidence indicates that shallow nonvolcanic earthquakes are satisfactorily modeled as shear failures on planar or at least tabular features we call faults. A seismic source zone, then, represents a geographic region that is judged to contain at least one and perhaps a collection of faults capable of generating earthquakes. Seismic parameters, principally the frequency-magnitude relation and maximum-magnitude earthquake, are assumed to be homogeneous throughout the zone. Along plate boundaries and throughout most of the western U.S., seismic source zones can be restricted rather confidently to mapped fault zones, although the presence of unrecognized source zones remains (e.g., the Coalinga earthquake for which the causative fault was concealed by an anticline ridge structure of Pliocene and younger age [Clark and others, 1983]).

In the central U.S., seismic source zones are generally large, a reflection of large uncertainty in their definition. Moreover, in an exercise in which 13 experts were requested by Lawrence Livermore National Laboratory to independently zone the central and eastern U.S., the divergence of the resulting maps was startling, as was the range of criteria that the experts used to delineate the source zones (Bernreuter and others, 1989; Anderson, 1986, Fig. 3). Most weight was given to historical seismicity patterns, with tectonic structure and orientation to the regional stress regime also ranking high in importance, but the emphasis and interpretation of each expert varied greatly.

The classification of intraplate seismic source zones (ISSZs) proposed by Johnston (1987) enables one to define seismic source zones in a systematic manner. This is useful because it helps characterize seismic hazard in these regions while incorporating the current level of uncertainty in the definition of the source zones. As used here, the term "intraplate" excludes all features on which plate contact seismicity occurs or zones directly associated with plate margins in which it is clear that relative plate motions are accommodated, even though slip vectors may not be oriented subparallel to the relative plate motion vector. (Examples of such interplate seismic source zones include actual plate boundaries, subsidiary faults in the San Andreas system, and outer-rise or overriding-wedge earthquakes in subduction zones.) The distinction between interplate and intraplate is most difficult in regions such as south-central Asia or portions of western North America, where plate motion is accommodated over a broad zone. Such distributed plate boundaries are commonly included in the intraplate category.

The intraplate designation can be further subdivided according to whether a region is subject to significant Mesozoic–Cenozoic tectonic activity. If this is absent, we term the region "stable continental interior" (SCI). In SCI regions active surface faulting is rare, and consequently, precision and confidence in delineating ISSZs is limited. Our study area, the central U.S., is a SCI region.

The proposed classification for continental, intraplate, seismic source zones is given in Table 2. All intraplate regions are assigned to one of six categories, depending on known (or unknown) tectonic, geologic, and seismologic characteristics. Categories 1 through 6 (Table 2) imply a step-like transition from abundant data that clearly define an ISSZ (category 1 and 2) to a virtual lack of data for background zones (category 6). In reality, the categories are gradational; as new data are acquired and knowledge improves, seismic sources can be redefined into new, better-constrained ISSZs. One of the primary objectives of seismic-hazard research is to upgrade category 3 through 6 zones

TABLE 2. CONTINENTAL INTRAPLATE SEISMIC SOURCE ZONES

Category		Name	Description
1	(A)	Aseismic	An ISSZ within which there is no known significant seismic activity. Moreover, the region is understood well enough geologically and geophysically to exclude with high confidence the possibility future significant earthquakes.
2	(SG)	Seismogenic	A specific geologic entity (usually a fault) that can be defined geologically or geophysically and, on which, earthquakes are known to have occurred, or there is evidence of prehistoric earthquakes.
3	(ST)	Seismotectonic	A clearly defined tectonic feature such as a fault zone, rift, suture, intrusion, etc., with which seismicity is spatially associated, but a clear association with a specific fault or faults is lacking.
4	(S)	Seismic	A region where seismicity is "enhanced over background" and spatial clustering is evident, but data are insufficient to associate the activity with seismogenic or seismotectonic crustal structures.
5	(T)	Tectonic	Geologic or geophysical data resolve a crustal feature that elsewhere is known to be associated with earthquakes, but in this case no instrumental, historical, or paleoseismic data exist that suggest the feature has experienced significant seismicity.
6	(B)	Background	A region with no known significant seismicity or known geologic/tectonic features capable of significant earthquakes, but the data are too poor to exclude their existence with confidence.

(where most continental intraplate ISSZs now would be classified) into category 1 or 2.

SEISMIC-SOURCE ZONATION

To zone the central U.S. for hazard analysis, we must: (1) delineate individual seismic source zones, (2) assign a maximum credible earthquake to each zone, (3) estimate the rate of seismic activity for each zone, and (4) determine the anelastic attenuation from each zone to sites of interest. Estimating the seismic activity and attenuation are beyond the scope of this study, but we will examine how to approach tasks 1 and 2 for the central U.S.

The previously cited study of Coppersmith and others (1987; see also Coppersmith and Youngs, 1989) that assessed the worldwide occurrence of seismicity in stable continental interiors (SCI) provides a comprehensive data base that can guide source zone definition and maximum-earthquake selection in the central U.S. To counter the probability that the observational record is neither sufficiently long nor complete, Coppersmith and others (1987) compiled data from magnitude ≥5.0 earthquakes from all stable continental regions. They found fewer than 20 known events of (seismic moment) magnitude ≥7.0 in these regions, and the level of seismic activity varies greatly on a continent-size scale. Most large events have been preceded by known historical or instrumental seismicity and have occurred in crust of Paleozoic rather than Precambrian age.

Other findings from the SCI study are applicable to seismic source zonation in the central U.S. They include: (1) a compressive, horizontal, deviatoric stress regime dominates in SCI regions worldwide, producing mostly thrust and strike-slip earthquakes; (2) from a total data set of nearly 800 events, $m_b \geq 5.0$ earthquakes are strongly associated with continental rifts of Mesozoic age and younger, and continental passive margins; (3) the rifted-crust association is even stronger for large earthquakes—those that exceed moment magnitude 7 occur exclusively in zones of Mesozoic–Cenozoic rifting, i.e., passive continental margins (successful rifts) or intracontinental (failed) rifts; and (4) surface fault rupture is extremely rare and has been confidently documented in only 1 percent of the SCI data set (8 occurrences).

Given the information compiled in Coppersmith and others (1987), how should one proceed with seismic zonation in SCI regions? The study imposes a strong constraint on source-zone delineation by limiting large (**M**≥7.0) SCI earthquakes to a few possible tectonic settings. Since a seismic zone must have the same maximum earthquake assigned to the entire zone, boundaries should be based on mapped or geophysically inferred structural boundaries, principally of Mesozoic or younger rifts.

The problem of defining the seismic source zone for maximum New Madrid earthquakes was addressed by Johnston and Nava (1985) in their analysis of recurrence probabilities of such events (Fig. 7). They concluded that, although the crustal elastic-strain storage volume for the 1811–1812 earthquake sequence must far exceed the Reelfoot rift boundaries of Hildenbrand and others (1982), major New Madrid earthquakes will be restricted to the principal fault segments within the boundaries of the rift. These segments are delineated by the concentrated pattern of instrumental earthquake epicenters shown in Figure 8. We conclude that the principal seismicity segments of the New Madrid seismic zone must be separately zoned from the rest of the Reelfoot rift complex because it has a different (higher) maximum earthquake potential.

The study of Coppersmith and others (1987) offers useful guidance in restricting the major **M**≥7 earthquakes of SCI regions to a few locales, but what of the significant hazard contributed by damaging, moderate-magnitude events? Background seismicity (e.g., Fig. 5) is an unreliable, even misleading, guide to where such events might occur—witness the **M** 5.2 Sharpsburg, Kentucky, earthquake in 1980; the **M** 5.6 New Brunswick earth-

quake in 1982; or the **M** 5.0 earthquake near Cleveland, Ohio, in 1986. We conclude that, while major earthquakes can be localized to certain types of primary tectonic structures, one must allow for the occurrence of magnitude 5.0 to 5.5 events virtually anywhere in the central U.S.

Having examined some of the issues involved in seismic source zoning and maximum-earthquake designation, we now proceed to zone the central U.S. In Figure 9, we subdivide the central U.S. into seismic source zones (SSZ) that are labeled according to the type of data used to define the zone (see Table 2). Two requirements controlled the selection of the SSZs in Figure 9. The most important criterion is that the maximum earthquake must be allowed to occur anywhere within the boundaries of the identified source zone. Because fault dimensions of even the largest midplate earthquakes will likely not exceed 100 km (Nuttli, 1983), the SSZs of Figure 9 obviously do not represent monolithic seismogenic structures; rather they are regions within which structures have similar seismogenic potential. In applying this criterion, we emphasize the maximum earthquake component of seismic potential rather than seismic activity rate.

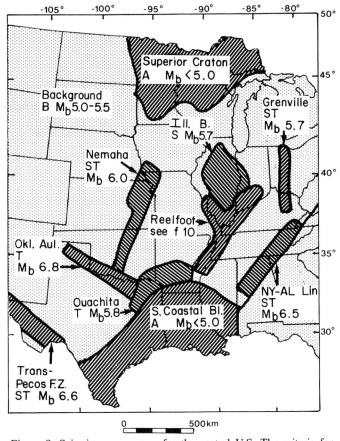

Figure 9. Seismic source zones for the central U.S. The criteria for defining each zone is indicated (see categories of Table 2). The estimated maximum earthquake and zone boundaries are derived from arguments presented in the text. See Figure 10 for detail on the Reelfoot rift–New Madrid seismic zone. Abbreviations: T, tectonic; ST, seismotectonic; S, seismic; B, background; SG, seismogenic; A, aseismic.

The first SSZ selection requirement leads directly to the second: boundaries of identified SSZs should be based primarily on the known or inferred extent of primary tectonic features (Fig. 3). This is a significant departure from the past practice of defining seismic source zones based on the record of historical seismicity.

The maximum earthquake estimated for each SSZ in Figure 9 is based on both the largest known earthquake for the zone and the earthquake record of similar SSZs in the global data base of Coppersmith and others (1987). Note that of all central U.S. seismic source zones, only the Reelfoot rift SSZ has experienced the estimated maximum earthquake in historic times.

We have defined fewer seismic source zones in Figure 9 than some previous studies (e.g., Nuttli and Herrmann, 1978; Bernreuter and others, 1989). This is because we recognize the possibility of a moderately large earthquake (m_b 5.0 to 5.5) over a very broad background SSZ (category 6, Table 2) based on the worldwide study (Coppersmith and others, 1987) that shows many such events in SCI environments cannot be associated with primary tectonic structures. Thus, our background SSZ combines many seismic source zones that previously had been treated separately (e.g., the Ozark uplift, the Colorado lineament, various intra-cratonic basins or uplifts). Past seismic activity and the orientation to the regional stress field are additional contributing factors that we considered.

The Reelfoot rift/New Madrid SSZ

The Reelfoot rift complex is subdivided into two separate SSZs (Fig. 10): a seismic SSZ (Zone A) and a seismotectonic SSZ (Zone B) (see Table 2). Zone A is delineated on the basis of the linear trends of the numerous small-earthquake epicenters (Fig. 8). The linearity of the pattern suggests that this zone is actually composed of several seismogenic fault segments; these probably last ruptured in their entirety in the great earthquake sequence of 1811–1812. Moreover, seismic-reflection profiles have actually imaged an upper-crust disturbed zone that is coincident with the southwestern arm of Zone A (e.g., Crone and others, 1985).

Zone B is defined by the geophysically inferred limits of the Reelfoot rift complex. Its borders are the margins of the rift as defined by magnetic and gravity data by Hildenbrand and others (1982) to the south, and by Braile and others (1984) to the north. The geophysical signature of the Reelfoot lobe is much clearer than the Saint Louis and Wabash Valley lobes to the north, but the geophysical data and seismic activity are significant enough that these northern branches should not be ignored in hazard zonations.

The east-west Rough Creek graben zone is included as a fourth lobe by Braile and others (1984). It is clearly a rift-type structure, but we classify it as a "tectonic" SSZ (category 5, Table 2) because it has no associated significant seismic activity. The lack of seismicity is probably related to the fact that its orientation is nearly parallel to the prevailing regional horizontal principal stress. We consider the probability of significant earth-

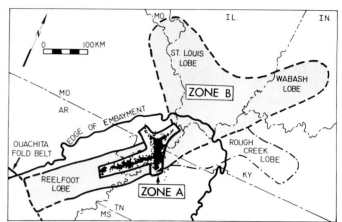

Figure 10. Subdivision of the Reelfoot rift complex into a seismic SSZ, Zone A, and a seismotectonic SSZ, Zone B. The two zones are separated on the basis of the type of data used for their definition and the estimated maximum-possible earthquake.

quakes ($m_b \geqslant 5.5$) in this zone to be much lower than the rest of Zone B; therefore, we remove it from Zone B on the map in Figures 9 and 10.

We assign as the southern boundary of Zone B the inferred extension of the Ouachita foldbelt beneath the Mississippi embayment. This choice of boundary is not based on hard data. It is unclear that the rift structure of Hildenbrand and others (1982) extends to the foldbelt, but there is no evidence that the rift extends south of the Ouachita belt. Therefore, it seems a logical place to truncate Zone B.

In terms of perceived seismic hazard, the distinction between Zone A and Zone B is important: both the maximum possible earthquake and the seismic activity rate differ substantially for the two subzones. We believe that a great earthquake of $m_b \geqslant 7.0$, $M_s \geqslant 8.0$ would be restricted to Zone A. A possible, although admittedly qualitative, explanation for this is that the crustal rock of stable continental interiors is normally strong enough to inhibit or confine coseismic rupture propagation; only within the faulted and weakened segments of Zone A can rupture propagate to sufficient dimensions to produce great earthquakes. Thus, we regard the New Madrid Zone A as a special case that is virtually unique in North America, with the possible exception of portions of the St. Lawrence rift valley.

Even though the boundaries of Zone B are fairly well defined by geophysical methods, its maximum-magnitude earthquake is difficult to estimate with any degree of confidence. On the basis of the Coppersmith and others (1987) study, we assign an m_b 6.5 as the maximum probable event. Low magnitude 6 events have occurred in continental-rift environments currently under compression in Europe (Rhine graben), India (Cambay and Godavari grabens), North America (St. Lawrence rift), Australia (Adelaide geosyncline, Fitzroy trough), and Africa (Sirte grabens). Events larger than m_b 6.5 have occurred in the St. Lawrence and Sirte regions, but we consider these analogous to New Madrid Zone A events. The assigned maximum earthquake of m_b 6.5 has not been experienced in historic times in Zone B, but the occurrence of similar-magnitude shocks in tectonically similar rift settings worldwide suggests such an event is possible in Zone B.

On the basis of the historical seismicity (Fig. 5) and instrumental seismicity (Fig. 8), significant earthquakes are more likely in Zone B north of latitude 35.5. One could argue for separate zones, but we feel this relies too heavily on the short historical record. Nevertheless, the relatively aseismic nature of Reelfoot rift south of Marked Tree, Arkansas, is an enigma.

Epilogue: The Meers fault

The Meers fault, located in the Oklahoma aulacogen (Fig. 3), represents a probable prehistoric exception to the domination of central U.S. seismicity by the New Madrid zone. Strong geologic evidence now indicates a magnitude 7^+ earthquake on this fault within the past 1,100 to 1,400 years (Luza and others, 1987; Ramelli and others, 1987; Madole, 1988). If the fault's dip is subvertical at hypocentral depths, its orientation is favorable for left-lateral strike-slip movement, which is the observed dominant slip component. It has been virtually aseismic throughout the historical past.

The Meers fault, with its prominent surface scarp, represents a western-style (e.g., surface rupture) active fault within the central U.S. stable interior. It is already forcing a reexamination of seismic-zonation practices, which in the past, have relied heavily on historical seismicity, because it violates the assumption of stationarity of seismicity on which much seismic-hazard analysis is based. It is an important reminder that we must continually question our assumptions and strive to improve our understanding of the tectonics underlying the seismogenic process in the central United States.

ACKNOWLEDGMENTS

The Nuclear Regulatory Commission (Contract NRC-04-86-120) and the Electric Power Research Institute (Project RP2556-12) supported portions of this work. We are also grateful for the support from the U.S. Army Corps of Engineers, particularly the encouragement of Ellis Krinitsky and the comprehensive critical review of Tony Crone; however, all interpretations in this study remain solely those of the authors. We thank Linda Johnson and Tanya George for manuscript and figure preparation, respectively.

REFERENCES CITED

Algermissen, S. T., Perkins, D. M., Thenhaus, P. C., Hanson, S. L., and Bender, B. L., 1982, Probabilistic estimates of maximum acceleration and velocity in rock in the contiguous United States: U.S. Geological Survey Open-File Report 82-1033, 99 p.

Anderson, J. G., 1986, Seismic strain rates in the central and eastern United States: Bulletin of the Seismological Society of America, v. 76, p. 273–290.

Bernreuter, D. L., Savy, J. B., Mensing, R. W., and Chen, J. C., 1989, Seismic hazard characterization of 69 nuclear plant sites east of the Rocky Mountains: U.S. Nuclear Regulatory Commission NUREG/CR-5250, 8 volumes, no sequential page numbers.

Bickford, M. E., Van Schmus, W. R., and Zietz, I., 1986, Proterozoic history of the midcontinent region of North America: Geology, v. 14, p. 492–496.

Braile, L., Hinze, W., Sexton, J., Keller, G. R., and Lidiak, E., 1984, Tectonic development of the New Madrid seismic zone, *in* Hays, W. W., and Gori, P. L., eds., Proceedings of the Symposium on "The New Madrid Seismic Zone": U.S. Geological Survey Open-File Report 84-770, p. 204–233.

Chase, C. G., and Gilmer, T. H., 1973, Precambrian plate tectonics; The midcontinent gravity high: Earth and Planetary Science Letters, v. 21, p. 70–78.

Clark, M. M., and 5 others, 1983, The May 2, 1983, earthquake at Coalinga, California; The search for surface faulting, *in* The Coalinga earthquake sequence commencing May 2, 1983: U.S. Geological Survey Open-File Report 83-511, p. 8–11.

Coppersmith, K. J., and Youngs, R. R., 1989, Issues regarding earthquake source characterization and seismic hazard analysis within passive margins and stable continental interiors, *in* Gregersen, S., and Basham, P. W., eds., Earthquakes at North Atlantic passive margins; Neotectonics and postglacial rebound: Dordrecht, Netherlands, Kluwer Academic Publishers, p. 601–631.

Coppersmith, K. J., Johnston, A. C., Metzger, A. G., and Arabasz, W. J., 1987, Methods for assessing maximum earthquakes in the central and eastern United States: Palo Alto, California, Electric Power Research Institute Working Report Project RP2556-12, 109 p.

Costain, J. K., Bollinger, G. A., and Speer, J. A., 1987, Hydroseismicity; A hypothesis for the role of water in the generation of intraplate seismicity: Seismological Research Letters, v. 58, p. 41–64.

Crone, A. J., and 5 others, 1985, Structure of the New Madrid seismic zone in southeastern Missouri and northeastern Arkansas: Geology, v. 13, p. 547–550.

Davis, S. D., Pennington, W. D., and Carlson, S. M., 1989, A compendium of earthquake activity in Texas: University of Texas at Austin, 29 p. plus appendices (in press).

Doser, D. I., 1987, The 16 August 1931 Valentine, Texas, earthquake; Evidence for normal faulting in West Texas: Bulletin of the Seismological Society of America, v. 77, p. 2005–2017.

DuBois, S. M., and Wilson, F. W., 1978, A revised and augmented list of earthquake intensities for Kansas 1867–1977: Washington, D.C., U.S. Nuclear Regulatory Commission NUREG/CR-0294, 56 p.

Electric Power Research Institute, 1986, Seismic-hazard methodology for the central and eastern United States: Electric Power Research Institute Project P101-19 Final Report NP-4726, volumes 1-10, including seismicity catalog, no sequential page numbers.

Gordon, D. W., 1988, Revised instrumental hypocenters and correlation of earthquake locations in the central United States: U.S. Geological Survey Professional Paper 1364, 69 p.

Gordon, D. W., Bennett, T. J., Herrmann, R. B., and Rogers, A. M., 1970, The south-central Illinois earthquake of November 9, 1968: Macroseismic studies: Bulletin of the Seismological Society of America, v. 60, p. 953–971.

Hatcher, R. D., Jr., Zietz, I., and Litehiser, J. J., 1987, Crustal subdivisions of the eastern and central United States and a seismic boundary hypothesis for eastern seismicity: Geology, v. 15, p. 528–532.

Herrmann, R. B., Langston, C. A., and Zollweg, J. E., 1982, The Sharpsburg, Kentucky, earthquake of 27 July 1980: Bulletin of the Seismological Society of America, v. 72, p. 1219–1239.

Hildenbrand, T. G., Kane, M. F., and Hendricks, J. D., 1982, Magnetic basement in the upper Mississippi embayment region; A preliminary report, *in* McKeown, F. A., and Pakiser, L. C., eds., Investigations of the New Madrid, Missouri, earthquake region: U.S. Geological Survey Professional Paper 1236, p. 39–53.

Hoffman, P. F., 1988, United plates of America, the birth of a craton; Early Proterozoic assembly and growth of Laurentia: Annual Review of Earth and Planetary Sciences, v. 16, p. 543–603.

Horner, R. B., and Hasegawa, H., 1978, The seismotectonics of southern Saskatchewan: Canadian Journal of Earth Sciences, v. 15, p. 1341–1355.

Johnston, A. C., 1982, A major earthquake zone on the Mississippi: Scientific American, v. 246, p. 60–68.

—— , 1987, Characterization of intraplate seismic source zones, *in* Crone, A. J., and Omdhal, E. M., eds., Directions in paleoseismology: U.S. Geological Survey Open-File Report 87-673, p. 404–413.

—— , 1989, The seismicity of 'stable continental interiors,' *in* Gregersen, S., and Basham, P. W., eds., Earthquakes at North Atlantic passive margins; Neotectonics and postglacial rebound: Dordrecht, Netherlands, Kluwer Academic Publishers, p. 581–599.

Johnston, A. C., and Nava, S. J., 1985, Recurrence rates and probability estimates for the New Madrid seismic zone: Journal of Geophysical Research, v. 90, p. 6737–6753.

Johnston, A. C., Reinbold, D. J., and Brewer, S. I., 1985, Seismotectonics of the southern Appalachians: Bulletin of the Seismological Society of America, v. 75, p. 291–312.

King, E. R., and Zietz, I., 1978, The New York–Alabama lineament; Geophysical evidence for a major crustal break in the basement beneath the Appalachian basin: Geology, v. 6, p. 312–318.

Luza, K. V., Madole, R. F., and Crone, A. J., 1987, Investigation of the Meers fault in southwestern Oklahoma: Washington, D.C., U.S. Nuclear Regulatory Commission NUREG/CR-4937, 55 p.

Madole, R. F., 1988, Stratigraphic evidence of Holocene faulting in the midcontinent; the Meers fault, southwestern Oklahoma: Geological Society of America Bulletin, v. 100, p. 392–401.

McGuire, R. K., 1979, Adequacy of simple probability models for calculating felt-shaking hazard, using the Chinese earthquake catalog: Bulletin of the Seismological Society of America, v. 69, p. 877–892.

Nava, S. J., and Johnston, A. C., 1984, Rivers and earthquakes; A correlation for New Madrid and the Mississippi River [abs.]: Earthquake Notes, v. 55, no. 3, p. 15.

Nicholson, C., Roeloffs, E., and Wesson, R. L., 1987, The northeastern Ohio earthquake of January 31, 1986; Was it induced?: Bulletin of the Seismological Society of America, v. 78, p. 188–217.

Nuttli, O. W., 1979, Seismicity of the central United States, *in* Hatheway, A. W., and McClure, C. R., Jr., eds., Geology in the siting of nuclear power plants: Geological Society of America Reviews in Engineering Geology, v. IV, p. 67–93.

—— , 1983, Average seismic-source parameter relations for mid-plate earthquakes: Bulletin of the Seismological Society of America, v. 73, p. 519–535.

Nuttli, O. W., and Brill, K. G., Jr., 1981, Catalog of central United States earthquakes since 1800 of $m_b \geqslant 3.0$, Part 2 and Appendix B-2, *in* Barstow, N. L., Brill, K. G., Jr., Nuttli, O. W., and Pomeroy, P. W., eds., An approach to seismic zonation for siting nuclear electric power generating facilities in the eastern United States: Washington, D.C., U.S. Nuclear Regulatory Commission NUREG/CR-1577, p. 97–143, B2-1–B2-31.

Nuttli, O. W., and Herrmann, R. B., 1978, Credible earthquakes for the central United States, *in* State-of-the-art for assessing earthquake hazards in the United States: Vicksburg, Mississippi, U.S. Army Corps of Engineers Geotechnical Lab Report 12, 99 p.

Ramelli, A. R., Slemmons, D. B., and Brocoum, S. J., 1987, The Meers fault; Tectonic activity in southwestern Oklahoma: Washington, D.C., U.S. Nuclear Regulatory Commission NUREG/CR-4852, 25 p.

Sims, P. K., and Peterman, Z. E., 1986, Early Proterozoic Central Plains orogen; A major buried structure in the north-central United States: Geology, v. 14, p. 488–491.

Steigert, F. W., 1984, Seismicity of the southern Appalachian seismic zone in Alabama: Tuscaloosa, Geological Survey of Alabama Circular 119, 106 p.

Street, R. L., 1980, The southern Illinois earthquake of September 27, 1891: Bulletin of the Seismological Society of America, v. 70, p. 915–920.

Street, R., and Nuttli, O. W., 1984, The central Mississippi Valley earthquakes of 1811–1812, *in* Hays, W. W., and Gori, P. L., eds., Proceedings of the Symposium on "The New Madrid Seismic Zone": U.S. Geological Survey Open-File Report 84-770, p. 33–63.

Taylor, K. B., Herrmann, R. B., Hamburger, M. W., Pavlis, G. L., Johnston, A. C., Langer, C., and Lam, C., 1989, The southeastern Illinois earthquake of 10 June 1987: Seismological Research Letters, v. 60, p. 101–110.

Van Schmus, W. R., and Hinze, W. J., 1985, The midcontinent rift system: Annual Review of Earth and Planetary Sciences, v. 13, p. 345–383.

Van Schmus, W. R., Bickford, M. E., and Zietz, I., 1987, Early and middle Proterozoic provinces in the central United States, *in* Kroner, A., ed., Proterozoic lithospheric evolution: American Geophysical Union Geodynamics Series, v. 17, p. 43–68.

Viele, G. W., 1979, Geologic map and cross section, eastern Ouachita Mountains, Arkansas: Geological Society of America Map and Chart Series MC-28F, 8 pages.

Zoback, M. L., and Zoback, M. D., 1980, State of stress in the conterminous United States: Journal of Geophysical Research, v. 85, p. 6113–6156.

—— , 1989, Tectonic stress field of the continental U.S., *in* Pakiser, L. C., and Mooney, W. D., eds., Geophysical framework of the continental United States: Geological Society of America Memoir 172, p. 523–540.

MANUSCRIPT ACCEPTED BY THE SOCIETY AUGUST 18, 1989

Geological Society of America
Reviews in Engineering Geology, Volume VIII
1990

Chapter 4

Implications of the Meers fault on seismic potential in the central United States

Alan R. Ramelli
Nevada Bureau of Mines and Geology, University of Nevada, Reno, Nevada 89557
D. Burton Slemmons
Center for Neotectonic Studies, Mackay School of Mines, University of Nevada, Reno, Nevada 89557

ABSTRACT

The Meers fault in southwestern Oklahoma, with a prominent scarp resulting from late Holocene surface displacement, is the best-expressed late Quaternary surface fault known to occur in a "stable" continental interior (or mid-plate) region (i.e., regions far removed from areas of high tectonic rates). The Meers fault is part of a major fault system that has not been the locus of major tectonic activity since the Paleozoic, and although recent surface displacements have been sizable, average late Quaternary rates have been low, based on a lack of geomorphic expression indicating significant cumulative displacement. Activity of the Meers fault is unusual, because in mid-plate regions, few large historical earthquakes have occurred and recognized cases of late Quaternary surface faulting are very rare.

Based on the extent of surface rupturing and amounts of displacement, the Meers fault appears capable of producing very large events (i.e., M > 7, or possibly even M > 7½). Recent events on the Meers fault produced surface displacements of a few to several meters. Such displacements are quite large, relative to the rupture length of about 40 km, and could result from a tendency for mid-plate or long-recurrence faults to rupture with higher stress drops than plate-margin or short-recurrence faults. Studies attempting to evaluate this possibility have produced conflicting results and may indicate this cannot be placed in as simple a context as plate-margin versus intraplate settings. A large earthquake on the Meers fault would produce strong ground motion throughout much of the south-central United States and could cause widespread damage. The existence of a potential source of large earthquakes in a region thought to be tectonically stable suggests that the seismic potential of this and other mid-plate regions may be underestimated.

INTRODUCTION

One of the greatest surprises in recent neotectonic studies is recognition of late Holocene activity of the Meers fault in southwestern Oklahoma (Fig. 1). This fault has been historically aseismic (Lawson and others, 1979; Lawson and Luza, 1980–1988) and lies within an intraplate region thought to be tectonically stable, yet it exhibits striking evidence of recent surface faulting. A prominent linear scarp trends N60°W across an area of fairly flat terrain for a distance of almost 40 km. Features with such fresh and impressive geomorphic expression are usually restricted to more tectonically active regions. Evidence of surface faulting is generally considered lacking in the central United States and other stable continental interior (SCI) regions. The Meers fault shows that in some cases such evidence does exist, but has not yet been recognized.

Ramelli, A. R., and Slemmons, D. B., 1990, Implications of the Meers fault on seismic potential in the central United States, *in* Krinitzsky, E. L., and Slemmons, D. B., Neotectonics in earthquake evaluation: Boulder, Colorado, Geological Society of America Reviews in Engineering Geology, v. 8.

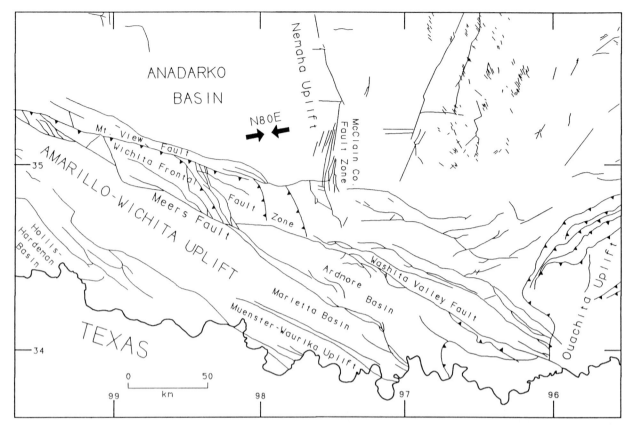

Figure 1. Principal faults and major structural features in southwestern Oklahoma (after Chenoweth, 1983). Direction of greatest horizontal stress (arrows) from Dart (1987).

The recent activity of the Meers fault presents several significant problems for analyses of seismic hazards of this and other similar regions. How great is the potential for a damaging earthquake along this fault? To what extent have potential sources of damaging earthquakes been overlooked or underestimated in SCI regions? What are the implications for areas where there have traditionally been no seismic design codes? Is this a one-of-a-kind feature, or does it suggest that conventional methods for evaluating seismic potential in SCI regions may be inadequate and misleading? An increased effort to identify and characterize paleoseismic surface ruptures throughout this region is warranted and could go a long way toward resolving these and other related issues.

The Meers fault scarp is well expressed at the surface (Figs. 2 and 3), but despite this fact, it escaped recognition as an active fault until only recently. Moody and Hill (1956) briefly mentioned its presence in Quaternary alluvium, but this observation went unrecognized, because it came prior to an increased effort to assess seismic hazards in the United States. Harlton (1951, 1963, 1972) accomplished detailed structural mapping of the area, but made no mention of evidence of recent activity. Not until the early 1980s was this area subjected to intensive geological study, when the recency of activity on the Meers fault became widely recognized. Gilbert (1983) and Donovan and others (1983) were

the first to present evidence for late Quaternary surface displacements. If not for their studies, this important feature would probably remain unknown.

GEOLOGIC/STRUCTURAL SETTING

Even though the Meers fault has been recently active, intense deformation has not occurred in the region since the late Paleozoic. This is a mid-plate region, far removed from plate margins and other areas of high tectonic activity. The regions to the east of the Rocky Mountains and the Rio Grande Rift form the stable continental interior of North America. SCI regions are subject to earthquake activity, so they are not completely "stable," but the term is useful to denote the level of tectonism, relative to regions like the western United States. The evidence of recent large earthquakes on the Meers fault is rather anomalous, because SCI regions usually have low seismic potential, and recognized cases of surface faulting are rare.

The Meers fault is generally considered to be the south-bounding fault of the Wichita frontal fault system. This fault system separates the Anadarko Basin, the deepest intracontinental basin in the United States, from the uplifted igneous complex of the Wichita Mountains, the exposed part of the Amarillo-Wichita uplift (Fig. 1). The frontal fault system has had a complex history

Figure 2. Oblique aerial view, looking NW, of Meers fault scarp in Post Oak Conglomerate, a resistant Permian carbonate boulder conglomerate. Contrast the geomorphic expression with Figure 3. This results from both the greater resistance of the material and the greater degree of brittle displacement. (Photo by D. B. Slemmons.)

of displacement. The earliest documented phase of deformation involved down-to-the-south normal displacement during Cambrian rifting associated with the opening of the proto-Atlantic ocean. The igneous complex emplaced within this rift, often called the southern Oklahoma aulacogen, is composed predominantly of layered gabbros, granites, and rhyolites and is now exposed at the surface (Ham and others, 1964).

A subsidence phase followed the rifting phase, forming the Anadarko Basin. Subsidence occurred throughout much of the Paleozoic, although most of it took place during late Cambrian and Ordovician time (Donovan, 1986). As much as 12 km of stratigraphic separation now occurs between the Anardarko Basin and the Wichita igneous complex (Donovan, 1986). The Anadarko Basin is asymmetric, with a depositional axis immediately adjacent and parallel to the frontal fault system.

During Pennsylvanian and Permian time, the closing of the proto-Atlantic ocean led to the Ouachita orogen to the east and reactivated the frontal fault zone (Donovan, 1986). The latter stage (Permian) of this deformational phase involved a component of down-to-the-south throw on the Meers fault, with Post Oak Conglomerate shed off the uplifting Wichita Mountains and Slick Hills into a narrow, elongate trough, which is roughly coincident with the present-day Meers Valley.

The Wichita frontal fault system has long been depicted with a vertical orientation extending to depth (e.g., Ham and others, 1964). However, recent studies, based principally on deep seismic profiling surveys and drill-hole data, have interpreted the frontal fault system to be south-dipping, with the Wichita Mountains thrust over sediments of the Anadarko Basin (Brewer and others, 1983). This interpretation calls for the Mountain View fault to be the main feature of this system and to dip to the south at about 30 to 40 degrees. A similar orientation was inferred for the Meers fault, but this seems improbable based on the subvertical to north-dipping orientation at the surface and the unlikeli-

hood of large normal displacements in a compressional regime. At present, connections between the fault expressed at the surface and specific structures at depth are not obvious.

In the Slick Hills, adjacent to the northwestern part of the Meers fault scarp (Fig. 4), about one-fourth of the total width of the frontal fault zone (6 km out a 24 km) is exposed at the surface. Structures exposed in this area may have resulted from transpressive deformation, with a considerable amount of left-lateral deformation (Donovan, 1982; Donovan and others, 1982; Beauchamp, 1983; McConnell, 1983; Donovan, 1986; McCoss and Donovan, 1986). A lateral deformational phase, in which the Meers fault played a major role, apparently followed a contractional phase (Donovan, 1986).

Recent displacements have occurred along a very linear fault trace (Fig. 4); nowhere does the strike of the fault scarp vary by more than a few degrees from its overall N60°W trend. This linearity persists through the Slick Hills, an area of slight relief (i.e., tens of meters), indicating that the fault is nearly vertical at the surface. Shallow seismic-reflection surveys (Harding, 1985; Myers and others, 1987) have suggested that the fault is steeply dipping throughout the shallow subsurface. A strike-slip history

Figure 3. Oblique aerial view, looking NW, of Meers fault scarp in Hennessey Shale. This unit is much less resistant than Post Oak Conglomerate and has accommodated surface displacements largely by warping, rather than brittle offset. It thus has a much more subdued geomorphic expression than the scarp on Post Oak (Fig. 2). (Photo by R. A. Whitney.)

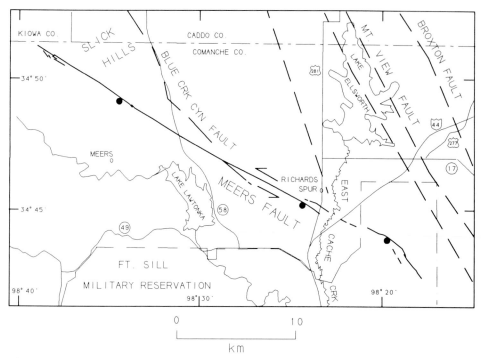

Figure 4. Map of late Quaternary surface displacements on the Meers fault as interpreted from field study and low-sun-angle photography. Balls on down-thrown (footwall) side of fault; intersecting structures as mapped by Harlton (1972).

for the Meers fault is likely, since linearity and vertical orientations are commonly characteristic of strike-slip faults.

SURFACE RUPTURE LENGTH

The prominent expression along almost the entire length of the Meers fault scarp allows for relatively simple length determination. Gilbert's (1983) initial reported length of 26 km remained unchanged until low-sun-angle aerial photographs revealed a significant extension to the southeast (Ramelli and others, 1987). The main fault scarp forms a continuous linear, topographic break extending from the Kiowa/Comanche County line to U.S. Highway 281, near Richard's Spur, where it intersects the active flood plain of East Cache Creek (Fig. 4). Inclusion of a scarp trending across the northeastern part of Fort Sill Military Reservation (Fig. 5) yields an end-to-end surface-rupture length of 37 km.

Several aspects of the Fort Sill scarp provide evidence of structural control. It is located on-line with, and in proximity to, the main fault scarp, has a WNW orientation, and is down-thrown on the south side, similar to the main fault scarp. A small drainage runs along the scarp for much of its length, but this is oriented transverse to the local drainage network. This scarp is discernible beginning about 4 km southeast of East Cache Creek and trending across most of the northeastern part of Fort Sill Military Reservation. Its location across an "impact area" for artillery practice will unfortunately limit access and study of this part of the fault. The eastern end of this scarp lies about 1 km

from the eastern border of Fort Sill. Connection of the main fault trace and the Fort Sill scarp is not completely clear cut. There is a moderate (⅓ km) left step from the main trace to the trace of the Fort Sill scarp near East Cache Creek. Recent flood-plain deposition has concealed most, if not all, surficial evidence of faulting in this area.

Subdued lineaments apparent on the low-sun-angle aerial photographs cross much of the East Cache Creek floodplain, but fault control of these is problematic without additional exploration. Between the Fort Sill scarp and the East Cache Creek floodplain lineaments is a subdued, linear, south-facing scarp. Fault control of this short scarp is not obvious, but its location and linearity suggest it is tectonic.

The three largest discontinuities in the surface fault trace lie along the eastern half of the scarp (Fig. 4). The westernmost of these is a splay from the main fault. While not obvious on aerial photographs, this splay was mapped by Harlton (1972) and forms a slight topographic break. The middle discontinuity, the step-over at East Cache Creek, is the largest of the three. The easternmost discontinuity is a bend near the end of the fault. These irregularities lie across an area where several NW- to NNW-trending faults (e.g., Mountain View, Blue Creek Canyon) are mapped as intersecting the Meers fault (Fig. 4). It is probable that interaction with these faults is responsible for these discontinuities.

Recently, "segmentation" of fault zones has been used increasingly to better characterize paleoseismic events. Individual seismic events rarely rupture the entire lengths of fault zones.

Figure 5. Oblique aerial view, looking ENE, of scarp trending across the northeastern part of Fort Sill Military Reservation. (Photo by R. A. Whitney.)

Segmentation of faults is an attempt to delineate the features that reflect the starting or stopping points of individual ruptures. These are commonly significant bends, step-overs, or other fault-zone discontinuities. Features along the southeastern part of the Meers fault scarp possibly reflect segment boundaries (the step-over at East Cache Creek, in particular), but this seems unlikely for the following reasons: (1) this would require displacement of at least a few meters, but a length of only about 10 km; (2) vertical displacement curves (Fig. 6) suggest that displacements do not die out at East Cache Creek; and (3) this would further complicate the displacement versus length problem discussed in Ramelli and others (1987) and in the section on seismic potential in this chapter.

DISPLACEMENT

The Meers fault scarp is south-facing along its entire length. Natural and trench exposures show reverse displacements along a steeply to moderately north-dipping fault. The recent interpretation of the Meers fault as south-dipping (Brewer and others, 1983) led to some speculation of normal displacement. However, because the fault has a subvertical to north-dipping orientation at the surface, and crustal stress in the region is recognized as compressional, normal displacement can be precluded. Donovan and others (1983) recognized a component of left-lateral displacement, similar to their interpretation of the late Paleozoic displacement. Left-lateral displacement is compatible with the

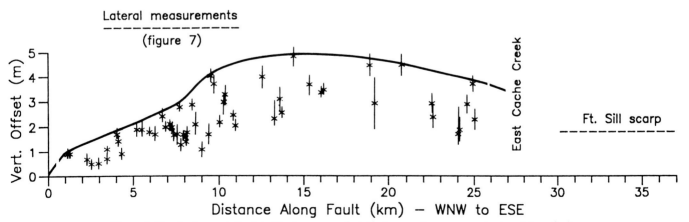

Figure 6. Graph of cumulative late Quaternary vertical-displacement measurements along Meers fault from NW to SE. Note the range and scale difference of Figure 7.

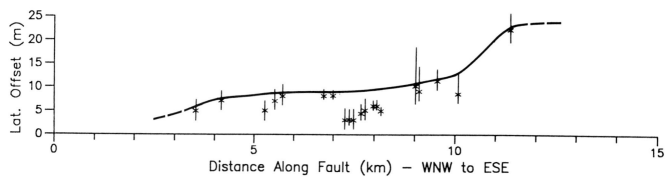

Figure 7. Graph of cumulative late Quaternary horizontal-displacement measurements along Meers fault from NW to SE. Note the scale difference of Figure 6.

ENE-WSW–oriented maximum horizontal stress direction in the south-central United States (see Fig. 1) as determined from hydraulic fracturing and borehole breakouts (Dart, 1987; Zoback, 1987). Displacement thus, is believed to be reverse-left oblique.

Due to the discrete narrow zone of deformation, the recency of scarp formation, and, for the Post Oak Conglomerate, the resistant nature of the faulted material, the Meers fault is well suited for estimation of displacement of surficial features. Although displaced surficial features provide only approximate piercing points, they can often be accurately measured. Measurements of separation of surficial features (Figs. 6 and 7) are considered to closely approximate the cumulative late Quaternary offsets. Thatcher and Bonilla (1989) showed that maximum surface displacements closely approximate geodetic estimates of displacement. The enveloping curves (Figs. 6 and 7) thus represent the current best estimates of displacement at depth. The vertical displacement can be easily determined by projecting the far-field slope across the scarp and measuring the mismatch of the original surface. Vertical displacement reaches almost 5 m; 2 to 3 m is common.

Determination of lateral displacements is usually much more ambiguous. Even in cases of historical events, it is often difficult or impossible to determine lateral offsets accurately more than a few years after the event, based on surficial expression alone. For example, documented lateral offsets from the 1932 Cedar Mountain earthquake in west-central Nevada (Gianella and Callahan, 1934) are now either erased or very subdued (Molinari, 1984).

In the case of the Meers fault scarp, the Post Oak Conglomerate is quite resistant and very closely retains the topography present prior to the most recent activity. Displacement of broad ridges and stream channels suggests that lateral displacement along this part of the fault slightly exceeds 10 m (Fig. 7). Although most streams have erased obvious evidence of this displacement, many of the less energetic streams retain sharp left bends at the fault. The cumulative late Quaternary lateral offset across the fault scarp may be slightly greater than 20 m. The data point in Figure 7 representing this amount of displacement is taken from a small stream with sharp right-angle bends at the

fault (Fig. 8). Although this is considerably greater than the lateral displacement to the west, it coincides approximately with an increase in vertical offset (Fig. 6). The displacement measurements obtained suggest that, on the average, the cumulative left-lateral displacement is about 3 to 5 times greater than the vertical displacement (Figs. 6 and 7). This is based on comparison of the enveloping curves. Through the area to the west, where the lateral displacement is best constrained, the ratio of lateral to vertical ranges from about 2:1 to 4:1.

The strike-slip history of the Meers fault and the recognition that the present land surface closely approximates the surface at earlier times (Donovan, 1986) led to speculation that lateral deflections of surficial features could be relics of older displacements now evident in an exhumed topography (Tilford and Westen, 1985). The lateral offsets, however, occur directly across the scarp. Assuming that fault scarps are short-lived geomorphic features, these measurements should represent recent activity.

The exact number of events accounting for the cumulative late Quaternary displacement is not well known, but several aspects suggest multiple events, including multiple flights of stream

Figure 8. Oblique aerial view, looking SSW, of small stream with a sharp left bend at the fault. This is located about at the Post Oak–Hennessey contact and suggests more than 20 m of left-lateral displacement. (Photo by A. R. Ramelli.)

terraces on the upthrown side of the fault, smaller scarps formed on stream terraces, and evidence from trenching. Scarps formed on stream terraces, and sharp knickpoints in stream channels cut into Post Oak Conglomerate are roughly one-half the total scarp height. Recent results from trenching (Crone, 1987; Swan, 1989) have indicated two events in the late Holocene that account for most, if not all, of the scarp height. Therefore, the scarps on stream terraces appear to have resulted from the most recent event.

The amount of lateral displacement evident from trenching (Swan, 1989) is significantly less than that indicated by offset of an immediately adjacent ridgeline. This may indicate either preservation of a lateral component from older similar events, or prior events with more dominantly lateral displacement. The former possibility appears unlikely, because evidence of associated vertical displacement is lacking. The existence of locally exposed subhorizontal slickensides may evidence the latter possibility. Because the most recent event accounts for as much as one-half the total scarp height, surface displacements during individual events probably reached several meters (i.e., ±5 m).

EVIDENCE FOR COSEISMIC SCARP FORMATION

Tilford (1987) raised the possibility that the Meers fault scarp could have formed by aseismic creep and that it is premature to designate it as a possible source of large-magnitude earthquakes. However, given our current understanding of faulting processes and observations of the Meers fault scarp, we believe that such events are required.

"Creeping" faults are usually identified by slow but persistent surface displacements. This results in cracking and/or misalignments of the ground surface, paved surfaces, buildings, gutters, underground lines, and other manmade features. No such damage was observed during field studies, nor is any known to have been reported along the trace of the Meers fault scarp. Additionally, the presence of a continuous scarp with steep slope angles should require rapid scarp formation. Even if conditions were such that a scarp could be formed (i.e., high slip rates and low erosion rates), it should be highly uneven, due to local variations in erosion.

The lack of microseismicity further suggests that the Meers fault is currently "locked," and that stress accumulation is released during sudden, stick-slip seismic events. Fault sections observed to be creeping typically have high levels of microseismicity. The creeping section of the San Andreas fault, approximately from Corralitos to Cholame, and parts of the Hayward and Calaveras faults, are clearly delineated by abundant microseismicity (Fig. 9). The noncreeping sections of the San Andreas fault, which ruptured during the 1857 and 1906 earthquakes (magnitudes about 8), show sparse seismic activity. Fault creep is presumed to occur along parts of fault zones that lack strong enough discontinuities (i.e., asperities) to lock the differential displacement across the zone.

IMPLICATIONS OF ACTIVITY ON THE MEERS FAULT

Recognition of recent activity on the Meers fault has several far-reaching implications for seismic hazards in stable continental interior (SCI) regions. This presents a potential source of strong ground motion in a region (south-central U.S.) generally thought to be tectonically stable and devoid of a potential for large-magnitude earthquakes. A repeat of the last scarp-forming event would likely produce strong ground motion over vast parts of Oklahoma and Texas and be felt over most of the central United States.

A second implication for seismic hazards is that the recently active section of the Meers fault may be only one part of an actively deforming zone capable of producing large-magnitude earthquakes along much of its length. Structures bounding the Amarillo-Wichita-Arbuckle uplift extend through most of southern Oklahoma and the Texas panhandle and may be linked with other regional structures to both the west and east. Possible evidence of regional activity includes numerous Pliocene to Holocene volcanics with WNW-trending source structures east of the Rio Grande rift valley in northeastern New Mexico (Dane and Bachman, 1965), historical seismicity and possible deformation of Pleistocene sediments in the Texas panhandle (McGookey and Budnik, 1983), possible Quaternary tectonic activity of the Washita Valley fault in south-central Oklahoma (Cox and VanArsdale, 1986; VanArsdale, 1989), and Holocene uplift of the Monroe uplift in northern Louisiana (Schumm, 1986). The Washita Valley fault (Fig. 1) lies about on-line with, and parallel to, the Meers fault. Its morphologic expression in bedrock suggests late Quaternary activity, with displacement characteristics similar to the Meers fault. Recent study of the Washita Valley fault has been able to demonstrate inactivity over about the last 20,000 years, but activity prior to this cannot be ruled out (VanArsdale, 1989).

In tectonically active regions, most significant faults are interconnected or branch from major fault zones, suggesting a high degree of fault interaction. If this holds true for fault systems in SCI regions, activity along these structures may be linked to extensions of the New Madrid seismic zone, and in turn to such faults as the Kentucky River fault system (VanArsdale, 1986). On the other hand, SCI earthquakes may typically result from failure along preexisting crustal flaws solely in response to the regional stress field and may not require much fault interaction. Much more work throughout this region is required before such potential relations can be fully evaluated.

A more far-reaching implication lies in the possibility of additional active structures throughout SCI regions and their impact on seismic hazards. If a feature as prominent as the Meers fault scarp can escape recognition for so long, it seems likely that less obvious features have likewise been overlooked. Methods of seismic-hazard analysis in the central United States have differed greatly from those in the West, where the existence of numerous

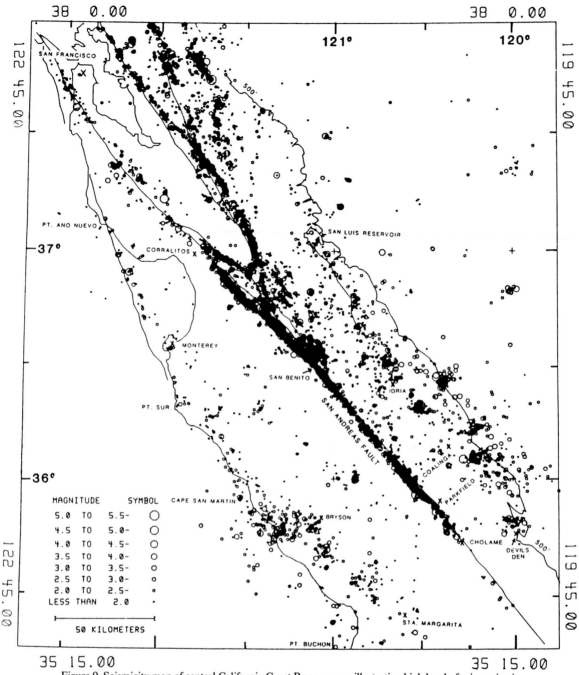

Figure 9. Seismicity map of central California Coast Ranges area, illustrating high level of microseismicity along creeping sections of San Andreas, Calaveras, and Hayward faults. $M_L \geqslant 1.5$ for January, 1972 through April, 1983 (Dehlinger and Bolt, 1987).

active structures has long been recognized. Relatively high rates of activity in the western U.S. have created distinctive landforms, which sometimes are well preserved by arid climates (e.g., the Basin and Range). Along with the occurrence of several large earthquakes over the last century, this has led to a methodology for seismic-hazard analyses whereby faults or fault zones are evaluated individually for their potential for producing large-magnitude earthquakes. For design purposes, a magnitude value

based on fault characteristics (e.g., fault or fault zone length, surface rupture lengths, displacements, geologic or structural setting, historical seismicity) is commonly considered for its ground-motion potential at the site of concern.

In contrast, rates of tectonic activity in the central U.S. are much lower. There have been no large earthquakes in this region over the last century. However, we know that they do occur, as evidenced by the remarkable series of three great earthquakes near New Madrid, Missouri in 1811–1812. Surface rupturing has rarely been documented even during large SCI earthquakes. Worldwide, only nine cases of historical surface rupture in SCI regions have been reliably documented (Coppersmith and others, 1987), and one of these, the 1819 earthquake at Kutch, India, possibly should not be considered an SCI event. Seismic-hazard analyses in SCI regions, thus, have not focused on fault-specific studies, but rather have been based largely on extrapolations of historical seismicity and/or general structural associations. Such methods can lead to a greatly underestimated seismic potential when the historical seismicity record is inadequate, as is often the case, or when structural associations are poorly understood.

It is often stated that evidence of large prehistoric earthquakes in the central U.S. is generally lacking. However, several studies in this region have revealed evidence suggesting tectonic activity. Known or suspected active structures or areas include the Meers fault (Gilbert, 1983; Donovan and others, 1983; Westen, 1985; Crone (1987); Ramelli and others, 1987; Luza and others, 1987; Madole, 1988; Ramelli, 1988), the Washita Valley (Cox and VanArsdale, 1986; VanArsdale and others, 1989) and Criner faults (Swan, personal communication, 1989) in Oklahoma, the New Madrid area in Missouri (Russ, 1979), the Kentucky River fault (VanArsdale, 1986), and the Pierre, South Dakota, area (Nichols and Collins, 1987; Fig. 10). It is likely that possible fault activity will be recognized at other locations in the future.

Moderate to large earthquakes in the central U.S. consistently affect much larger areas than similar-sized events in the West. In the central U.S., homogeneity of the crust allows more efficient transmission of seismic wave energy, whereas in the western states, structural and lithologic complexity cause this energy to be attenuated over much shorter distances. Comparison of areas damaged by large historical earthquakes in the United States (Fig. 11) illustrates this. The 1906 San Francisco earthquake is one of the strongest earthquakes to occur in U.S. history, but the area it affected is far smaller than the areas affected by large earthquakes in the eastern half of the country.

The surface offsets from the recent Meers fault earthquakes indicate large magnitudes (i.e., M >7). It appears reasonable to assume that levels of ground motion and felt and damage areas would be similar to the 1811–1812 New Madrid, Missouri, and 1886 Charleston, South Carolina, earthquakes. From Figure 11, it is obvious that only a few such seismic sources could subject much of the central U.S. to at least moderate levels of damage.

This raises several questions about what level of hazard mitigation is appropriate. These questions must be answered based on what is considered to be an acceptable level of risk. Many potential natural hazards are rare enough that it is necessary to consider their low probabilities of occurrence in hazard analyses. However, care should be taken in assigning probabilities, particularly when we have so little information on the late Quaternary tectonics of the region. Is it appropriate to constrain probabilities by historical seismicity levels, by the recency of large-magnitude events, or by apparent recurrence intervals? Sev-

eral historical events suggest that such bases often will not identify future sources of large earthquakes. In order to deal with this problem, common practice has called for certain critical structures (e.g., nuclear power plants and large dams) to be designed to withstand such events; low probabilities of occurrence are considered for less critical structures.

SEISMIC POTENTIAL

Estimation of the maximum size that can reasonably be expected for future earthquakes on the Meers fault or other faults of this zone is important for seismic-hazard evaluation of this and other tectonically similar regions. Determination of surface rupture characteristics (e.g., rupture length and distribution, style and amount of displacement, timing of events, structural setting) for large prehistoric earthquakes can provide a firm basis for estimating seismic potential through comparisons to historical events. Such estimates are not without limitations, given the high degree of variability in fault behavior and the uncertainties involved in analyzing rupture histories. However, they are generally the best estimates that can be made, because they are based on real and directly applicable data, rather than on extrapolations or general comparisons. The prominent surface expression of the Meers fault scarp suggests that paleoseismological analyses can sometimes be conducted in stable continental interior (SCI) regions.

Data used in studies relating earthquake magnitude to rupture length and/or displacement are typically grouped by fault type (e.g., strike-slip versus reverse) or region (e.g., interplate versus intraplate). Comparisons by fault type are relatively straightforward. However, there have not been enough large, historical SCI earthquakes to allow regional comparisons to be made with much confidence. If it is assumed that no significant differences exist, regression analyses (e.g., Slemmons, 1982; Bonilla and others, 1984) yield magnitude estimates for the Meers fault of between about 6¾ and 7½, based on rupture length and maximum displacement, respectively. The wide range in these values (about ¾ of a magnitude) result from the unusually large displacements with respect to surface-rupture length. While the exact amount of displacement per event is not well constrained, it is at least a few, and possibly several, meters. This is well above the average for historical events (Fig. 12).

Historical surface rupture data are too sparse to determine whether large displacements, relative to rupture lengths, are typical in SCI regions. Many earthquakes have occurred in continental interior regions, but nearly all these occurred in tectonically active areas, e.g., extensional faulting in the Basin and Range Province in western North America and compressional faulting throughout much of Asia. Australia is the only SCI region with multiple well-documented historical surface ruptures. The Australian events do not show a significant difference in displacement versus length relative to worldwide events (Fig. 12), but they do plot slightly above average.

The surface patterns of all the Australian events are quite different from the Meers fault. All had highly arcuate to

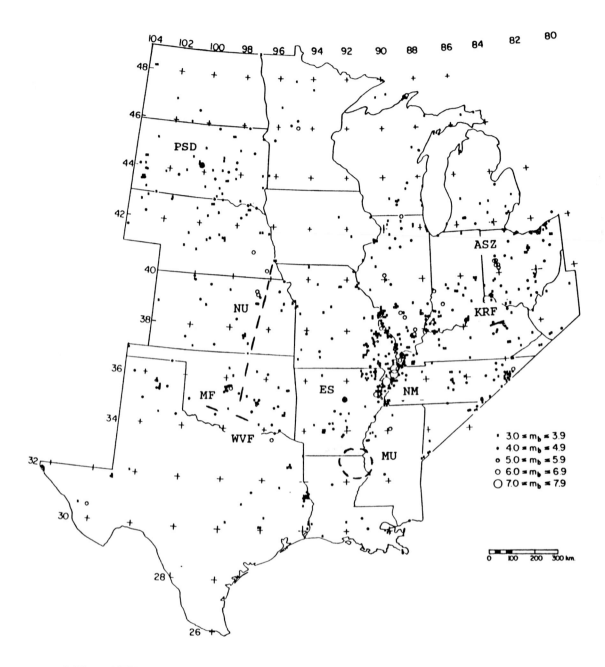

ASZ – ANNA SEISMIC ZONE   NM – NEW MADRID

ES – ENOLA SWARM   NU – NEMAHA UPLIFT

KRF – KENTUCKY RIVER FAULT   PSD – PIERRE, SOUTH DAKOTA

MF – MEERS FAULT   WVF – WASHITA VALLEY FAULT

MU – MONROE UPLIFT

Figure 10. Historical seismicity and areas of known or suspected late Quaternary tectonic activity in the central U.S. (after Nuttli, 1979).

boomerang-shaped surface rupture patterns. This may represent thrust "slivers" associated with localized faulting in response to high levels of horizontal compressive stress, rather than rupture along a throughgoing fault system. The linear surface pattern and large offsets on the Meers fault are more likely to evidence deep-seated faulting. Without sufficient seismic data, it is difficult to conclude whether the differences between the Meers fault events and the Australian events signify differences in seismic potential. The Australian events are not necessarily any less typical of SCI earthquakes than the recent Meers fault events, but this shows the high degree of variability in earthquake behavior. Each large earthquake is unique, and comparing a handful of events will rarely yield obvious relations.

Other historical SCI surface-faulting events are not documented well enough to allow inclusion in such analyses. Most of these are moderate-sized events with limited surface rupture. In such cases, surface rupture is often not sufficiently representative of rupture in the subsurface. Surface rupture occurred from the 1983 Guinea, West Africa, earthquake (Langer and others, 1987), but the mapping of surface breaks is described as incomplete; measured displacements were taken across individual fault traces, rather than across the entire zone. An additional problem is posed by the uncertainty about what should be considered an SCI setting. One of the largest reported SCI events (Coppersmith and others, 1987) is the 1819 Kutch, India, earthquake (M >8). This should possibly not be considered an SCI event, because it occurred in a near-coastal mudflat area, probably indicating active subsidence, and within a zone of high seismicity.

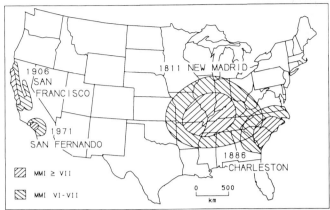

Figure 11. Damage areas (Modified Mercalli Intensity VI and greater) for large historical earthquakes in the United States (after Nuttli, 1979). Lower attenuation of seismic waves in the central and eastern U.S. result in much larger damage areas relative to the West.

Another way in which earthquake size can be estimated is through input of surface rupture parameters into calculations of seismic moment (M_o), using the equation:

$$M_o = DA\mu$$

where D = average displacement over the rupture surface, A = area of the rupture surface, and μ = shear modulus of faulted materials. Although this requires several assumptions, possible

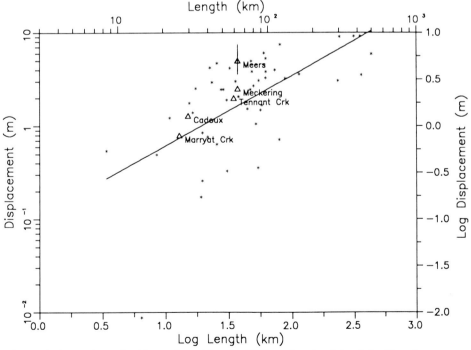

Figure 12. Comparison of stable continental interior (SCI) earthquakes (triangles) with surface rupture length versus surface displacement for large-magnitude historical earthquakes (after Bonilla and others, 1984).

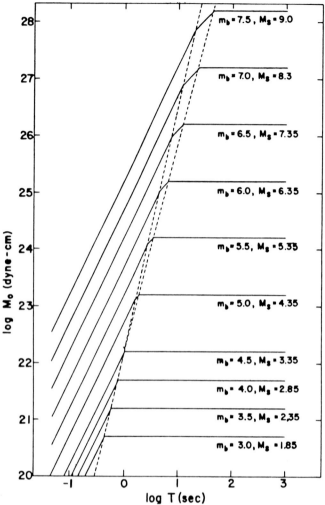

Figure 13. Proposed spectral scaling relation for mid-plate earthquakes (Nuttli, 1983b).

the Australia events (Denham, 1988), since they appear to be confined to shallow crustal depths (15 km and above).

The length of a rupture area can be approximated by using surface rupture length. For small events that barely reach the surface, this can drastically underestimate rupture length in the subsurface; but as length increases, the surface length should approach the subsurface length percentagewise. It is unlikely that a particular limit exists at which surface length becomes an accurate approximation of subsurface length, but this may occur with lengths equal to or greater than about two times the down-dip width of the rupture surface (Bonilla and others, 1984).

Assuming (1) a commonly used shear modulus value of 3×10^{11} dyne/cm^2 (Bonilla and others, 1984), (2) surface-rupture parameters reasonably approximating the entire rupture surface, (3) a simple length times width rupture model, (4) rupture of the entire width of a 20-km-thick seismogenic zone, and (5) an average displacement of 5 m, a calculated seismic moment of about 1×10^{27} dyne-cm can be derived. This is a very large event, corresponding to a moment magnitude (M_w) of about 7½.

Most historical earthquakes have occurred at or near tectonic plate margins, and relations like those discussed above are dominated by them. Examination of the few historical "intraplate" events suggests that these events may have differences from their "interplate" counterparts. Intraplate events may rupture with higher stress drops, and thus have greater displacements and larger magnitudes for a given rupture length.

Nuttli (1983a, 1983b) examined reported values of m_b (body wave magnitude taken at 1-second periods), M_s (surface wave magnitude), and M_o (seismic moment) for mid-plate and plate-margin earthquakes. From the derived empirical relations, Nuttli concluded that, for mid-plate earthquakes, seismic moment varies as the fourth power of the corner period (Fig. 13), implying increasing stress drop with increasing moment. Nuttli thus proposed that, with higher stress drop at larger magnitudes, large rupture lengths are not required for mid-plate events.

Scholz and others (1986) compared 30 large earthquakes for their relations of length and seismic moment (Fig. 14), and distinguished these events by fault type and tectonic setting (see Table 1). Their interpretation held that a simple scaling relation is maintained for both interplate and intraplate settings, with a scal-

variations in the assumptions used are limited enough that useful estimates can be derived.

The down-dip width of a rupture surface is limited by the vertical extent of the seismogenic zone, the base of which can most reliably be determined from the depth distribution of aftershocks of large-magnitude events. Earthquakes are generally confined above a fairly abrupt cut-off, taken to represent a rapid brittle-ductile transition (Sibson, 1984). This is well constrained at a depth of about 10 to 15 km in many tectonically active regions. It is less well constrained in SCI regions due to less seismic activity, but it should be deeper and is likely in the range of 20 to 25 km (Chen and Molnar, 1983) or even deeper. In many regions, large-magnitude events usually propagate upward and outward from near the base of the seismogenic zone, but whether this is the case in SCI regions is unknown. The lower crust should be stronger if a thicker seismogenic zone exists. SCI events might commonly be confined to the upper crust, with a stronger lower crust that resists rupture. This may be the case for

TABLE 1. CLASSIFICATION OF TECTONIC EARTHQUAKES*

Type	Description	Slip Rate of Causative Fault (cm yr^{-1})	Recurrence Time (yr)
I	Interplate	$v > 1$	$\approx 10^2$
II	Intraplate (plate boundary-related)	$0.01 < v < 1$	$\approx 10^3 \text{-} 10^4$
III	Intraplate (mid-plate)	$v < 0.01$	$> 10^4$

*Scholz and others, 1986.

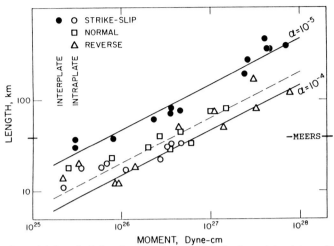

Figure 14. Log fault length versus log moment for large interplate and intraplate earthquakes (Scholz and others, 1986).

Kanamori and Allen (1985) have suggested that such relations are an effect of repeat times (or recurrence intervals) between large events. With an increase in repeat time, a fault has a greater chance to "heal," allowing a greater amount of stress accumulation and subsequent release, resulting in high stress drop when the fault eventually ruptures. This relation of repeat time, rupture length, and magnitude shows definite correlation, even though there is a large scatter of data (Fig. 15). By this treatment, a fault of about 40 km length with a repeat time >2,000 years would be expected to have the potential for generating earthquakes of approximately M_s 7½. Recent study suggests the occurrence of two late Holocene events, preceded by a long period of quiescence, along this part of the Meers fault (Swan, 1989). If the relation proposed by Kanamori and Allen (1985) is a dominant factor, temporal clustering of events might be expected to result in smaller magnitudes for the latter event. Although poorly constrained, it appears that the recent Meers fault events were roughly of equal size. A relation of magnitude and repeat time may be valid, but might act in combination with other factors, such as the influence of rupture-controlling discontinuities and increasing strength associated with greater seismogenic depths.

ing constant about six times higher for intraplate events. They suggested that, on the average, displacements are six times greater during intraplate earthquakes. Using this relation, an estimated seismic moment of about 1×10^{27} dyne-cm, similar to that calculated above, would be inferred for an intraplate event with a rupture length of about 40 km.

Relations showing differences between intraplate and interplate earthquakes have been developed based on events in regions with higher levels of activity than the south-central United States. Scholz and others (1986) treat these intraplate events as an intermediate case (Table 1), where faults are subject to plate-margin

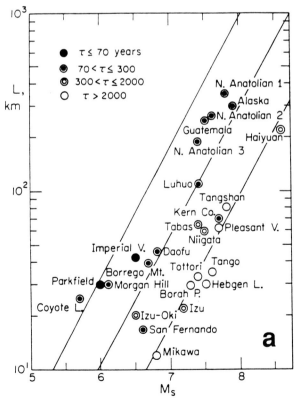

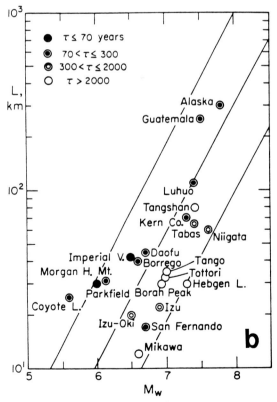

Figure 15. Relation between: (15a) surface-wave magnitude (M_s) (15b) moment magnitude (M_w), fault length (L), and repeat time for large historical earthquakes (Kanamori and Allen, 1985).

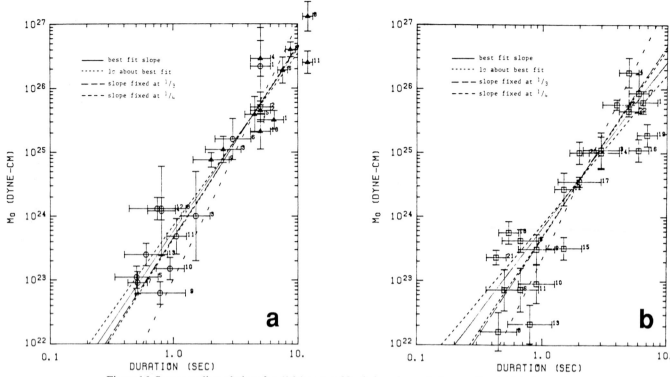

Figure 16. Source scaling relations for: (16a) eastern North America and other continental interiors and (16b) western North America Somerville and others, 1987).

influences, distinguishing them from mid-plate cases (e.g., Meers fault). There are too few historical mid-plate events to determine the extent to which these differences hold true far from plate-margin influences, but it seems likely that mid-plate events would bear these relations out even more strongly. This suggests that an earthquake of between 7½ and 8 magnitude on the Meers fault may be possible, but the paucity of surface rupture data for historical SCI earthquakes makes this difficult to fully evaluate.

Several studies on scaling relations of principally small to moderate events (i.e., M <6) have suggested that no such case exists. Somerville and others (1987) compared source parameters of a number of earthquakes in the eastern U.S., other continental interiors, and the western U.S. Most of the eastern U.S. events are taken from the St. Lawrence region along the U.S.–Canada border. Somerville and others (1987) found no significant difference between the data sets (Fig. 16) and inferred that the same constant scaling relation applies in both regions, disagreeing with Nuttli's (1983a, b) interpretation. Haar and others (1984) similarly found no obvious differences between a series of well-recorded events of the 1983 Enola, Arkansas earthquake swarm and aftershocks of earthquakes in the Mammoth and Oroville, California areas.

It should be noted that these studies have all used different data sets. This is essential to demonstrate whether hypothesized relations are valid, but it raises questions about what is being compared. For instance, is it necessarily valid to equate a compar-

ison of central versus western U.S. earthquakes with a plate-margin versus mid-plate comparison? Is a zone such as the St. Lawrence Seaway, which has a high level of historical seismic activity, representative of SCI regions? Similarly, many earthquakes in the western states have occurred on previously unrecognized or poorly defined faults that are often referred to as "intraplate." It is possible that there is much more variability between individual events in the West, considering the much broader range of structural settings. Somerville (1986) suggested this possibility and speculated that, if the relations proposed by Kanamori and Allen (1985) are valid, this is probably due to increases in fault zone strength and size of asperities over time.

Currently, the greatest problem in evaluating these differing interpretations appears to hinge on classification. Several questions can be raised in this regard. Should both mid-plate oceanic and continental seismic events be lumped together? When should an event be considered a plate-margin event? If an event does not lie on a plate-margin, but is within a highly active region (e.g., Basin and Range Province), should it be classified as intraplate, or would subclasses of active tectonic domains be more appropriate? Do certain mid-plate areas (e.g., St. Lawrence Seaway) more closely resemble the western U.S. than surrounding regions, due to higher rates of activity? It is hoped that systematic examination of various classification schemes will resolve these questions. A promising approach toward classification for worldwide events was undertaken by Coppersmith and others (1987). They grouped events by associations with differing types and ages of geologic structures and age of affected crust. However, with so few large-magnitude events, it is not possible to make fine distinctions between surface faulting events and still retain large enough data sets to make valid statistical arguments.

IMPACT OF A LARGE EARTHQUAKE IN THE CENTRAL U.S.

A large-magnitude earthquake (M >7) in a heavily populated area of the central United States would likely be one of the most catastrophic natural disasters in our nation's history. In many parts of the western United States the recognition of a significant seismic potential has led to numerous measures to reduce losses due to earthquakes. Much more could yet be done in the West, but such measures lag far behind in the central part of the country.

Historical seismic events in the central U.S., notably the 1811–1812 New Madrid earthquakes, have affected much larger areas than those in the west. The New Madrid series of three great earthquakes were probably felt over all of the U.S. and southern Canada east of the Rocky Mountains (Nuttli, 1982). The crust in this region is more structurally homogeneous than that in the West, resulting in lower attenuation of seismic energy.

We currently cannot hope to predict accurately when and where all large earthquakes will occur in the near future, but we can try to recognize potential seismic sources and estimate the sizes and probabilities of events that could be expected. Without a long historical record, geologic indicators can provide the only available evidence of late Quaternary seismic activity. An increased emphasis on such studies could lead to a much better understanding of the overall seismic potential in this region. Even in the western states, intensive paleoseismic study is new. Most data on ages, extents, and recurrence intervals of prehistoric surface ruptures have been collected in recent years. Collection of such data is a formidable, but not overwhelming, task.

Large-magnitude earthquakes in the central U.S. are infrequent events. On the one hand, this is fortunate, since most people stand a low probability of being directly affected by such an event, and the expected lifespan of most structures is much less than the repeat times of potentially damaging earthquakes. On the other hand, this causes a lower awareness of seismic hazards and hampers efforts to implement earthquake-hazard reduction programs. This can make the occurrence of such events all the more damaging.

If a great enough probability for large-magnitude earthquakes exists, it is important to assess what impact such events might have on existing critical structures, and what design requirements should be imposed on new structures. Most damage and loss of life during earthquakes results from improperly designed structures. If the potential for large earthquakes can be recognized and accurately characterized, steps can be taken to mitigate their impact. It is impractical to retrofit every existing structure, but a large-magnitude earthquake would cause much more damage if no improvements were made on critical structures.

CONCLUSION

The Meers fault exhibits clear evidence of large-magnitude earthquakes during the late Holocene. This is not entirely surprising, since large-magnitude earthquakes do occasionally occur in the central United States, and this fault lies within a major structural zone. However, the prominent expression of this fault scarp is very surprising, because no other such features are known in cratonic regions. The fact that this fault scarp escaped recognition for so long implies that there is much we need to learn about late Quaternary tectonic activity and frequency of large-magnitude earthquakes in stable continental interior regions.

Many key questions remain about the late Quaternary activity of the Meers fault, including more specific information on the number, timing, displacements, and sizes of late Quaternary earthquakes. Nonetheless, it seems clear that the most recent surface-rupturing earthquakes on this fault caused surface displacements of a few to several meters, indicating large magnitudes (M >7). It is less clear whether these events are representative of seismic events on this or other faults in SCI regions, or whether they are simply indicative of the high degree of earthquake variability.

Earthquakes in the central U.S. and other SCI regions may typically rupture with shorter lengths and larger displacements than similar-sized earthquakes in plate-margin settings. If this is true, the underlying cause is likely to be the various processes that act to strengthen fault zones during quiescent periods between large-magnitude events. A fault zone with a high rate of activity (e.g., San Andreas fault zone) does not have a long enough interseismic interval to allow prolonged growth of asperities and strengthening of the fault zone. With displacements of several meters and a length of only about 40 km, the most recent large-magnitude events on the Meers fault may support this interpretation.

The possibility that fault zones with low rates of activity have the potential for larger-magnitude events than previously believed presents a situation that contradicts conventional methods of assessing seismic hazards. In the past, the larger, more active fault zones were considered to have a higher seismic potential than less active zones. While this holds true for the probability of earthquake occurrence, it may not be valid to assume large-magnitude events are confined to highly active zones.

ACKNOWLEDGMENTS

The authors thank the many individuals who provided information and/or comments, including Steve Brocoum, Randy Cox, Tony Crone, Craig dePolo, Nowell Donovan, Charles Gilbert, Bill Lettis, Ken Luza, Rich Madole, Tom Sawyer, Bert Swan, Norm Tilford, Roy VanArsdale, Diane Westen and Bob Whitney. We also thank the many hospitable landowners who made this work much more enjoyable. This project was supported in part by the U.S. Nuclear Regulatory Commission.

REFERENCES CITED

Beauchamp, W. H., 1983, The structural geology of the southern Slick Hills, Oklahoma [M.S. thesis]: Stillwater, Oklahoma State University, 119 p.

Bonilla, M. G., Mark, R. K., and Lienkaemper, J. J., 1984, Statistical relations among earthquake magnitude, surface rupture length, and surface fault displacement: Bulletin of the Seismological Society of America, v. 74, no. 6, p. 2379–2411.

Brewer, J. A., Good, R., Oliver, J. E., Brown, L. D., and Kaufman, S., 1983, COCORP profiling across the southern Oklahoma aulacogen; Overthrusting of the Wichita Mountains: Geology, v. 11, p. 109–114.

Chen, W., and Molnar, P., 1983, Focal depths of intracontinental and intraplate earthquakes and their implications for the thermal and mechanical properties of the lithosphere: Journal of Geophysical Research, v. 88, no. B5, p. 4183–4214.

Chenoweth, P. A., 1983, Principal structural features of Oklahoma: Tulsa, Oklahoma, PennWell Publishing Co., scale 1:500,000.

Coppersmith, K. J., Johnston, A. C., Metzger, A. G., and Arabasz, W. J., 1987, Methods for assessing maximum earthquakes in the central and eastern United States: Palo Alto, California, Electric Power Research Institute Working Report Project RP2556-12, 109 p.

Cox, R., and VanArsdale, R., 1986, Style and timing of displacement along the Washita Valley fault, Oklahoma [abs.]: Geological Society of America Abstracts with Programs, v. 18, p. 573.

Crone, A. J., 1987, The Meers fault, southwest Oklahoma; Evidence of multiple episodes of Quaternary surface faulting [abs.]: Geological Society of America Abstracts with Programs, v. 19, p. 630.

Dane, C. H., and Bachman, G. O., 1965, Geologic map of New Mexico: U.S. Geological Survey, scale 1:500,000.

Dart, R. L., 1987, South-central United States well-bore breakout-data catalog: U.S. Geological Survey Open-File Report 87-405, 95 p.

Dehlinger, P., and Bolt, B. A., 1987, Earthquakes and associated tectonics in a part of coastal central California: Bulletin of the Seismological Society of America, v. 77, no. 6, p. 2056–2073.

Denham, D., 1988, Australian seismicity; The puzzle of the not-so-stable continent: Seismological Research Letters, v. 59, no. 4, p. 235–240.

Donovan, R. N., 1982, Geology of the Blue Creek Canyon, Wichita Mountains area, in Gilbert, M. C., and Donovan, R. N., eds., Geology of the eastern Wichita Mountains, southwestern Oklahoma: Oklahoma Geological Survey Guidebook 21, p. 65–77.

—— , 1986, Geology of the Slick Hills, in Donovan, R. N., ed., The Slick Hills of southwestern Oklahoma; Fragments of an aulacogen?: Oklahoma Geological Survey Guidebook 24, p. 1–12.

Donovan, R. N., Sanderson, D. J., and Marchini, D., 1982, An analysis of structures resulting from left-lateral strike-slip movement between the Wichita Mountains and Anadarko Basin, southwestern Oklahoma: Geological Society of America Abstracts with Programs, v. 14, p. 476.

Donovan, R. N., Gilbert, M. C., Luza, K. V., Marchini, D., and Sanderson, D., 1983, Possible Quaternary movement on the Meers fault, southwestern Oklahoma: Oklahoma Geological Survey Geology Notes, v. 43, no. 5, p. 124–133.

Gianella, V. P., and Callahan, E., 1934, The Cedar Mountain earthquake of December 20, 1932: Bulletin of the Seismological Society of America, v. 24, p. 345–377.

Gilbert, M. C., 1983, The Meers fault of southwestern Oklahoma; Evidence for possible strong Quaternary seismicity in the midcontinent [abs.]: EOS Transactions of the American Geophysical Union, v. 64, no. 18, p. 313.

Haar, L. A., Fletcher, J. B., and Mueller, C. S., 1984, The 1982 Enola, Arkansas, swarm and scaling of ground motion in the eastern U.S.: Bulletin of the Seismological Society of America, v. 74, no. 6, p. 2463–2482.

Ham, W. E., Denison, R. E., and Merritt, C. A., 1964, Basement rocks and structural evolution of southern Oklahoma: Oklahoma Geological Survey Bulletin 95, 302 p.

Harding, S. T., 1985, Preliminary results of a high-resolution reflection survey across the Meers fault, Comanche County, Oklahoma [abs.]: Seismological Society of America Earthquakes Notes, v. 55, p. 2.

Harlton, B. H., 1951, Faults in the sedimentary part of Wichita Mountains of Oklahoma: American Association of Petroleum Geologists Bulletin, v. 35, no. 5, p. 988–999.

—— , 1963, Frontal Wichita fault system of southwestern Oklahoma: American Association of Petroleum Geologists Bulletin, v. 47, no. 8, p. 1552–1580.

—— , 1972, Fault fold belts of southern Anadarko Basin adjacent to frontal Wichitas: American Association of Petroleum Geologists Bulletin, v. 56, no. 8, p. 1544–1551.

Kanamori, H., and Allen, C., 1985, Earthquake repeat time and average stress-drop, in Das, S., Boatwright, J., and Scholz, C., eds., Earthquake source mechanics: American Geophysical Union Maurice Ewing Series, v. 6, p. 227–235.

Langer, C. J., Bonilla, M. G., and Bollinger, G. A., 1987, Aftershocks and surface faulting associated with the intraplate Guinea, West Africa, earthquake of 22 December 1983: Bulletin of the Seismological Society of America, v. 77, no. 5, p. 1579–1601.

Lawson, J. E., Jr., and Luza, K. V., 1980–1988, Annual seismicity reports: Oklahoma Geology Notes: Norman, Oklahoma Geological Survey, University of Oklahoma.

Lawson, J. E., Jr., Dubois, R. L., Foster, P. H., and Luza, K. V., 1979, Earthquake map of Oklahoma: Oklahoma Geological Survey Map GM-19.

Luza, K. V., Madole, R. F., and Crone, A. J., 1987, Investigation of the Meers fault, southwestern Oklahoma: Oklahoma Geological Survey Special Publication 87-1, 75 p.

McConnell, D., 1983, The mapping and interpretation of the structure of the northern Slick Hills, southwest Oklahoma [M.S. thesis]: Stillwater, Oklahoma State University, 131 p.

McCoss, A. M., and Donovan, R. N., 1986, Application of a construction for determining deformation in zones of transpression to the Slick Hills in southern Oklahoma, in Donovan, R. N., ed., The Slick Hills of southwestern Oklahoma; Fragments of an aulacogen?: Oklahoma Geological Survey Guidebook 24, p. 40–44.

McGookey, D. A., and Budnik, R. T., 1983, Tectonic history and influence on sedimentation of rhomb horsts and grabens associated with Amarillo uplift, Texas Panhandle [abs.]: American Association of Petroleum Geologists Bulletin, v. 67, no. 3, p. 511.

Madole, R. F., 1988, Stratigraphic evidence of Holocene faulting in the midcontinent; The Meers fault, southwestern Oklahoma: Geological Society of America Bulletin, v. 100, p. 392–401.

Molinari, M. P., 1984, Late Cenozoic geology and tectonics of the Stewart and Monte Cristo Valleys, west-central Nevada [M.S. thesis]: Reno, University of Nevada, 124 p.

Moody, J. D., and Hill, M. J., 1956, Wrench-fault tectonics: Geological Society of America Bulletin, v. 67, p. 1207–1246.

Myers, P. B., Miller, R. D., and Steeples, D. W., 1987, Shallow seismic reflection profile of the Meers fault, Comanche County, Oklahoma: American Geophysical Union Geophysical Research Letters, v. 14, no. 7, p. 749–752.

Nichols, T. C., Jr., and Collins, D. S., 1987, Active faults and potential earthquakes in central South Dakota [abs.]: Geological Society of America Abstracts with Programs, v. 19, p. 788.

Nuttli, O. W., 1979, Seismicity of the central United States, in Hatheway, A. W., and McClure, C. R., Jr., eds., Geology in the siting of nuclear power plants: Geological Society of America Reviews in Engineering Geology, v. IV, p. 67–93.

—— , 1982, Effects of major earthquakes in the New Madrid fault zone and other earthquake zones of the eastern United States, in Hays, W. E., ed., Proceedings of a workshop on "Preparing for and Responding to a Damaging Earthquake in the Eastern United States": U.S. Geological Survey Open-

File Report 82-220, 200 p.

——, 1983a, Empirical magnitude and spectral scaling relation for mid-plate and plate-margin earthquakes: Tectonophysics, v. 93, p. 207–223.

——, 1983b, Average seismic source-parameter relations for mid-plate earthquakes: Bulletin of the Seismological Society of America, v. 73, no. 2, p. 519–535.

Ramelli, A. R., 1988, Late Quaternary tectonic activity of the Meers fault, southwestern Oklahoma [M.S. thesis]: Reno, University of Nevada, 123 p.

Ramelli, A. R., Slemmons, D. B., and Brocoum, S. J., 1987, The Meers fault; Tectonic activity in southwestern Oklahoma: Washington, D.C., U.S. Nuclear Regulatory Commission NUREG/CR-4852, 25 p.

Russ, D. P., 1979, Late Holocene faulting and earthquake recurrence in the Reelfoot Lake area, northwestern Tennessee: Geological Society of America Bulletin, part 1, v. 90, p. 1013–1018.

Scholz, C. H., Aviles, C. A., and Wesnousky, S. G., 1986, Scaling differences between large interplate and intraplate earthquakes: Bulletin of the Seismological Society of America, v. 76, no. 1, p. 65–70.

Schumm, S. A., 1986, Alluvial river response to active tectonics, *in* Wallace, R. E., Active tectonics; Studies in geophysics: Washington, D.C., National Academy of Science, 266 p.

Sibson, R. H., 1984, Roughness at the base of the seismogenic zone; Contributing factors: Journal of Geophysical Research, v. 89, no. B7, p. 5791–5799.

Slemmons, D. B., 1982, Determination of design earthquake magnitudes for microzonation, *in* Proceedings of the 3rd International Earthquake Microzonation Conference: Seattle, Washington, v. 1, p. 119–130.

Somerville, P. G., 1986, Source scaling relations of large eastern North American earthquakes and implications for strong ground motions, *in* Proceedings of the 3rd National Conference on Earthquake Engineering, Charleston, South Carolina: El Cerrito, California, Earthquake Engineering Research Institute, v. 1, p. 117–124.

Somerville, P. G., McLaren, J. P., LeFevre, L. V., Burger, R. W., and Helmberger, D. V., 1987, Comparison of source scaling relations of eastern and western North American earthquakes: Bulletin of the Seismological Society of America, v. 77, no. 2, p. 322–346.

Swan, F. H., 1989, Preliminary results of paleoseismic investigations along the Meers Valley fault, southwestern Oklahoma [abs.]: Geological Association of Canada Annual Meeting, Montreal, Quebec.

Thatcher, W., and Bonilla, M. G., 1989, Earthquake fault slip estimation from geologic, geodetic, and seismologic observations; Implications for earthquake mechanics and fault segmentation, *in* Schwartz, D. P., and Sibson, R. H., eds., Workshop on Fault Segmentation and Controls of Rupture Initiation and Termination: U.S. Geological Survey Open-File Report 89-315, p. 386–399.

Tilford, N. R., 1987, Deformation and seismicity along the Meers fault, Oklahoma [abs.]: Geological Society of America Abstracts with Programs, v. 19, p. 869.

Tilford, N. R., and Westen, D. P., 1985, The Meers fault in southwestern Oklahoma; Implications of the sense of recent movement [abs.]: Winston-Salem, North Carolina, 28th Annual Meeting, Association of Engineering Geologists, p. 77.

VanArsdale, R. B., 1986, Quaternary displacement on faults within the Kentucky River fault system of east-central Kentucky: Geological Society of America Bulletin, v. 97, p. 1382–1392.

VanArsdale, R., Ward, C., and Cox, R. 1989, Post-Pennsylvanian reactivation along the Washita Valley fault, southern Oklahoma: Washington, D.C., U.S. Nuclear Regulatory Commission NUREG CR-5375, 48 p.

Westen, D. P., 1985, Recognition criteria for young multiple surface ruptures along the Meers fault in southwestern Oklahoma [M.S. thesis]: College Station, Texas A&M University, 69 p.

Zoback, M. L., 1987, Global pattern of intraplate tectonic stress [abs.]: EOS Transactions of the American Geophysical Union, v. 68, no. 44, p. 1209.

MANUSCRIPT ACCEPTED BY THE SOCIETY AUGUST 18, 1989

Printed in U.S.A.

Geological Society of America
Reviews in Engineering Geology, Volume VIII
1990

Chapter 5

Neotectonic movement and earthquake assessment in the eastern United States

Patrick J. Barosh
P. J. Barosh and Associates, 35 Potter Street, Concord, Massachusetts 01742

ABSTRACT

Neotectonic movement in the United States east of the Rocky Mountains results from various superimposed intraplate adjustments related to movement in the North Atlantic Basin and glacial rebound. Some movements, such as slight southward tilt in the north from waning rebound and northward tilt of the entire region, appear aseismic. Others form a rectilinear grid pattern of zones of fractures and vertical movement and coincide with the distribution of seismicity. Most seismic source areas occur along northwest-trending fracture zones, which commonly have some right-lateral strike-slip displacement. They have broad, northeast-trending belts of rising highlands and sinking lowlands and are concentrated at their intersections. These belts are the Atlantic Coast Lowland, Southern and Central Appalachian Highland, Arkansas–St. Lawrence Lowland, and Mid-continent Arch. The northwest-trending fracture zones also apparently control the positions of northwest-trending synclinal basins—embayments—on the coastal plains and continue seaward as the larger transform fracture zones. The embayments are relatively subsiding and have significant associated seismicity. Some earthquakes also occur along north-trending extensional faults, whose movement seems related to lateral displacement on northwest-trending fracture zones, and a few occur along northeast-trending faults at structural intersections. The fracture zones continue into the western United States; the difference between "western" and "eastern" seismicity is more of degree than kind.

Earthquakes in the eastern United States thus are shown to be controlled by neotectonic movement and structural zones despite the lack of recent surface faulting, and a firm basis exists for seismic zoning.

INTRODUCTION

The knowledge that large earthquakes have occurred in the eastern United States, coupled with the lack of any information on recent faulting, pose many difficulties in evaluating the seismic hazard to sites for nuclear power plants and dams in the region. Sites were, and are, evaluated separately with little regard to the overall cause of seismicity across the region. Various assumptions were argued and many causes of earthquakes hypothesized in proposing seismic ground-motion values for construction at a site. Some excellent work was done, but the understanding of the regional cause of seismicity was only slightly advanced, and there

was scant scientific basis for establishing earthquake zonation and return times.

The main problems were that the recording of earthquakes and the accuracy in their epicentral locations were inadequate, and the historic earthquake records were in need of revision. Most importantly, the critical geologic data were missing, and each area was being evaluated separately without comparison with others. An attempt to circumvent these problems led to the development of probabilistic methods of producing a quantified seismic risk using semi-statistical means, but in which the critical

Barosh, P. J., 1990, Neotectonic movement and earthquake assessment in the eastern United States, *in* Krinitzsky, E. L., and Slemmons, D. B., Neotectonics in earthquake evaluation: Boulder, Colorado, Geological Society of America Reviews in Engineering Geology, v. 8.

data are assumed. Therefore, the results are essentially assumed and, hence, have little scientific credibility. The problems of evaluating the earthquake hazard remained.

The need for a more comprehensive and regional evaluation of the seismic hazard led the U.S. Nuclear Regulatory Commission in 1976 to begin a series of regional seismotectonic studies under the general direction of Neil B. Steuer. Information from a wide variety of geological, geophysical, geodetic, and other studies was used to improve seismograph networks and revise historic records. This vast amount of new information was augmented by other studies for the U.S. Geological Survey and the U.S. Army Corps of Engineers. The results of this work not only provide a better understanding of local areas with relatively high seismic activity, but reveal a regional pattern of neotectonic movement that apparently controls that activity.

The method followed herein in analyzing this information is: first, to evaluate the local data on geologic structure and crustal movement for relations that match the distribution of epicenters in each of the relatively more seismically active areas; second, to seek common features among these areas; and third, to combine these results with an analysis of the pattern of regional data. This pattern-recognition process was approached in an empirical manner without an encompassing theory. This slow process has been conducted during the past 10 years and reported on periodically (Barosh, 1981a, 1986a, 1986c, 1990a). These reports contain much of the detail summarized below.

The results of this analysis show a variety of neotectonic movements are taking place in the eastern U.S. Some are apparently aseismic, but others are closely related spatially to the distribution of earthquakes. The crustal deformation that is spatially related to the earthquakes in the source zones is caused by a complex interplay of structures. Earthquakes are mainly spatially related to northwest- and north-trending fault zones, and generally occur at structural intersections. The activity is concentrated where these fault zones cross broad, northeast-trending, fault-controlled belts undergoing vertical movement. The deformation has a structural pattern similar to the western North Atlantic Basin, and both regions apparently move under the same intraplate stress.

Once the cause of seismicity was recognized and local seismogenic zones delineated, an earthquake zonation map could be produced and return times estimated.

The purpose of this chapter is to present a summary of the presently known neotectonic movements in the U.S. east of the Rocky Mountains, and the structures controlling them, and to show the application of these data to evaluating the seismic hazard.

EARTHQUAKE CHARACTERISTICS AND PROPOSED CAUSES

Earthquakes occur far less frequently in the U.S. east of the Rocky Mountains than in the West. However, when large ones do occur, the damage produced is much more widespread as the attenuation rate is much less than in the West (Nuttli, 1973a). They also tend to be shallow. Most earthquakes are less than 10 km in depth, and therefore are related to surface and near-surface geologic features that can be identified. Because the earthquakes occur near the surface, they are noisy, as the high frequencies are generally not filtered out. In fact, some earthquakes are heard, but not felt. The earthquakes are more evenly distributed around a source area and do not show as strong a directional variation related to the structure as characterizes the West Coast (Barosh, 1969), although there are notable exceptions. The isoseismal maps are commonly generalized into bullseye patterns, but where contoured carefully, they are irregular and reflect the structural grain (Barosh, 1986b).

The distribution of earthquakes is highly irregular, with many local active areas commonly separated by regions with little or no seismicity. The active areas have remained stationary throughout the time of historic records, although the rate of activity may change. Most importantly, surface faulting has not been seen to accompany earthquakes, with the possible exception of the February 7, 1812, New Madrid, Missouri, earthquake (Fig. 1). Faulting could have accompanied the uplift that caused the formation of falls across the Mississippi River and a temporary reversal of its flow (McGee, 1892). It appears that surface breaks occur less readily in the east even though some other large earthquakes were located beneath water and could not be checked. Also, few faults with evidence for Holocene movement have been found. Thus, it is more difficult to evaluate earthquakes in this area than it is in the western U.S.

Some characteristic of eastern earthquakes makes it difficult to produce reasonable focal-plane solutions. The solutions show an extreme scatter of trends, wide variation between preparers, and little correspondence with the distribution of seismicity or structural trends, and they do not match the geology where investigated (Graham, 1979; Isachsen and Geraghty, 1979; Graham and Chiburis, 1980; Pulli and Toksoz, 1981; Barosh, 1986c; Ravat and others, 1987). Only a few in South Carolina appear to show a significant correlation with the geology and seismicity. This lack of reasonable solutions may be due to poor determination of focal depth (McKenzie, 1969) or techniques used. To date, the focal-plane solutions constructed have no known geological validity; the more that are produced, the greater the confusion.

A wide variety of causes of earthquakes have been and are still being proposed for the eastern U.S., largely because of the lack of Holocene faults or faults shown near the epicenters. Earthquakes have been ascribed to glacial rebound (Leet and Linehan, 1942), rebound from a meteorite impact (Leblanc and others, 1973; Hasegawa, 1986), granitic plutons (Collins, 1927), basic plutons (Kane, 1977; Long and Champion, 1977; Simmons, 1977), reactivation of ancient deep thrust faults (Behrendt and others, 1981; Behrendt and others, 1983; Seeber and Armbruster, 1981), reactivation of Mesozoic rifts (Page and others, 1968; Ratcliff, 1971, 1980), post-Cretaceous reverse faulting

Figure 1. Index map of the eastern U.S. and adjacent Canada.

(Wentworth and Mergner-Keefer, 1981), northeast-southwest–oriented compression (Zoback and Zoback, 1980), pure random occurrence (J. F. Devine, U.S. Geological Survey, written communication, 1982), and intersections of major structural zones (Hobbs, 1907). Except for the last, all of these fail the test of adequately matching the distribution of seismicity. The pattern of seismicity shows no relation to post-glacial rebound (Woollard, 1958); the activity extends across the area of rebound into the southern states. A few of these proposed causes were attempts to provide a nonfault explanation of seismicity prior to discovery of faulting in the region. In some, a local peculiar feature was assigned the cause, such as a possible meteorite crater near La Malbaie, Quebec, but the activity at La Malbaie is part of a large zone of activity and is not due to a local unique feature.

Other explanations suffer from an attempt to attribute all seismicity to one simple type of structure without adequate consideration for the complex interrelations of geologic structure and tectonic movements. An example is the Boston-Ottawa seismic zone, shown by Hobbs (1907), that was proposed as a broad, continuous, northwest-trending seismic zone passing through Boston, Massachusetts, and Ottawa, Ontario (Sbar and Sykes, 1973). However, in detail, the proposed zone crosses both seismically quiet and active areas with trends generally different from the zone, and the proposed active structures are oblique to it and show little relation to the seismicity. The basic problem is that the critical geologic structures, which are generally not shown on the published geologic maps, and the neotectonic movements are not considered adequately.

NEOTECTONIC MOVEMENT

Considerable information indicates that neotectonic movement is taking place in the eastern United States. These data are derived from geomorphic studies, shoreline changes, tidal-gage readings, geodetic measurements, and other investigations, coupled with indications of movement from the recent geologic past as shown by stratigraphic studies, fission-track analysis, and post-Cretaceous fault movements. A bewildering variety of movement is shown, not all of which appears to be compatible. The principal indicated movement now appears to represent a composite of several different motions.

Geomorphology provides the best indicator of movement. It indicates the general motion, smoothing out small temporal variations, and may provide a history of development. The landforms are the result of differential erosion, deposition, and crustal deformation. Much of the geomorphology is controlled directly or indirectly by structure. Most of the relief in the east has been ascribed to differential erosion, but indicators of vertical motion suggest more is due to crustal movement than previously thought. The stream pattern in New England is closely controlled by the structure in the exposed basement rock (Hobbs, 1901). Elsewhere in the east where the basement is deeply buried, the major river valleys still commonly coincide with basement fracture zones. This relation indicates that much of the surface drainage reflects deformation and is not a random development. The geomorphic data provide the general fabric on which to pin the other data.

Some movement appears spurious and due to residual strain release and frost activity rather than neotectonic movement. This includes the small offsets of Pleistocene bedrock surfaces in the northeast (Dale, 1907; Woodworth, 1907; Thompson, 1979; Adams, 1981), offsets in roadcuts and quarry faces, and pop ups (Block and others, 1979; Schafer, 1983). Investigations show the highly strained rock apparently moves from natural or man-caused unloading, ice prying, and probably local frostquakes (Feld, 1966; Barosh, 1986c).

The general movement appears to be a superposition of a regional north tilt, a south tilt in the north, broad northeast-trending belts of vertical movement, and more local northwest-trending subsiding areas along the coastal plain.

North tilt

Much of the eastern United States appears to be undergoing a regional tilt to the north. This is shown by the coastal plain, which is raised and extends far inland in the south, slopes northward to plunge beneath the sea near New York City, and lies submerged off of New England (Fig. 2). Correspondingly, the exposed southern end of the Appalachian Mountains lies far inland, whereas its northeast end plunges seaward, allowing the sea to breach it in the Gulf of St. Lawrence and extend along its west side up the St. Lawrence River. In balance, the offshore carbonate banks have risen in the south to form the Florida Peninsula and the Bahama Islands to the southeast of it.

The edge of the continental shelf deepens from several meters off Florida to about 140 m near the Canadian border (Johnson, 1925; Officer and Drake, 1982). Miami, Florida, has been raised at a rate of 0.8 cm/yr with respect to the shelf off southern Canada during the past 18,000 yr (Officer and Drake, 1982). This northward tilt is continuing today along the Atlantic coast, as shown by sea-level changes in tidal-gage stations (Holdahl and Morrison, 1974), releveling data (Brown, 1978), and changes in coastal marshes (Walcott, 1972).

The progressive shoreward shift in position of the Tertiary contacts in the Gulf Coastal Plain shows the tilt has been active since the Cretaceous, and not, as Walcott (1972) suggested, due to peripheral effects of post-Pleistocene glacial rebound. The raised Pliocene shorelines above the Pleistocene ones in the south Atlantic and east Gulf Coasts (Winkler and Howard, 1977a, b) also demonstrate that the rise was underway earlier.

Because the tilt is regional, there is no apparent structural control; the cause must lie in overall plate movement. Rising coasts, such as along the West Coast, tend to be associated with convergent boundaries. Perhaps North America is moving relative to the Gulf of Mexico.

South tilt

A south tilt of the northern part of the eastern U.S. due to post-glacial rebound is well known (Flint, 1963). This tilt, in conjunction with the post-Pleistocene rise in sea level, has resulted in the late Pleistocene Atlantic shoreline being deeply submerged south of Long Island, at present sea level just south of Boston, and progressively rising onshore to the north. The tilt across central New England is a uniform 90 cm/km (Koteff and Larsen *in* Larsen, 1987).

The rebound was mainly completed about 6,000 yr ago (Farrand, 1962; Kaye and Barghoorn, 1964) and it appears to be finished in the U.S., except near the northern Great Lakes (Vanicek and Nagy, 1980), although it has amounted to about 30 m over Hudson Bay in the last 2,000 yr (Walcott, 1972; Fig. 3). At present, much of the New England coast is subsiding (Atwood, 1940; Tyler and Ladd, 1981) in excess of sea-level rise.

There does not appear to be any structural control of this regional effect caused by a climatic fluctuation, except indirectly in the structural control of topography, which affected ice thickness and direction of flow.

Northeast-trending belts of vertical movement

The principal geomorphic features in the eastern U.S. are a northwest-trending lowland that stretches from the Mississippi River Valley in southeast Arkansas through the lower Great Lakes and St. Lawrence River Valley to the Gulf of St. Lawrence, and the paralleling highland of the southern and central Appalachian Mountains (Fig. 4). The former is a major waterway except where it is filled in by Pleistocene deposits in western Ohio and Indiana (Wayne, 1956; Teller, 1973). There is

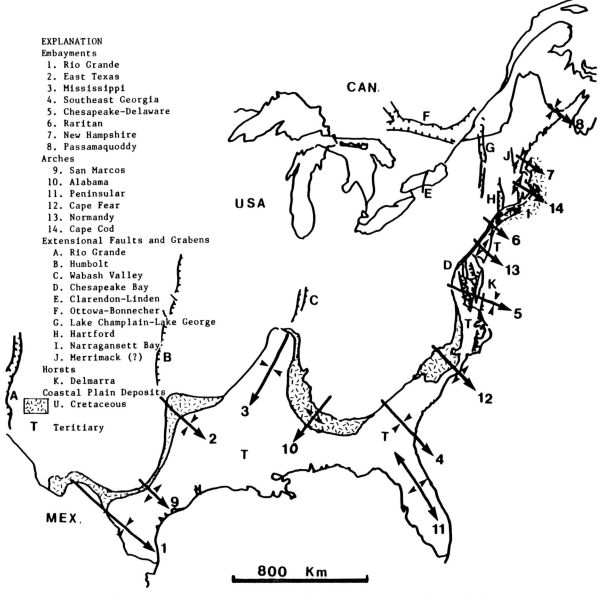

EXPLANATION
Embayments
   1. Rio Grande
   2. East Texas
   3. Mississippi
   4. Southeast Georgia
   5. Chesapeake-Delaware
   6. Raritan
   7. New Hampshire
   8. Passamaquoddy
Arches
   9. San Marcos
  10. Alabama
  11. Peninsular
  12. Cape Fear
  13. Normandy
  14. Cape Cod
Extensional Faults and Grabens
   A. Rio Grande
   B. Humbolt
   C. Wabash Valley
   D. Chesapeake Bay
   E. Clarendon-Linden
   F. Ottowa-Bonnecher
   G. Lake Champlain-Lake George
   H. Hartford
   I. Narragansett Bay
   J. Merrimack (?)
Horsts
   K. Delmarra
Coastal Plain Deposits
   [figure] U. Cretaceous
   T Teritiary

Figure 2. Map of the eastern U.S. and adjacent Canada showing embayments along the Late Cretaceous continental margin that are also areas of known or probable present-day relative subsidence, arches and selected extensional faults, grabens, and horsts, which may be active (Barosh, 1986c).

considerable evidence that the Appalachian Mountains are rising, and some indications exist that the Arkansas–St. Lawrence lowland is subsiding (Meade, 1971; Dames and Moore, 1978; Barosh, 1980, 1981a, 1986c). The relative uplift of central Tennessee with respect to the Mississippi River Valley is indicated to be about 4.6 m/m.y. in post-Cretaceous time and greatly accelerated in the last 2 m.y. (Stearns and Reesman, 1986). The Adirondack Mountains are also rising (Isachsen, 1975; Zimmerman, 1976; Barnett and Isachsen, 1980). A parallel feature farther northwest, across Minnesota and South Dakota, forms a much more subtle surface feature, the Mid-continent Arch, which also has indications of uplift (U.S. Geodynamics Committee, 1973).

In addition, there may be some general subsidence along the Atlantic Coastal Plain and coastal New England (Durham and Murray, 1967; Meade, 1971). In all these, the highlands are rising and the lowlands subsiding.

All of the belts are underlain by northeast-trending structural zones (Barosh, 1986c). The Mid-continent Arch follows the fault zones of the Precambrian Colorado Lineament (Warner, 1978) and Great Lakes Tectonic Zone (Mooney and Walton, 1980), where arching has taken place at various times. The south and central Appalachian Mountains also coincide with many late Precambrian and Paleozoic faults (Cohee, 1961) and have undergone episodes of arching during the Tertiary (Keith,

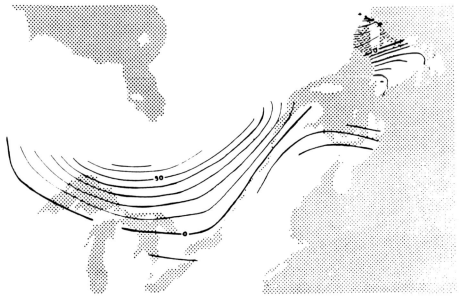

Figure 3. Map of southeastern Canada and adjacent U.S. showing vertical movements in centimeters per century from geodetic data (surface of 2nd degree) (from Vanicek and Nagy, 1980).

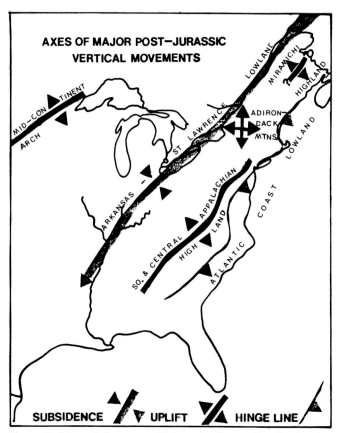

Figure 4. Map of the eastern U.S. and adjacent Canada showing northeast-trending belts of apparently subsiding lowlands and rising uplands and arches.

1923; Atwood, 1940; Zimmerman, 1980). Both the lowlands overlie zones of grabens and normal faults. Those along the Arkansas–St. Lawrence zone are late Precambrian and early Paleozoic (Kumarapeli and Saull, 1966; Kumarapeli, 1978, 1986), and pass between flanking domes of lower Paleozoic rock and across a sag in the Precambrian surface northwest of the Adirondack Mountains. The coastal plain and near-shore New England overlies a zone of early Mesozoic grabens (Ballard and Uchupi, 1975; Wentworth and Mergner-Keefer, 1983), apparently controlled by older faults.

These movements parallel those associated with the rifting and opening of the North Atlantic Basin and are apparently a minor continuation of the process. They seem to have moved progressively inland. The East Coast began to subside in the Triassic as a series of grabens as rifting started, then as a more general seaward tilt as the ocean basin opened and the initial Atlantic Coastal Plain deposits were laid down in the Middle Jurassic. The Appalachian Mountains rose about the same time to supply sediments to the coastal plain along the new edge of the continent. The Arkansas–St. Lawrence lowland started sinking during the Late Cretaceous, at least at the southwest end, as shown by deposits in the Mississippi Embayment. The Midcontinent Arch began to rise again slightly later to deform deposits of this age (Dutch, 1981).

Movements similar to those taking place today in these belts have occurred previously, and these mobile belts seem to be longstanding tectonic features. The rising uplands have suffered intermittent arching. The subsiding lowlands follow zones of normal faults, suggesting that these extensional movements are still important. Some of the subsidence along the coastal plain is attributed to cooling of the crust (Watts, 1981), and some may be

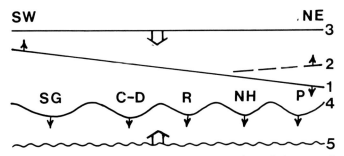

Figure 5. Schematic diagram showing present-day relative crustal movements and sea-level change along the East Coast of the U.S. Arrows represent relative direction of movement. 1, epeirogenic north tilt; 2, glacial rebound south tilt; 3, Atlantic Coastal Plain subsidence and seaward tilt; 4, embayment subsidence; 5, sea level rise; SG, southeast Georgia; C-D, Chesapeake–Delaware; R, Raritan; NH, New Hampshire; P, Passamaquoddy (Barosh, 1986c).

due to compaction of sediments, but this appears only to add to a continuing tectonic process.

Northwest-trending subsiding zones

A series of transverse basins of thicker sediments, referred to as embayments, along the Atlantic Coastal Plain shows evidence of continuing relative subsidence (Barosh, 1981a, 1986a, 1986c; Fig. 2). All of these form bays along the coast, except for the Southeast Georgia Embayment, where the north tilt has apparently counterbalanced the subsidence (Fig. 5). The embayments on the Gulf Coastal Plain are now inland from the sea, and evidence for present-day relative subsidence is not as clear, but each is the site of a major river drainage. They all trend northwest, except for the Mississippi Embayment, which is part of the Arkansas–St. Lawrence lowland. The intervening arches appear relatively stable.

Stratigraphic evidence shows these embayments were established by the Late Cretaceous and continued through the Tertiary. Prior to this, many basins within the Atlantic Coastal Plain tended to overlie the buried northeast-trending grabens (Brown and others, 1972; Miller, 1982). The positions of the embayments are controlled by large, underlying, northwest-trending fault zones and are aligned with the large, offshore transform fracture zones, although the evidence is incomplete for some embayments (Fig. 6). Some, such as the Rio Grande and East Texas Embayments, are clearly controlled by reactivated Precambrian fault zones, but for some the initial age of the faults is not yet known. Relative uplift between the reactivated fault and transform fracture zones and perhaps within large fracture zones has shifted basement blocks to control the overlying basins and arches (Barosh, 1986a).

A close relation between faults, present deformation, and the edge of a basin is displayed along a zone that crosses central Florida and southwestern Alabama (Fig. 6). The offshore Bahamas transform fracture zone crosses central Florida and di-

rectly into a zone of normal faults across southwestern Alabama and adjacent Mississippi (Daniels and others, 1983; Wilson, 1975). These form the northeastern side of a Late Jurassic salt-bearing basin. The fault zone also crosses a low in the basement that separates the buried southwestern end of the Appalachian Mountains from a basement high, the Wiggens Arch, to the southwest. The zone is marked by present deformation in Alabama and Mississippi as shown by both geodetic and geomorphic evidence (Holdahl and Morrison, 1974; Schumm, 1986).

EARTHQUAKE DISTRIBUTION AND CONTROLS

The distribution of earthquakes corresponds closely to the combined neotectonic movement of the northeast-trending belts of vertical movement and the northwest-trending subsiding areas. However, both the regional north tilt and the south tilt appear to be unrelated to earthquakes and to be epeirogenic.

The distribution of earthquakes is highly irregular; local active areas are commonly separated by regions with little or no seismicity. The contouring of the rate of seismic activity across the region shows this well (Hadley and Devine, 1974; Fig. 7). Where the activity can be looked at in more detail, as in the northeast with its earthquake record of 400 years, the local nature of the seismic activity is even more striking (Barosh, 1979; Chiburis, 1981; Fig. 8). An even more detailed view using the

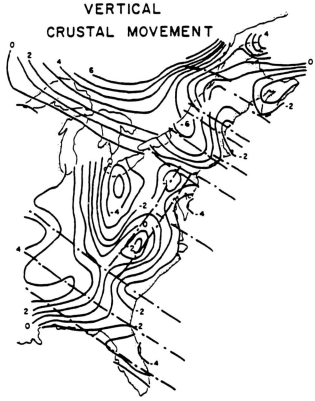

Figure 6. Map of the eastern U.S. and adjacent Canada showing apparent vertical movement in mm/yr (data compiled by Brown and Reilinger, 1986) and basement fracture zones controlling embayments (Barosh, 1990a).

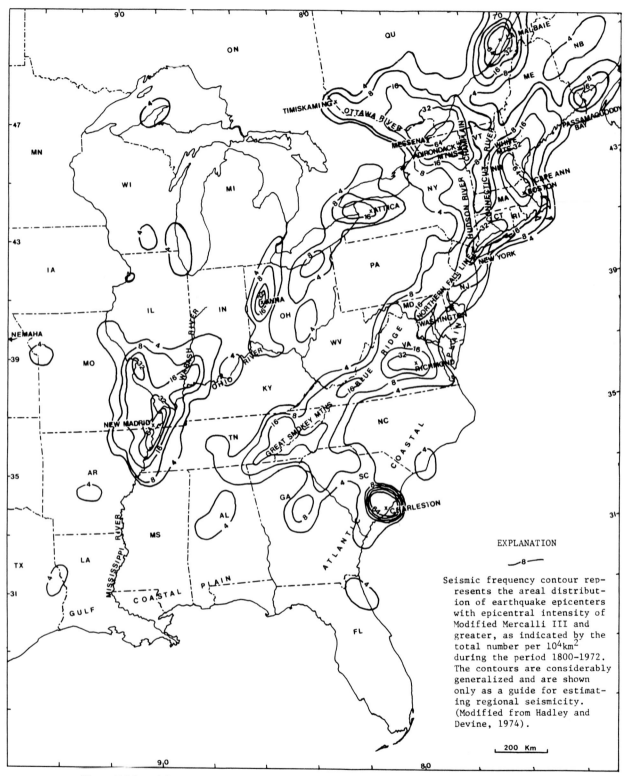

Figure 7. Map of the eastern U.S. and adjacent Canada showing the seismic frequency for the period 1800–1972 (from Hadley and Devine, 1974).

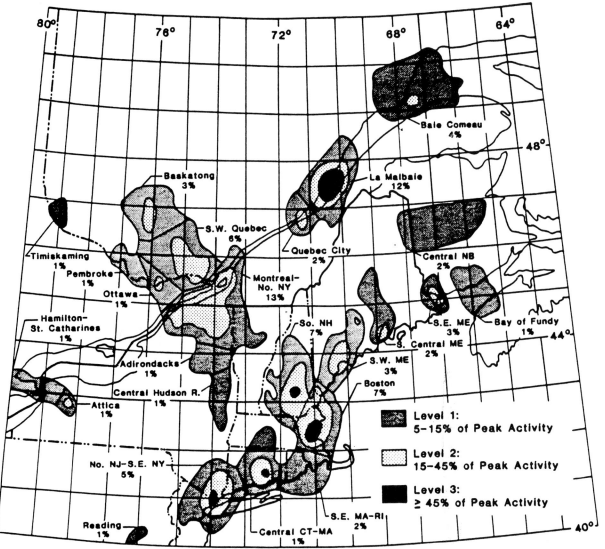

Figure 8. Map of the northeastern U.S. and adjacent Canada showing seismic subregions contoured at three levels of relative activity for the time period 1534–1977 and their percentage of the overall activity (Chiburis, 1981).

well-located epicenters of the past 10 years shows alignments of epicenters within these clusters (Barosh, 1986b). This variable distribution is real and not an artifact of population or instrumental distribution. The population distribution in the northeast has not had a significant effect on this variation (Boston Edison, 1976), nor has the array of seismographs, except near the Ramapo fault, north of New York City (Nottis and Mitronovas, 1983). The advent of a greatly increased seismograph network beginning in 1976 has revealed much more activity and some minor events where they were not known before, but has not changed this pattern of activity. The improved epicentral locations and the removal of spurious events from the record has tended to reduce the size of these clusters. The activity recorded over a few months in the northeast for example, will reproduce the historic pattern (Barosh, 1979, 1981a; Chiburis, 1981; Ebel,

1984) and in the New Madrid area the pattern may be reproduced in only several days. The rate of activity of an active area may vary over the years (Shakal and Toksoz, 1977), but its location does not. The known distribution of earthquakes, thus, fairly accurately reflects the position of the seismogenic zones in the region. The zones on the East Coast, with nearly 400 years of records, are correspondingly better defined than many farther west where the record is only a third as long. However, some areas of minor earthquakes, such as in Florida and southern Alabama, are probably underrepresented by the present distribution of seismographs.

Not only does the general distribution of earthquakes match well the positions of the northeast-trending belts of vertical movement, but the degree of seismic activity corresponds to their geomorphic prominence. Most earthquakes occur along the Ar-

P. J. Barosh

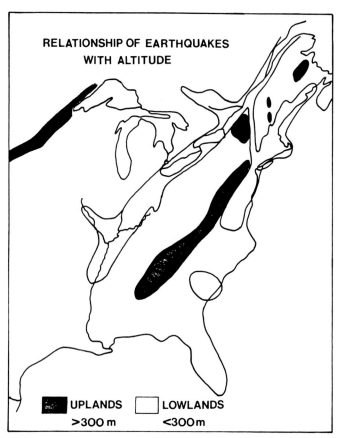

RELATIONSHIP OF EARTHQUAKES
WITH ALTITUDE

UPLANDS >300 m   LOWLANDS <300m

Figure 9. Map of the eastern U.S. and adjacent Canada showing generalized areas of seismic activity in relation to altitude (Barosh, 1986c).

kansas–St. Lawrence lowland, and the two centers of the largest earthquakes and greatest number of small shocks—New Madrid and La Malbaie—lie near either end (Fig. 1). The southern and central Appalachian Mountains stand out as a distinct zone of earthquakes centered along the Great Smoky Mountains and the Blue Ridge. A lesser, but definable zone of seismic events occurs along the Mid-continent Arch (not shown on Fig. 7). In a simplified way, these relations can be used to sort earthquakes that have evidence of movement into those occurring in uplands (rising) and those occurring in lowlands (subsiding) (Fig. 9).

The embayments along the Atlantic Coast also correspond to concentrations of seismic activity. In addition, the spacing of the embayments and their clusters of activity along the Atlantic Coast match the spacing of the centers of activity along the Arkansas–St. Lawrence lowland to the northwest (Fig. 7). This must have some tectonic significance.

The regional distribution of earthquakes thus is explained by its correspondence to northeast- and northwest-trending areas of movement. This match also indicates the general structural control of eastern earthquakes, as these earthquake-prone areas of movement coincide with fault zones of these trends. The distribution also shows that the larger earthquakes and most areas of

activity are related to subsidence rather than uplift. These general relations are upheld in detailed studies of individual seismically active areas, where additional relations are also revealed. These areas may be quite complex and show a wide structural variation between them, but they also show several common features. The northwest- and north-trending (north to north-northeast) faults are the youngest ones found in the seismic areas of the northeastern U.S., and probably elsewhere in the east as well (Barosh, 1981a, 1986a). Earthquakes occur at intersections of faults of these two trends with northeast-trending faults and with each other. They also occur locally along the northwest- and perhaps north-trending faults. Several studies of local seismogenic zones in different sections of the eastern U.S. are described below to show these relations.

Central

The New Madrid, Missouri, area is a good example of earthquakes controlled by the intersection of northeast- and northwest-trending structures. This is the site of the largest known earthquakes in the United States (December 16, 1811; January 23, 1812; and February 7, 1912), and small earthquakes are recorded almost daily (Fuller, 1912; Nuttli, 1973b; Stauder and others, 1980). A few months of recordings shows an elongated X pattern of epicenters in the epicentral area of the great earthquakes (Fig. 10). The X is aligned with the intersection of the buried Reelfoot Rift and the Pascola Arch (Fig. 11). One trend follows the northeast-trending late Precambrian rift, and the other the northeastern side of the crest of the northwest-trending basement arch. Where the arch crosses the rift near New Madrid it is deflected and strikes north-northwest locally (Buschbach, 1980), exactly matching one of the epicentral trends. The precise fit of the epicentral distribution and structure demonstrates that the earthquakes are controlled by the intersection of faults along the arch with those of the rift (Barosh, 1981a; O'Leary and Hildenbrand, 1981; Johnston, 1982). The two basement structures have been intermittently active, as shown by their effect on the thickness of Paleozoic formations. The last major activity along the arch was prior to the Late Cretaceous when the rift began to subside, resulting in the formation of a synclinal basin of Late Cretaceous and early Tertiary deposits above it (Fig. 11). Normal faults associated with these structures are exposed to the northeast beyond the Cretaceous strata and to the northwest where the basement arch rises to the surface in the Ozark Plateau; remote sensing studies indicate many more (Cohee, 1961; Heyl and Brock, 1961; Heyl and McKeown, 1978; Buschbach, 1980; O'Leary and Hildenbrand, 1981).

The most seismically active area is confined to the rift (Erwin and McGinnis, 1975; Hildenbrand and others, 1977), and the pattern of activity corresponds with faults and surface deformation. The northeastern arm of epicenters follows the northwestern side of the rift, and Holocene surface faults are found locally along the other arms (Russ, 1981; Fig. 10). Doming related to Holocene deformation also follows the active seismic

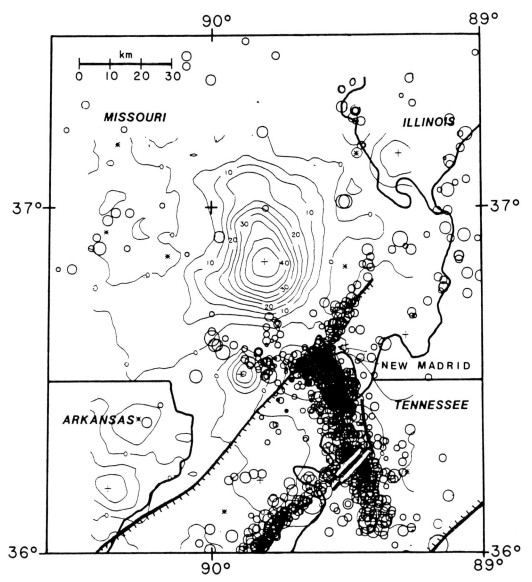

Figure 10. Map of New Madrid, Missouri, and vicinity showing earthquake epicenters from June 1974 to June 1983, residual gravity anomaly map (Ravat and others, 1987), and the Reelfoot Rift boundaries and other faults (Russ, 1981).

arms, and areas of local subsidence lie adjacent (Stearns, 1979). During the 1811–1812 earthquakes, the epicenters of the main shocks may have been spaced slightly apart and have had a northeast-trending alignment (Nuttli, 1973b), as do the areas of sand blows (Heyl and McKeown, 1978). The largest earthquake (February 7, 1812), however, caused a partial uplift of the north-northwest–trending Tiptonville and related domes, which strike toward New Madrid; the uplift created two falls across the Mississippi River (McGee, 1892; Fuller, 1912; Stearns, 1979). Holocene faults have been identified along the side of the dome (Russ, 1981), and some surface faulting may have accompanied the earthquake.

The Pascola Arch rises to the surface to the northwest and merges with the Ozark Uplift. A zone of lesser seismicity also extends northwest from New Madrid but is stepped slightly northward and lies along the Mississippi River above Cairo, Illinois (Figs. 1 and 7). This follows a zone of northwest-striking faults along the northeastern flank of the uplift (Heyl and McKeown, 1978).

Seismically active areas occur farther northeast along the Arkansas–St. Lawrence lowland where more northerly striking normal faults cross it. Activity is present in the Wabash Valley of Illinois and Indiana in a zone of normal faults (Bristol and Treworgy, 1979). In the Anna area of western Ohio, seismicity occurs where faults and probable faults lie along the west side of a north-trending basement arch, particularly where it is crossed by a northwest-striking fault zone (Cole and others, 1987; Fig. 12). The buried pre-Pleistocene river system in this region is con-

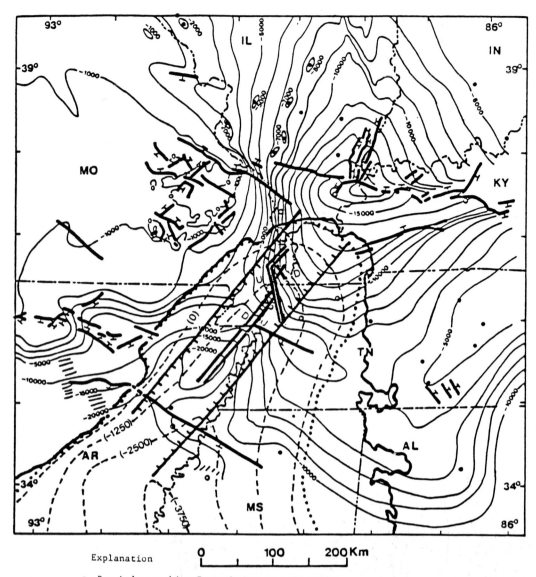

Explanation

●   Borehole reaching Precambrian igneous rocks.

○   Other significant deep borehole.

Structural contours drawn on top of Precambrian igneous rocks, showing elevation below sea level.

Border of Coastal Plain rocks of the Mississippi embayment.

Contact of Tertiary rocks.

Structural contour drawn on top of Cretaceous rocks showing elevation below sea level.

Generalized border of graben in Precambrian rocks interpreted from geophysical data, ticks indicate downthrown side.

Trend of seismicity, letters indicate relative movement (D, down; U, up) based on slope of Precambrian surface, if seismicity occurs on faults.

X   New Madrid, Missouri, approximate epicenter of 1811–1812 earthquakes.

Normal fault cutting Precambrian rocks, ticks on downthrown side.

Figure 11. Map of New Madrid, Missouri, and vicinity showing the configuration of the top of the Precambrian rock (Buschbach, 1980) and the base of Tertiary rock (Cohee, 1961), borders of a late Precambrian graben (Hildenbrand and others, 1977), the presently active seismic zone (Herrmann, 1980), and possible present-day movements (from Barosh, 1981a).

trolled by the known faults and probably others. The recent earthquake at Sharpsville, Kentucky, appears to lie on the south end of this same zone (Fig. 12).

Northeast

The northeastern United States and adjacent Canada contains about a dozen separate seismogenic areas (Barosh, 1979; Chiburis, 1981; Fig. 8). The relations shown in the separate active areas indicate that the earthquakes are associated with high-angle northwest-, north-, and northeast-trending faults (Barosh, 1981a, 1986a; Sanford and others, 1984). The numerous low-angle Paleozoic thrust faults in the region are not related to the seismicity.

These faults associated with the various seismically active areas can be extended to form a regional seismotectonic map (Fig. 13). They are well displayed in the landscape and are followed by the major rivers and streams. Many of the northwest- and north-trending faults are shown to have post–middle or late Mesozoic movement. The faults are not active everywhere, but appear concentrated in the areas of general vertical movement. The New York region shows this well. Structural zones may cross the region, but are active only where they intersect the regions of neotectonic movement: The Arkansas–St. Lawrence lowland, central Appalachian and Adirondack Mountains, and the Raritan Embayment (Fig. 13).

The earthquakes are primarily spatially associated with the northwest- and north-trending faults, the youngest in the region. The northeast-trending ones appear active only where intersected. However, the isoseismal patterns show elongation along both northwestern and northeastern trends. The two young trends are both high angle. The north-trending ones are normal and form horst and graben systems in Lake Champlain–Lake George and lower Narragansett Bay, and father south in Chesapeake Bay (Barosh, 1986c). Some also show left-lateral strike-slip movement (Sawyer and Carroll, 1982). The northwest-trending ones appear to have more strike-slip movement, usually right-lateral. These faults, where seen, tend to form wide disruptive zones, but with modest offset. The largest offset known is along the Little Androscoggin fault, in southwestern Maine, with 11 km of right-lateral offset (Barosh, 1990b). Some northwest-trending faults can be extended out to sea using geophysical and bathymetric data and show an approximate alignment with the offshore transform fracture zones.

Some of these faults appear to have larger geophysical expression than is warranted by the surface offset (Barosh, 1986c) and others to affect the thickness of Paleozoic formations (Fakundiny, 1981). These and other features suggest that many are old, deep-seated faults that have been reactivated.

The various kinds of seismogenic structural situations are found along a broad northwest-trending zone of faults, the Winooski-Winnipesaukee zone, that crosses central New England (Barosh, 1981a, 1986b, d). This zone of faults, as shown by prominent topographic, bathymetric, radar, LANDSAT, geophysical, and field data, extends from the Ontario-Quebec border

area southeastward across the New Hampshire Embayment at the coast of New Hampshire and southernmost Maine, and into the Gulf of Maine to align with transform fracture zones farther at sea (Fig. 13). This zone roughly coincides with the "Boston-Ottawa seismic zone," but earthquakes vary greatly in number and frequency along it (Figs. 7 and 8). It is particularly active where it crosses northeast-trending faults along the Arkansas–St. Lawrence lowland at Messena, New York, and Montreal, Quebec, and others of this trend near the coast and offshore Cape Ann. The central part appears more controlled by north-trending extensional faults such as in the Lake Champlain–Lake George graben. Earthquakes are aligned locally along apparent northwest-trending faults within the zone, as in the northern Adirondack Mountains and near the White Mountains in New Hampshire and southern Maine (Barosh, 1986a, b). Even in these areas, intersections with north-trending faults may control the earthquakes as they apparently controlled the emplacement of Cretaceous plutons there (Barosh, 1990b).

The geology as the active Moodus area in south-central Connecticut is complex, but most structures are ancient and inactive. The earthquakes occur where a northwest-trending fault zone with 6 km of left-lateral movement crosses a northeast-trending Early Jurassic dike system that extends a few hundred kilometers (Barosh and others, 1977, 1982; Fig. 14). No significant faults are known along the dike at the surface, but such a large straight feature must be controlled by a fault zone at depth. The dike itself is offset laterally by small, northwest- and

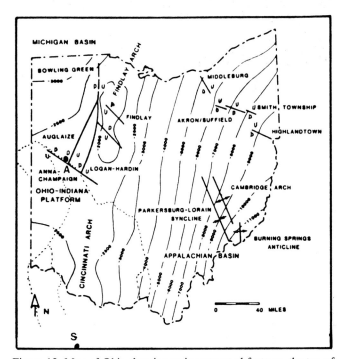

Figure 12. Map of Ohio showing major structural features, the top of Precambrian basement (compiled by Cole and others, 1987), and pre-glacial rivers (dotted lines) (Wayne, 1956; Teller, 1973) that may follow faults. A, Anna, Ohio; S, Sharpsburg, Kentucky.

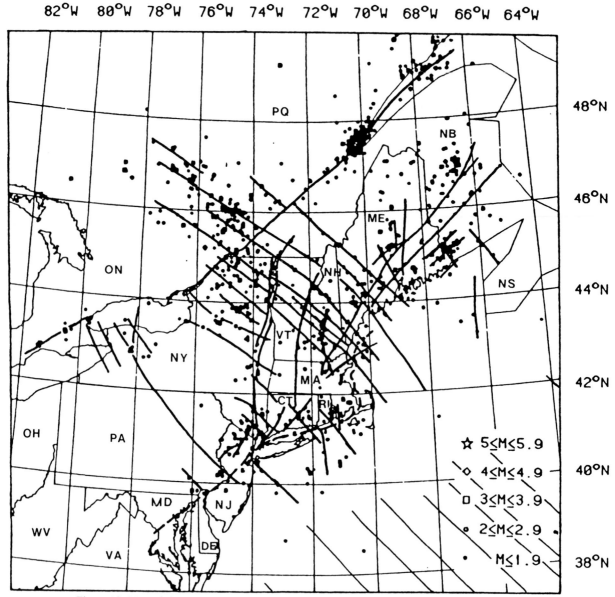

Figure 13. Map of the northeastern U.S. and adjacent areas showing earthquakes during the period October 1975 to March 1984 (Foley and others, 1985), generalized fault and probable fault zones spatially related to earthquakes (solid lines), the border of the Coastal Plain deposits (dashed line), and offshore transform fracture zones (Klitgord and Behrendt, 1979; modified from Barosh, 1986c).

north-trending faults (Sawyer and Carroll, 1982). The northwest-trending faults are offset in a right-lateral direction, and this also may be the latest direction of movement along the main fault zone. A northwest-trending fault zone, lying between two major northeast-trending zones, is also the locus of earthquakes in the subsiding Passamaquoddy Bay area of Maine and New Brunswick (Barosh, 1981c, 1986a; Fig. 15).

At Attica, in northwestern New York, the shocks are concentrated at an intersection of a northwest- and north-trending fault zone (Barosh, 1985, 1986b), similar to the situation at Anna, Ohio to the southwest. The area of mild seismicity in lower Narragansett Bay also appears to be spatially associated with

north-trending extensional faults near an intersection with a northwest-trending zone (McMaster and others, 1980; Barosh, 1986c).

The north-trending Lake Champlain–Lake George graben system that contains faults with apparent Holocene offset (Young and Putnam, 1979; Geraghty and Isachsen, 1981; Hunt and Dowling, 1981; Putnam and others, 1983; McHone, 1987) seems to relieve strain in the region to allow central Vermont and western Massachusetts to remain seismically quiet. Similarly, the north-trending Penobscot lineament, which extends northward from Penobscot Bay across east-central Maine, separates a mildly active area from an aseismic one (Barosh, 1981a, b).

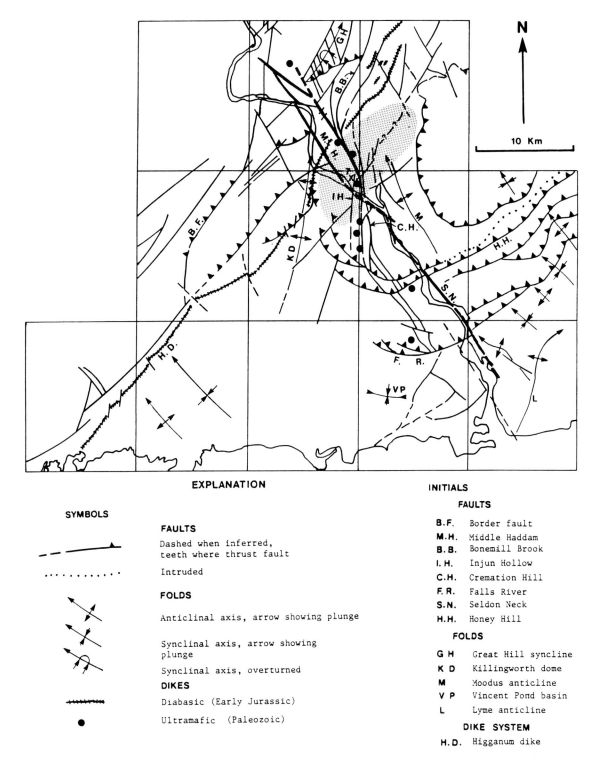

EXPLANATION

SYMBOLS

FAULTS

Dashed when inferred,
teeth where thrust fault

Intruded

FOLDS

Anticlinal axis, arrow showing plunge

Synclinal axis, arrow showing
plunge

Synclinal axis, overturned

DIKES

Diabasic (Early Jurassic)

Ultramafic (Paleozoic)

INITIALS

FAULTS

B.F.	Border fault
M.H.	Middle Haddam
B.B.	Bonemill Brook
I.H.	Injun Hollow
C.H.	Cremation Hill
F.R.	Falls River
S.N.	Seldon Neck
H.H.	Honey Hill

FOLDS

G H	Great Hill syncline
K D	Killingworth dome
M	Moodus anticline
V P	Vincent Pond basin
L	Lyme anticline

DIKE SYSTEM

H.D.	Higganum dike

Figure 14. Map of Moodus, Connecticut, and vicinity showing structural features and general area of seismic activity (stippled). Seldon Neck and Middle Haddam fault zones shown heavier (modified from Barosh and others, 1982).

Southeast

The southeastern United States displays an excellent correlation of northeast- and northwest-trending epicentral patterns coinciding with areas of structurally controlled neotectonic movement, some of which tie in closely with offshore transform fracture zones (Barosh, 1983). There are three principal seismic zones with local concentrations, rather than the more distinct and numerous small source areas in the northeast. These are the Southern Appalachian, South Carolina–Georgia, and Central Virginia seismic zones (Bollinger, 1973). The former lies along the rising, northeast-trending Southern Appalachian Mountains upland. The South Carolina–Georgia and Central Virginia seismic zones lie to the southeast along the northwest-trending Southeast Georgia and Chesapeake–Delaware embayments, respectively. The principal seismic activity in both embayments lies more toward the flanks of the Cape Fear Arch. The general division between the upland and lowland trends is marked by the Brevard fault zone, but they do overlap (Fig. 16). Most of the epicenters in the Southern Appalachian seismic zone are concentrated where a projection of the Southeast Georgia zone crosses it, and a small cluster occurs northwest of the Chesapeake-Delaware Embayment.

The Southeast Georgia embayment and its offshore extension lie between the Blake Spur and Jacksonville transform fracture zones (Klitgord and others, 1983) buried Triassic graben along the extension of the Jacksonville zone (Chowns and Wil-

liams, 1983) and a fault cuts the coastal plain deposits, at least locally, along that of the Blake Spur (Talwani, 1982, and oral communication, 1984). There are numerous northwest-trending early Mesozoic basic dikes on land between the projections of these two zones; they indicate extensive fractures of this trend. Northeast of the Blake Spur and its seismically active projection the dikes trend north.

Charleston, South Carolina, the site of the 1886 Modified Mercalli intensity X earthquake, lies along a prominent northwest-trending line of epicenters along the northeast side of the Southeast Georgia Embayment (Talwani, 1982; Rinehart, 1983) and is aligned with the Blake Spur fracture zone (Sykes, 1978). Some of these earthquakes produced northwest-trending isoseismal patterns (Bollinger and Visvanathan, 1977; Tarr, 1977; Bagwell, 1981; Bollinger, 1983), and some faulting of this trend has been identified. Near Charleston, other northeast-trending faults and isoseismal patterns have been found; the activity there appears to be the result of a fault intersection with the prominent seismic zone (Bollinger, 1983). Another northwest seismic zone follows the nearby Savannah River, and the most active part of Florida is the northeastern corner where the Jacksonville fracture zone projects onshore.

Thrust sheets conceal the basement structure of the most active part of the Southern Appalachian seismic zone opposite the Southeast Georgia Embayment. However, geophysical studies reveal a major northeast-trending fault zone and several northwest-trending ones in the basement (Watkins, 1964). The northeast-trending zone extends from central Alabama to northeast Kentucky (and perhaps to southern New York); it appears to be associated with local seismicity and to separate the region of activity in the southern Appalachian zone from the minor activity to the northwest in the Appalachian Plateaus (Watkins, 1964). Some of the northwest faults also appear to be seismically active and to control local centers of activity at intersections with other faults (Watkins, 1964; Barosh, 1986a). The Southern Appalachian zone may end to the southeast against fracture zones along the extension of the Pascola Arch. Minor activity occurs farther to the southwest along a northern northwest-trending zone of neotectonic movement, which may be increased by salt flow along border faults of a Jurassic salt basin.

The principal structure in the Chesapeake-Delaware Embayment appears to be a northwest-trending structural zone that is approximately on line with the Norfolk fracture zone along the southern side of the north-trending graben forming Chesapeake Bay (Brown and others, 1972). Local faults that cut Miocene coastal plain deposits (Ward and Blackwelder, 1980) lie near both features. Triassic grabens are offset by faults along this northwest-trending zone (Pavlides, 1981), and small Eocene intrusive bodies, which are the youngest along the East Coast (Johnson and Milton, 1955; Metcalf, 1982), lie along it. Earthquakes occur along the northwest-trending zone near Richmond, Virginia, and also form a north-trending zone along the faulted border of the coastal plain in eastern Virginia, adjacent to the

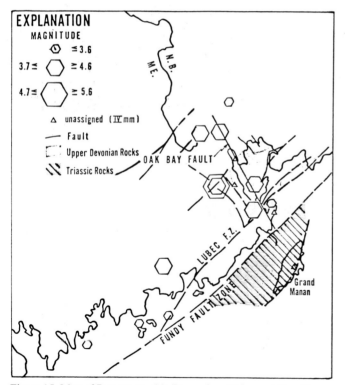

EXPLANATION

MAGNITUDE

⬡ ≤ 3.6

3.7 ≤ ⬡ ≥ 4.6

4.7 ≤ ⬡ ≥ 5.6

△ unassigned (IXmm)

— Fault

▭ Upper Devonian Rocks

◹ Triassic Rocks

OAK BAY FAULT

N.B.

ME.

LUBEC F.Z.

FUNDY FAULT ZONE

Grand Manan

Figure 15. Map of Passamaquoddy Bay region, Maine and New Brunswick, showing earthquake epicenters and major faults and grabens.

graben of Chesapeake Bay. The seismicity of central Virginia thus appears related to the intersection of these two structural zones.

The seismicity at Giles County, Virginia, to the west in the Southern Appalachian zone is probably due to an intersection of north- and northeast-trending structures, judging by the epicentral trends (Bollinger and Wheeler, 1983). This area is also covered by a thrust sheet, but the incised New River and several small transverse faults in a north-striking alignment (Schultz and others, 1986) may reflect a controlling north-trending basement fault that intersects a regional northeast-trending fault, which follows a magnetic low in the basement shown by Dean and others (1979).

An unusual seismic feature that lies mostly within the southeast is the Appalachian Plateau quiet zone, which follows the Appalachian Plateaus from the Cumberland Plateau of central Tennessee northeastward to the Catskill Mountains of central New York. This is a zone of very low seismicity that separates the active area of the Appalachian Mountains from that in the lowland farther northwest. The Rough Creek–Kentucky River fault zone forms its northwestern side (Fig. 16). Only minor seismicity along a few northwest-trending geophysical discontinuities, which probably represent basement faults, occurs in this zone (Barosh, 1986a; Black, 1986). The region is relatively undeformed and characterized by Paleozoic strata with gentle dips or in simple folds. Even the area of the buried Precambrian east-trending Rough Creek graben in Kentucky appears quiet.

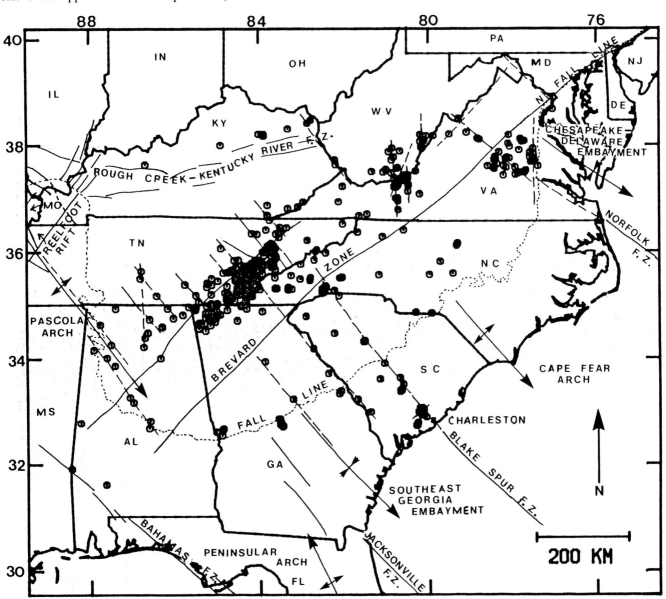

Figure 16. Map of the southeastern U.S. showing earthquakes during the period July 1977 through June 1986 (Sibol and others, 1986) and selected faults, probable faults, and folds (data from Cohee, 1961; Watkins, 1964; King and Beikman, 1974; Klitgord and Behrendt, 1979; Chowns and Williams, 1983; Rinehart, 1983; and others).

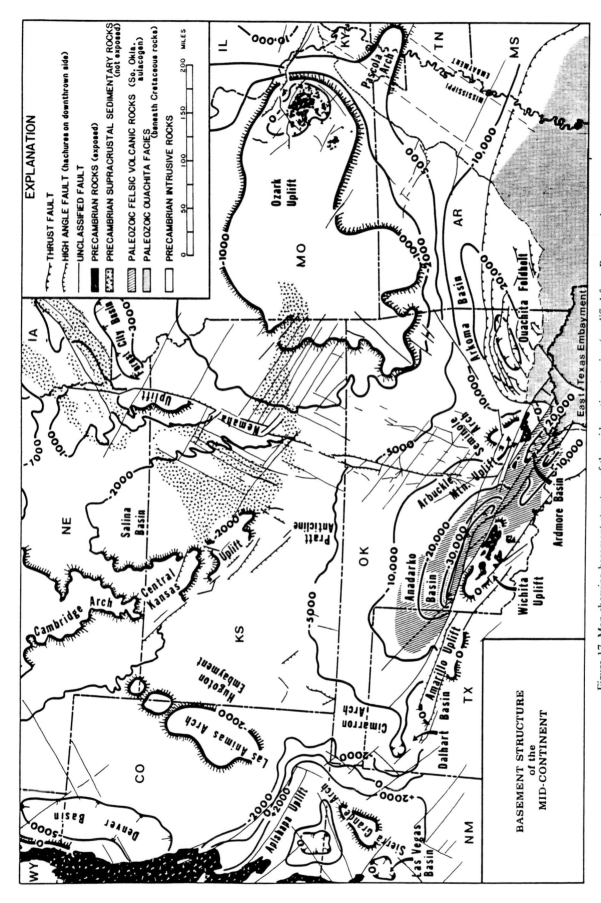

Figure 17. Map showing basement structure of the mid-continent region (modified from Rascoe and Adler, 1983, with data from Maughan, 1966; Warner, 1978; Buschbach, 1980; Berendsen and others, 1981; Dickas, 1986; Budnik, 1986; Barosh, 1986a).

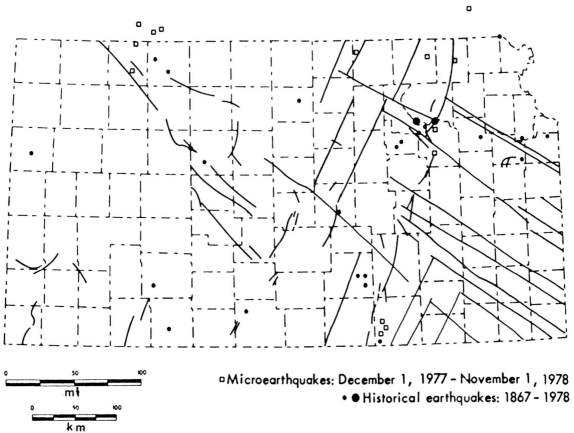

Figure 18. Map of Kansas showing basement faults and location of historic earthquakes and recent microearthquakes (Wilson, 1979; Berendsen and others, 1981).

Midwest

The midwest region also displays spatial relations of earthquakes with northwest-, north-, and northeast-trending structures, notably at their intersections, although the lower level of seismic activity and lack of major concentrations here makes this less obvious. A few general seismic zones are present: the Wichita zone trends west-northwest across northeast Texas, southern Oklahoma, and northern Texas; the Nemaha zone extends along the buried Nemaha Uplift from central Oklahoma north to southeast Nebraska; and the northwest-trending Missouri River zone lies across eastern Nebraska and into central South Dakota. In addition, there is a zone along the Mid-continental Arch and a few other scattered small clusters of activity.

The Wichita zone follows a major late Precambrian structural zone (Ham and others, 1964; Feinstein, 1981; Budnik, 1986; Fig. 17) that seems to control the East Texas embayment and the general Red River drainage. The lower Red River Valley and a seismically active zone across Louisiana are on a southeastward extension of this zone and may be part of it. Holocene movement has occurred along the Meers fault in this zone in Oklahoma (Donovan and others, 1983; Budnik, 1985).

The Nemaha zone follows a zone of subsurface normal faults along a buried uplifted basement block. This major structure was active mainly in Pennsylvanian time when the Wichita

Uplift was also rising in Oklahoma, but existed as a positive element since Early Cambrian time or earlier (Berendsen and others, 1981). The Nemaha structures show up well in the surface drainage, and some Holocene movement along the Nemaha zone is indicated by changes in glacial till (Dubois, 1978). The activity along it appears to lie near intersections with northwest-trending basement faults in Kansas (Berendsen and others, 1981; Wilson, 1979; Fig. 18) and Oklahoma (Barosh, 1986a); these faults also appear to control small Cretaceous intrusive bodies (Berendsen and others, 1981). The largest recorded earthquake along this zone, the 1952 El Reno earthquake (intensity VII), and numerous small ones (Lawson and others, 1979; Luza and Lawson, 1982) occur where it meets the northern edge of the Wichita zone near Oklahoma City.

The Missouri River zone follows a basement fault zone that offsets a buried late Precambrian graben system (Dickas, 1986) and is postulated to be active (Maroney and Burchett, 1979). Where this structural zone crosses the Mid-continent Arch near Pierre in central South Dakota (Shurr, 1981), there is a concentration of activity and also evidence of recent fault movement (Nichols and Collins, this volume). Activity along the Mid-continent Arch in Minnesota also appears to be located at intersections with northwest-trending structures (Mooney and Walton, 1980; Fig. 19).

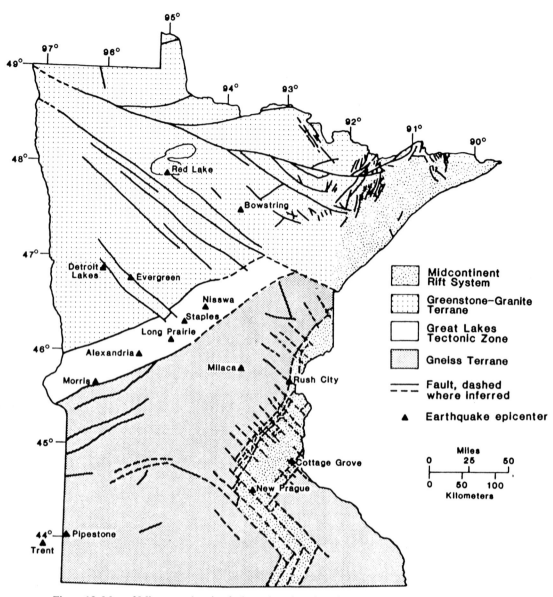

Figure 19. Map of Minnesota showing faults and earthquake epicenters (Mooney and Walton, 1980).

The Southwest and the relation between "eastern" and "western" seismicity

General structural control of the distribution of earthquakes in the west Texas–New Mexico region, which lies astride the southern Rocky Mountains front, is clear. Earthquakes are related to active faulting, and surface offsets have occurred during seismic events. This region also shows the mechanical relations between the northwest- and north-trending faults. Neotectonic structures grade from those in New Mexico that are typical of the western U.S. to features in south Texas characteristic of the east (Barosh, 1986a).

The earthquakes are related to a major northwest-trending system of faults along the Mexican border, the large north-trending Rio Grande Rift in New Mexico, and a lesser northeast-

trending fault zone, the Jemez lineament, that crosses the rift (Fig. 20). Together they control the position of the Rio Grande. The system of faults, referred to as the Texas lineament (Albritten and Smith, 1957), is a Precambrian zone that has been reactivated periodically (Dickerson, 1983; Muehlberger, 1980). It has numerous faults with Tertiary and Holocene offsets; some have moved during earthquakes (Dickerson, 1980, Muehlberger, 1980). The Rio Grande Rift is a prominent active rift valley with many normal faults. It extends northward from the Texas lineament across New Mexico and southern Colorado, just west of the Rocky Mountain front (Chapin, 1979). The rift is crossed in northern New Mexico by the northeast-trending Jemez lineament, a zone of Tertiary to Holocene volcanoes that has undergone recent faulting and some earthquakes (Aldrich and others, 1983, 1986).

The Rio Grande Rift began forming in Miocene time in response to extension accompanied by right-lateral strike-slip movement along the Texas lineament (Dickerson, 1980; Muehlberger, 1980). The Jemez lineament also began reactivating at this time with some extension, which facilitated the rise of volcanic fluids, and some small, left-lateral strike-slip movement (Aldrich and others, 1983).

This system of well-displayed structural trends and movements matches the trends and most movements known less perfectly in the eastern U.S. The Texas lineament plunges southeastward into and beneath the Rio Grande Embayment, which it apparently controls (Fig. 20). This, in turn, is aligned with a major transform fracture zone in the Gulf of Mexico. Thus, the general neotectonic features typically associated with western seismicity in New Mexico grade eastward to features near the Gulf that are typical of eastern seismicity. The structural controls appear to be the same: seismicity is distributed more widely along the more active features in the west and is concentrated more locally along the less active structures in the east. Eastern and western seismicity, therefore, vary in degree rather than kind. Appearances also vary as the relatively more active, northwest-trending structures parallel the West Coast and cross the East Coast. However, the difference in rate of attenuation remains, probably due to the average crustal thickness being greater in the east.

TECTONIC CONTROL

Neotectonic framework

Similar structural relations, thus, are found to account for the distribution of earthquakes and neotectonic movements in the seismically active areas across the eastern U.S. A compilation of these structures reveals an overall neotectonic framework that controls earthquakes in the region (Barosh, 1986c; Fig. 21). The framework consists of a rectilinear grid of northwest- and northeast-trending elements, with north-trending zones extending locally from, or lying between, the northwest-trending zones. Hobbs (1907) recognized such a pattern related to seismicity along the East Coast, and Bollinger (1973) noted the importance of vertical movement to part of it.

The north-trending fault zones are high-angle faults with known or probable extensional movement. Most northwest-trending zones appear to have strike-slip movement along them. Many appear to have right-lateral movement, but some may have left-lateral. In the Wichita zone, the Holocene movement along the Meers fault appears to be left-lateral (Donovan and others, 1983; Budnik, 1986), but farther to the northwest in Colorado the same zone appears to have right-lateral Holocene movement (Baars, 1979; Stevenson and Baars, 1981). Also, a few zones crossing the mid-Atlantic coast are aligned with transform fracture zones (Klitgord and Behrendt, 1979) that have evidence for left-lateral movement, as shown by the offset of the magnetic high along the continental shelf. Some faults reversed direction from left-lateral to right-lateral (Thomas, 1979). The principal

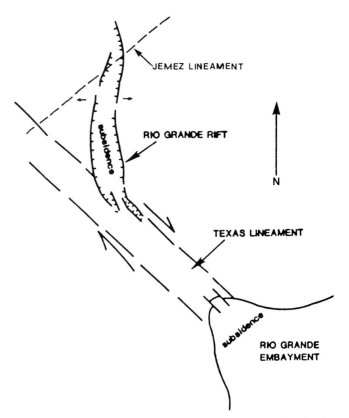

Figure 20. Sketch map of southwestern Texas and New Mexico showing relations of the principal neotectonic structures (Barosh, 1986a).

northwest-trending fault at Moodus, Connecticut, for example, had significant left-lateral movement early, but the latest may be right-lateral. Some also have vertical movement that controls the overlying embayments. The northwest-trending faults seen in the field in New England appear to have wide broken zones in regards to the amount of measurable offset.

Evidence for general movement along the northeast-trending zones is not as clear. Where areas are subsiding above normal faults, it would seem that these faults are again active. Faults in the uplifts, however, may be acting as minor hinges in broad arching without much movement. A few zones have evidence suggesting some left-lateral strike-slip movement (Baars, 1979; Aldrich and others, 1983), and perhaps a minor movement of this direction that occurred along the Appalachian Mountains during the Mesozoic (Ballard and Uchupi, 1975; Manspeizer, 1981) is still occurring. Possibly no great amount of offset is taking place. No post-Mesozoic movement along faults of this trend is known in New England. A few cut the Cretaceous coastal plain deposits farther south, but at least some of these are nontectonic gravity-growth faults (Hutchinson and Grow, 1985).

Stress

Earthquakes are the result of fault movement caused by the release of strain resulting from stress in the crust. The relative stress orientation of a region, therefore, can be determined by analysis of the type of movement and geometry of the active faults present. The maximum principal horizontal stress is found by this means to be fairly similar across the eastern U.S. It appears to be oriented approximately north-south, based mainly on the presence of north-trending extension faults, northwest-trending faults with mostly right-lateral strike-slip, and northeast-trending faults with possible left-lateral movement. Several local studies in New England and elsewhere in the midcontinent (Mollard, 1990) confirm this, and no other post-Mesozoic fault orien-

tations are indicated. The orientation of the maximum horizontal stress in the North Atlantic Basin is similar (N8°E, S8°W; Brian Tucholke, oral communication, 1989), and thus the intraplate stress realm is approximately the same from the Rocky Mountains to the central North Atlantic.

Stress at particular points can also be determined by the use of strain measurements in rock by overcoring and other methods. A synthesis of such data has been put forth as indicating the present-day stress orientation (Zoback and Zoback, 1980, 1981), but this is not a viable method (Barosh, 1986c). The hypothesis is

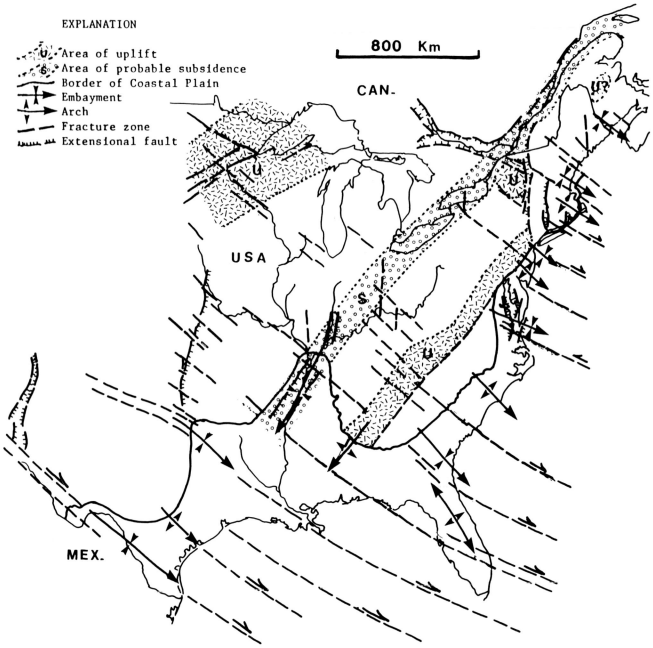

Figure 21. Map of the eastern U.S. and adjacent Canada showing selected neotectonic features (Barosh, 1986c).

based on the premise that the measured strain is a result of present-day stress, whereas it is a composite of the stress on the rock since its lithification. Where these are investigated in the northeast, they tend to agree with lower Paleozoic strain and apparently represent residual strain. In other areas, they are clearly contradictory to the strain indicated from active faulting. Also, like all point data, they have no significance unless integrated with the local geology and cannot be used as raw data. Local structures demonstrate that the orientation and kind of strain may vary greatly at any one time from place to place, even along a single active fault. The results of Zoback and Zoback (1980) do not correlate well with the structural movements associated with earthquakes, nor are there any indications of the existence of separate subrealms with different stress orientations, as they proposed. Where all the data are shown, there is a variety of inconsistent orientations. In any case, an interpreted stress direction derived from the strain has no meaning for earthquake-hazard evaluation unless the structures acted upon are known and a reason is given for the persistent local strain concentrations.

Basement tectonic control

Many of the fault zones associated with modern seismicity are known to have formed in the Precambrian, and many others may have also. This raises the prospect that selective reactivation of ancient structural zones may be controlling the present-day deformation (Barosh, 1986c; Hasegawa, 1986). A compilation and synthesis of basement fracture zones bears this out (Barosh, 1990a). Many of these zones have been discovered many times and in different ways that reflect on the influence of these zones through time. They have been noted in field mapping, studies of stratigraphic thickness and facies change, various geophysical investigations, remote sensing and geomorphic studies, studies of variations in the age and configuration of basement terranes, and other investigations. Several long basement fracture zones are indicated to cross the western and central United States (Cary, 1958, 1976; Maughan, 1966; King, 1975; Warner, 1978; Baars, 1979; Thomas, 1979). A number of others were indicated to cross the East Coast from studies of early Paleozoic strata (Thomas, 1981). Recently a number of these basement features were indicated to control basin development across Canada and the adjacent central U.S. (Sanford and others, 1985; Mollard, 1990). These and many other studies were utilized in compiling the data, leaving out a few east-west zones, as such zones do not appear to be active at present. The results show a system of fundamental fracture zones that have exerted a strong influence on the structural development of the eastern U.S. since the Precambrian (Fig. 22). Such zones commonly appear to consist of a number of faults and may have an enechelon arrangement.

The pattern of these basement fracture zones (Fig. 22) coincides with that of the neotectonic framework (Fig. 21) and demonstrates a close genetic relation. The present-day neotectonic movement and earthquakes thus appear to be controlled by reactivation of parts of a basement fracture system under the present-day stress field.

Crustal thickness

Large deep-seated fracture systems are of a site that may reflect changes in crustal thickness. The variation in crustal thickness in the eastern U.S. shows a good match not only with the positions of the basement fracture zones, but also with areas of neotectonic movement and sites of large earthquakes. The northeast-trending zones tend to parallel the major changes of crustal thickness in the eastern U.S., and the northwest-trending zones occur along smaller transverse changes in thickness (Fig. 23).

The northeast-trending belts of vertical movement have an inverse relation with the crustal thickness. The axial trends of the rising uplands match the axes of belts of relatively thicker crust and those of the subsiding lowlands the axes of thinner crust. These crustal features are the most prominent ones seen, just as the geomorphic expression of the mobile belts are the most prominent ones in the eastern U.S. The inverse relation is what would be expected from the structures that appear to control them. The extensional features along the Arkansas–St. Lawrence lowland have apparently resulted in a stretched and thinned crust. A local narrow subsiding zone across the southern Appalachian Mountains is also marked by thinner crust, suggesting some extension, as does a slightly broader transverse zone across central New England. Conversely, the Pascola arch overlies a narrow zone of thicker crust.

The sites of the major seismogenic areas show a correspondence with the major changes in crustal thickness. The upland earthquakes of the southern and central Appalachian Mountains lie along the axis of thicker crust there. Where the crust is thinner in New England, upland earthquakes are generally absent, but they appear again in the highlands of New Brunswick where the crust thickens again. Earthquakes of the Arkansas–St. Lawrence lowland occur along the axis of thinner crust, and the sites of the largest earthquakes in the east, New Madrid and La Malbaie, are near both ends, where cross-features lie. The two main earthquake areas on the East Coast, Charleston and Cape Ann, each with zones of earthquakes extending to the northwest, lie at the two northwest-trending zones of thinner crust shown to cross the Appalachian Mountains (Fig. 23). The only unusual area of thin crust without large earthquakes lies centered in southern Alabama, although the crustal warping is occurring there.

Intraplate movement

The pattern of neotectonic movement in the eastern U.S. is the same as that in the western North Atlantic Basin. Both are deforming together in a single system of intraplate movement resulting from crustal adjustments due to the continual opening of the North Atlantic Basin. The Mesozoic framework of the ocean basin mimics the essentially Precambrian structural framework on land. The rifting of the ocean basin closely followed the position of the late Precambrian collision boundary along the East Coast, and the transform fractures in the initial ocean basin ex-

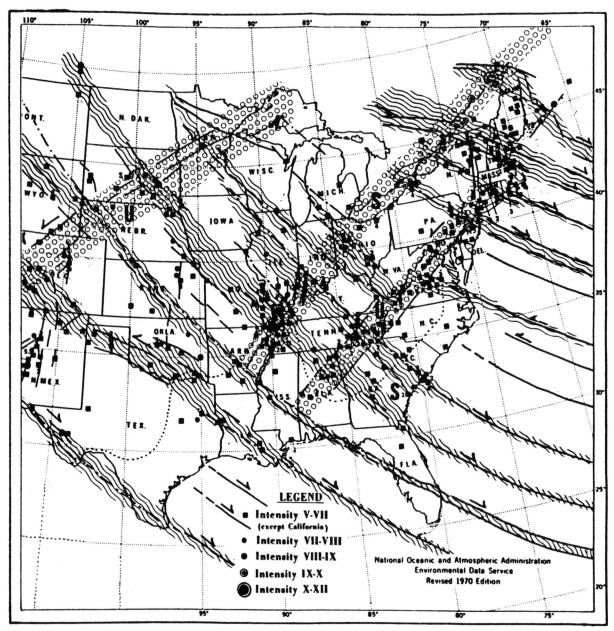

Figure 22. Map of the eastern U.S. showing earthquake epicenters (Coffman and others, 1982) and major basement fracture zones (modified from Barosh, 1990a).

tended seaward from the large transverse fracture zones on the continent (Wilson, 1965; Barosh, 1981a, 1990a; Bryan, 1986). Deformation associated with the transform fracture zones at sea occurs onshore along the older fractures; any movement affecting the longitudinal structure in the ocean basin may also affect parallel structures onshore. Thus, movements in the ocean basin and on land are tightly coupled.

Various kinds of movement have been hypothesized to affect the North Atlantic Basin, but the only well-documented movements are extension normal to the center of the basin and lateral movement along the transform fracture zones, plus some vertical movement between blocks bounded by major transform

zones. These are the same kinds of movement that satisfy the neotectonic movements onshore. Extensional movements that began in the Triassic along the Atlantic appear to have moved progressively inland, reaching the Arkansas–St. Lawrence zone by the Late Cretaceous. Rifting appears to have ended along the Atlantic Coast prior to the Late Cretaceous when northwest-trending embayments were well-established across the rifts. The formation of the embayments is apparently the result of differential vertical movement across the transforms and their landward counterparts. North-trending extensional faulting probably became active at this time also.

The change from northeast-trending rifts to the present

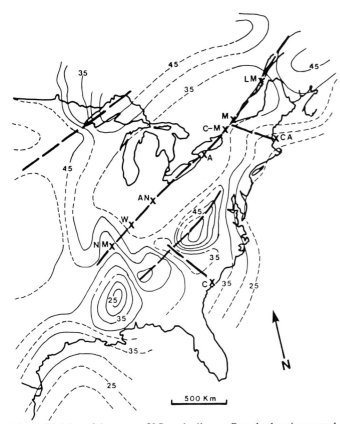

Figure 23. Map of the eastern U.S. and adjacent Canada showing crustal thickness in kilometers (dashed where very approximate) (Allenby and Schnetzler, 1983), the axes of principal zones of neotectonic movement, and major earthquake centers. NM, New Madrid; W, Wabash Valley; AN, Anna; A, Attica; C-M, Cornwall–Messena; M, Montreal, LM, La Malbaie; CA, Cape Ann; C, Charleston.

of appropriate structural intersections to release strain, or being too weak to store much strain for release as earthquakes.

The east-west extension across the plate may be due to subcrustal convection currents moving away from the Mid-Atlantic Ridge, or perhaps an overall southward movement of the plate that would stretch it over a wider portion of the Earth. There is evidence of a worldwide general pole-fleeing force operating, due to changes in rotation and precession of the Earth, which results in north-south compression and southward movement in the northern hemisphere (Taylor, 1910; Moody and Hill, 1956; Brown and others, 1972). The northward tilt of the eastern U.S. would be compatible with such a southward movement and convergence in the Caribbean.

EARTHQUAKE HAZARD

Once the seismogenic structures and cause of earthquakes are known, a proper assessment of the hazard posed by earthquakes can be made. The source zones can be delineated and a proper determination of the maximum credible earthquakes, along with the expected rate of activity, can be accomplished.

Earthquakes do not occur everywhere, but are controlled by specific local structural situations. Relations of earthquakes with faults in the east demonstrate that large amounts of strain can accumulate at structural intersections and not just along single fault zones. The general situation of strain buildup at intersecting structural zones is different from that on the West Coast, where longer segments of fault zones move, and calls for different approaches in evaluating it. The concept of "seismic gaps" to indi-

north-trending rifts, such as Lake Champlain, appears due to the rotation of the continent away from the North Atlantic Ridge as the ocean basin widened. The continent slowly rotated clockwise relative to the Mid-Atlantic Ridge as the basin opened, changing the originally north-trending rifting and west-trending transform zones to northeast- and northwest-trending zones, respectively (Cary, 1958; Fig. 24). The principal orientation, as seen today along the North Atlantic Ridge, remained essentially north-trending. The Triassic rifts along the Atlantic Coast thus rotated out of a favorable position with respect to the stress, and new north-trending extensional faults began to operate.

Continued widening of the North Atlantic Basin and east-west extension, with lateral adjustments along the northwest-trending transform fracture zones, can account for the seismicity in the eastern United States. Seismic activity is concentrated along zones of vertical movement related to the Atlantic margin, and earthquakes are concentrated at structural intersections on land just as they are along the North Atlantic Ridge where it is cut by the transform fracture zones. The intervening oceanic crust experiences few earthquakes, perhaps due to relatively uniform movement that does not build up local areas of high strain, lack

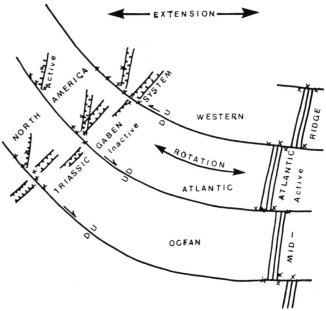

Figure 24. Diagrammatic sketch showing geometric relations between principal neotectonic elements of the western North Atlantic Basin and eastern North America, and their relation with the Triassic graben system and the location of earthquakes (X).

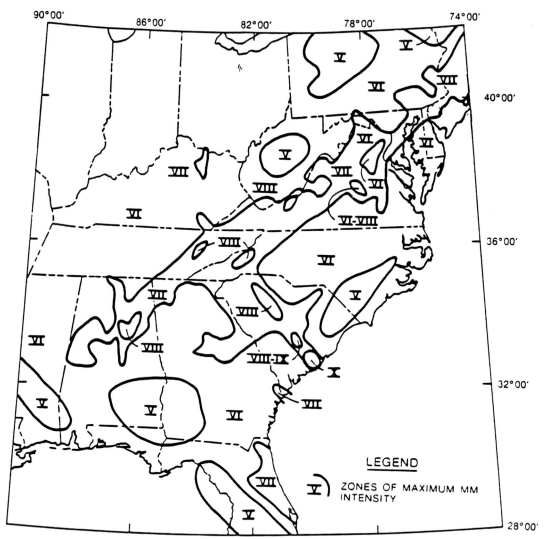

Figure 25. Earthquake zonation map of the southeastern U.S. (Barosh, 1986a). See Table 1 for explanation of values used.

cate areas of unrelieved strain with a potential for future large earthquakes does not apply to the East Coast. The main controlling structures are perpendicular to the coast and are separate rather than part of a single zone paralleling the coast. Even along single seismogenic zones in the eastern U.S., earthquakes do not occur everywhere, but may be restricted to structural intersections. Similarly, the use of fault length to estimate maximum credible earthquakes does not apply to zones that may be active only locally. The problem of surface rupture appears to be much less severe than in the west. Again, this is probably the result of strain release at intersections rather than along a single fault. The ratio between earthquake size and expected surface fault displacement needs to be scaled down for the East. Criteria for evaluating the hazard must be consistent with the nature of the seismogenic structures.

Earthquake zonation

Delineation of the seismogenic zones allows an earthquake zonation to be constructed on a scientific basis. A zonation of the eastern seaboard has been made by estimating the maximum credible earthquake, in terms of maximum expected epicentral intensity on firm ground, for each source area (Barosh, 1984, 1986a; Figs. 25 and 26). The maximum is estimated individually for each source zone and then compared to others in a similar tectonic environment. Most active areas have probably not experienced the maximum earthquake allowed for their tectonic situation, but some have in the 300-plus years of records for the region. These show up in a regional analysis and aid in setting limits. The zonation is in terms of intensity to reduce conversion errors and render it more useful. Most of the records are in terms

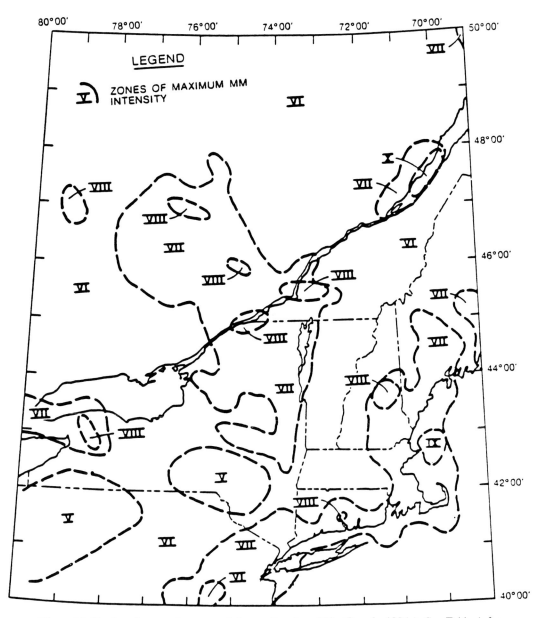

Figure 26. Earthquake zonation map of the northeastern U.S. (Barosh, 1986a). See Table 1 for explanation of values used.

of intensity, and the relation between intensity and magnitude along the East Coast is poorly known. The intensity values can be directly converted to ground-motion parameters (Krinitzsky and Chang, 1987).

SUMMARY AND CONCLUSIONS

Neotectonic movement in the United States east of the Rocky Mountains appears to be the superposition of at least four separate movements: a regional north tilt, a south tilt at the northern edge, broad northeast-trending belts of vertical movement, and local northwest-trending subsiding basins along the coastal plain. The former two show no spatial relation to the distribution of earthquakes and are aseismic; the first appears to be due to a general movement of the North American Plate, and the second to waning glacial rebound. The combination of the latter two movements matches the general distribution of earthquakes and is therefore directly related to their cause. These movements and their related earthquakes are structurally controlled. The northeast-trending belts are the rising uplands of the southern and central Appalachian Mountains and Mid-continent Arch, and the subsiding lowlands of the Atlantic Coastal Plain and the Arkansas–St. Lawrence lowland, which all parallel the Atlantic Coast. They are controlled by parallel fault systems that began by the

TABLE 1. VALUES USED IN FIGURES 25 AND 26 FOR MAXIMUM EPICENTRAL INTENSITY EXPECTED ON FIRM GROUND IN SEISMIC SOURCE ZONES IN THE EASTERN UNITED STATES

Value	Explanation
V	Areas of no known earthquakes. Generalized boundaries avoid large known or suspected fracture zones, but otherwise not drawn on geological basis. The level chosen at V because rapid freezing may produce this intensity locally in the northern half of the area.
VI	Areas that have experienced only scattered intensity V earthquakes. Most of the area is considered to rate at intensity V level, but it contains local, more active areas with potential for VI (might separate with more detailed zonation).
VII	Areas with identifiable clusters of earthquakes forming a seismic zone that has experienced only intensity VI and probably has potential for intensity VII in general vicinity of the experienced VI, or areas where an experienced intensity VII is the estimated maximum. Boundaries related to geologic features and generally drawn on them, but modified locally to conform to earthquake distribution.
VIII	Areas with clusters of epicenters within a seismic zone with an experienced intensity of or near VII, or areas where an experienced intensity VIII is the estimated maximum. Where near (intensity VII changed to VI by recent reevaluations), the areas have geologic environments similar to other areas with an experienced VIII. Related to geologic source zone and boundaries generalized around source zone and related earthquakes.
IX	Areas with cluster of epicenters within a seismic zone with an experienced intensity of VIII. Probably approaching limit of strain buildup in areas of shallow earthquakes. Related to geologic source zone and boundaries generalized around source zone and related earthquakes.
X	Areas with clusters of numerous epicenters within a seismic zone with an experienced intensity of IX or X. Probable limit of strain buildup on the U.S. East Coast. Related to geologic source zone and boundaries generalized around source zone and related earthquakes.

late Precambrian. The lowland structures are characterized by grabens and normal faults. The present vertical movements started on the East Coast in the Triassic and moved progressively inland, reaching the midcontinent at the end of the Cretaceous.

The northwest-trending coastal basins, referred to as embayments, are controlled by downdropped basement blocks bounded by ancient northwest-trending faults onshore, which continue seaward as transform fracture zones. The basins were established by Late Cretaceous time along the shoreline as it existed then. Structures controlling the basins continue inland, and their intersections with the northeast-trending belts form the most seismically active segments of these belts. Thus, the spacing of the active basins on the Atlantic Coast matches that of the most active areas along the Arkansas–St. Lawrence lowland.

The structure of individual earthquake source areas varies greatly from one to another, but the controlling faults are in decreasing order of activity, northwest-trending faults with mainly lateral movement, north-trending extensional faults, and northeast-trending high-angle faults. Most of the activity is concentrated at structural intersections. Northwest-trending faults seem to dominate. North-trending ones appear to extend from them and be due to the same crustal movement, and northeast-trending faults are active primarily where crossed by them.

This neotectonic framework of earthquake-related movements and associated structures forms a regional rectilinear grid pattern of northwest and northeast elements. These structural

elements appear to reflect portions of Precambrian basement fracture zones, which have been selectively reactivated under the present stress field. These large basement structures are reflected in changes in crustal thickness. The general variation in crustal thickness shows a close inverse relation with the northeast-trending belts of vertical movement and indicates the sites of the larger earthquakes are in subsiding areas with thinner, and therefore stretched, crusts. The northwest-trending zones show up as transverse irregularities in this pattern. The two main sites of earthquakes on the coast, Charleston and Cape Ann, are marked by transverse zones of thinner crust. The principal seismogenic areas to the west, New Madrid and La Malbaie, also occur where transverse changes occur along the axis of a northeast-trending belt of thinner crust.

The structural movements causing the earthquakes are closely related to those involved in the continued opening of the North Atlantic Basin. Eastern North America and the western North Atlantic Basin deform together in a single system of intraplate movement affected by approximately east-west extension, and north-south orientation of maximum compressive stress.

Understanding the causative relation of earthquakes to neotectonic deformation and structure allows the earthquake hazard to be assessed on a scientific basis. The source areas can be delineated and maximum credible earthquakes calculated for tectonically similar sources to produce useful earthquake zonation maps. The seismogenic sources in the East arising from structural intersections need to be evaluated differently from those in the West that occur more along single fault zones. The concept of "seismic gap" does not apply along the East Coast, in general, because different structural zones control the different sources along the coast. Even along the same structural zone it does not apply because the active areas lie at intersections rather than occurring everywhere. Similarly, the use of fault length cannot be used to estimate the maximum credible earthquake for a zone. In addition, surface fault rupture is less likely in the east because the activity at intersections may keep the strain from building up as much as in a single fault. Further improvement in the assessment of earthquake hazards will follow increased understanding of their geologic controls.

ACKNOWLEDGMENTS

This chapter draws heavily on the work of participants in the various seismotectonic studies, particularly that in the northeastern U.S., which the author directed. I especially wish to thank the directors of the other studies: T. C. Buschbach, F. W. Wilson, and K. V. Luza for their aid, and also M. H. Pease, Jr., for the valuable help in New England. This work was funded by the U.S. Nuclear Regulatory Commission and the U.S. Army Corps of Engineers.

REFERENCES CITED

Adams, J., 1981, Postglacial faulting; A literature survey of occurrences in eastern Canada and comparable glaciated areas: Atomic Energy of Canada Limited Report TR-142, 63 p.

Albritten, D. D., Jr., and Smith, J. F., Jr., 1957, The Texas lineament: International Geological Congress Proceedings, Mexico City, section 5, p. 501–518 (1961).

Aldrich, M. J., Jr., Ander, M. E., and Laughlin, A. W., 1983, Geological and geophysical signatures of the Jemez lineament; A reactivated Precambrian structure, *in* Gabrielsen, R. H., and others, eds., Proceedings 4th International Conference on Basement Tectonics: Salt Lake City, Utah, International Basement Tectonics Association, p. 77–85.

Aldrich, M. J., Jr., Ander, M. E., Laughlin, A. W., Meade, J. S., and Pierce, H. W., 1986, The Jemez lineament's structural boundaries and control of sedimentary facies, tectonism, and mineralization, *in* Aldrich, M. J., Jr., and Laughlin, A. W., eds., Proceedings 6th International Conference on Basement Tectonics: Salt Lake City, Utah, International Basement Tectonic Association, p. 104–113.

Allenby, R. J., and Schnetzler, C. C., 1983, United States crustal thickness: Tectonophysics, v. 93, p. 13–31.

Atwood, W. W., 1940, The physiographic provinces of North America: Boston and New York, Ginn and Co., 336 p.

Baars, D. L., 1979, The Colorado Plateau aulacogen; Key to continental scale basement rifting, *in* Podwysocky, M. H., and Earle, J. L., eds., Proceedings 2nd International Conference on Basement Tectonics: Denver, Colorado, Basement Tectonics Committee Inc., Publication 2, p. 157–164.

Bagwell, J. B., 1981, An isoseismal study of September 1, 1980, Summersville, South Carolina, earthquake: Earthquake Notes, v. 52, no. 3, p. 8.

Ballard, R. D., and Uchupi, E., 1975, Triassic rift structure in Gulf of Maine: American Association of Petroleum Geologists Bulletin, v. 59, p. 1041–1072.

Barnett, S. G., and Isachsen, Y. W., 1980, The application of Lake Champlain water level studies to the investigation of Adirondack and Lake Champlain crustal movements: Vermont Geology, v. 1, p. 5–11.

Barosh, P. J., 1969, Use of seismic intensity data to predict the effects of earthquakes and underground nuclear explosions in various geologic settings: U.S. Geological Survey Bulletin 1279, 93 p.

—— , 1979, Earthquake zonation in the northeastern United States: American Society of Civil Engineers Preprint 3602, 22 p.

—— , 1980, Relationship of earthquakes with vertical crustal movements in the eastern United States and adjacent Canada: Earthquake Notes, v. 51, no. 3, p. 10, and Seismological Society of America Eastern Section Annual Meeting, State College, Pennsylvania, Abstracts with Program, p. 5.

—— , 1981a, Cause of seismicity in the eastern United States; A preliminary appraisal, *in* Beavers, J. E., ed., Earthquakes and earthquake engineering:

The eastern United States: Ann Arbor Science, v. 1, p. 397–417.

—— , 1981b, The Penobscot lineament, Maine, *in* O'Leary, D. W., and Earle, J. L., eds., Proceedings 3rd International Conference on Basement Tectonics: Denver, Colorado, Basement Tectonics Committee Publication 3, p. 119–135, and *in* U.S. Nuclear Regulatory Commission Report NUREG/CR-2291, 36 p.

—— , 1981c, Seismicity and tectonics in the Passamaquoddy Bay area, Maine and New Brunswick: Geological Society of America Abstracts with Programs, v. 13, p. 122.

—— , 1983, Use of seismicity and tectonic fraamework to define the seismic hazard in the region encompassing Charleston, South Carolina, *in* Hayes, W. W., and Gori, P. L., eds., A workshop on "The 1886 Charleston, South Carolina, earthquake and its implications for today": U.S. Geological Survey Open-File Report 83-843, p. 380–390.

—— , 1984, Earthquake zonation of the eastern United States: 27th Annual Meeting of the Association of Engineering Geologists Abstracts and Program, p. 45.

—— , 1985, Earthquake controls and zonation in New York: U.S. Geological Survey Open-File Report 85-836, p. 54–75.

—— , 1986a, Seismic source zones of the eastern U.S. and seismic zoning of the Atlantic seaboard and Appalachian regions, *in* State-of-the-art for assessing earthquake hazards in the United States: U.S. Army Corps of Engineers Waterways Experiment Station Miscellaneous Paper Report 21, 287 p.

—— , 1986b, Summary and analysis of the 1982 Gaza, New Hampshire, earthquake, *in* Krinitzsky, E. L., and Dunbar, J., Geological-seismological evaluation of earthquake hazards at Franklin Falls dam, New Hampshire: U.S. Army Corps of Engineers Waterway Experiment Station Technical Report GL-86-16, appendix C, p. C1–C75.

—— , 1986c, Neotectonic movement, earthquakes, and stress state in the eastern United States: Tectonophysics, v. 132, no. 1-3, p. 117–152.

—— , 1986d, An evaluation of earthquakes and active faults in the area of the Sebago Lake Batholith, Maine, and the hazard they pose to a high-level radioactive waste facility located there: Lakes Environmental Association unpublished report, 23 p.

—— , 1990a, Intraplate tectonic movement and earthquake hazards in the United States, *in* State-of-the-art for assessing earthquake hazards in the United States: U.S. Army Corp of Engineers Waterways Experiment Station Miscellaneous Paper Report 86 (in press).

—— , 1990b, Northwest-trending basement fracture zones in the eastern United States and their role in controlling neotectonic movement and earthquakes, *in* Baars, D. L., ed., Proceedings 6th International Conference on Basement Tectonics: Denver, Colorado, Basement Tectonics Committee, Inc., Publication 6 (in press).

Barosh, P. J., Pease, M. H., Jr., Schnabel, R. W., Bell, K. G., and Peper, J. P.,

1977, Aeromagnetic lineament map of southern New England showing relation of lineaments to bedrock geology: U.S. Geological Survey Miscellaneous Field Studies Map MF-885, scale 1:250,000.

Barosh, P. J., London, D., and de Boer, J., 1982, The structural geology of the Moodus seismic area, south-central Connecticut, *in* Joesten, R., and Quarrier, S. S., eds., Guidebook for fieldtrips in Connecticut and south-central Massachusetts; 74th Annual Meeting, New England Intercollegiate Geological Conference, University of Connecticut: Connecticut Geological and Natural History Survey Guidebook 5, p. 419–452.

Behrendt, J. C., Hamilton, R. M., Ackerman, H. D., and Henry, V. J., 1981, Cenozoic faulting in the vicinity of the Charleston, South Carolina, 1886 earthquake: Geology, v. 9, p. 117.

Behrendt, J. C., Hamilton, R. M., Ackerman, H. D., Henry, V. J., and Bayer, K. C., 1983, Marine multichannel seismic-reflection evidence for Cenozoic faulting and deep crustal structure near Charleston, South Carolina: U.S. Geological Survey Professional Paper 1313-J, 29 p.

Berendsen, P., Wilson, F. W., Yarger, H. L., and Steeples, D. W., 1981, New data on major basement fractures in the tectonic development of eastern Kansas, *in* O'Leary, D. W., and Earle, J. L., eds., Proceedings 3rd International Conference on Basement Tectonics: Denver, Colorado, Basement Tectonics Committee, Inc., Publication 3, p. 227–240.

Black, D.F.B., 1986, Basement faulting in Kentucky, *in* Aldrich, M. J., Jr., and Laughlin, A. W., eds., Proceedings 6th International Conference on Basement Tectonics: Salt Lake City, Utah, International Basement Tectonics Association, p. 125–139.

Block, J. W., Clement, R. C., Lew, L. R., and de Boer, J., 1979, Recent thrust faulting in southeastern Connecticut: Geology, v. 7, p. 79–82.

Bollinger, G. A., 1973, Seismicity and crustal uplift in the southeastern United States: American Journal of Science, v. 273-A, p. 396–408.

—— , 1983, Speculations on the nature of seismicity at Charleston, South Carolina: U.S. Geological Survey Professional Paper 1313-T, 11 p.

Bollinger, G. A., and Visvanathan, T. R., 1977, The seismicity of South Carolina prior to 1886: U.S. Geological Survey Professional Paper 1028-C, p. 33–42.

Bollinger, G. A., and Wheeler, R. L., 1983, The Giles County, Virginia, seismic zone: Science, v. 219, p. 1063–1065.

Boston Edison Co., 1976, Summary report geologic and seismologic investigations; Boston Edison Company Pilgrim Unit: Boston Edison Co. BE-SG7602, 185 p.

Bristol, H. M., and Treworgy, J. D., 1979, The Wabash fault system in southeastern Illinois: Illinois State Geological Survey Division Circular 509, 19 p.

Brown, L D., 1978, Recent vertical crustal movement along the east coast of the United States: Tectonophysics, v. 44, p. 205–231.

Brown, L. P., and Reilinger, R. E., 1986, Epeirogenic and intraplate movements, *in* National Research Council, Active tectonics: Washington, D.C., National Academy Press, p. 30–44.

Brown, P. M., Miller, J. A., and Swain, F. M., 1972, Structural and stratigraphic framework, and spatial distribution of permeability of the Atlantic Coastal Plain, North Carolina to New York: U.S. Geological Survey Professional Paper 796, 79 p.

Bryan, W. B., 1986, Tectonic controls on initial continental rifting and the evolution of young ocean basins; A planetary perspective: Tectonophysics, v. 132, p. 103–115.

Budnik, R. T., 1985, Tectonic history of the Amarillo–Wichita uplift and its bearing on recent deformation along the Meers fault: Earthquake Notes, v. 55, no. 1, p. 2.

—— , 1986, Left-lateral intraplate deformation along the ancestral Rocky Mountains; Implications for late Paleozoic plate motions: Tectonophysics, v. 132, p. 195–214.

Buschbach, T. C., 1980, New Madrid seismotectonic study activities during fiscal year 1979: U.S. Nuclear Regulatory Commission Report NUREG/CR-0977, 149 p.

Carey, S. W., 1958, The tectonic approach to continental drift, *in* Carey, S. W., ed., Continental drift; A symposium: Hobart, Tasmania University Geological Department, p. 177–355.

—— , 1976, The expanding Earth; Developments in geotectonics: Amsterdam, Elsevier Science Publication Co., no. 10, p. 377–380.

Chapin, C. E., 1979, Evaluation of the Rio Grande Rift; A summary, *in* Riecker, R. E., ed., Rio Grande Rift; Tectonics and magmatism: Washington, D.C., American Geophysical Union, p. 1–5.

Chiburis, E. F., 1981, Seismicity, recurrence rates, and regionalization of the northeastern United States and adjacent southeastern Canada: U.S. Nuclear Regulatory Commission Report NUREG/CR 2309, 76 p.

Chowns, T. M., and Williams, C. T., 1983, Pre-Cretaceous rocks beneath the Georgia Coastal Plain; Regional implications: U.S. Geological Survey Professional Paper 1313-L, 42 p.

Coffman, J. L., von Hake, C. A., and Stover, C. W., eds., 1982, Earthquake history of the United States: U.S. National Oceanic and Atmospheric Administration Publication 41-1, revised with supplement, 208 p., supplement 50 p.

Cohee, G. W., chairman, 1961, Tectonic map of the United States: U.S. Geological Survey, scale 1:2,500,000.

Cole, G. A., Prozd, R. J., Sedivy, R. A., and Halpern, H. I., 1987, Organic geochemistry and oil-source correlations, Paleozoic of Ohio: American Association of Petroleum Geologists Bulletin, v. 71, p. 788–809.

Collins, M. P., 1927, The New Hampshire earthquakes of November 9, 1936, and further data on New England travel times: Bulletin of the Seismological Society of America, v. 27, p. 99–107.

Dale, T. N., 1907, The granites of Maine, *with an Introduction by* G. O. Smith: U.S. Geological Survey Bulletin 313, 202 p.

Dames and Moore, 1978, Geologic investigation, Nine Mile Point nuclear station unit 2: Niagara Mohawk Corp. Report, Docket no. 50-410, v. 2, sec. 2.0.

Daniels, D. L., Zietz, I., and Popenoe, P., 1983, Distribution of subsurface lower Mesozoic rocks in the southeastern United States as interpreted from regional aeromagnetic and gravity maps: U.S. Geological Survey Professional Paper 1313-K, 24 p.

Dean, S. L., Kulander, B. R., and Williams, R. E., 1979, Regional tectonics, systematic fractures, and photolinears in southeastern West Virginia, *in* Podwysocki, M. H., and Earle, J. L., eds., Proceedings 2nd International Conference on Basement Tectonics: Denver, Colorado, International Basement Tectonics Committee, Inc., p. 10–53.

Dickas, A. B., 1986, Comparative Precambrian stratigraphy and structure along the Mid-continent Rift: American Association of Petroleum Geologists Bulletin, v. 70, p. 225–235.

Dickerson, P. W., 1980, Structural zones transecting the southern Rio Grande Rift; Preliminary observations, *in* Dickerson, P. W., and Hoffer, J. M., eds., Trans Pecos region, southeastern New Mexico, and West Texas: 31st New Mexico Geological Society Field Conference Guidebook, p. 63–70.

—— , 1983, Evidence for basement control of structural zones transected by the southern Rio Grande Rift, *in* Gabrielsen, R. H., and others, eds., Proceedings 4th International Conference on Basement Tectonics: Salt Lake City, Utah, International Basement Tectonics Association Publication 4, p. 103–114.

Donovan, R. N., Gilbert, M. C., Luza, K. V., Marchini, D., and Sanderson, D., 1983, Possible Quaternary movement on the Meers Fault, southwestern Oklahoma: Oklahoma Geological Notes, v. 43, p. 124–133.

Dubois, S. M., 1978, The origin of surface lineaments in Nemaha County, Kansas: U.S. Nuclear Regulatory Commission Report NUREG/CR-0321, 50 p.

Durham, C. O., Jr., and Murray, G. E., 1967, Tectonism of Atlantic and Gulf Coastal Province: American Journal of Science, v. 265, p. 428–441.

Dutch, S. I., 1981, Post-Cretaceous vertical motions in the eastern midcontinent, USA: Zeitschrift fur Geomorphologie, v. 40, p. 13–25.

Ebel, J. E., 1984, Statistical aspects of New England seismicity from 1975 to 1982 and implications for the past and future earthquake activity: Bulletin of the Seismological Society of America, v. 74, p. 1311–1329.

Ervin, C. P., and McGinnis, L. D., 1975, Reactivated precursor to the Mississippi embayment: Geological Society of America Bulletin, v. 86, p. 1287–1295.

Fakundiny, R. H., 1981, Basement tectonics and seismicity in New York State: Geological Society of America Abstracts with Programs, v. 13, p. 132.

Farrand, W. R., 1962, Post glacial uplift in North America: American Journal of

Science, v. 260, p. 181–199.

Feinstein, S., 1981, Subsidence and thermal history of southern Oklahoma aulacogen; Implications for petroleum exploration: American Association of Petroleum Geologists Bulletin, v. 65, p. 2521–2533.

Feld, J., 1966, Rock movements from load release in excavated cuts, *in* Proceedings 1st International Congress of the Society for Rock Mechanics, Lisbon, 1966: Pergamon, Oxford, p. 139–140.

Flint, R. F., 1963, Glacial and Pleistocene geology: New York, John Wiley and Sons, Inc., 553 p.

Foley, J. E., Doll, C., Filipkowski, F., and Lorsbach, G., 1985, Seismicity of the northeastern United States January 01–March 31, 1984: Chestnut Hill, Massachusetts, Boston College, Western Observatory Northeastern U.S. Seismic Network Bulletin 34, 43 p.

Fuller, M. L., 1912, The New Madrid earthquake: U.S. Geological Survey Bulletin 494, 119 p.

Geraghty, E. P., and Isachsen, Y. W., 1981, Investigation of the McGregor–Saratoga–Ballston Lake fault system east-central New York: U.S. Nuclear Regulatory Commission Report NUREG/CR-1866, 44 p.

Graham, T., 1979, A study of fault plane solutions for six New England earthquakes [M.S. thesis]: Storrs, University of Connecticut, 97 p.

Graham, T., and Chiburis, E. F., 1980, Fault plane solutions and state of stress in New England: Earthquake Notes, v. 51, no. 2, p. 3–12.

Hadley, J. B., and Devine, J. F., 1974, Seismotectonic map of the eastern United States: U.S. Geological Survey Miscellaneous Field Studies Map MF-620, scale 1:5,000,000.

Ham, W. E., Denison, E. E., and Merritt, C. A., 1964, Basement rocks and structural evolution of southern Oklahoma: Oklahoma Geological Survey Bulletin 95, 203 p.

Hasegawa, H. S., 1986, Seismotectonics in eastern Canada; An overview with emphasis on the Charlevoix and Miramichi regions: Earthquake Notes, v. 57, p. 83–94.

Herrmann, R. B., 1980, A seismological study of the northern extent of the New Madrid seismic zone, *in* Buschbach, T. C., New Madrid seismotectonic study activities during fiscal year 1979: U.S. Nuclear Regulatory Commission Report NUREG/CR-0977, p. 126–136.

Heyl, A. V., and Brock, M. R., 1961, Structural framework of the Illinois–Kentucky mining district and its relation to mineral deposits, *in* Geological Survey Research, 1961: U.S. Geological Survey Professional Paper 424-D, p. D3–D6.

Heyl, A. V. and McKeown, F. A., 1978, Preliminary seismotectonic map of the central Mississippi Valley and environs: U.S. Geological Survey Miscellaneous Field Studies Map MF-1011, scale 1:250,000.

Hildenbrand, T. G., and others, 1977, Magnetic and gravity anomalies in the northern Mississippi embayment and their spatial relation to seismicity: U.S. Geological Survey Miscellaneous Field Studies Map MF-914, scale 1:1,000,000.

Hobbs, W. H., 1901, The river system of Connecticut: Journal of Geology, v. 10, p. 469–484.

—— , 1907, Earthquakes; An introduction to seismic geology: New York, D. Appleton and Co., 336 p.

Holdahl, S. R., and Morrison, N. L., 1974, Regional investigations of vertical crustal movements in the U.S. using precise relevelings and mareograph data: Tectonophysics, v. 23, p. 373–390.

Hunt, A. S., and Dowling, J. J., 1981, Geophysical investigations of Lake Champlain, *in* Barosh, P. J., ed., New England seismotectonic study activities during fiscal year 1979: U.S. Nuclear Regulatory Commission Report NUREG/CR-2131, p. 46–54.

Hutchinson, D. R., and Grow, J. A., 1985, New York Bight fault: Geological Society of America Bulletin, v. 96, p. 975–989.

Isachsen, Y. W., 1975, Possible evidence for contemporary doming of the Adirondack Mountains, New York, and suggested implications for regional tectonics and seismicity: Tectonophysics, v. 29, p. 169–181.

Isachsen, Y. W., and Geraghty, E. P., 1979, Ground investigations of projected traces of focal mechanisms for earthquakes at Blue Mountain Lake, Raquette

Lake, and Chazy Lake, Adirondack Uplift, New York: U.S. Nuclear Regulatory Commission Report NUREG/CR-0888, 33 p.

Johnson, D., 1925, The New England–Acadian shoreline: New York and London, Hafner Publication Co., 608 p.

Johnson, R. W., Jr., and Milton, C., 1955, Dike rock of central western Virginia: Geological Society of America Bulletin, v. 66, p. 1689–1690.

Johnston, A. C., 1982, A major earthquake zone on the Mississippi: Scientific American, v. 246, no. 4, p. 60–68.

Kane, M. F., 1977, Correlation of major eastern earthquake center with mafic/ultramafic basement masses: U.S. Geological Survey Professional Paper 1028-O, p. 199–204.

Kaye, C. A., and Barghoorn, E. S., 1964, Quaternary sea-level change and crustal rise at Boston, Massachusetts, with notes on the autocompaction of peat: Geological Society of America Bulletin, v. 75, p. 63–80.

Keith, A., 1923, Outlines of Appalachian structure: Geological Society of America Bulletin, v. 34, p. 309.

King, P. B., 1975, Ancient southern margin of North America: Geology, v. 3, p. 732–734.

King, P. B., and Beikman, H. M., compilers, 1974, Geologic map of the United States: U.S. Geological Survey, scale 1:2,500,000.

Klitgord, K. D., and Behrendt, J. C., 1979, Basin structure of the U.S. Atlantic margin, *in* Watkins, J. S., Mondedert, L., and Dickerson, P. W., eds., Geological and geophysical investigations of continental margins: American Association of Petroleum Geologists Memoir 29, p. 85–112.

Klitgord, K. D., Dillon, W. P., and Popenoe, P., 1983, Mesozoic tectonics of the southeastern United States Coastal Plain and continental margin: U.S. Geological Survey Professional Paper 1313-P, 15 p.

Krinitzsky, E. L., and Chang, F. K., 1987, Parameters for specifying intensity-related earthquake ground motions, *in* State-of-the-art for assessing earthquake hazards in the United States: U.S. Army Corps of Engineers Waterways Experiment Station Miscellaneous Paper S-73-1, Report 25, 43 p., appendix 41 p.

Kumarapeli, P. S., 1978, The St. Lawrence paleo-rift system; A comparative study, *in* Ramberg, I. B., and Neumann, E. R., eds., Tectonics and geophysics of continental rifts: Holland, Reidel Publication Co., p. 367–384.

—— , 1986, Iapetan aulacogens and fracture zones in the Canadian Shield, *in* Riad, S., and Baars, D. L., eds., Proceedings 5th International Conference on Basement Tectonics: Salt Lake City, Utah, International Basement Tectonics Association Publication 5, p. 235–243.

Kumarapeli, P. S., and Saull, V. A., 1966, The St. Lawrence Valley system; A North American equivalent to the East African rift valley system: Canadian Journal of Earth Sciences, v. 3, p. 639–659.

Larsen, F. D., 1987, Glacial Lake Hitchcock in the valleys of the White and Ottauquechee Rivers, east-central Vermont, *in* Westerman, D. S., ed., Guidebook for field trips in Vermont, v. 2: Montpelier, Vermont, 79th Annual Meeting, New England Intercollegiate Geological Conference, p. 30–52.

Lawson, J. E., Jr., Dubois, R. L., Foster, P. H., and Luza, K. V., 1979, Earthquake map of Oklahoma: Oklahoma Geological Survey Map GM-19, scale 1:750,000.

Leblanc, G., Stevens, A. E., Wetmiller, R. J., and others, 1973, A microearthquake survey of the St. Lawrence valley near La Malbaie, Quebec: Canadian Journal of Earth Sciences, v. 10, no. 1, p. 42–53.

Leet, L. D., and Linehan, D., 1942, Instrumental study of the New Hampshire earthquakes of December 1940: Bulletin of the Seismological Society of America, v. 32, no. 1, p. 75–82.

Long, L. T., and Champion, J. W., Jr., 1977, Bouger gravity map of the Summerville–Charleston, South Carolina, epicentral zone and tectonic implications: U.S. Geological Survey Professional Paper 1028-K, p. 150–166.

Luza, K. V., and Lawson, J. E., Jr., 1982, Seismicity and tectonic relationships of the Nemaha uplift in Oklahoma: Oklahoma Geological Survey Special Publication 82-1, 52 p.

Manspeizer, W., 1981, Early Mesozoic basins of the central Atlantic passive margins, *in* Geology of passive continental margins; History, structure, and sedimentologic record, with special emphasis on the Atlantic margin: American Association of Petroleum Geologists Educational Course Note Series 19, p. 4-1–4-60.

Maroney, D. G., and Burchett, R. R., 1979, A detailed geophysical investigation of western Richardson and eastern Pawnee Counties in southeastern Nebraska, *in* Regional tectonics and seismicity of eastern Nebraska, Annual Report June 1977-May 1978: U.S. Nuclear Regulatory Commission Report NUREG/CR-0876, p. 19–54.

Maughan, E. K., 1966, Environment of deposition of Permian salt in the Williston and Alliance Basins, *in* Second Symposium on Salt: Northern Ohio Geological Society, p. 35–47.

McGee, W. J., 1982, A fossil earthquake: Geological Society of America Bulletin, v. 4, p. 411–414.

McHone, J. G., 1987, Cretaceous intrusions and rift features in the Champlain Valley of Vermont, *in* Westerman, D. S., ed., Guidebook for field trips in Vermont, v. 2; 79th Annual Meeting New England Intercollegiate Geological Conference: Norwich University, Department of Earth Sciences, p. 237–253.

McKenzie, D. P., 1969, The relation between fault plane solutions for earthquakes and directions of the principal stresses: Bulletin of the Seismological Society of America, v. 59, p. 591–601.

McMaster, R. L., de Boer, J., and Collins, B. P., 1980, Tectonic development of southern Narragansett Bay and offshore Rhode Island: Geology, v. 8, p. 496–500.

Meade, B. K., 1971, Report of the sub-commission of recent crustal movements in North America, *in* Recent crustal movements, Symposium 15, 15th General Assembly of the International Union of Geodesy and Geophysics International Association of Geodesy, Moscow, 28 p.

Metcalf, T. P., 1982, Intraplate tectonics of the Appalachians in post-Triassic time [M.S. thesis]: Middleton, Connecticut, Wesleyan University, 238 p.

Miller, J. A., 1982, Geology and configuration of the base of the Tertiary limestone aquifer system, southeastern United States: U.S. Geological Survey Open-File Report 81-1176, scale 1:1,000,000.

Mollard, V. D., 1990, Fracture lineament research and applications on the Canadian Prairies: Canadian Geotechnical Society, 41 p. (in press).

Moody, J. P., and Hill, M. J., 1956, Wrench-fault tectonics: Geological Society of America Bulletin, v. 67, p. 1207–1246.

Mooney, H. M., and Walton, M., 1980, Seismicity and tectonic relationships for upper Great Lakes Precambrian Shield province: U.S. Nuclear Regulatory Commission Report NUREG/CR-1569, 85 p.

Muehlberger, W. R., 1980, Texas lineament revisited, *in* Dickerson, P. W., and Hoffer, J. M., eds., Trans-Pecos region, southeastern New Mexico and west Texas: New Mexico Geological Society 31st Field Conference Guidebook, p. 113–121.

Nottis, G. N., and Mitronovas, W., 1983, Documentation of the felt earthquakes in the Coastal Plain of southeastern New York and east-central New Jersey; 1847–1954: U.S. Nuclear Regulatory Commission Report NRC B 5961, 74 p.

Nuttli, O. W., 1973a, Seismic wave attenuation and magnitude relations for eastern North America: Journal of Geophysical Research, v. 78, no. 5, p. 876.

——, 1973b, The Mississippi Valley earthquakes of 1811 and 1812; Intensities, ground motion, and magnitudes: Bulletin of the Seismological Society of America, v. 63, p. 231.

Officer, C. B., and Drake, C. L., 1982, Epeirogenic plate movements: Journal of Geology, v. 90, p. 139–153.

O'Leary, D. W., and Hildenbrand, T. G., 1981, Structural significance of lineament and aeromagnetic patterns in the Mississippi embayment, *in* O'Leary, D. W., and Earle, J. L., eds., Proceedings 3rd International Conference on Basement Tectonics: Salt Lake City, Utah, International Basement Tectonic Committee, p. 305–313.

Page, R. A., Molnar, P. H., and Oliver, J., 1968, Seismicity in the vicinity of the Ramapo fault, New Jersey–New York: Bulletin of the Seismological Society of America, v. 58, p. 681–687.

Pavlides, L., 1981, The central Virginia volcanic–plutonic belt; An island arc of Cambrian(?) age: U.S. Geological Survey Professional Paper 1231-A, 34 p.

Pulli, J. J., and Toksoz, M. N., 1981, Fault plane solutions for northeastern United States earthquakes: Bulletin of the Seismological Society of America, v. 71, p. 1875–1882.

Putnam, G. W., Young, J. R., and Willems, H. T., 1983, Preliminary study of possible fault displacements of Holocene age near Saratoga Springs, New York, *in* Barosh, P. J., and Smith, P. V., New England seismotectonic study activities during fiscal year 1981: U.S. Nuclear Regulatory Commission Report NUREG/CR-3253, p. 43–49.

Rascoe, B., Jr., and Adler, F. J., 1983, Permo-Carboniferous hydrocarbon accumulations, mid-continent, U.S.A.: American Association of Petroleum Geologists Bulletin, v. 67, p. 979–1001.

Ratcliffe, N. M., 1971, The Ramapo fault system in New York and adjacent northern New Jersey; A case of tectonic heredity: Geological Society of America Bulletin, v. 82, p. 125–142.

——, 1980, Brittle faults (Ramapo fault) and phyllanitic ductile shear zones in the basement rocks of the Ramapo seismic zones New York and New Jersey, and their relationship to current seismicity, *in* Manspeizer, W., ed., Field studies of New Jersey geology and guide to field trips; 52nd Annual Meeting New York State Geological Association, Rutgers University, Newark, New Jersey: Newark, New Jersey, Rutgers University Geology Department, p. 278–311.

Ravat, D. N., Braile, L. W., and Hinze, W. J., 1987, Earthquakes and plutons in the midcontinent; Evidence from the Bloomfield pluton, New Madrid Rift complex: Seismological Research Letters, v. 58, p. 41–52.

Rinehart, W. A., 1983, Epicentral map of the southeastern U.S. showing historic and recorded earthquakes through 1980: National Oceanic and Atmospheric Administration National Geophysical Data Center unpublished map.

Russ, D. P., 1981, Model for assessing earthquake potential and fault activity in the New Madrid seismic zone, *in* Beavers, J. E., ed., Earthquakes and earthquake engineering, eastern United States: Ann Arbor, Michigan, Ann Arbor Science, p. 309–335.

Sanford, B. V., Thompson, F. J., and McFall, G. H., 1984, Phanerozoic and recent tectonic movements in the Canadian Shield and their significance to the Nuclear Waste Management Program, *in* Workshop on transitional processes: Proceedings, Atomic Energy of Canada Limited Report 78822, p. 73–96.

——, 1985, Plate tectonics; A possible controlling mechanism in the development of hydrocarbon traps in southwestern Ontario: Canadian Petroleum Geologists Bulletin, v. 33, p. 52–71.

Sawyer, J. S., and Carroll, S. E., 1982, Fracture deformation of the Higganum dike, south-central Connecticut: U.S. Nuclear Regulatory Commission Report NUREG/CR-24-79, 52 p.

Sbar, M. L., and Sykes, L. R., 1973, Contemporary compressive stress and seismicity in eastern North America; An example of intraplate tectonics: Geological Society of America Buletin, v. 84, p. 1861–1882.

Schafer, K., 1983, Current compressive tectonics in Paleozoic mountain belts; Evidence from the Appalachians (USA) and the Dividing range (Australia), *in* Gabrielson, R. H., and others, eds., Proceedings 4th International Conference on Basement Tectonics: Salt Lake City, Utah, Basement Tectonics Association Publication 4, p. 379–380.

Schultz, A. P., and 6 others, 1986, Geologic map of Giles County, Virginia: Virginia Department of Mines, Minerals, and Energy, scale 1:50,000.

Schumm, S. A., 1986, Alluvial river response to active tectonics, *in* National Research Council Active tectonics: Washington, D.C., National Academy Press, p. 80–94.

Seeber, L., and Armbruster, J. G., 1981, The 1886 Charleston, South Carolina, earthquake and the Appalachian detachment: Journal of Geophysical Research, v. 86, p. 7874.

Shakal, A. F., and Toksoz, M. N., 1977, Earthquake hazard in New England: Science, v. 195, p. 171–173.

Shurr, G. W., 1981, Lineaments as basement-block boundaries in western South Dakota, *in* O'Leary, D. W., and Earle, J. L., eds., Proceedings 3rd International Conference on Basement Tectonics: Salt Lake City, Utah, Basement Tectonics Commission Publication 3, p. 177–198.

Sibol, M. S., Bollinger, G. A., and Mathena, E. C., 1986, Seismicity of the southeastern United States; January 1, 1986–June 30, 1986: Southeastern U.S. Seismic Network Bulletin, v. 18, 82 p.

Simmonss, E., 1977, Our New England earthquakes: Boston, Massachusetts, Boston Edison Co., 18 p.

Stauder, W., and 7 others, 1980, Central Mississippi Valley earthquake bulletin: St. Louis, Missouri, Saint Louis University Department of Earth and Atmospheric Science Quarterly Bulletin 25, 31 p.

Stearns, R. G., 1979, Recent vertical movement of the land surface in the Lake County uplift and Reelfoot Lake Basin areas, Tennessee, Missouri, and Kentucky: U.S. Nuclear Regulatory Commission Report NUREG/CR-0871, 37 p.

Stearns, R. G., and Reesman, A. L., 1986, Cambrian to Holocene structural and burial history of Nashville Dome: American Association of Petroleum Geologists Bulletin, v. 70, p. 143–154.

Stevenson, G. M., and Baars, P. L., 1981, Pre-Carboniferous paleotectonics of the San Juan Basin, *in* O'Leary, D. W., and Earle, J. L., eds., Proceedings 3rd International Conference on Basement Tectonics: Salt Lake City, Utah, International Basement Tectonics Association Publication 3, p. 331–346.

Sykes, L. R., 1978, Intraplate seismicity, reactivation of pre-existing zones of weakness, alkaline magmatism, and other tectonism postdating continental fragmentation: Reviews of Geophysics and Space Physics, v. 16, no. 4, p. 621–688.

Talwani, P., 1982, An internally consistent pattern of seismicity near Charleston, South Carolina: Geology, v. 10, p. 654–658.

Tarr, A. C., 1977, Recent seismicity near Charleston, South Carolina, and its relationship to the August 31, 1886, earthquake: U.S. Geological Survey Professional Paper 1028-D, p. 43–57.

Taylor, F. B., 1910, Bearing of the Tertiary mountain belt on the origin of the Earth's plan: Geological Society of America Bulletin, v. 21, p. 179–226.

Teller, J. Y., 1973, Preglacial (Teays) and early glacial drainage in the Cincinnati area, Ohio, Kentucky, and Indiana: Geological Society of America Bulletin, v. 84, p. 3677–3688.

Thomas, G. E., 1979, Lineament-block tectonics; North America-Cordilleran orogen, *in* Padwysocki, M. H., and Earle, J. L., eds., Proceedings 2nd International Conference on Basement Tectonics: Salt Lake City, Utah, International Basement Tectonics Association Publication 2, p. 361–370.

Thomas, W. A., 1981, Basement faults along the Appalachian–Ouachita continental margin, *in* O'Leary, D. W., and Earle, J. L., eds., Proceedings 3rd International Conference on Basement Tectonics: Denver, Colorado, Basement Tectonics Committee Publication 3, p. 347–355.

Thompson, W. B., 1979, Postglacial faulting along the Norumbega fault zone, eastern Maine: Geological Society of America Abstracts with Programs, v. 11, p. 56.

Tyler, D. A., and Ladd, J. W., 1981, Vertical crustal movement in Maine, *in* Barosh, P. J., and Smith, P. V., eds., New England seismotectonic study activities during fiscal year 1980: U.S. Nuclear Regulatory Commission Report NUREG/CR-3252, p. 158–159.

U.S. Geodynamics Committee, 1973, U.S. program for the geodynamics project: Washington, D.C., National Academy of Sciences, 235 p.

Vanicek, P., and Nagy, D., 1980, Report on the correlation of the map of vertical crustal movements in Canada: Energy, Mines, and Resources Canada, Earth Physics Branch Open-File Report 80-2, p. 59.

Walcott, R. I., 1972, Late Quaternary vertical movements in eastern North America; Quantitative evidence of glacio-isostatic rebound: Reviews of Geophysics and Space Physics, v. 10, no. 4, p. 849–884.

Ward, L. W., and Blackwelder, B. W., 1980, Stratigraphic revision of upper Miocene and lower Pliocene beds of the Chesapeake Group, Middle Atlantic Coastal Plain: U.S. Geological Survey Bulletin 1482-D, 72 p.

Warner, L. A., 1978, The Colorado lineament; A middle Precambrian wrench fault system?: Geological Society of America Bulletin, v. 89, p. 161–171.

Watkins, J. S., 1964, Regional geologic implications of the gravity and magnetic fields of a part of eastern Tennessee and southern Kentucky: U.S. Geological Survey Professional Paper 516-A, p. A1–A17.

Watts, A. B., 1981, The U.S. Atlantic continental margin; Subsidence history, crustal structure, and thermal evolution, *in* Geology of passive continental margins; History, structure, and sedimentologic record, with special emphasis on the Atlantic margin: American Association of Petroleum Geologists Education Course Note Series 19, p. 2-1-2-75.

Wayne, W. J., 1956, Thickness of drift and bedrock physiography of Indiana north of the Wisconsin glacial boundary: Indiana Geological Survey Report of Progress, no. 7, 70 p.

Wentworth, C. M., and Mergner-Keefer, M., 1981, Reverse faulting along the eastern seaboard and the potential for large earthquakes, *in* Beavers, J. E., ed., Earthquakes and earthquake engineering; The eastern United States: Ann Arbor, Michigan, Ann Arbor Science, p. 109–128.

—— , 1983, Regenerate faults of small Cenozoic offset; Probable earthquake sources in the southeastern United States: U.S. Geological Survey Professional Paper 1313-S, 20 p.

Wilson, F. W., 1979, A study of the regional tectonics and seismicity of eastern Kansas; Summary of project activities and results to the end of the second year, or September 30, 1978: U.S. Nuclear Regulatory Commission Report NUREG/CR-0666, 69 p.

Wilson, G. V., 1975, Early differential subsidence and configuration of the northern Gulf Coast Basin in southwest Alabama and northeast Florida: Gulf Coast Association of Geological Societies Transactions, v. 25, p. 196–206.

Wilson, J. T., 1965, A new class of faults and their bearing on continental drift: Nature, v. 207, p. 343, 347.

Winkler, C. D., and Howard, J. D., 1977a, Correlation of tectonically deformed shorelines on the southern Atlantic Coastal Plain: Geology, v. 5, p. 123–127.

—— , 1977b, Plio-Pleistocene paleogeography of the Florida Gulf Coast interpreted from relict shorelines: Gulf Coast Association of Geological Societies Transactions, v. 27, p. 409–420.

Wollard, G. P., 1958, Areas of tectonic activity in the United States as indicated by earthquake epicenters: EOS Transactions of the American Geophysical Union, v. 39, p. 1135–1150.

Woodworth, J. B., 1907, Post glacial faults of eastern New York: New York State Museum Bulletin 107, p. 4–28.

Young, J. R., and Putnam, G. W., 1979, Stratigraphy, structure, and mineral waters of Saratoga Springs; Implications for Neogene rifting: New York State Geological Association 51st Annual Meeting Guidebook, p. 272–291.

Zimmerman, R. A., 1976, Fission-track tectonics, regional uplift in eastern North America: Geological Society of America Abstracts with Programs, v. 8, p. 1181–1182.

—— , 1980, Patterns of post-Triassic uplift and inferred fall zone faulting in the eastern United States: Geological Society of America Abstracts with Programs, v. 12, p. 554.

Zoback, M. L., and Zoback, M., 1980, State of stress in the conterminous United States: Journal of Geophysical Research, v. 85, p. 6113–6156.

Zoback, M. S., and Zoback, M. L., 1981, State of stress and intraplate earthquakes in the United States: Science, v. 213, no. 4503, p. 96–110.

MANUSCRIPT ACCEPTED BY THE SOCIETY AUGUST 18, 1989

Geological Society of America
Reviews in Engineering Geology, Volume VIII
1990

Chapter 6

Neotectonics in the southeastern United States with emphasis on the Charleston, South Carolina, area

Pradeep Talwani
Department of Geological Sciences, University of South Carolina, Columbia, South Carolina 29208

ABSTRACT

A study of neotectonics in the southeastern United States was carried out by examining a variety of parameters, including the state of stress, pattern of seismicity, ground deformation, and estimation of recurrence rate for larger events. The direction of maximum horizontal stress (S_{Hmax}) was found to be uniform over the region, oriented in an ENE-WSW direction, and due to plate-tectonic forces. The current, historic, and prehistoric seismicity was found to occur in local clusters that displayed spatial stationarity over the historical period (300 yr). Ground deformation inferred from releveling, geoarcheological, and shallow sedimentary data was found to occur both on a regional and a local scale, the rates of deformation varying over the region. Statistical and paleoseismological data suggest a recurrence period of about 1,000 to 2,000 yr for the larger events in the Charleston, South Carolina, area.

These observations lead to the conclusion that neotectonic activity is episodic and is due to the interaction of a uniform stress field with local, preexisting zones of weakness. In the current episode of neotectonic activity (>300 yr and <2 m.y.), most of the dominant patterns of seismicity display spatial stationarity; thus, the current distribution of activity can be used for assessing seismic hazards.

INTRODUCTION

According to the National Academy of Sciences (1986), neotectonics pertains to the tectonics of the past few million years, or from the latest Neogene and Quaternary time. In this chapter, the neotectonics of the southeastern United States will be described, with special emphasis on the Charleston-Summerville region of South Carolina where most data have been gathered. However, available data from other parts of the region are also included in order to present a regional picture.

In the southeastern U.S. there is an absence of any exposed, seismically active faults that could be studied directly. Neotectonic studies in this region, therefore, were carried out indirectly and consisted of six elements (Table 1). Because neotectonics, or recent earth movements, are primarily in response to states of stress in the lithosphere, the state of tectonic stress in the region will be described first. All reliable data suggest that the region is in a compressional stress regime, with the direction of maximum horizontal stress oriented about N60°E. An evaluation of current,

historic, and prehistoric seismicity in the region suggests that it is not uniformly distributed, but is characterized by spatial and temporal clustering, while the predominant source zones display stationarity. The nature of ground movement at various time scales was found to be nonuniform over the region. Although the data are sparse and sometimes of questionable quality, some pockets of active vertical tectonics were detected. Recurrence rates for the larger earthquakes, similar to the 1886 Charleston event, were obtained both statistically and from paleoseismological data. In the Charleston area, they range from about 1,000 to 2,000 yr. There is a lack of consensus on the causative seismogenic structure or mechanisms responsible for the current seismicity, although several hypotheses have appeared in the literature.

A review of these elements leads to two conclusions: (1) there is an absence of uniform neotectonic activity over the entire southeastern U.S., and (2) the various neotectonic manifestations are the response of anomalous (weaker?) local structures to a uniform tectonic stress field.

Talwani, P., 1990, Neotectonics in the southeastern United States with emphasis on the Charleston, South Carolina, area, *in* Krinitsky, E. L., and Slemmons, D. B., Neotectonics in earthquake evaluation: Boulder, Colorado, Geological Society of America Reviews in Engineering Geology, v. 8.

**TABLE 1. NEOTECTONIC STUDIES
IN THE SOUTHEASTERN U.S.**

Element	Time/Scale	Data Source
1. State of stress	Current	Focal mechanisms In-situ measurements Geological indicators
2. Seismicity	Current Historical Prehistorical	Seismic networks Archival Paleoseismology
3. Sense and rate of ground deformation	Short 10s yrs 10^2-10^3 yrs 10^3-10^6 yrs	Focal Mechanisms Releveling Geoarcheology Geomorphology Shallow stratigraphy
4. Recurrence rates	10^2 yrs 10^2-10^3 yrs	Historical accounts Statistical analysis Paleoseismology
5. Seismotectonics	Integration of seismicity, stress, geological and geophysical data Current studies in South Carolina, Virginia, Tennessee, etc.	
6. Mechanisms	Several mechanisms have been proposed for discrete areas	

STATE OF STRESS

Any observed neotectonic activity is the response of local structures to the stress field. Seismicity can result due to the action of anomalous local stress concentrations or a tectonic stress field acting on preexisting zones of weakness or both. Hence it is of great importance to determine the state of the ambient in situ stress field.

The orientation of the maximum horizontal principal stress (S_{Hmax}) can be determined from a variety of data. These include earthquake focal mechanisms, in situ stress measurements by hydrofracture and overcoring techniques, and from geologic evidence of recent deformation (see e.g., McGarr and Gay, 1978; Zoback and Zoback, 1980). In recent years, analysis of stress-induced wellbore elongation (or breakouts) has been increasingly used to determine the direction of S_{Hmax} (see e.g., Bell and Gough, 1979).

In the southeastern U.S., several studies have described the direction of S_{Hmax}. Some of the initial results were conflicting due to inclusion of few, poor, or questionable data (e.g., Sbar and Sykes, 1973; Zoback and others, 1978; Zoback and Zoback, 1980; Talwani, 1985). In the latest compilation by Zoback and others (1987), the questionable data have been weeded out and additional data incorporated (especially from wellbore break-

outs). The results describe a clearer picture. In the southeastern U.S., Zoback and others (1987) found that the geological, seismological, and in situ stress data all suggest a NE to ENE compressive stress regime (characterized by strike-slip or reverse faulting). This direction is consistent with plate-tectonic-ridge push forces for the North American plate (Zoback and others, 1987). One implication of this observation, that the observed stress regime in the region can be explained by plate-tectonic sources, is that the probable cause of most of the observed seismicity at the active locations is due to the action of tectonic stress on zones of locally weak structures, rather than to inherently local stress concentrations.

SEISMICITY

In this section the historic, instrumental, and prehistoric seismicity in the region is described. Seismicity is of concern because large felt earthquakes have occurred in the historic past. The most notable and largest event (MMI = X, m_b = 6.7, M_s = 7.7) was the 1886 Charleston, South Carolina, earthquake.

Historical and instrumental seismicity

The historical activity was studied by Bollinger (1973), who divided the felt activity from 1754 to 1970 into distinct seismic zones, with the southern Appalachian seismic zone parallel and the central Virginia and South Carolina–Georgia seismic zones transverse to the Appalachian trend. Later Bollinger and Visvanathan (1977) extended the historical seismicity back to 1698 without a change in the pattern.

The first seismic network in the region was deployed in late 1973. By 1977, several networks had been deployed, and the results were catalogued bi-annually in the Southeastern U.S. Seismic Network (SEUSSN) bulletins. Bollinger and others (1990) reviewed the seismicity of the southeastern U.S. from 1698 to 1986; that work should be referred to for details. In the section below, some of the important results relative to the study of neotectonics are taken from that review.

Bollinger and others (1990) note that their catalog lists 1,088 events (483 with M >3) for the pre-network period, 1698 to 1977 (Fig. 1), and 474 events (43 with M >3) for the network period, 1977 to 1985 (Fig. 2). The authors further note that the historical seismicity was characterized by "the decidedly non-random spatial distribution of epicenters with patterns that are parallel as well as oblique to the northeasterly tectonic fabric of the host region. . . ." Seismicity was observed throughout the extent of the Appalachian highlands (south of 40°N), while the seismicity was observed in the Piedmont province only in Virginia, South Carolina, and Georgia. Only the Coastal Plain of South Carolina was seismically active.

The instrumentally recorded seismicity lowered the detection threshold, allowing for more accurate depth determinations and the construction of focal mechanism solutions.

A comparison of the epicenters located by network monitor-

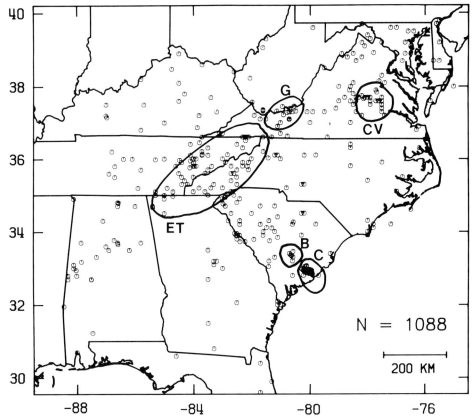

Figure 1. Historical seismicity of the southeastern U.S. (1698 to 1977). The open circles are the locations of felt events (from Bollinger and others, 1990). C, B, CV, G, and ET are the Charleston-Summerville, Bowman, central Virginia, Giles County, and eastern Tennessee (southern Appalachians) seismic zones.

ing (Fig. 2) and the noninstrumental historical epicenters (Fig. 1) shows that they both display the same general spatial patterns—some local clusters in the Piedmont and Coastal Plain and an elongated trend along the Appalachian highlands. Thus, the pattern of historical activity, which is based on larger magnitude felt events, is also seen in the pattern of smaller, instrumentally located events. Temporally, however, some distinctions are noted. To quote Bollinger and others (1990), "modern seismic activity decreases are seen in the northern Virginia Appalachians and the South Carolina Piedmont while relative increases of seismicity have occurred recently in the northeastern Kentucky Plateau and on the southeastern Tennessee Appalachians. . . ."

Seismic zones

The most active seismic zones (Fig. 1) identified in the historic and instrumental data are as follows:

(i) The Charleston-Summerville and Bowman seismic zones in the coastal plain of South Carolina (Tarr and others, 1981). The Charleston-Summerville region has been the scene of multidisciplinary studies aimed at determining its cause (Rankin, 1977; Gohn, 1983). Based on the planar distribution of hypocenters and on seismic reflection data, Talwani (1982) suggested that the observed seismicity was occurring on the shallow (4 to 7 km

deep) NW-trending Ashley River fault and on the deeper (8 to 13 km) NNE-trending Woodstock fault (Fig. 3). These faults were associated with reverse and strike-slip faulting, respectively. Subsequent studies incorporating a variety of geological and geophysical data (Talwani, 1986) have lent further support to the seismogenic nature of the Ashley River fault, while the existence of the Woodstock fault has not been confirmed by other data.

Smith and Talwani (1988) studied the seismotectonics of the Bowman seismic zone (Fig. 1) and noted that the shallow seismicity occurred near the intersection of a northwest feature (collinear with the Ashley River fault, 50 km to its southeast) and the NE-trending fault of an inferred basin of Triassic age.

(ii) The seismic zones in eastern Tennessee and Giles County, southwestern Virginia, are both elongated in a northeasterly direction along the Appalachians (Fig. 1). The nearly 200-km-long eastern Tennessee seismic zone has been the most active in the region since the deployment of networks. The mode of faulting is predominantly by strike-slip motion (Bollinger and others, 1985; Johnston and others, 1985; Teague and others, 1986). In both of these areas the seismicity is found to occur below the postulated décollement (see e.g., Bollinger and Wheeler, 1983).

(iii) The nearly circular (map view), central Virginia seis-

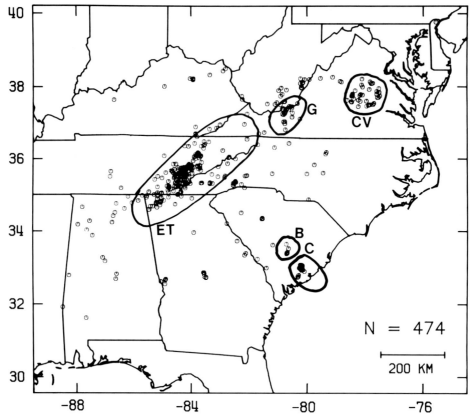

Figure 2. Network seismicity of the southeastern U.S. (1977–1985). The open circles are the locations of events with $M_D \geqslant 0.0$ (modified from Bollinger and others, 1990).

mic zone is the most active area in the Piedmont (Bollinger and Sibol, 1985). Munsey and Bollinger (1985) suggested from their focal mechanism studies that there was a stress discontinuity at about the depth of the décollement with the orientation of S_{Hmax} northeasterly above 7 km and northwesterly below that. However, using the same data but compositing differently, Nelson and Talwani (1985) obtained a new set of focal mechanisms, all of which were compatible in the S_{Hmax} oriented in a northeasterly direction.

Depths

Bollinger and others (1990) noted that there was a systematic difference in the pattern of depths between the Appalachian highlands, and the Piedmont and Coastal Plain earthquakes. In the Appalachian highlands the 90 percent depth (i.e., the depth above which 90 percent of all the foci lie) is 19 km, with a peak in the focal depth distributions at 10 to 11 km. The corresponding depths for the Piedmont and Coastal Plain earthquakes are 13 km and 7 to 8 km, respectively. Bollinger and others (1990) argue that there is a significant difference in the thickness of the seismogenic crust between the adjacent provinces. The details of a study of the depth characteristics can be found in Bollinger and others (1990).

Focal mechanisms

Bollinger and others (1990) also describe the available focal mechanism data for the region. Various focal mechanisms for the larger single events and composites of focal mechanisms for the smaller events are shown in Figure 4. Most of the focal mechanisms indicate thrust or strike-slip faulting, with the direction of the P-axis (inferred to be the direction of maximum horizontal stress, S_{Hmax}) oriented in a NE-SW to ENE-WSW direction. This result is compatible with the stress data discussed in an earlier section.

Prehistoric data

In order to extend the seismicity data back in time, a relatively new field—paleoseismology—has emerged. A search is underway for evidence of prehistoric earthquakes in the geologic record. Results of these studies in paleoseismology are discussed in a later section on the determination of recurrence rates of large earthquakes.

In the southeastern U.S., paleoseismological studies have been carried out only in the Charleston region. In one study, Obermeier and others (1987) described the discovery of several earthquake-induced sand blows manifested as filled craters in the

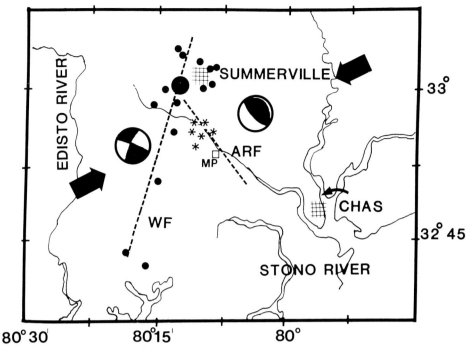

Figure 3. Locations of shallow earthquakes (4 to 7 km, asterisks) used to define the Ashley River fault (ARF) and deeper earthquakes (8 to 13 km, solid circles) used to define the Woodstock fault (WF). Lower-hemisphere equal-area projections of composite fault-plane solutions of earthquakes used to define these faults yield reverse faulting for the ARF, with a steep, SW-dipping fault plane, and right-lateral strike-slip on the WF. Compressional quadrants are shaded. The inferred orientation of the maximum horizontal stress (parallel to the P-axes) is shown by solid arrows. MP and CHAS are Middleton Place and Charleston, respectively (modified from Talwani, 1986).

coastal region of South Carolina and in the southeastern edge of North Carolina. They noted a decrease in the size and frequency of these craters away from the meizoseismal area of the 1886 Charleston earthquake, "although the susceptibility of the widespread beach deposit sites to earthquake-induced liquefaction is approximately the same throughout the area. . . ." They concluded: "These data indicated that, in this coastal region, the strongest earthquake shaking during the Holocene has taken place repeatedly near Charleston. . . ."

Conclusions

Our main conclusions from a review of the seismicity data in the southeastern United States are as follows: (1) a comparison of the historical (since 1698) and instrumental (since 1977) data suggests that, spatially, the seismicity is nonrandomly distributed, wherein the principal source zones over the period from 1698 to present display stationarity; (2) the pattern of seismicity within a given source zone displays temporal clustering; (3) paleoseismological studies in South Carolina revealed the occurrence of prehistoric earthquakes, but supported only the Charleston region as the source zone for these prehistoric earthquakes—further arguing for the nonrandom location of seismicity in the southeastern U.S.; (4) instrumental data suggest that the focal depths are all in

the upper crust, being on average deeper in the Appalachian highlands than in the Piedmont or Coastal Plain provinces; and (5) focal mechanisms for most regional seismic events support a compressional stress regime with S_{Hmax} oriented in a NE-SW to ENE-WSW direction.

GROUND DEFORMATION

In the western United States, where seismogenic faults like the San Andreas are exposed, ground deformation can be directly observed. However, in the southeastern U.S., where there is an absence of surface faulting, indirect methods have to be employed to study ground deformation. This is especially true in areas like Charleston, South Carolina, which lie on a wedge of Coastal Plain sediments. Here the evidence of ground deformation is quickly obliterated by erosion and by the deposition of sediments. Deformation of these sedimentary features is expressed generally by uplift and subsidence that is spread laterally over several kilometers as compared to discrete offsets observed in the western U.S.

In the Southeast, ground deformation has been studied at different time scales. Data from focal mechanism solutions give an instantaneous view of the ground deformation. These data are available in various seismically active regions and extend to large depths compared to other indicators of ground deformation. The focal mechanisms have been described earlier (Fig. 4) and indicate crustal shortening and offsets by thrust and strike-slip faulting, presumably on preexisting faults. In a general way, thrust faulting appears to be associated with shallow earthquakes (on an average above about 7 km), and strike-slip faulting with the deeper events. This observation is concordant with the existence of a compressional stress regime in the area.

Ground deformation on a time scale of tens of years is detected from a study of releveling data. Although there have been many studies of releveling data in the region (e.g., Brown and Oliver, 1976; Reilinger and Brown, 1981), focused studies in tectonically active regions have been carried out at only a few locations in South Carolina (Lyttle and others, 1979; Poley, 1984; Poley and Talwani, 1986), Virginia (Nelson, 1985; Nelson

and Talwani, 1985), and the Gulf Coastal Plain (Jurkowski and others, 1984). The results of these studies are discussed in a later section.

Ground deformation on a time scale of hundreds to thousands of years is studied from geomorphological and geoarcheological data. In the Charleston region, there is an absence of any systematic studies of geomorphological data with a view toward detecting neotectonic ground deformation. However, some recent geoarcheological studies by Colquhoun and Brooks (1986) in the Charleston region have extended information on ground deformation back about 4,000 years.

Mapping of shallow stratigraphy has allowed for detection of ground deformation in the last several million years. Some of the more detailed studies have taken place in the South Carolina Coastal Plain (e.g., Colquhoun and others, 1983). Evaluation of ground deformation on the different time scales described above

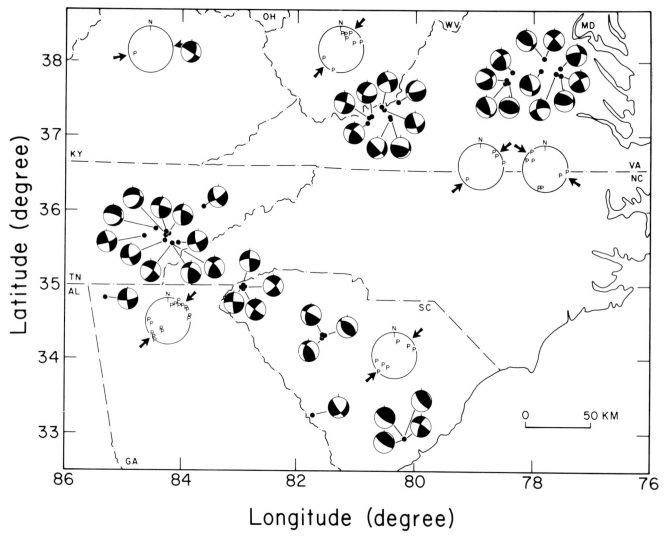

Figure 4. Focal mechanism solutions for the southeastern U.S. Shown are lower-hemisphere equal-area projections. Compressional quadrants are shown in black. Larger circles are plots of P-axes (maximum compressive stress), one axis point (P) per focal mechanism, and are adjacent to the group of focal mechanism solutions they represent. Heavy arrows indicate average P-axis directions (from Bollinger and others, 1990).

suggests the occurrence of localized vertical ground movements in the region.

Releveling

The analyses of releveling measurements have proven effective in monitoring ground deformation due to tectonic activity (e.g., Savage and Church, 1974; Stein and Thatcher, 1981). In large-scale studies, deformation has been detected on a regional scale (e.g., Brown and Oliver, 1976; Vanicek and Nagy, 1980). In an analysis of releveling data in the eastern U.S. Coastal Plain province, Brown and Oliver (1976) observed a consistent regional tilt toward the Atlantic Ocean; a large northward tilt of the Atlantic Coastal Plain between Harrington, Delaware, and Savannah, Georgia; and local uplifts near the Cape Fear Arch, at Kiptopeke, Virginia, and Savannah, Georgia. An apparent uplift of the Appalachians relative to the coastal regions was also indicated. However, these inferred crustal movements may result from tectonic deformation, near-surface movements, and/or systematic errors (e.g., Reilinger and Brown, 1981; Chi and Reilinger, 1984). Local subsidence has also resulted from subsurface fluid withdrawal in the Gulf Coast (Holdahl and Morrison, 1974; Jurkowski and others, 1984). In many areas, ground-water withdrawal in the vicinity of growing cities has led to localized ground subsidence; for example, near Charleston and Columbia, South Carolina, Augusta and Savannah, Georgia (Holdahl and Morrison, 1974; Lyttle and others, 1979; Poley and Talwani, 1986; Davis, 1987). Brown and Reilinger (1986) point out that "before ascribing these motions to some new, unheralded form of intraplate tectonics, it is important to recognize that there are major questions about the accuracy of geodetic measurements on which most of these studies are based. . . ."

In this section, results of three local studies where the releveling data had been carefully screened by the National Geodetic Survey for systematic and rod calibration errors will be described. Two of these studies, Poley and Talwani (1986) and Nelson (1985), were specifically designed to seek evidence of any ground deformation in the South Carolina and Virginia seismic zones.

Releveling studies in the Coastal Plain of South Carolina

Poley and Talwani (1986) analyzed first-order releveling data for the South Carolina Coastal Plain along several lines (Fig. 5). Although leveling data extended back to 1918, in view of bench-mark recovery, rod calibrations, etc., reliable evidence of vertical movement was best obtained from leveling profiles in the 1960s and 1970s. It was also recognized that localized subsidence in the vicinity of larger towns may be due to groundwater withdrawal and that this observed subsidence may mask ground movements due to tectonic causes.

Poley and Talwani (1986) noted a general subsidence toward the Atlantic Ocean together with evidence for localized

recent vertical crustal movements along some profiles. One of these, an east-west profile frm Yemassee to Charleston (Fig. 6) surveyed in 1961 and 1974, runs across an area of observed seismicity. Poley and Talwani (1986) interpret the releveling data (Fig. 6) as showing regional subsidence at a velocity of 5.4 to 3.1 mm/yr in the Charleston area, with a distinct local uplift approximately 20 km west of Charleston. The subsidence in the immediate vicinity of Charleston was attributed to be primarily due to ground-water withdrawal. This uplift was also detected in an earlier study by Lyttle and others (1979). This local uplift lies to the southwestern side of the proposed northwest-trending Ashley River fault (Talwani, 1982, 1986), and is parallel and to the southwest of the Charleston fault, interpreted in the shallow stratigraphic data by Colquhoun and others (1983). Focal mechanisms by Talwani (1982) suggest that the southwestern side of the Ashley River fault is upthrown, in general agreement with the observed uplift seen on the releveling and stratigraphic data (Fig. 13).

Among the other profiles examined by Poley and Talwani (1986) were line GA (from Augusta to Savannah, Georgia) and line 57 (from Fairfax, South Carolina, to Savannah; Fig. 5). Line 9 from Yemassee to Savannah was analyzed by Lyttle and others (1979). In all three profiles, regional tilting was observed toward the east, with localized subsidence in the vicinity of Savannah, which has been attributed by many authors (e.g., Poley and Talwani, 1986; Davis, 1987) to local ground-water withdrawal. In these profiles, Smith (personal communication, 1987) observed a localized uplift occurring about 15 to 20 km from Savannah (Fig. 7). This northeast-trending uplift is tentatively interpreted to be spatially associated with the middle Eocene Garner-Edisto fault inferred by Colquhoun and others (1983) from shallow stratigraphic data.

Releveling studies in Virginia

In a recent study, Nelson (1985) examined releveling data in Virginia with particular attention on the Giles County and central Virginia seismic zones. The various releveling data are along profiles shown in Figure 8. Where possible, the results of this analysis were compared with focal mechanism solutions of recent earthquakes.

In the Giles County seismic zone in southwestern Virginia, focal mechanism solution A of Munsey (1985) was from some earthquakes in the immediate vicinity of the second-order level line extending from Rich Creek to Pembroke. The profile from Wytheville to Roanoke lies within 7 km of the epicenters of events used in composite focal mechanism C by Munsey (1985). The observed strike-slip motion is in agreement with the leveling results, which showed essentially no vertical motion along these profiles (Nelson, 1985). Also, it must be noted that motion may be occurring at hypocentral depths (as much as 25 km) too great to be detected by measures of crustal motion at the surface.

The areas from Talcott, West Virginia, to Moss Run, Virginia, and Covington to Buchanan, Virginia, lie to the north and

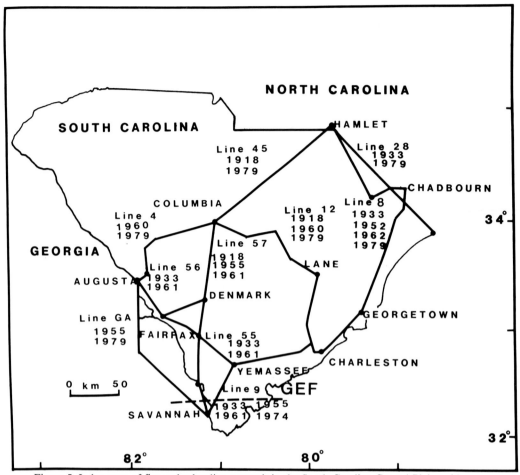

Figure 5. Index map of first-order leveling network in the South Carolina Coastal Plain, with survey years indicated for each line (from Poley and Talwani, 1986). Also shown is the Garner-Edisto fault (GEF) (after Colquhoun and others, 1983).

northeast of the network-monitored events in the Giles County seismic zone. This is not an area in which seismicity has recently been recorded; therefore, no focal mechanisms have been obtained for this area. Small vertical ground motion was detected along these lines, however; Covington moved up relative to Buchanan and Talcott. With no seismicity in the area, the cause of this uplift is not clear.

In the central Virginia seismic zone the location of the leveling lines was not optimal for a direct comparison with the focal mechanisms for various earthquake clusters in the zone. Along a SW-NE profile from Lynchburg to Scottsville the sense of ground motion (down to the northeast) is consistent with focal mechanism solutions 4 and 5 obtained by Nelson (1985) for two clusters of events near Scottsville.

Evidence of vertical ground movement was seen on profiles not in the seismic zones. The profile extending from Greensboro to Raleigh, North Carolina, showed substantial subsidence of Raleigh relative to Greensboro (−2.51 ± 0.42 mm/yr). It is important to note, however, that loop misclosure analysis indicated the possible presence of (unquantifiable) distance-dependent er-

rors in this profile. Tilt to the east at −0.43 ± 0.01 μrad/yr agreed in both sense and magnitude with results obtained by Citron and Brown (1979) for a line that ran west from the Greensboro area. Along the profile from Lynchberg to Greensboro, rates of change were small (~1.0 mm/yr).

Both the Lynchburg-to-Scottsville and the Briery-to-Richmond profiles indicated that the Richmond area has subsided relative to points to its west and south. This pattern was not observed between Richmond and points east; the Richmond-to-Toano line exhibited no apparent motion. This would be expected, however, if subsidence of the coastal plain was also occurring, as only relative changes were measured. Subsidence near Richmond may have been due, at least in part, to loading of the ground surface by urbanization, or to ground-water withdrawal.

Releveling studies in the Gulf Coastal Plain

Releveling studies in the Gulf Coastal Plain show regional tilting (subsidence) toward the Gulf of Mexico. Contour maps of

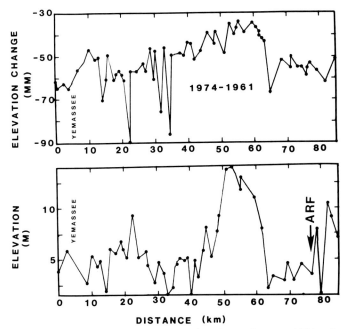

Figure 6. Profile showing observed elevation changes between 1974 and 1961 (1961 being held fixed), along line 9 from Yemassee to Charleston, South Carolina. Data points indicate individual benchmarks. The profile ends at BM X67, which is located about 8 km NW of Charleston. The profile crosses the projection of the ARF near BM-60 (modified from Poley and Talwani, 1986).

uplift rates in the region, based on geodetic releveling data, reveal an elliptical area of uplift in southeastern Mississippi and southwestern Alabama, with rates from 2 to 4 mm/yr (Fig. 9; Holdahl and Morrison, 1974). Within the region, there are also localities of crustal warping that have been attributed to possible subsurface fluid withdrawal (Holdahl and Morrison, 1974; Jurkowski and others, 1984). However, Jurkowski and others (1984) suggest that the subsurface fluid withdrawal and systematic errors do not fully explain the wavelength and magnitude of the observed elevation changes; therefore, they attribute them to neotectonic processes.

In summary, analyses of releveling data have revealed the evidence of crustal deformation on both a regional and local scale. Where other data are available, the local anomalies appear to be associated with other indicators of neotectonic activity.

Geoarcheological studies

In South Carolina, geoarcheological data have been analyzed for possible indications of neotectonic movements. Colquhoun and Brooks (1986) examined the locations of shell midden deposits dating from about 4,200 B.P., along the estuaries of the South Carolina coast. The observed spatial and temporal changes in locations of these deposits were interpreted by them as being in response to local variations in sea level. These sea-level

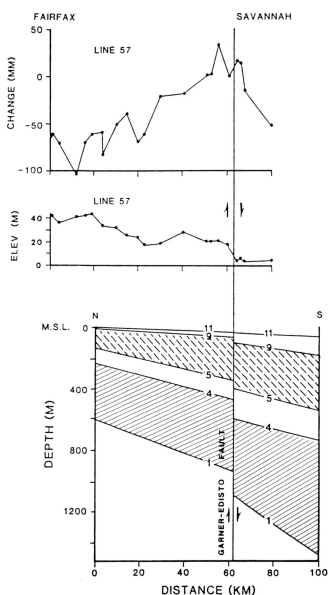

Figure 7. Geodetic and stratigraphic profiles across the Garner-Edisto fault. The top two profiles are from releveling data (line 57 as shown in Fig. 5) during the period 1918–1955, showing elevation changes and topography from Fairfax, South Carolina, to Savannah, Georgia (after Poley and Talwani, 1986). The profiles are approximately aligned with the position of the Garner-Edisto fault. Data points are individual benchmarks. The lower profile is a north-south stratigraphic cross section showing the depth to regional unconformities across the Garner-Edisto fault (after Colquhoun and others, 1983). The ages of the unconformities are: (1) middle Cretaceous, (4 and 5) Upper Cretaceous, (9) middle Eocene and (11) lower Miocene.

fluctuations were attributed, at least in part, to neotectonic movements in the area.

Brooks and others (1979) had discovered several interriverine archeological sites in Pleistocene barrier-island areas in the coastal zone of South Carolina. Colquhoun and Brooks

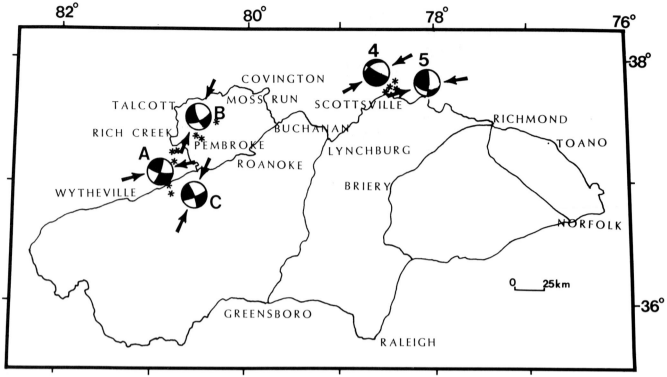

Figure 8. Index map of first-order leveling lines in Virginia and North Carolina. Composite focal
mechanisms A through C are from Munsey (1985); 4 and 5 are from Nelson (1985). Asterisks are
seismic events.

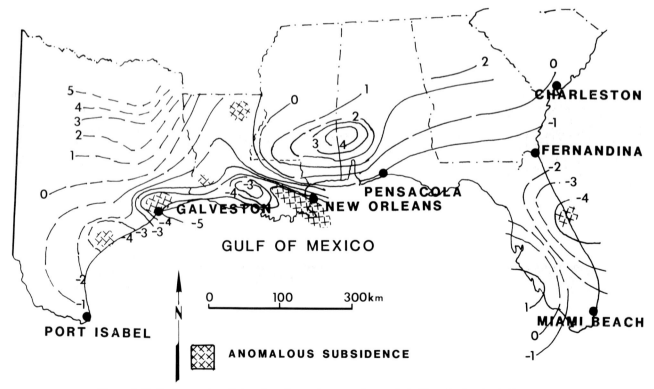

Figure 9. Preliminary rates of elevation change (contours in mm/yr). Note the local subsidence near
Galveston, New Orleans, etc. and the uplift on the Alabama-Mississippi border (from Holdahl and
Morrison, 1974).

(1986) studied a possible relation between the occurrence of these sites and sea-level changes. They found that the number of such interriverine sites was greater when there was a rise in the sea level. They further suggest that the locations of such episodes of interriverine settlements were spatially controlled by the locations of faults undergoing vertical movement. They offer the following explanation.

Human populations in the coastal zone since at least 4,200 B.P. exploited two major food sources, from the sea and from the land. This resulted in two different archeological site types, or prehistoric garbage dumps, consisting of estuarine shell middens and interriverine subsistence camps. The shell middens, which included a variety of food types from both land and sea, suggested a sedentary existence. The interriverine sites, however, indicate short-term exploitation of deer and other game during periods of sea-level rise. Colquhoun and Brooks (1986) suggest that as there was a rise in the sea level there was a relative scarcity in the food resources from the estuaries. Part of the human population moved upriver, away from the estuaries to interriverine sites where they exploited game and other foods. In the South Carolina Coastal Plain, Colquhoun and Brooks (1986) found that the ages of the interriverine sites were temporally clustered during periods of sea-level rise.

Figure 10 shows the location of four interrriverine sites in South Carolina. The Winyah Bay study area lies to the south of Cape Fear Arch. The Wando River site is to the northeast of the Ashley River fault (Talwani, 1982), whereas the Stono River site is to its south. The North Edisto River site is to the northeast and upthrown side of the Garner-Edisto fault. According to Colquhoun and Brooks' (1986) hypothesis, during periods of sea-level rise (or relative downward movement of the coast) there is an increase in the number of sites occupied. The frequency of occurrence of these interriverine sites is shown in Figure 11. Before about 2,200 B.P. there appears to have been little difference in the frequency of occupation. Since then, however, Colquhoun and Brooks (1986) claim the frequency of occurrence is not uniform and is correlatable with inferred tectonic activity on the faults.

Although these observations suggest a different sense of vertical deformation on adjacent sides of a fault, they are not conclusive in that they ignore other possible reasons for population shifts.

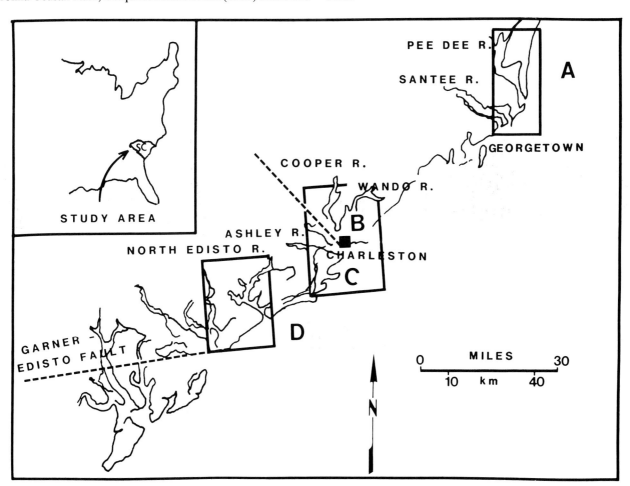

Figure 10. Locations of the four intensely studied sites for geoarcheological evidence of neotectonics. A, Winyah Bay; B, Wando River; C, Stono River; D, North Edisto River (from Colquhoun and Brooks, 1986).

Shallow stratigraphic studies in the South Carolina Coastal Plain

In South Carolina, the Atlantic Coastal Plain consists of a wedge of southeast-dipping, unconsolidated to semiconsolidated, sedimentary rocks formed in river, coastal, and continental-shelf environments. The wedge thickens seaward from the fall line to a maximum thickness of about 1.1 km along the coast near Charleston and is underlain by a basement of Precambrian, Paleozoic, and Mesozoic rocks. The results of over 20 years of shallow stratigraphic drilling through the Cretaceous, Tertiary, and Quaternary sediments and the recognition of a number of erosional unconformities separating depositional unit sequences were compiled by Colquhoun and others (1983) into a series of structure, lithofacies, and isopach maps. From these maps they noted the influence of older, basement-controlled structures on subsequent deposition. Since the number of wells penetrating to deeper strata are sparse, the accuracy of these maps of deeper unconformities is subject to some uncertainty. However, several general features were recognized.

The maps revealed that major structural features, such as the Cape Fear Arch and the Southeast Georgia embayment, have affected the depositional environment and thicknesses of Coastal Plain sediments. This also led to the discovery of the northwest-trending Charleston and ENE-trending Garner-Edisto faults, which have affected the sedimentary thickness but not the depositional environments.

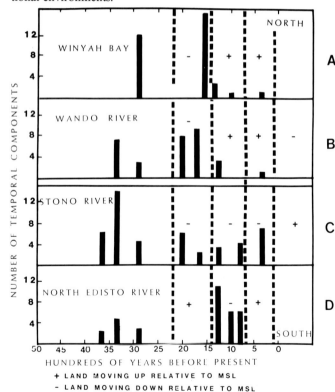

Figure 11. Frequency of interriverine camps at sites A through D (see Fig. 10). Time zero refers to present (from Colquhoun and Brooks, 1986).

Since 1984, additional shallow stratigraphic studies were undertaken with the objective of seeking evidence of neotectonic activity in sediments and its possible association with other indicators of neotectonic activity. This allowed an increase in the data base on neotectonic activity by several million years. The studies began in the Summerville-Charleston seismic zone (Lennon, 1985) and were subsequently extended to the Bowman seismic zone (Muthanna and others, 1987).

Regional chronostratigraphy

Three Tertiary markers were identified in the Charleston-Summerville area by drilling. The individual markers were identified by their characteristic signatures in well logs, changes in lithology, microfossils, or drilling speeds. The three mapped unconformities include the base of the Orangeburg Group (48 Ma, unconformity 8), which ranges in depth from about 60 to more than 150 m; the base of the Cooper Group (43 Ma, unconformity 9), with a depth range from about 20 to 100 m; and the base of the Ashley Member of the Cooper Formation (38 Ma) at depths from 15 to 60 m. The updip limit of the Fishburne Formation was obtained from earlier (deeper) well data (Gohn and others, 1984a).

Unconformity 8, at the basee of the Orangeburg Group underlies the entire region, being eroded only in the extreme northeastern part of Orangeburg County (to the northeast of Bowman). This 48-Ma unconformity has been identified by a marked gamma-ray log anomaly in the available water-well data in the region. This gamma-ray anomaly is due to a well-developed phosphate-rich zone at the base of the Santee limestone.

Unconformity 9, at the base of the Cooper Group, lies south of Bowman and extends to the coast. The updip subcrop limit of this unconformity (under Pliocene strata) was generally known from earlier work in the area. It is the contact between the underlying Santee limestone and the overlying Cooper Formation. These two units have sharply contrasting lithologies, which allow for precise identification through lithologic examination.

Results

In the Summerville-Charleston area, Lennon (1985) described a northwest-oriented rectangular depression (graben) defined by the surfaces of three successive Tertiary formations in the Charleston-Summerville area (see e.g., Fig. 12). This feature is anomalous in an otherwise featureless, gently dipping, regional unconformity. The 40-km-long and 18-km-wide graben is bounded on three sides by inferred faults drawn on stratigraphic contour anomalies and distortion in the near-surface Tertiary and Quaternary sediments.

The fault on the northeastern boundary of the observed graben-like features is the Charleston fault of Colquhoun and others (1983). It is a low-angle, normal growth fault, dipping to the southwest, and has been active since the Paleocene. The

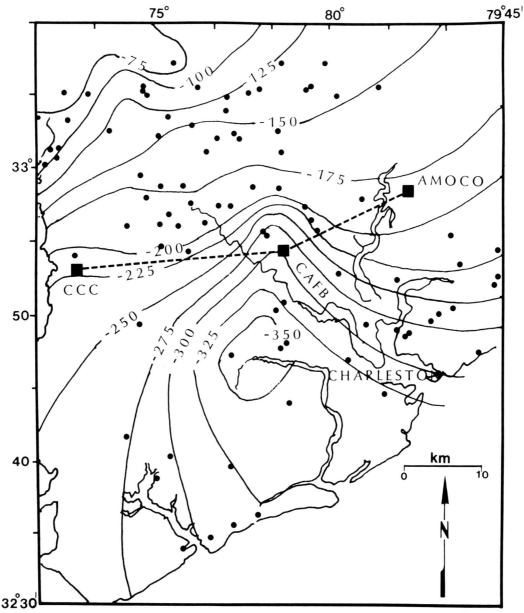

Figure 12. Well control (solid dots) and elevations in feet at the base of the Cooper Formation in the Charleston-Summerville area (contour interval 25 ft). Note the dense control to the north and relatively sparse control to the SW. The E-W dashed line connects the location of deep wells at Clubhouse Crossroads (CCC), Charleston Air Force Base (CAFB), and the Amoco Company (AMOCO). A cross section along this line is shown in Figure 13 (from Lennon, 1985).

position and orientation of the updip limit of the Fishburne Formation suggest that it has been removed by middle Eocene erosion on the northeastern flank (Fig. 13). Stratigraphic data indicate that the Charleston fault is displaced to the northeast as it shallows, and is consistent with the near-surface observation of Malde (1959) and McCartan and others (1984). The Charleston fault (in the top 150 m) is parallel to, and possibly associated with, the seismically defined subsurface (4 to 7 km deep) Ashley River fault.

To the northwest is a fault possibly related to the Wood-stock fault (Talwani, 1982), or a subsurface horst-like feature discovered by Ackermann (1983).

The subsurface control for the southern and southwestern flanks of the depression is inadequate to define it unambiguously. However, the southwestern flank is characterized by uplift and distortion in the Fishburn Formation and Santee limestone (Fig. 13). Also, it possibly is correlated with the uplift observed by Poley and Talwani (1986) in the releveling line from

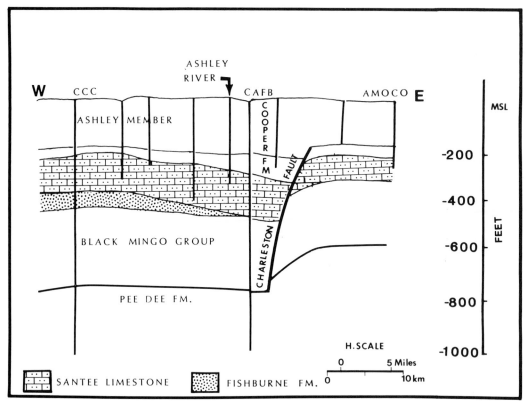

Figure 13. Subsurface projection of the Charleston fault. The projection of the Ashley River fault lies about 5 km to the west of CAFB (arrow), suggesting it may be related to the downward projection of the Charleston fault. Note the distortions on the Tertiary formations probably associated with vertical displacement on the ARF. Well control is shown and the depths are in feet (modified from Lennon, 1985).

Yemassee to Charleston. Both of these uplifts, stratigraphic and surficial, can possibly be explained by uplift to the southwest on a southwest-dipping Ashley River fault, as suggested by focal mechanism solutions. This association is tenuous at present, and more data are needed to confirm it.

Drilling of an additional 70 holes in the Bowman area in the summer and fall of 1985 revealed that unconformity 9 (the boundary between the Cooper marl and Santee limestone) had not been distorted there. In order to examine the structure on the deeper unconformity 8, additional holes were drilled through the Santee limestone to the Black Mingo Group. These data were added to the existing data base on the 48-Ma unconformity 8 (Muthanna and others, 1987). The resulting map of unconformity 8 (Muthanna, 1988), which includes both the Summerville-Charleston and Bowman seismic zones, is shown in Figure 14.

It should be noted that the regional ENE-WSW to E-W trend of contours is perturbed near Bowman and Charleston along two collinear NW-trending basins. The seismicity of the two zones (Ashley River fault and a trend of epicenters in the Bowman seismic zone) appears to be spatially associated with these basins, which are separated by an inferred Triassic-age basin. Thus, the seismicity in the two zones appears to be clustered at the intersections of NW-SE and NE-SW features, the former being collinear.

Colquhoun and others (1983) constructed an isopach map of the Upper Cretaceous interval (Fig. 15). In that map there is evidence of a rapid change in the thickness of the sediments from approximately 90 to 180 m (300 to 600 ft) within 10 km. This feature, called the Bamberg Warp (Colquhoun and others, 1983), is parallel to the main rift-basin boundary fault (Behrendt, 1985; Smith and Talwani, 1988) as well as other regional geophysical trends along-strike to the SW (e.g., Zietz and others, 1982).

The presence of two collinear NW-trending basins and NW distortions of the depth contours of the 48-Ma unconformity 8, and the absence of any NW distortion in the Cretaceous are noted by comparing Figures 14 and 15. This suggests that the NW feature, if it existed during the Cretaceous, was inactive. However, it has been active (at least episodically) since 48 Ma. Thus, the current seismicity observed along the Ashley River fault and at Bowman can be traced back approximately 48 m.y. It is not clear if the activity has been continuous or episodic.

RECURRENCE RATES

One of the important parameters in estimating seismic hazard at any location is the determination of the recurrence rate of larger events. In China, where the historical record extends back over 1,000 years, it has been possible to observe cyclic patterns in the temporal distribution of large events. In the southeastern U.S., the historical record covers only about 300 years, and in that time, there have been only two larger events: the 1886 Charleston, South Carolina (m_b = 6.7, M_s = 7.7), and the 1897 Giles County, Virginia (m_b ≈ M_s = 5.8), earthquakes. The historical data, therefore, are inadequate to establish the recurrence rates. Two other approaches have been used to obtain the recurrence rate. These are, statistically, from the frequency-magnitude (or frequency-intensity) distributions and from paleoseismology.

Statistical methods

The magnitude-frequency distribution of earthquakes are conventionally represented by the Gutenberg and Richter (1944) relation:

$$\log N = a - b\,M \tag{1}$$

where N is the number of earthquakes occurring within a region in a given time period with magnitude greater than or equal to M, and M is the magnitude (such as M_L, m_b, M_D, or m_{bLg}). Values a

and b are constants; a depends on the size of the area chosen and the length of the time period, and is an overall measure of the level of seismicity of the area. The fit to the equation of a plot of log N versus M is a straight line and yields a value for the slope, b. The b value varies with source region, focal depth, type of earthquake process, stress level, and in some cases, with time. For most earthquakes the b value lies between 0.5 and 1.5.

If a linear relation exists between magnitude and intensity, such as the M = 1 + (⅔)I relation suggested by Gutenberg and Richter (1956) for southern California, then the relation between the frequency and intensity can be expressed as:

$$\log N_c = a - b I_o \tag{2}$$

where N_c is the number of events occurring within a region in a given time period with epicentral intensity ≥I_o, and constants a and b describe the level of seismicity and its distribution with respect to I_o, respectively, realizing that the constants a and b are different from those for the frequency-magnitude relation (1). As Chinnery and Rogers (1973) point out, relation (2) allows for the use of data for smaller, more plentiful earthquakes to estimate the frequency of large earthquakes, which are rare. Instead of using

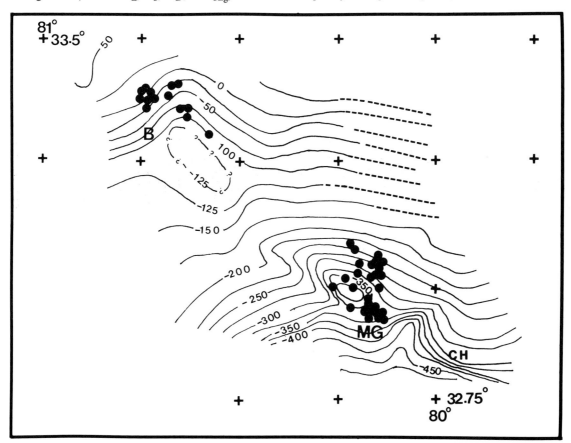

Figure 14. Map of the elevations at the top of unconformity 8 (contour interval 25 ft) in the area between Charleston (CH) and Bowman (B). Solid dots in the vicinity of Middleton Gardens (MG) and Bowman show recent epicenters. Note the presence of two collinear NW-trending basins near B and MG. The seismicity appears to be concentrated in the vicinity of these basins with the regional E-W to ENE-WSW contours (from Muthanna, 1988).

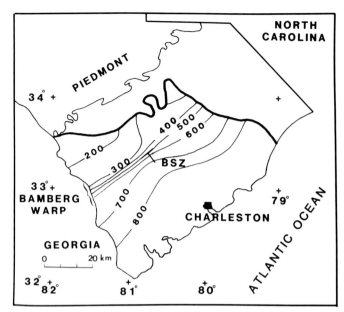

Figure 15. Isopach map of the Upper Cretaceous, with thickness in feet. Note that the Bamberg Warp, defined by a sharp gradient in the contours, does not show any NW distortion near the Bowman seismic zone (BSZ) (modified from Colquhoun and others, 1983).

N_c, it is more convenient to define the mean return (or recurrence) period, τ of an earthquake, which is the average time between earthquakes with a given intensity I_0 (or magnitude), and is equal to $1/N_c$ time periods. Conversely, it can be used to estimate the largest event for a given return period. It is important to realize that the maximum size of the earthquake is more closely related to local geology, fractures, and stress conditions that must be considered before final conclusions can be drawn from statistical analyses.

Results for the Southeastern U.S.

Earlier attempts to obtain recurrence rate estimates were based exclusively on historical data (see e.g., Bollinger, 1972, 1973, 1974; Tarr, 1977). These estimates have now been revised with the incorporation of instrumental data.

Bollinger and others (1989) have developed recurrence relations for the southeastern U.S. from a combination of historical (1698 to 1977) and network (1978 to 1986) earthquake catalogs. They obtained the recurrence relations for the region as a whole and for a series of subregions consisting of three geologic provinces and four seismic zones. To combine the historical and network data, they established a relation between MM intensity and m_{bLg} values. An updated version of their results is summarized in Table 2.

Thus, for the Charleston region, the estimated return times for a m_b 6.4 to 6.7 (estimated magnitude of the 1886 event) are 1,963 to 3,350 yr. These values are greater than estimates obtained by Amick and Talwani (1986), who considered the inten-

sity data from 1893 to 1984. They argued that the aftershock sequence of the 1886 earthquake lasted through 1892. Amick and Talwani (1986) obtained a recurrence time of 1,585 yr for an intensity X event. These differences probably reflect the accuracy of the recurrence estimates from statistical data.

Paleoseismology studies

Paleoseismology involves the search for evidence of prehistoric earthquakes preserved in the geologic record. Sieh (1981) and Wallace (1981) have described various geologic settings where paleoseismological investigations can be carried out. One recoverable indicator of ancient earthquakes in the southeastern U.S., where causative faults are inaccessible, is soft sediment that is deformed due to seismically induced liquefaction.

Following the 1886 Charleston earthquake, sand blows due to liquefaction of underlying sands covered the area of over 1,500 km². They were especially intense in the meizoseismal area of the earthquake (Dutton, 1889).

Following the discovery of an 1886 sand blow (Cox and Talwani, 1983; Cox, 1984), a search was made for evidence of pre-1886 events. An intense effort in the following years led to the discovery of several pre-1886 sand blows and a discussion of the optimum conditions for their formation and preservation (see e.g., Cox, 1984; Gohn and others, 1984b; Talwani and Cox, 1985; Obermeier and others, 1985, 1986, 1987; Ebasco Services, 1987). Two types of liquefaction features seen in other locations were also identified in the region. These are the abundant sandblow explosion craters and lateral-spread landslides (Ebasco Services, 1987).

To obtain recurrence rates for these prehistoric earthquakes, it was necessary to date them. Talwani and Cox (1985) studied a sand crater in the meizoseismal area of the 1886 earthquake and found evidence of two prehistoric earthquakes. Using ^{14}C ages of roots that had cut the crater and other roots that had been cut by the extruded sand, they bracketed the two events between about 3,700 and 1,200 B.P., or possibly between about 3,000 and 1,200 B.P. By including the 1886 event, they obtained an initial average for maximum recurrence interval of about 1,500 to 1,800 yr.

Weems and others (1986) found evidence of three pre-1986 earthquakes dating back to 7,200 B.P. In addition to ^{14}C ages of roots, they estimated the ages of humate soils that had fallen into the liquefied craters and those that overlie them. They obtained an estimate of average recurrence rates of 1,800 yr or less—in general agreement with the results of Talwani and Cox (1985).

Conclusions

The available methods for obtaining the recurrence rates of earthquakes similar to the 1886 Charleston event lead to crude estimates. However, the results from statistical and paleoseismological data are consistent and suggest a maximum recurrence rate of about 1,000 to 2,000 yr.

SEISMOTECTONICS AND MECHANISMS

To understand the various elements of neotectonics, the subject must be cast in a framework of seismotectonics where the additional element is the definition of the seismogenic structure. Studies are underway in the Charleston-Summerville and Bowman areas of the South Carolina Coastal Plain (see e.g., Talwani, 1986; Smith and Talwani, 1988); central Virginia; Giles County, Virginia; and the southern Appalachian seismic zones (see e.g., Johnston and others, 1985; Bollinger and others, 1990). An analysis of these studies is beyond the scope of this chapter.

Many mechanisms have been suggested to explain the observed seismicity; most of these studies have been aimed at explaining the seismicity near Charleston. For a review of the various models and hypotheses, see Talwani (1985) and Dewey (1985).

CONCLUSIONS

Due to a lack of exposed seismogenic faults in the southeastern U.S., in contrast to the western U.S., a different approach had to be adopted to study neotectonics and to assess the seismic hazard. The results of this study are summarized below (see also Table 1):

1. The observed pattern of the majority of current and historical ($\sim$300 yr) seismicity is spatially clustered.

2. At these locations, the seismicity displays stationarity since historical times.

3. Neotectonic deformation is not uniform at different locations, but is characterized by local differences in rates and styles of ground deformation.

4. The direction of the maximum horizontal compressive stress (S_{Hmax}) is uniform over the region and oriented in the ENE-WSW direction. The implication of this observation is that plate tectonics accounts for the mechanism generating the stress. Therefore, it can be argued that the driving force for earthquakes in the southeastern U.S. is the interaction of this uniform stress field with local, preexisting zones of weakness.

5. If the relatively high rates of ground deformation and long return periods of larger events (thousands of years) had persisted for millions of years, one would expect major uplifts of sediments, in spite of erosion. These are not seen, suggesting that either the vertical ground deformation was episodic rather than continuous, or it was interrupted by deformation in an opposite sense. There is no evidence for reversal of the stress field in the recent geologic past, which argues for episodic neotectonic activity lasting longer than the historical period (300 yr) but shorter than the Quaternary record (2 m.y.).

6. Therefore, to estimate the seismic hazard in the southeastern U.S., one needs to consider the neotectonic activity in the current episode, i.e., treat the neotectonic activity as a spatially stationary process rather than anticipate new locations of major seismicity.

ACKNOWLEDGMENTS

I thank Ellis Krinitzsky for inviting me to participate in the symposium on "Neotectonics in Earthquake Evaluation," and for his patience while the paper was written. I also thank Gil Bollinger for his insightful comments, Bill Smith for help with the references and drafting Figure 7, Steve Acree for help with the other figures, and Andrea Conkle for typing the manuscript. The studies reported here were supported in part by U.S. Nuclear Regulatory Commission contract NRC-04-86-119.

TABLE 2. RECURRENCE RELATIONS FOR SOUTHEASTERN U.S.*

Region	a	b	n
Southeastern U.S.	3.126 ± 0.084	0.844 ± 0.024	860
Valley Ridge and Blue Ridge	2.667 ± 0.081	0.824 ± 0.027	398
Piedmont	2.164 ± 0.184	0.812 ± 0.053	191
Coastal Plain	2.191 ± 0.164	0.784 ± 0.048	188
Giles County, Virginia	1.042 ± 0.247	0.656 ± 0.078	28
Central Virginia	1.004 ± 0.201	0.628 ± 0.062	94
Eastern Tennessee	2.753 ± 0.100	0.900 ± 0.035	198
Charleston, South Carolina	1.654 ± 0.254	0.773 ± 0.080	84

*Note:

$$\log N_1 = a - b \, m_{bLg}$$

where N_1 = no/yr in ± 0.25 magnitude intervals, and n = number of earthquakes after deletion of aftershocks (from Bollinger and others, 1989).

REFERENCES CITED

Ackermann, H. D., 1983, Seismic-refraction study in the area of the Charleston, South Carolina, 1886 earthquake, in Gohn, G. S., ed., Studies related to the Charleston, South Carolina, earthquake of 1886; Tectonics and seismicity: U.S. Geological Survey Professional Paper 1313, p. F-1–F-20.

Amick, D., and Talwani, P., 1986, Earthquake recurrence rates and probability estimates for the occurrence of significant seismic activity in the Charleston area; The next 100 years, in Proceedings of the 3rd U.S. National Conference on Earthquake Engineering, v. 1: Earthquake Engineering Research Institute, p. 55–64.

Behrendt, J. C., 1985, Interpretations from multichannel seismic-reflection profiles of the deep crust crossing South Carolina and Georgia from the Appalachian mountains to the Atlantic coast: U.S. Geological Survey Miscellaneous Field Studies Map MF 1656.

Bell, J. S., and Gough, D. I., 1979, Northeast-southwest compressive stress in Alberta; Evidence from oil wells: Earth and Planetary Science Letters, v. 45, p. 475–482.

Bollinger, G. A., 1972, Historical and recent seismic activity in South Carolina: Bulletin of the Seismological Society of America, v. 62, p. 851–864.

—— , 1973, Seismicity of the southeastern United States: Bulletin of the Seismological Society of America, v. 63, p. 1785–1808.

—— , 1974, Errata; Seismicity of the southeastern United States: Bulletin of the Seismological Society of America, v. 64, p. 733.

Bollinger, G. A., and Sibol, M. S., 1985, Seismicity, seismic-reflection studies, gravity, and geology of the central Virginia seismic zone; Part 1, seismicity: Geological Society of America Bulletin, v. 96, p. 49–57.

Bollinger, G. A., and Visvanathan, T. R., 1977, The seismicity of South Carolina prior to 1886, in Rankin, D. W., ed., Studies related to the Charleston, South Carolina, earthquake of 1886; A preliminary report: U.S. Geological Survey Professional Paper 1028, p. 33–42.

Bollinger, G. A., and Wheeler, R. L., 1983, The Giles County, Virginia, seismic zone: Science, v. 219, p. 1063–1065.

Bollinger, G. A., Teague, A. G., and Munsey, J. W., 1985, Focal mechanism analysis for Virginia and eastern Tennessee earthquakes, 1978–1984: U.S. Nuclear Regulatory Commission Report NUREG/CR-4288, 83 p.

Bollinger, G. A., Davison, F. C., Sibol, M. S., and Birch, J. B., 1989, Magnitude recurrence relations for the southeastern U.S. and its subdivisions: Journal of Geophysical Research v. 94, p. 2857–2873.

Bollinger, G. A., and 6 others, 1990, Seismicity of the southeastern U.S., 1698 to 1986, in Slemmons, D. B., Engdahl, E. R., Blackwell, D., and Schwartz, D., eds. Neotectonics of North America: Boulder, Colorado, Geological Society of America, Decade Map Volume (in press).

Brooks, M. J., Colquhoun, D. J., Pardi, R. R., Newman, W. S., and Abbott, W. H., 1979, Preliminary archaeological and geological evidence for Holocene sea level fluctuations in the lower Cooper River Valley, South Carolina: Florida Anthropologist, v. 32, p. 85–103.

Brown, L. D., and Oliver, J. E., 1976, Vertical crustal movements from leveling data and their relation to geologic structure in the eastern United States: Reviews in Geophysics and Space Physics, v. 14, p. 13–35.

Brown, L. D., and Reilinger, R. E., 1986, Epeirogenic and intraplate movements, in Active tectonics: Washington, D.C., National Academy Press Studies in Geophysics series, p. 30–44.

Chi, S. C., and Reilinger, R. E., 1984, Geodetic evidence for subsidence due to groundwater withdrawal in many parts of the United States of America: Journal of Hydrology, v. 67, p. 155–182.

Chinnery, M. A., and Rogers, D. A., 1973, Earthquake statistics in southern New England: Earthquake Notes, v. 44, p. 89–103.

Citron, G. P., and Brown, L. D., 1979, Recent vertical crustal movements from precise leveling surveys in the Blue Ridge and Piedmont provinces of North Carolina and Georgia: Tectonophysics, v. 52, p. 223–236.

Colquhoun, D. J., and Brooks, M. J., 1986, New evidence from the southeastern

U.S. for eustatic components in the late Holocene sea levels: Geoarchaeology, v. 1, p. 275–291.

Colquhoun, D. J., and 7 others, 1983, Surface and subsurface stratigraphy structure, and aquifers of the South Carolina Coastal Plain; Report for the Department of Health and Environmental Control, Ground Water Protection Division: Columbia, State of South Carolina, published through the Office of the Governor, 78 p.

Cox, J.H.M., 1984, Paleoseismology studies in South Carolina [M.S. thesis]: Columbia, University of South Carolina, 75 p.

Cox, J.H.M., and Talwani, P., 1983, Discovery of the first seismically induced paleoliquefaction site near Charleston, South Carolina: Earthquake Notes, v. 54, p. 16.

Davis, G. H., 1987, Land subsidence and sea level rise on the Atlantic Coastal Plain of the United States: Environmental Geology and Water Science, v. 10, p. 67–80.

Dewey, J. W., 1985, A review of recent research on the seismotectonics of the southeastern seaboard and an evaluation of hypotheses on the source of the 1886 Charleston, South Carolina, earthquake: U.S. Nuclear Regulatory Report NUREG/CR-4339, 45 p.

Dutton, C. W., 1889, The Charleston earthquake of August 31, 1886: U.S. Geological Survey Annual Report, 1887–1888, p. 209–558.

Ebasco Services, 1987, Paleoliquefaction features on the Atlantic seaboard; Task 1 report: U.S. Nuclear Regulatory Commission contract NRC-04-86-117, 68 p.

Gohn, G. S., ed., 1983, Studies related to the Charleston, South Carolina, earthquake of 1886; Tectonics and seismicity: U.S. Geological Survey Professional Paper 1313, 375 p.

Gohn, G. S., Hazel, J. E., Bybell, L. M., and Edwards, L. E., 1984a, The Fishburne Formation (lower Eocene); A newly defined subsurface unit in the South Carolina Coastal Plain: U.S. Geological Survey Bulletin 1537-C, 16 p.

Gohn, G. S., Weems, R. E., Obermeier, S. F., and Gelinas, R. L., 1984b, Field studies of earthquake induced liquefaction flowage features in the Charleston, South Carolina, area; Preliminary report: U.S. Geological Survey Open-file Report 84-670, 26 p.

Gutenberg, B., and Richter, C. F., 1944, Frequency of earthquakes in California: Bulletin of the Seismological Society of America, v. 34, p. 185–188.

—— , 1956, Earthquake magnitude, intensity, energy, and acceleration: Bulletin of the Seismological Society of America, v. 46, p. 105–145.

Holdahl, S. R., and Morrison, N. L., 1974, Regional investigations of vertical crustal movements in the U.S. using precise releveling and mareograph data: Tectonophysics, v. 23, p. 373–390.

Johnston, A. C., Reinbold, D. J., and Brewer, S. I., 1984, Seismotectonics of the southern Appalachians: Bulletin of the Seismological Society of America, v. 75, p. 291–312.

Jurkowski, G., Ni, J., and Brown, L., 1984, Modern uparching of the Gulf Coastal Plain: Journal of Geophysical Research, v. 89, p. 6247–6255.

Lennon, G., 1985, Identification of a northwest-trending seismogenic graben near Charleston, South Carolina [M.S. thesis]: Columbia, University of South Carolina, 92 p.

Lyttle, P. T., Gohn, G. S., Higgins, B. B., and Wright, D. S., 1979, Vertical crustal movements in the Charleston, South Carolina–Savannah, Georgia, area: Tectonophysics, v. 52, p. 183–189.

Malde, H. E., 1959, Geology of the Charleston phosphate area, South Carolina: U.S. Geological Survey Bulletin 1079, 105 p.

McCartan, L., Lemon, E. M., Jr, and Weems, R. E., 1984, Geologic map of the area between Charleston and Orangeburg, South Carolina: U.S. Geological Survey Miscellaneous Investigations Map I-1472, scale 1:250,000.

McGarr, A., and Gay, N. C., 1978, State of stress in the Earth's crust: Annual Review of Earth and Planetary Science, v. 6, p. 405–436.

Munsey, J. W., 1985, Focal mechanism analysis for recent (1978-1984) Virginia earthquakes [M.S. thesis]: Blacksburg, Virginia Polytechnic Institute and State University, 214 p.

Munsey, J. W., and Bollinger, G. A., 1985, Focal mechanism analyses for Virginia earthquakes (1978-1984): Bulletin of the Seismological Society of America, v. 75, p. 1613 1636.

Muthanna, A., 1988, An integrated geophysical and geological study of the central South Carolina Coastal Plain [M.S. thesis]: Columbia, University of South Carolina, 97 p.

Muthanna, A., Talwani, P., and Colquhoun, D. J., 1987, Preliminary results from integration of stratigraphic and geophysical observations in the central South Carolina Coastal Plain: Seismological Research Letters, v. 58, p. 102.

National Academy of Science, 1986, Active tectonics: Washington, D.C., National Academy Press Geophysics Series, 266 p.

Nelson, K., 1985, Vertical crustal motion in and around the central Virginia and Giles County seismogenic zones [M.S. thesis]: Columbia, University of South Carolina, 129 p.

Nelson, K., and Talwani, P., 1985, Reanalysis of focal mechanism data for the central Virginia seismogenic zone: Earthquake Notes, v. 56, p. 76.

Obermeier, S. F., Gohn, G. S., Weems, R. E., Gelinas, R. L., and Rubin, M., 1985, Geologic evidence for recurrent moderate to large earthquakes near Charleston, South Carolina: Science, v. 227, p. 408–411.

Obermeier, S. F., and 6 others, 1986, Holocene and late Pleistocene(?) earthquake-induced sand blows in coastal South Carolina, *in* Proceedings of the 3rd U.S. National Conference on Earthquake Engineering, Charleston, South Carolina: Earthquake Engineering Research Institute, p. 197–208.

Obermeier, S. F., Weems, R. E., and Jacobson, R. B., 1987, Earthquake induced liquefaction features in the coastal South Carolina region: U.S. Geological Survey Open-File Report 87-504, 20 p.

Poley, C. M., 1984, Recent vertical crustal movements in the South Carolina Coastal Plain; Implications for neotectonic activity [M.S. thesis]: Columbia, University of South Carolina, 95 p.

Poley, C. M., and Talwani, P., 1986, Recent vertical crustal movements near Charleston, South Carolina: Journal of Geophysical Research, v. 91, p. 9056–9066.

Rankin, D. W., ed., 1977, Studies related to the Charleston, South Carolina, earthquake of 1886; A preliminary report: U.S. Geological Survey Professional Paper 1028, 204 p.

Reilinger, R. E., and Brown, L. D., 1981, Neotectonic deformation, near surface movements, and systematic errors in U.S. releveling measurements; Implications for earthquake prediction, *in* Simpson, D. W., and Richards, P. G., eds., Earthquake prediction; An international review: American Geophysical Union Maurice Ewing Series, v. 4, p. 422–440.

Savage, J. C., and Church, J. P., 1974, Evidence for post-earthquake slip in the Fairview Peak, Dixie Valley, and Rainbow Mountain fault areas of Nevada: Bulletin of the Seismological Society of America, v. 64, p. 687–698.

Sbar, M. L., and Sykes, L. R., 1973, Contemporary compressive stress and seismicity in eastern North America; An example of intraplate tectonics: Geological Society of America Bulletin, v. 84, p. 1861–1881.

Sieh, K. E., 1981, A review of geological evidence for recurrence times of large earthquakes, *in* Simpson, D. W., and Richards, P. G., eds., Earthquake prediction; An international review: American Geophysical Union Maurice Ewing Series, v. 4, p. 181–207.

Smith, W. A., and Talwani, P., 1988, An integrated study of the northern flank of a buried Mesozoic rift basin, South Carolina [abs.]: Geological Society of America Abstracts with Programs, v. 20, p. 316.

Stein, R. S., and Thatcher, W., 1981, Seismic and aseismic deformation associated with the 1952 Kern County, California, earthquake and relationship to the Quaternary history of the White Wolf fault: Journal of Geophysical Research, v. 86, p. 4913–4928.

Talwani, P., 1982, An internally consistent pattern of seismicity near Charleston, South Carolina: Geology, v. 10, p. 654–658.

—— , 1985, Current thoughts on the cause of the Charleston, South Carolina, earthquakes: South Carolina Geology, v. 29, p. 19–38.

—— , 1986, Seismotectonics of the Charleston region, *in* Proceedings of the 3rd U.S. National Conference on Earthquake Engineering: Earthquake Engineering Research Institute, v. 1, p. 15–24.

Talwani, P., and Cox, J., 1985, Paleoseismic evidence for recurrence of earthquakes near Charleston, South Carolina: Science, v. 229, p. 379–381.

Tarr, A. C., 1977, Recent seismicity near Charleston, South Carolina, and its relationship to the August 31, 1886, earthquake, *in* Rankin, D. W., ed., Studies related to the Charleston, South Carolina, earthquake of 1886; A preliminary report: U.S. Geological Survey Professional Paper 1028, p. 43–57.

Tarr, A. C., Talwani, P., Rhea, S., Carver, D., and Amick, D., 1981, Results of recent South Carolina seismological studies: Bulletin of the Seismological Society of America, v. 71, p. 1883–1902.

Teague, A. G., Bollinger, G. A., and Johnston, A. C., 1986, Focal mechanism analyses for eastern Tennessee earthquakes (1981–1983): Bulletin of the Seismological Society of America, v. 76, p. 95–105.

Vanicek, P., and Nagy, D., 1980, The map of contemporary vertical crustal movements in Canada: EOS Transactions of the American Geophysical Union, v. 61, p. 145–147.

Wallace, R. E., 1981, Active faults, paleoseismicity, and earthquake hazards in the western United States, *in* Simpson, D. W., and Richards, P. G., eds., Earthquake prediction; An international review: American Geophysical Union Maurice Ewing Series, v. 4, p. 209–216.

Weems, R. E., and 6 others, 1986, Evidence for three moderate to large prehistoric Holocene earthquakes near Charleston, S.C., *in* Proceedings of the 3rd U.S. National Conference on Earthquake Engineering, Charleston, South Carolina: Earthquake Engineering Research Institute, p. 3–13.

Zietz, I., Riggle, F. E., and Daniels, D. L., 1982, Aeromagnetic map of South Carolina: U.S. Geological Survey Geophysical Investigations Map GP-951, scale 1:1,000,000.

Zoback, M. D., Healy, J. H., Roller, J. C., Gohn, G. S. and Higgins, B. B., 1978, Normal faulting and in situ stress in the South Carolina Coastal Plain near Charleston: Geology, v. 6, p. 147–152.

Zoback, M. L., and Zoback, M. D., 1980, State of stress in the coterminous United States: Journal of Geophysical Research, v. 85, p. 6113–6156.

Zoback, M. L., Nishenko, S. P., Richardson, R. M., Hasegawa, H. S., and Zoback, M. D., 1987, Mid-plate stress, deformation, and seismicity, *in* Vogt, P. R., and Tucholke, B. E., eds., The western North Atlantic region: Boulder, Colorado, Geological Society of America, Geology of North America, v. M, p. 297–312.

MANUSCRIPT ACCEPTED BY THE SOCIETY AUGUST 18, 1989

Geological Society of America
Reviews in Engineering Geology, Volume VIII
1990

Chapter 7

Late Quaternary fault scarps, mountain-front landforms, and Pliocene-Quaternary segmentation on the range-bounding fault zone, Sangre de Cristo Mountains, New Mexico

Christopher M. Menges*
Department of Geology, University of New Mexico, Albuquerque, New Mexico 87131

ABSTRACT

The morphology of a 1,200-m-high bedrock mountain front in the Rio Grande rift of northern New Mexico demonstrates the persistence through Pliocene-Quaternary time of temporal and spatial patterns of late Quaternary rupture along the range-bounding fault zone. Detailed mapping of the surface trace of the fault zone suggests a complex geometric segmentation pattern consisting of four primary segments, each containing two to four 5- to 10-km-long subsegments. The central to south-central part of a subsegment *or* segment is defined by a narrow zone of single- to double-strand fault scarps commonly at the base of a reentrant in the range front. The narrow zones typically change along strike into more complex zones of mixed piedmont fault scarps and multiple bedrock fault splays that bound structural benches. These diffuse terminations of subsegments or segments preferentially are at salients and/or abrupt deflections in the mountain front. Variations in fault-scarp morphology and displaced geomorphic surfaces suggest that several latest Pleistocene and Holocene ruptures are nonuniformly distributed along a 50-km-long section of fault scarps at or near the base of the mountain front. Morphologic age estimates from height-slope regressions and diffusion modeling of fault scarps suggest that: (1) one or several temporally clustered rupture(s) of mid- to early Holocene age may have extended 30 to 50 km across three primary segments of the range-bounding fault; and (2) a late to mid-Holocene rupture may have occurred on one 6- to 10-km-long subsegment. These two rupture lengths are associated with average vertical displacements of 1.2 and 0.8 m, respectively, which suggests potentially different scales of paleoearthquakes with estimated magnitudes of 6.7 to 7.1 (multiple segment) and 5.8 to 6.3 (single segment only), with probable recurrence intervals of 10^4 yr between events at a given site on the fault zone.

This time-space segmentation of the fault zone influences the morphology of large-scale tectonic landforms such as facets and spurs, which have developed in the adjacent bedrock escarpment over longer Quaternary time spans. Basal triangular facets above the central parts of subsegments or segments have greater relief and size, steeper mean slopes, fewer benches, less dissection, and thicker colluvial mantles, compared to facets at adjacent subsegment boundaries. Similar morphologic patterns characterize the overall profiles of the larger facet-spur systems of the range front. These patterns extend

*Present address: U.S. Geological Survey—Al Ain Mission, National Drilling Company, P.O. Box 15287, Al Ain, United Arab Emirates.

Menges, C. M., 1990, Late Quaternary fault scarps, mountain-front landforms, and Pliocene-Quaternary segmentation on the range-bounding fault zone, Sangre de Cristo Mountains, New Mexico, *in* Krinitzsky, E. L., and Slemmons, D. B., Neotectonics in earthquake evaluation: Boulder, Colorado, Geological Society of America Reviews in Engineering Geology, v. 8.

upward on the mountain front to at least the level of a prominent mid-escarpment bench that correlates with a 4.3-Ma basalt flow overlying an erosional surface at the northern end of the range block. The subsegment containing the morphologically youngest fault scarps also coincides with an unusually high, steep, and undissected set of basal facets, and the greatest amount of post-Pliocene vertical displacement, as estimated from the elevation of the mid-escarpment bench above correlative basalt flows in the adjacent basin. These collective relations suggest that cumulative amounts and rates (120 to 230 m/m.y.) of vertical displacements since mid-Pliocene time may increase by a factor of 1.5 to 2 near the south ends of some primary segments of the range-bounding fault zone. Post-Pliocene displacement rates are several times greater than those estimated solely from late Pleistocene and Holocene fault scarps (0.1 to 0.2 mm/yr versus 0.3 to 0.6 mm/yr, respectively), and are sufficient to generate most of the total relief of the Sangre de Cristo range block within a middle Miocene to Quaternary time interval. The width and internal complexity of the fault trace also increase northward along most primary segments; this structural asymmetry may reflect a small component of left-lateral slip related to unilateral northward propagation of seismogenic rupture from depth at non-conservative boundaries on the southern ends of some fault segments.

INTRODUCTION

Most of the tectonically active fault zones in the Basin and Range Province and Rio Grande rift of the western United States are located along or near the base of large mountain fronts. A few faults in the Basin and Range are associated with historical surface ruptures that produced topographic scarps during large-magnitude earthquakes (e.g., the 1915 Pleasant Valley, the 1954 Dixie Valley–Fairview Peak, and the 1983 Borah Peak earthquakes; see Wallace, 1977, 1984, 1987; Crone and others, 1987). Many other fault zones in these provinces are not associated with historical earthquakes, but still display geomorphic or stratigraphic evidence for surface ruptures in late Quaternary time. Limited data on the rates and timing of multiple ruptures on some of these faults suggest recurrence intervals of 10^3 to 10^5 yr and that faulting may be nonuniformly clustered in time and space (Machette, 1987; Pearthree and others, 1983; Wallace, 1984, 1987; Pearthree and Calvo, 1987).

There is a need to evaluate the short- (10^3 to 10^4 yr) and long-term (10^5 to 10^6 yr) Quaternary paleoseismicity of the many potentially active faults in regions that lack any record of historical seismicity. Degraded fault scarps developed in alluvium along many of these faults are one of the most important sources of data for estimating short-term patterns and rates of paleoseismicity. Several analytical techniques have recently been developed for using the morphology of fault scarps to directly estimate the rupture age of the associated fault zone (e.g., Wallace, 1977; Bucknam and Anderson, 1979; Nash, 1980, 1984, 1986; Colman and Watson, 1983; Mayer, 1984; Crone and others, 1987). Fault-scarp analyses also provide geomorphic data on key seismic source parameters, such as the length, amount, and number of individual surface ruptures, which in turn commonly form the basis for estimating the magnitude of large, prehistoric earthquakes.

Recent paleoseismic studies suggest that many of the active normal faults that bound long (>30 km), high-relief (>1,000 m)

range blocks are subdivided into segments with differing patterns and timing of surface rupture. Coseismic rupture patterns on a given segment appear to commonly repeat in "characteristic earthquakes" over at least late Quaternary time intervals (Schwartz and Coppersmith, 1984, 1986; Scott and others, 1985; Wallace, 1987). Accurate assessment of the seismotectonic hazards posed by this type of range-bounding fault should rely on data collected at many sites in order to adequately characterize any patterns of fault segmentation and their effect on the generation of past earthquakes.

The presence and morphology of large bedrock escarpments provide direct evidence for significant Quaternary tectonic activity that extends over much longer time intervals than are recorded in late Quaternary fault scarps (Bull and McFadden, 1977; Bull, 1984; Schwartz and Coppersmith, 1984; Scott and others, 1985; Menges, 1987a, b; Menges and Wells, 1987). There is a need to establish the degree to which segmentation and slip patterns of fault scarps persist over long time intervals in the Quaternary. Statistical analyses of some large-scale geologic and geomorphic characteristics of the Wasatch Mountains suggest that certain fault segments persist over the long time intervals—10^6 to 10^7 yr—that are reflected in the morphology of the range block (Maclean, 1985; Mayer and Maclean, 1986; Wheeler and Krystinik, 1987). It is still not clear, however, to what extent, and over what time intervals, various scales of fault segmentation influence the form and evolution of mountain front landforms such as bedrock facets and spurs.

This chapter summarizes a study of the tectonic geomorphology of a 50-km-long section of the southern Sangre de Cristo fault zone at the base of a large mountain-front escarpment in the Rio Grande rift of northern New Mexico (Fig. 1; Menges, 1987a, b; 1988). The main objectives of this chapter are to identify geometric segmentation along this range-bounding fault zone and to estimate the relations between these segmentation patterns and

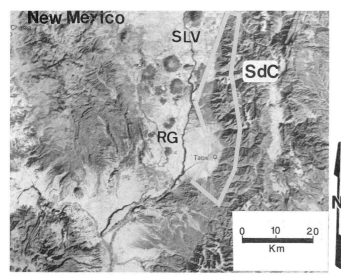

Figure 1. Location of study areas in the southern Sangre de Cristo Mountains near Taos. Large box in center outlines the part of the range-bounding fault zone and adjoining mountain front included in this study. Abbreviations: Rio Grande gorge (RG), Sangre de Cristo Mountains (SdC), southern San Luis Valley (SLV). Northern limit of map coincides with the Colorado and New Mexico border. (Adapted from composite Landsat image; New Mexico Geological Society, 1982.)

late Quaternary surface ruptures on the fault. This phase of the study emphasizes comparison of the geometry of the fault trace with individual rupture events estimated from morphologic analyses of fault scarps. The persistence of late Quaternary segmentation patterns is then evaluated by comparing fault geometry and the rupture ages of fault scarps with the morphology of facets and spurs on the range front. These latter bedrock landforms record intervals of faulting and landscape evolution on the order of 10^5 to 10^6 yr (Menges, 1988).

METHODS

The patterns of surface faulting along this part of the Sangre de Cristo fault zone were identified in several stages. The geometry of the surface trace of the fault zone at the base of the 70-km-long mountain front between Taos and the New Mexico border (Fig. 1) was identified, based primarily on detailed photointerpretive mapping of fault scarps and the basal topographic junction of the range front on color and black and white aerial photographs (nominal scales of 1:15,780 and 1:70,000, respectively). Field data on scarp morphology and the amount of surface offset were collected at eight sites distributed along a 50-km-long section of the range-front escarpment selected for detailed study (Fig. 2a). Field studies consisted of: (1) measuring 40 profiles of undissected fault scarps with rod and Abney level; (2) estimating the fault displacement of middle to upper Quaternary surfaces across fault scarps from the field profiles; and (3) using correlations of the degree of soil development on the piedmont with local and

regional soil chronosequences (see below) to estimate the approximate ages of displaced surfaces.

The map and field data were first used to define objectively the geometric segmentation along the fault zone. This segmentation scheme is based mainly on systematic along-strike variation in the geometry of the surface trace of the fault zone. The fault scarp data were used to estimate the relative lengths, sizes, and general timing of discrete surface ruptures among the individual geometric segments on this fault zone. Ages of fault scarps were derived primarily from both linear regression and diffusion modeling techniques of morphologic age estimation (see section on fault scarps below). Both methods were used in order to assess their relative efficiency and resolution in estimating the age of the most recent event on this type of range-bounding fault zone. These data and age interpretations were then used to infer the probable magnitudes and frequency of late Quaternary paleoseismicity on various segments of the range-bounding fault zone.

The forms, or morphologies, of selected bedrock landforms such as facets, spurs, benches, and range-crest summits on the mountain front were defined quantitatively by field transects and morphometric measurements on topographic maps (USGS 7½-min quadrangle with 40- or 20-ft contour intervals). Specific types of morphologic data include: (1) topographic cross sections of triangular facets and spurs constructed from field transects (basal facets only) and topographic maps (full mountain front); (2) the height (i.e., local relief), average slope gradient, and slope area (corrected for gradient) of basal triangular facets measured from topographic maps; and (3) vertical projections of the mountain-front base, range crest, and a set of mid-escarpment topographic benches that correlate with dated Pliocene basalt flows on the mountain front (see below). The elevations and relative positions of all three of the latter surfaces and benches were plotted together in vertical projections that parallel the average trend of the mountain front.

Nonparametric and parametric (ANOVA) analyses of variance were used to compare observed variations in landform morphology with spatial changes in both major tectonic and nontectonic variables. These include geometric segmentation and ages of late Quaternary surface rupture on the range-bounding fault, bedrock lithology, and the degree of piedmont dissection related to downcutting of the axial Rio Grande drainage. These statistical analyses isolated the extent to which the morphology of mountain-front landforms correlate with the time-space segmentation patterns, which were independently identified from fault-trace geometry and the morphology of late Quaternary fault scarps on the range-bounding fault (see Menges, 1988, for details of mountain-front study).

STUDY AREA

The study area is a 50-km-long section of the bedrock mountain front that forms the western structural boundary of the southern Sangre de Cristo Mountains between Taos and the New Mexico–Colorado border (Figs. 1 and 2). This prominent topo-

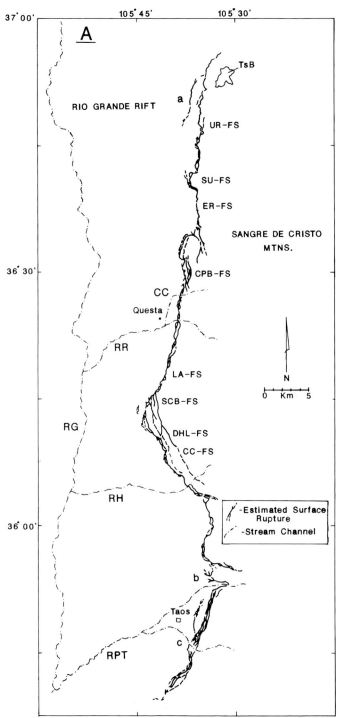

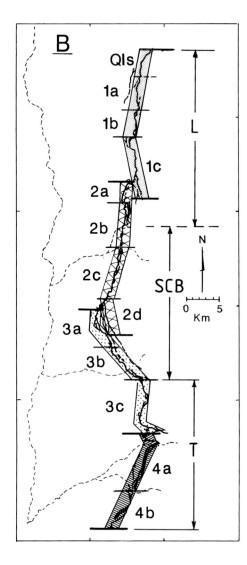

Figure 2. Map of the late Quaternary rupture pattern along the range-bounding fault zone of the Sangre de Cristo Mountains interpreted from selected geomorphic and structural features along the mountain front. A. Map of fault scarps, the basal topographic junction of the mountain front, and selected bedrock faults considered to be part of the boundary fault zone (defined in text). Mapping based on interpretation of aerial photographs and detailed fieldwork at 8 sites (labeled in capital letters, e.g., UR-FS). Three sites identified as a, b, and c are from

Machette and Personius (1984). River abbreviations: Rio Grande gorge (RG), Red River (RR), Cabresto Creek (CC), and Rio Hondo (RH). TsB is an outcrop of Pliocene basalt (Servilleta basalts of Lipman and others, 1986) preserved at San Pedro Mesa on the north end of the range front. B. Map of geometric segmentation patterns of the range-bounding fault zone based on variations in the features presented in Figure 2a (see text for details). Four primary segments are bounded by the heavy lines and are indicated by numbers 1 through 4; subsegments are outlined by fine lines and are labeled with combination of lowercase letters and numbers. L (Latir) and SCB (San Cristobal) and T (Taos) refer to gross physiographic subdivisions of the mountain front defined primarily on the basis of relative elevation of the range crest. The boundary between the Land SCB sections lies at a low section of the mountain front coincident with Cabresto Creek (CC, Fig. 2a). These general subdivisions were later replaced by the more systematic geometric fault segmentation scheme. C (facing page). Enlargement of fault segment 1 and northern part of segment 2 from Figure 2a, showing several examples of type A and type B rupture patterns (described in text) that are used to define geometric fault segmentation. Both types of ruptures are illustrated at segment and subsegment scales.

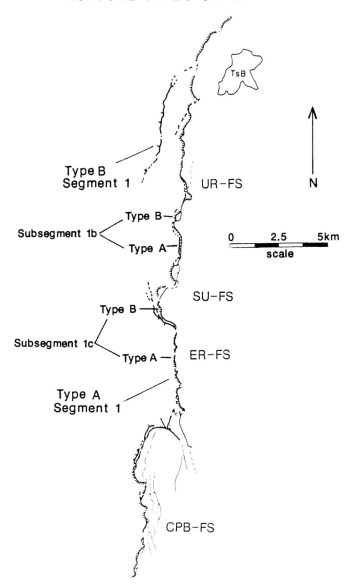

C

RUPTURE TYPES ON SEGMENT 1

TsB

Type B
Segment 1

UR-FS

N

Type B

Subsegment 1b

Type A

0   2.5   5km
scale

SU-FS

Type B

Subsegment 1c

Type A   ER-FS

Type A
Segment 1

CPB-FS

and intruded by mid- to late Tertiary volcanic and plutonic rocks (Reed and others, 1983; Reed, 1984). Most of the volcanic rocks are related to the formation of the Questa caldera and Latir volcanic field in late Oligocene time (Lipman and others, 1986). Paleozoic sediments are exposed in the southernmost part of the mountain front adjacent to Taos.

The base of the main bedrock escarpment is marked by a complex but well-delineated normal fault zone that dips at steep to moderate angles ($\geqslant 50°$) to the west. The fault zone forms the main eastern boundary of a narrow (5 to 15 km wide) graben in the adjacent part of the southeastern San Luis basin. This graben has an estimated depth of 2,500 to 3,000 m to the base of Tertiary fill (Keller and others, 1984). Together this Sangre de Cristo fault zone and adjoining mountain front compose the primary tectonic and physiographic boundary along the eastern margin of this part of the Rio Grande rift.

Pliocene basalt flows with K-Ar ages of 4.3 Ma are locally preserved on the north end of the range block near the Colorado–New Mexico border (Fig. 2a; Lipman and others, 1986). These rocks are correlated with the 3- to 5-Ma Servilleta basalts of the Taos Plateau volcanic field that are exposed extensively throughout the Rio Grande gorge and are interbedded with basin-fill sediment in the shallow subsurface of the San Luis Basin (Lipman and Mehnert, 1979; Lipman and others, 1986; Summers and Hargis, 1984; Winograd, 1959, 1985). Thus, the difference in altitude between the basalt flows on the range block and those in the adjoining basin provides an approximate measure of the cumulative vertical offset along the range-bounding fault zone since 4.3 Ma.

GEOMORPHIC AND GEOLOGIC SETTING OF FAULT SCARPS

The surface trace of the fault zone in the study area is marked along much of its length by discontinuous fault scarps of Holocene to middle Pleistocene age (see later section on fault scarps; Figs. 2a and 3). The topographic scarps occur in piedmont alluvium, or alluvial- or colluvial-mantled bedrock at or slightly basinward of the base of the mountain front. Bedrock is not exposed at the surface of any of the fault scarps analyzed in this study. Scarp parent materials consist of unconsolidated pebble, cobble, and small boulder gravels with a matrix of sand and silt.

The geomorphic surfaces affected by the fault scarps are associated with a range of poorly to well-developed soils. The best-developed soils are generally characterized by Bt (argillic?) horizons as much as a meter in thickness and contain no to very sparse accumulations of pedogenic carbonate, which in a few places attain Stage II to III morphologies (e.g., Gile and others, 1966; Birkeland, 1984). Detailed studies of the soils and stratigraphy of alluvial and glacial deposits have recently been conducted in parts of the San Luis basin (Hacker and Carleton, 1976; McCalpin, 1982; Kelson, 1986; Kelson and Wells, 1987), Sangre de Cristo Mountains (Hacker and Carleton, 1976; McCalpin, 1982; Karas, 1987; Kelson, 1986; Wesling, 1987;

graphic escarpment trends north-south and slopes westward with 500 to 1,200 m of local relief. The range front contains a well-developed suite of erosional landforms, including triangular facets, spur ridgecrests, drainage basins, and range-crest summits, all of which are characteristic of tectonically active mountain fronts in the Basin and Range province (Wallace, 1978; Mayer, 1986). In the Taos area, the highest summits reach elevations of 3,700 m above the adjacent basalt flows, basin fill, and piedmont alluvial fans of the southeastern San Luis Basin at 2,000- to 2,700-m elevations (Upson, 1939; Lambert, 1966).

The lithologies of bedrock in the study area include Precambrian granitic rocks, and mafic gneisses and schists overlain

Figure 3. Photographs of fault scarps on range-bounding fault zone below western mountain front of the Sangre de Cristo Mountains north of Taos, New Mexico. A. Fault scarps (FS, below central grassy area) developed on apex of upper Pleistocene alluvial fan at Urraca Ranch site (UR-FS, Fig. 2a). B. Fault scarps (FS) and structural benches (B) at Canada Pinabete site (CPB-FS, Fig. 2a). Fault scarps offset alluvial fans at canyon mouths. Similar scarps define the outer margin of bedrock benches mantled with alluvium and/or colluvium at the base of bedrock facets on the mountain front. The topographic benches are interpreted as structural blocks bounded by splays within the range-bounding fault zone. C. Large, gently sloping bedrock bench located between two fault-bounded escarpments at the piedmont junction boundary (left) and interior (right) of the overall mountain front. This complex multiple escarpment occurs at site SCB on the boundary between segments 2 and 3 of the range-front fault (Fig. 2b).

Wesling and McFadden, 1986), and Espanola basin (Dethier and others, 1988). This research provides important calibration for soil-based estimates of the ages of geomorphic surfaces, which in turn furnish limiting time control for the fault scarps analyzed in the present study.

Most fault scarps face west (±45°) in the study area and are at elevations ranging from 2,300 to 2,700 m, due mainly to lateral variations in the elevation of the base of the range front (described in next section). The type and density of vegetation on the scarps vary laterally with these changes in elevation, ranging from sparse mixed grasses and sagebrush at lower elevations, to mixed assemblages of scrub oak–pinyon–juniper or dense ponderosa pine forest at the highest elevations. Throughout the study area the climate at the base of the range front is generally semiarid continental, having mean annual temperatures and precipitation of 4° and 35 to 45 cm, respectively (Hacker and Carleton, 1976).

Machette and Personius (1984) and Personius and Machette (1984) made a reconnaissance survey of a few piedmont fault scarps located at the north and south ends of the Taos section of the Sangre de Cristo fault zone (Fig. 2a). Dungan and others (1984) studied late Cenozoic volcanism, localized faulting, and surface warping in the Rio Grande gorge and adjacent parts of the southeastern San Luis Basin, but they did not investigate Quater-

nary deformation on the boundary fault of the Sangre de Cristo Mountains between Taos and Costilla. The lack of neotectonic data on the main range-bounding fault probably results from general difficulty in recognizing fault scarps in the dense vegetation, the steep topography at the base of the mountain front, and generally poor access to the range-bounding fault zone.

DISTRIBUTION AND GEOMETRY OF SURFACE FAULTING ALONG THE RANGE-FRONT FAULT ZONE

Several types of geomorphic and structural data were used to map the spatial distribution of late Quaternary displacements along the fault zone (Fig. 2a). These data, listed in order of decreasing reliability, include: (1) piedmont fault scarps and low-relief bedrock fault benches; (2) the basal topographic junction of the main set of triangular facets; and (3) a few faults in the lower bedrock escarpment that generally strike parallel to and mimic the geometry of the other tectonic landforms along the base of the range front. Most of these latter faults lie at the base of prominent topographic steps with significant down-to-the-basin relief (e.g., Fig. 3c).

Physiographic and geomorphic expression of late Quaternary surface rupture

The geometry and geomorphic position of surface faulting varies laterally along the range front. Topographically distinct fault scarps are developed in alluvial fan deposits on less than 10 to 20 percent of the total length of the fault. Such scarps typically are located on the upper piedmont within 1 km of the base of the small salients in the mountain front (e.g., sites SCB-FS and SU-FS, Fig. 2a), or in narrow fanhead embayments where large drainages exist from the mountain front (e.g., sites LER-FS and UR-FS, Figs. 2a and 3a).

Geomorphic evidence for middle to late Quaternary surface faulting is more subtle displayed along the large sections of the boundary fault situated directly at the base of the bedrock escarpment. Subhorizontal to gently basinward sloping benches are located between small fault scarps (commonly ≤30 m high) and the base of the main set of bedrock facets on many parts of the range front (e.g., sites LA-FS and DHL-FS, Figs. 2a and 3b). These narrow (≤100 m wide) benches are commonly mantled by thin (less than 1 m thick) veneers of colluvium and/or alluvium overlying weathered bedrock. Most of these bedrock benches have very linear boundaries, which are locally associated with exposed fault zones and/or abrupt discontinuities in bedrock lithology. These benches, therefore, are interpreted as the topographic expression of elongate structural blocks bounded to either side by subparallel fault strands that mainly dip basinward within a complex boundary-fault zone. Elsewhere the topographic junction between the piedmont and the mountain front is defined by a sharp to gradual increase in slope related to deposition of a wedge of colluvium across the range-bounding fault at the base of triangular facets. Many of these basal wedges are disrupted by small but distinct benches or slope breaks, which may be the degraded remnants of late Quaternary fault scarps.

Geometric segmentation of the range-bounding fault zone

The surface trace of the range-bounding fault zone displays two fundamental geometric patterns or styles. These patterns are distinguished on the basis of the degree of internal complexity of fault scarps and their position relative to the topographic base of the mountain front. Along some sections, evidence for late Quaternary faulting is confined to a narrow zone (type A, Fig. 2c) at or slightly basinward of (<100 m) the base of the bedrock escarpment. Type A fault patterns have relatively simple geometries, characterized by either a single fault scarp or slope break (e.g., ER—FS, Fig. 2c) or more commonly by one of the narrow alluvial- or colluvial-mantled bedrock benches described above (e.g., north of SU-FS, Fig. 2C). Type A fault geometries typically change along strike into wide, complex zones of distributed surface faulting (type B, Fig. 2c). Type B sections of the fault typically contain one or more piedmont fault scarps as much as 1 km basinward from bedrock fault splays that bound multiple structural benches at the base of the main topographic escarpment (e.g., SU-FS, CPB-FS, and SCB-FS; Figs. 2a and 2c). These two fault types represent opposite extremes in the range of fault trace geometries observed along the mountain-front fault zone.

The two main types of fault geometries are not randomly distributed along the mountain front, but are concentrated in alternating patterns suggesting several scales of spatial segmentation in the trace of the fault zone. They therefore provide a means for defining geometric segments along the fault zone without a priori reference to any rupture-age criteria. Geometric variations are emphasized because: (1) they may be consistently and objectively identified on aerial photography, and (2) recent research in seismology and fracture mechanics suggests that fault geometry is an important factor in the nucleation and propagation of ruptures on normal fault zones (e.g., the barrier model of Bruhn and others, 1987; see Discussion section below). The timing data acquired from fault-scarp analysis may subsequently be added to the geometric framework of the fault zone in order to define those geometric segments and boundaries that have the greatest influence on specific surface-rupture events.

The geometric patterns described above have been used to subdivide the 70-km length of the mountain-front fault zone between Taos and the Colorado border into four primary geometric segments (labeled 1 through 4 in Fig. 2b). Each fault segment is 15 to 20 km in length, although only the northern two and one-half segments lie in the specific 50-km section of the fault in the detailed study area (Fig. 1). The middle, or central, reaches of fault segments are characterized by narrow, simple, type A fault geometries. The terminal or boundary reaches of primary segments are defined by broad, complex zones of type B faulting. Type A patterns are particularly narrow and simple in geometry near the southern ends of most segments (e.g., segment 1, Fig. 2c). Trace geometry generally increases both in width and in topographic and structural complexity northward along each primary segment.

Most of the lateral boundaries between primary segments in the fault zone also coincide with major changes in gross morphology and/or bedrock geology of the mountain front (Fig. 2). These include one or more of the following: (1) abrupt transverse jumps in the base of the mountain front that typically step 1 to 2 km to the right (looking northward along strike) between subparallel sections of the range front; (2) major spurs or deflections in the average trend of the range front; (3) broad (≥1 to 2 km wide) subhorizontal benches in the mountain front that are bounded by internal and external (i.e., range-bounding) bedrock escarpments commonly exceeding 100 m in height (Fig. 3c); (4) large elevation gaps in range-crest summits; and (5) major faults and/or lithologic contacts in the range block oriented transverse to the mountain front. These large-scale changes in the range front are difficult to define precisely and do not vary systematically along the mountain front, compared to variation in fault-trace geometry. The range-front characteristics listed above were used as auxiliary, rather than primary, criteria for identifying geometric fault segments.

The internal geometry of primary fault segments contains considerable small-scale variation along strike that may be used to subdivide each segment into two to four subsegments having lengths of 5 to 10 km. The central to south-central reaches of subsegments typically have narrow type A geometries. These zones grade laterally into the more complex type B fault patterns defining subsegment terminations. Thus, subsegments resemble segments in geometry, although the average range of geometric variation is smaller and less distinct at subsegment scales. The lateral boundaries between most subsegments also are not associated with the major discontinuities or changes in the mountain front that commonly occur at the boundaries between primary segments (see above).

The internal geometric patterns of fault segments and subsegments also coincide with pronounced changes in the relative position and elevation of the base of the mountain front. The narrow type A zones of segments and subsegments typically coincide with reentrants in the mountain front, whereas type B boundaries form on adjacent salients or spurs in the range front (Figs. 2b and 2c). Mountain-front salients are commonly 100 to 400 m lower in altitude than adjacent reentrants (Fig. 4). Adjacent Subsegments and segments thus tend to produce distinct lateral and vertical shifts in the base of the mountain front. The scale of variation and average elevation of the base of the mountain front generally increase irregularly to the south along most primary fault segments. This elevation rise continues to the southern termination of a given segment. At that point the base of the range front abruptly deflects or drops in altitude across the boundary to the next major segment to the south (Figs. 2, 3c, and 4). Many of these boundaries also are marked by a short (≤5 km) zone of overlap between the ends of adjoining segments, which typically coincides with a distinctly higher-elevation section of the range crest (Fig. 4).

AMOUNT AND TIMING OF LATE QUATERNARY SURFACE RUPTURE ALONG FAULT SCARPS

Data

Fault scarps of probable middle to late Quaternary age (see below) were studied on six subsegments of the three primary segments that make up the northern two-thirds of the range-bounding fault zone (Fig. 2a). The fault-scarp data were initially subdivided for geomorphic and morphologic analyses into two general groups on the mountain front defined by relative position to the north (Latir section) or south (San Cristobal section) of Cabresto Creek, a major, deeply incised stream in the mountain front (CC, Figs. 2 and 4). This stream canyon corresponds to a distinct low area in the average elevation of the range crest, and was originally considered to potentially represent a major discontinuity in the range front and boundary fault zone. This general two-part subdivision was not supported by subsequent analyses of fault geometry and scarp morphology (see below). Thus, it was later replaced by a more detailed classification of scarps by individual sites and small groups of 2 to 4 sites, arranged according to their position within the various fault segments and subsegments defined above.

The fault-scarp data are required to derive paleoseismic parameters such as the length and displacement size of coseismic surface rupture and slip; these are critical inputs for estimating the magnitude of associated earthquakes. In this study the vertical components of rupture are estimated from scarp heights, and the net vertical tectonic displacements are measured directly from field profiles using the graphical techniques of Machette and Personius (1984). Rupture lengths are defined from mapping of fault scarps, as constrained by spatial variations in the age of the most recent rupture estimated from the morphologies of degraded scarp profiles (see below). Scarp heights and displacements, plus the maximum scarp-slope angle, are also the key parameters used in techniques of morphologic-age estimation (described below).

Fault scarp heights and amounts of vertical offset

Scarp profiles indicate that both single-rupture and composite (multiple superimposed ruptures) fault scarps are present at most study sites, although the former are more commonly developed at sites on segment 1 and the northern part of segment 2. Most of the fault scarps in the study area exceed 4 to 5 m in height on upper Pleistocene or older structures (Hm, Table 1; Menges, 1988). These large composite scarps probably represent two or more individual surface ruptures along the same fault trace for the following reasons. The height and amount of offset typically increase in composite fault scarps formed in older geomorphic surfaces. The topographic profiles of most composite fault scarps also contain at least one, and in some cases two, slope sections (compound elements of Wallace, 1977), with distinctly steeper slope angles than adjoining parts of the profile. The graphical solutions of Machette and Personius (1984) were applied to these profiles to determine one to two smaller increments of height (Hs) and vertical surface displacement (S1) that at many sites correspond well with the heights and offsets estimated from adjacent single-rupture fault scarps (see below; Table 1).

Small fault scarps ≤2 to 3 m in height are locally interspersed among large composite scarps in areas where the fault zone crosses relatively young, upper Pleistocene or Holocene geomorphic surfaces. These small scarps are considered to represent the most recent event at a particular site on the range-front fault (Table 1). This single-event interpretation is based on the following criteria: (1) the development of only small scarps on the youngest (middle to early Holocene) geomorphic surfaces displaced on the fault zone; (2) the absence of any detectable smaller scarps in any Holocene surface; (3) the consistency (e.g., low dispersion) in scarp heights and displacement values estimated from small scarps measured at many different sites on the fault; and (4) the absence of any distinct, steeply sloping elements on the profiles of small scarps that resemble those observed on most large composite scarps (see above). The range in heights and vertical displacements of the small, single-event scarps in the study area are consistent with the most recent Holocene rupture event proposed by McCalpin (1982) for the northern end of the Sangre de Cristo fault zone from scarp morphology and offset relations in trenches.

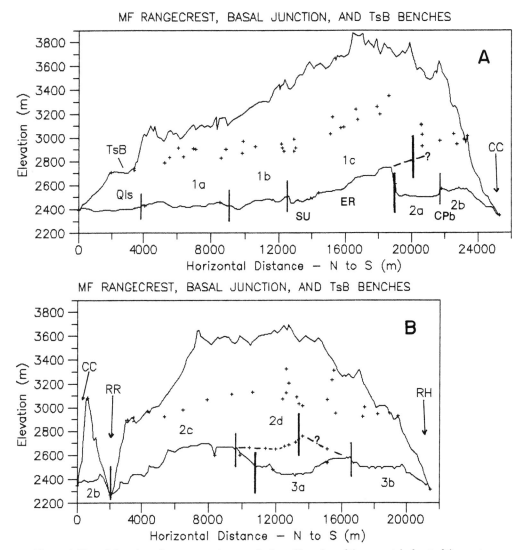

Figure 4. Plot of elevation of range crest, base, and selected benches of the mountain front of the western Sangre de Cristo Mountains, subdivided into sections north and south of Cabresto Creek (CC). Altitudes from 1:100,000 and 1:24,000 scale maps are projected approximately perpendicular to the mountain front into a common vertical plane (5.4× vertical exaggeration) oriented parallel to base of range front. Crosses indicate the projected positions of a set of prominent topographic benches at mid-escarpment levels on most facet-spur systems that correlate with Pliocene basalt flows (TsB; Fig. 2a) at the north end of the range crest (see text for details; also Fig. 14). Alpha-numeric labels refer to segments and subsegments of Figure 2b, with heavy and fine vertical lines indicating approximate segment and subsegment boundaries, respectively. Dashed horizontal lines indicate projected altitudes of the base of interior mountain fronts, i.e., large escarpments above subhorizontal bedrock benches within the main bedrock mountain front (see Fig. 2c). Qls: areas of Quaternary landslides, derived from basalt flows (TsB), that bury range-front fault. Other symbols are river abbreviations of Figure 2a. A. Projections of elevation surfaces on northern (Latir) section of range front. B. Projections of elevation surfaces on southern (San Cristobal) section of the mountain front.

The profiles of both single-rupture and composite fault scarps from all sites indicate that scarp heights and estimated vertical displacements of the most recent rupture average 2.2 and 1.2 m, respectively (Table 1). Composite scarps developed on middle to upper Pleistocene alluvial surfaces have mean cumulative heights and vertical displacements of 5.6 and 3.6 m, respectively (Table 1). A broad, 130 to 200 ka age range is estimated

for most of these surfaces, based on soil-stratigraphic comparisons with deposits of Bull Lake age in the southern Rocky Mountain region with assigned ages of ≈130 to 140 ka (Colman and Pierce, 1981; McCalpin, 1982; Birkeland, 1984). The largest composite scarps are formed on geomorphic surfaces of probable mid-Pleistocene age, and reach maximum heights of 12 to 15 m and vertical surface offsets of 9 to 10 m. The amounts of net vertical

C. M. Menges

tectonic displacement of geomorphic surfaces estimated from scarp profiles typically represent 50 to 70 percent of the height of the topographic scarps. The height and displacement of large composite scarps may be graphically underestimated by as much as 10 to 30 percent, however, if the presence of locally thick wedges of colluvial and/or eolian material deposited above the lower original surface at the base of the scarp is not accounted for in profile reconstructions.

Variations among sites along the range-front fault zone. Scarp heights and net vertical displacements are generally similar in size at a given site along the mountain front. Only minor differences are detectable among sites along segment 1 on the northern part of the mountain front. Two sites (ER-FS and SU-FS) on subsegment 1c (Fig. 2a; Table 1) have slightly smaller values in the heights and displacements of single-rupture scarps, relative to adjacent sites. Site ER-FS also contains 5- to 6-m-high composite fault scarps on upper Pleistocene surfaces that have more weakly developed soils than are observed typically at other sites along the range front.

Fault scarps at sites along segments 2 and 3 on the southern

TABLE 1. SUMMARY OF MORPHOLOGIC DATA OF 40 FAULT SCARPS GROUPED BY EIGHT SITES ALONG RANGE-FRONT FAULT, LISTED FROM NORTH TO SOUTH IN FIGURE 2a

Site		Scarp Height										
		Hm*(m)			$Hs^{\dagger}$(m) $C^{\S}$ + SR**				Hs (m) SR only			
Name	n	n	Max.	Min.	n	Max.	Min.	Avg.	n	Max.	Min.	Avg.
UR-FS	10	5	12.0	5.5	9	4.4	1.6	3.0 ± 1.0	5	3.5	1.6	2.6 ± 0.9
SU-FS	10	3	6.3	5.4	10	3.2	0.75	1.7 ± 0.9	5	1.5	0.75	1.1 ± 0.3
ER-FS	7	3	6.5	4.3	6	2.4	0.9	1.8 ± 0.6	4	2.1	0.9	1.5 ± 0.5
CPB-FS	4	2	6.0	4.4	4	3.5	1.4	2.5 ± 0.9	2	2.5	1.4	2.0 ± 0.8
LA-FS	1	1	14.2	....	0	....	....	....	0	....	....	......
SCB-FS	3	3	11.0	5.5	1	3.3	....	....	1	3.3	....	......
DHL-FS	5	2	12.4	4.5	4	4.2	2.3	3.1 ± 0.9	3	4.2	2.55	3.4 ± 0.8
CC-FS	2	2	15.0	10.1	1	3.0	....	....	0	....	....	......

Site		Surface Offsets							Max. Slope Angle		
		$S1^{\ddagger}$(m) C only			$S2^{\S\S}$(m) C + SR				Θ (deg)/H (m)		
Name	n	n	Max.	Min.	n	Max	Min.	Avg.	n	Max.	Min.
UR-FS	10	5	10.2	2.4	9	2.4	0.5	1.4 ± 0.6	10	25.5°/12.0	14.5°/1.6
SU-FS	10	3	4.6	3.5	8	1.2	0.7	0.8 ± 0.2	10	25.5°/6.3	11.5°/1.2
ER-FS	7	3	4.5	2.6	6	0.95	0.7	0.8 ± 0.2	7	29.5°/6.5	13.0°/0.9
CPB-FS	4	2	3.8	2.8	4	1.25	0.9	1.0 ± 0.2	4	26.0°/6.0	17.0°/1.4
LA-FS	1	1	9.0	....	....	....	....	....	1	26.5°/14	....
SCB-FS	3	2	6.5	4.0	2	2.15	2.1	2.1 ± 0.1	1	17.5°/9.4	13.0°/11
DHL-FS	5	4	7.2	2.0	5	2.2	0.7	1.3 ± 0.7	5	23.0°/4.5	16.5°/2.6
CC-FS	2	2	10.0	4.8	2	2.7	1.65	2.2 ± 0.8	2	24.0°/15	23.5°/10

Data includes number (n), maximum (max.) , and minimum (min.) values, and average and standard deviation (avg.) of scarp heights, net tectonic vertical displacements of surfaces, and maximum slope angles, as determined graphically from field profiles (after Machette and Personium, 1984).

Heights and displacements of most recent events	Hs	S2
Entire mountain front (average–all sites)	2.2 ± 1.0 m	1.2 ± 0.6 m
Average cumulative displacements of upper middle		
Pleistocene surfaces	Hm	S1
(≈Bull Lake age; all sites)	5.6 ± 1.2 m	3.6 ± 1.2 m

*Hm - Total height of composite scarp
†Hs - Height of steepest section of composite scarp, or height of single rupture scarp
§C - Composite scarp
**SR - Single-rupture scarp
‡S1 - Total vertical tectonic displacement of composite scarp
§§S2 - Vertical tectonic displacement, steepest section of composite scarp, or single-rupture scarp

section of the range-front fault display a greater range in heights, displacements, and maximum slope angles (Table 1). Several composite fault scarps at site SCB-FS are unusually high and degraded, with anomalously low slope angles, despite development in dissected alluvium of probable early(?) to middle Pleistocene age. Scarps exceeding 5 m in height lack the steeper slope sections ($>20°$) that are present on most composite fault scarps of that size elsewhere on the mountain front; this relation suggests an absence at this site of the youngest rupture event observed at most other sites on the range-bounding fault. Sites farther to the south on segment 3 (DhL-FS and CC-FS, Fig. 2), however, contain a few degraded scarps similar to site SCB-FS intermixed with morphologically younger scarps resembling those at sites on segment 2 and 3 to the north (e.g., UR-FS and CPB-FS, Fig. 2).

Morphologic age estimates of most recent rupture along fault scarps

Least-squares linear regressions. The first type of morphologic analysis used least-squares linear regressions of log scarp height versus maximum slope angle, following the procedures of Bucknam and Anderson (1979) and Machette and Personius (1984). The regression lines of undated fault scarps in the Taos area were compared in these analyses with a number of published regression lines of reference scarps that span a wide range of estimated ages (Fig. 5; Bucknam and Anderson, 1979; Machette and Personius, 1984). Least-square regression lines were initially fit to the height–slope-angle data from only single-rupture scarps: the single-event data were then combined with the heights of the steepest, youngest slope elements (Hs) of composite fault scarps. The regression equations derived from scarp data at all sites on the Latir section of the mountain front were essentially identical, whether they were restricted to only single-rupture scarps ($\theta_s = 15.1 + 13.7 \log H$; $R^2 = 0.52$), or included data from both single-rupture and composite scarps (Hs: $\theta_s = 15.6 + 13.8 \log Hs$; $R^2 = 0.58$). This supports the correlation of Hs slope elements on composite scarps with the most recent event recorded by the single-rupture scarps. Subsequent analysis of scarps by site and groups of scarps incorporated the latter set of mixed scarp data in order to ensure the largest possible sample sizes for statistical estimations of scarp ages. The full heights (Hm) of composite fault scarps were not utilized in estimating the age of the most recent rupture at any sites in the study area. Colman and others (1985) and Machette and Personius (1984) suggest that height–slope-angle plots with Hm data commonly yield spurious regression lines indicating excessively old scarp ages. This mainly reflects the inclusion of data points related to several different ages of surface rupture.

The results of the linear-regression analyses illustrate the difficulties in applying this technique to this type of range-bounding fault zone where multiple surface ruptures are commonly repeated on the same trace. Considerable scatter exists in the semilog scatter diagram of combined Hs morphologic data from all sites along the mountain front (Fig. 5). Most of the data

fall within the general area between the Fish Springs (FS) and Bonneville shoreline (BV) reference scarps (Fig. 5). This places only a very broadly defined age constraint of 2 to 15 ka for the most recent rupture(s) along all fault scarps developed along the range-front fault zone.

The large amount of scatter evident in this plot suggests that the observed scarp morphologies in this data set probably record more than one rupture age along the section of the range-front fault in the study area. An additional unknown, but probably significant, amount of morphologic variation may arise from differences in the parent material, microclimate, vegetation, and geomorphic setting of scarps. The combined data were therefore subdivided prior to analysis, according to general position relative to the Latir and San Cristobal subdivisions of the mountain front (see above, Figs. 2 and 4). This partition did decrease somewhat the amount of dispersion in each data subdivision (Fig. 5). For example, a regression line fit through the Latir scarp data, which includes data from segments 1 and 2 (north half), displays a moderate correlation with a fairly steep slope (13.8) and high intercept (15.6) generally associated with young rupture ages. The data from scarps along segment 3 on the southern (San Cristobal) section of the mountain front, however, still contain considerable scatter that is reflected in the low coefficient of determination (R^2) of the regression. No further regression analyses were applied to this data subset because of difficulty in clearly distinguishing the most recent rupture on many of the large composite scarps on this part of the fault zone.

The linear regressions for scarp data from the two northern fault segments are improved further by additional subdivision into groups of individual sites. Regressions of data from two sites (ER- and SU-FS) on the Latir section produce a steeply sloping line with a significantly higher correlation coefficient that clearly lies in the late to middle Holocene age field (Fig. 6). Analyses of more scattered data from the other two sites on the northern section (UR- and CPB-FS) produce a best-fit line with a lower R^2 and a position on the graph suggesting a broadly defined, mid-Holocene age range. These estimates suggest that the most recent rupture at the ER-SU sites may be slightly younger, relative to sites on either site. This age difference cannot be uniquely established from the regression analyses, however, due to the overlap of the 95-percent confidence intervals associated with the regression lines of each site group.

Diffusion modeling. The second morphologic analysis consisted of diffusion modeling of slope degradation (Nash, 1980, 1984, 1986; Colman and Watson, 1983; Mayer, 1984; Hanks and others, 1984; Andrews and Hanks, 1985). This method was applied to 20 single-rupture fault scarps (see Appendix C, Menges, 1988) using the finite difference solution of Nash (1984, 1987).

There are two principal sources of uncertainty in this type of diffusion modeling (Appendix C, Menges, 1988). First, analytical results are affected by the exact form of the initial scarp morphology assumed in diffusion modeling of subsequent scarp degradation (Nash, 1984, 1986). The numerical solution used in this

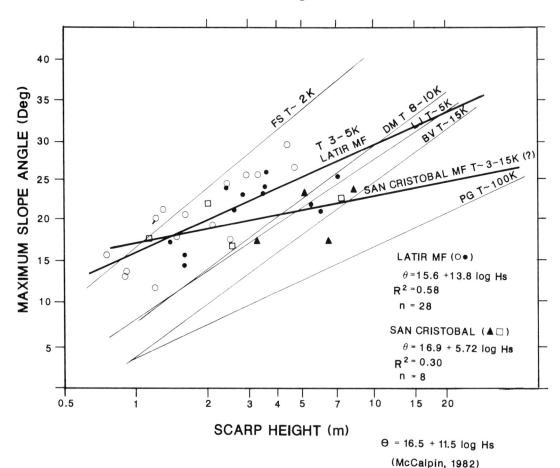

Figure 5. Linear regression analyses of log height versus maximum slope angle data from fault scarps at all sites along range-bounding fault zone. Plot includes morphologic data from single-rupture scarps combined with steepest sections of composite scarps (Hs). Data is subdivided by position on the mountain front, i.e., north (Latir section) and south (San Cristobal section) of Cabresto Creek (see Figs. 2a, b, and 4). Open and closed symbols for each section refer to scarp data from specific site groups (labeled in Fig. 6 and text). Regression equation for post-Pinedale fault scarps on northern Sangre de Cristo fault in Colorado included from McCalpin (1982) for comparison. Thin reference lines are regressions fitted to fault and wavecut scarps with independent age estimates. These reference scarps are located in parts of western Utah, central Idaho, and central New Mexico and include a range of parent material and climates generally similar to those of the Taos study area. Names and estimated ages (T, in ka) of reference scarps are labeled in the diagram. Abbreviations and sources for each scarp are: FS, Fish Springs fault scarp (Bucknam and Anderson, 1979); DM, Drum Mountain fault scarp (Bucknam and Anderson, 1979; Pierce and Colman, 1986); LJ, La Jencia fault scarp (Machette and Personius, 1984) (written communication, 1988); BV, Bonneville shoreline (Bucknam and Anderson, 1979; Machette and Personius, 1984; Pierce and Colman, 1986); PG, Panguitch fault scarp (Bucknam and Anderson, 1979).

study is especially sensitive to two parameters that must be specified in modeling each initial morphology. These are: (1) the degree of symmetry of the initial profile about its slope midpoint, and (2) whether the slopes of the upper and lower original surfaces (γ) are equal (i.e., parallel to one another).

Secondly, any diffusion technique produces a diffusion age (tc) for the fault scarp that consists of the product of time (t) since "formation" (that is, onset of diffusion-modeled degradation after surface rupture) and a diffusivity constant (c). The latter is assumed to incorporate the cumulative effects of all time-independent factors that influence the rate of scarp degradation,

such as parent material, climate, vegetation, and slope aspect (Mayer, 1984; Pierce and Colman, 1986). The "constant," c, may itself exhibit some dependence on the height and initial offset of the scarp in addition to these other variables (Pierce and Colman, 1986; Pearthree and others, 1988). Past changes in climate can also affect the diffusion rate if the scarp formed prior to the Holocene (Machette, 1986).

A model histogram technique adapted from Mayer (1984) was used to statistically incorporate these inherent analytical uncertainties into diffusion-age estimates (Fig. 7). Diffusion ages (tc) were derived from several possible initial scarp morphologies

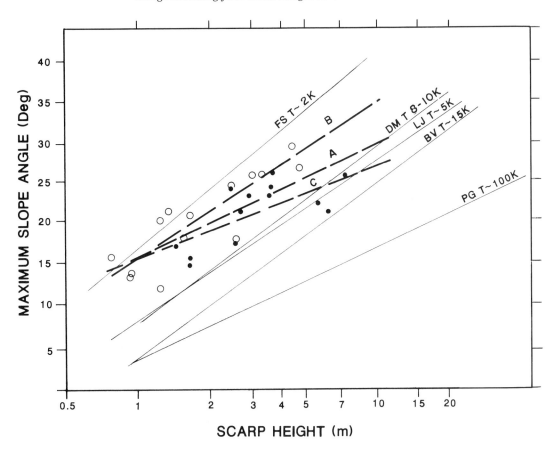

A: All LMF (o ●)
θ = 15.6 + 13.8 log HS
R² = 0.58
n = 28

B: Er — Su Only (o)
θ = 15.5 + 19.5 log HS
R² = 0.80
n = 14

C: Ur — CPb only (●)
θ = 15.3 + 11.7 log HS
R² = 0.48
n = 11

Figure 6. Linear-regression analyses applied to morphologic data from fault scarps along segments 1 and 2 (north part) on the Latir section of the mountain front only. The Lmf regression line is reproduced from Figure 5. Additional regressions have been fit to two subpopulations in the data subdivided by pairs of sites (located in Fig. 2). Note the improvement in R^2 for each site group, relative to that derived from all sites on the Lmf section of the range front. Reference lines are defined in Figure 5.

constructed for each single-event scarp analyzed. Three published diffusivity constants that span an order of magnitude in scarp degradation rates (i.e., c-Yellowstone from Nash, 1984; and height-corrected values of c-Idaho and c-Drum Mountain, Utah, from Pierce and Colman, 1986) were applied to each diffusion age to produce a range in age estimates for each scarp model (Appendix C, Menges, 1988). The c value of the Drum Mountains scarps is probably most directly applicable to the single-event scarps in the study because both formed in the Holocene, whereas the ages of Bonneville and Yellowstone scarps include part of the latest Pleistocene (Machette, written communication, 1988). The total age ranges derived for all models of all scarps analyzed at a given site or group of sites were compiled together to form a composite age histogram (Fig. 7). The median and modal peak of the histogram provide general composite age estimates for each group of scarps.

The results of the diffusion modeling of single-event fault-scarp profiles are much clearer than the linear-regression analyses, particularly in differentiating the morphologic ages of the most recent rupture at various sites on the fault zone. Composite histograms (defined above) for single-rupture scarps at all sites on segment 1 and 2 of the northern (Latir) section of the mountain front indicate a broadly defined, Holocene age distribution with a distinct late to middle Holocene modal peak (Fig. 8). Subdivision of this population into the same by-site groupings used in the regression analyses isolates two component histograms with partially overlapping ranges but distinct median values and modal peaks. The histogram for scarps from the ER-SU sites suggests a late Holocene median for the most recent rupture, which contrasts with the older mid-Holocene median of the age histogram from scarps located at the UR-CPB sites to either side (Fig. 8). Nonparametric Mann-Whitney rank tests (Davis, 1986; Hayes,

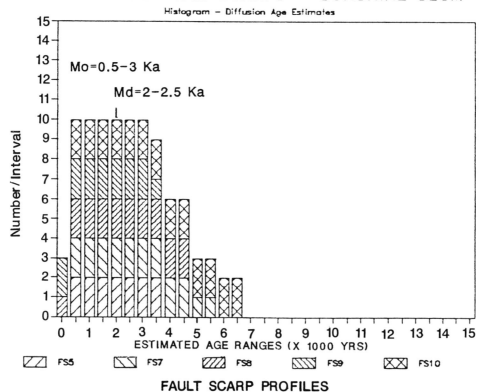

Figure 7. Example of modal-age histogram derived from modeling of single-rupture fault scarps (labeled individually below and within histogram) at SU-FS site. Age ranges are estimated for each fault scarp from three different diffusivity constants (c), applied to the diffusion ages (tc) of several possible initial morphologies (described in text). The total number (N) of age range estimates that fall within 500-yr class intervals are plotted as composite histograms. Mo and Md refer to the age interval of the modal peak and median value in the histogram, respectively.

1988) were directly applied to the age estimates that were derived from the diffusion modeling used to construct this histogram. The tests indicate that the ER-SU and UR-CPB site groups are statistically distinct at a 97.5 percent significance level, whereas individual sites within each group are not distinct at the same level of significance.

Several distinct histograms are also evident in the results of diffusion modeling of single-rupture fault scarps at sites on segment 3 of the range-front fault (Fig. 9). The composite age histograms for all sites is broadly dispersed and right-skewed, with a distinct early Holocene modal peak and a wide latest Pleistocene tail. The histogram of scarps located only at the San Cristobal site on the boundary to segment 3 (Fig. 2) spans a broad latest Pleistocene age range and lacks any Holocene peak. Similar late Pleistocene ages are estimated for several scarps at the DHL site to the south; this site, however, also contains a distinct subset of morphologically younger scarps with composite histograms and middle to early Holocene median ages similar to those derived from the UR- and CPB-FS sites to the north (Figs. 2, 8, and 9).

The diffusion-based age histograms for each site are grouped in Figure 10 by similarities in general form and median ages

instead of location on the mountain front. This rearrangement isolates three distinct categories in the estimated ages of the most recent rupture along the range-bounding fault. Each category is marked by an intra-group similarity in age parameters and general shape of the component histogram. This similarity among sites is especially significant, given the considerable modeling uncertainties deliberately included in the statistical treatment of the age-estimate data. There is an equally strong contrast in the general form and population characteristics of different age groups. These qualitative comparisons of within- and among-group histograms are statistically supported at the 97.5 percent significance level by Mann-Whitney rank sum tests (Davis, 1986; Hayes, 1988) of the original age estimates.

Temporal and spatial patterns in morphologic age estimates

The combined morphologic estimates from all sites indicate a probable age of latest Pleistocene to Holocene for the most recent rupture along most of the 50-km section of the mountain

TAOS RANGE FAULT SCARPS–DIFFUSION ANALYSES

AGE ESTIMATES–MODEL HISTOGRAMS
16 FAULT SCARP–35 MODELS

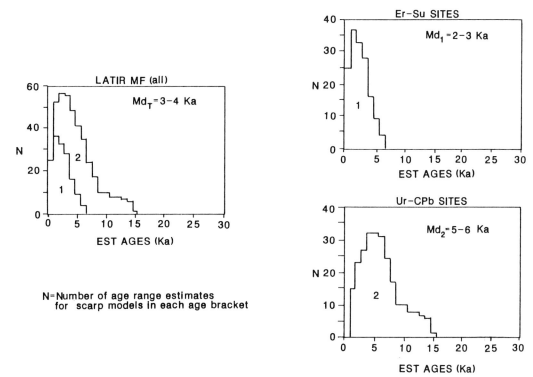

N=Number of age range estimates
for scarp models in each age bracket

Figure 8. Modal-age histograms from diffusion analyses of 16 single-rupture fault scarps, with 35 different models for initial scarp morphologies, along segments 1 and 2 on the Latir section of the mountain front. Histograms on left includes all fault scarps, subdivided by sites into two groups: 1, ER-SR sites; and 2, UR-CPB sites. A separate histogram has been constructed for each of these site groups on the right. Md_T, Md_1, and Md_2 indicate the median-age classes of the total population and subgroups 1 and 2, respectively. The preparation and labeling of histograms are described in text and in Figure 6.

front included in the fault scarp study. The best evidence for Holocene rupture is along segments 1 and 2 on the northern end of the range front (Fig. 2). Morphologic data from sites on segment 3 to the south suggest other early Holocene to latest Pleistocene rupture(s) on this part of fault zone.

These general age assignments for the most recent events on the range-front fault are consistent with the results of the regression analyses independently derived by McCalpin (1982) for fault scarps at the northern end of the range-bounding fault zone of the Sangre de Cristo Mountains in the northeastern San Luis Valley of Colorado. The slope and intercept of regression lines computed for the fault scarps along segments 1 and 2 of the range front in the study area are nearly identical to those calculated by McCalpin (1982) for post-Pinedale–age scarps on the northern Sangre de Cristo fault zone in Colorado (Fig. 5). McCalpin estimated a middle to early Holocene age for the most recent rupture at

several sites along this part of the range-front fault zone, based on relations of radiometrically dated and offset surficial deposits in several trenches across the fault zone.

The diffusion modeling of scarp morphologies in particular suggests a more complicated pattern of rupture segmentation in the study area. Three distinct age ranges for the most recent rupture are distributed among various geometric fault segments and subsegments (Figs. 2, 10, and 11): (1) the youngest rupture of late to middle Holocene age (medium age, Md, = 2.5 to 3.0 ka) restricted to scarps on subsegment 1c only; (2) a slightly older rupture of middle to early Holocene age (Md = 5 to 6 ka) found on scarps at sites on five subsegments of three primary fault segments; and (3) one or more latest Pleistocene ruptures (Md = 12 to 13 ka) detectable only on more degraded, old piedmont fault scarps at the northern ends of three of the primary fault segments.

TAOS RANGE FAULT SCARPS–DIFFUSION ANALYSES

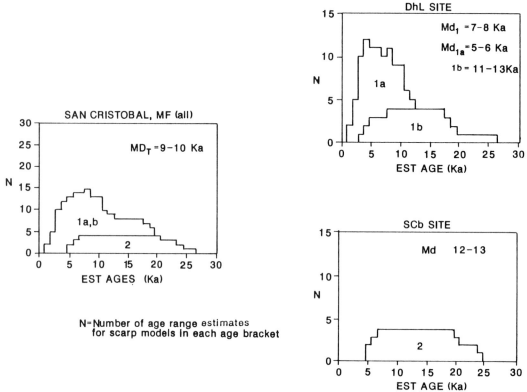

Figure 9. Modal-age histograms from diffusion analyses of 5 single-rupture fault scarps, with 18 different models for initial scarp morphologies, along segment 3 on the southern (San Cristobal) section of the mountain front. Histogram on left includes all fault scarps, subdivided by site into two major groups: 1a, b. DHL site; and 2, SCB site. A separate histogram has been constructed for each of these groups on the right. Group 1 also has been subdivided into two morphologically different sets of scarps that yield statistically distinct age estimates (1a, 1b), using Mann-Whitney rank sum tests at 97.5 percent significance level. Md_T, Md_{1a}, Md_{1b}, and Md_2 refer to median-age classes of the total population and the subdivisions described above. Preparation and labeling of histograms are described in text and Figure 6.

The morphologic age estimates are not precise enough to determine whether the fault scarps at the sites within age groups (2) or (3) in Figure 10 formed in one simultaneous coseismic event, or whether they record smaller-magnitude events clustered in a relatively short time interval. The age difference between the two groups of Holocene rupture in the diffusion histograms, though statistically significant (see above), is probably near the resolution of the morphologic analyses (Kneupfer and Turko, 1987). Assuming that there are two distinct groups of Holocene scarps, the morphologic data do not indicate whether the youngest faulting recorded by late Holocene single-rupture scarps on subsegment 1c was superimposed on a slightly older set of middle Holocene and Pleistocene scarps, or filled a gap in the prior mid-Holocene rupture event(s) to either side (Fig. 11).

Possible patterns of surface rupture among fault segments

The spatial distribution of these age estimates suggests that several possible patterns and scales of surface rupturing may have produced the youngest set of fault scarps in the study area (Fig. 11; Table 2).

1. One small, discrete, mid-Holocene rupture with a relatively small vertical displacement of 0.8 is restricted to a single subsegment. Machette (1986) identified several segments with similar small lengths along the La Jencia fault zone in central New Mexico and proposed that they ruptured independently at different times in the Holocene and latest Pleistocene. He based these conclusions on variations in scarp morphology and the soil stratigraphy of colluvial wedges.

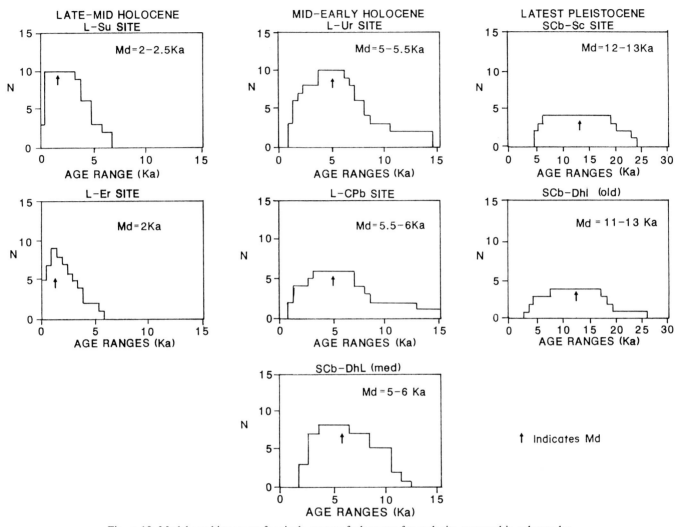

Figure 10. Modal-age histograms for single-rupture fault scarps for each site, arranged in columns by similarities in general form of histogram and median age (Md). The 8-site histograms define 3 general-age categories labeled above each column. Nonparametric tests indicate that these age categories are statistically distinct from one another (discussed in text).

2. One large, older, Holocene rupture (or several smaller ruptures) is (are) evident on at least three of the four primary geometric fault segments. This raises the possibility that a large coseismic event with a total length of 30 to 50 km and average vertical displacements of 1.2 m may have ruptured across several geometric subsegment and segment boundaries along the fault zone.

Crone and Machette (1984) and Crone and others (1987) defined lateral variations in the amount of surface displacement along the coseismic rupture associated with the 1983 Borah Peak earthquake in Idaho. The vertical component of surface rupture in that event alternately increases and decreases laterally along small, 5- to 10-km-long sections of the range-bounding Lost

River fault zone. The scale and size of this variation closely resembles the geometric subsegments that may have ruptured together in one large event or series of clustered events on the Sangre de Cristo fault zone.

3. There is a notable lack of any Holocene ruptures at site SCB-FS (Figs. 2 and 11) or at three sites from Machette and Personius (1984; sites a, b, and c, Figs. 2 and 11). Piedmont fault scarps at these sites are basinward from prominent salients or low parts of the range front that coincide with the northern boundaries of three of the four primary fault segments. The lack of Holocene fault scarps at these sites may mark persistent zones of less frequent rupture and/or smaller net displacement at the boundaries of major segments. Crone and others (1987) describe

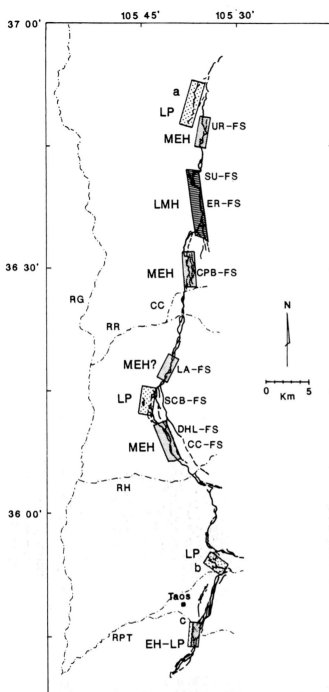

Figure 11. Map of the distribution of estimated ages for the most-recent single-event fault scarps along the range-bounding fault zone. Data for estimates include: (1) combined diffusion modeling and regression analyses at sites identified by capital letters (e.g., UR-FS; see Figs. 2, and 7 through 10); and (2) regression analyses of piedmont fault scarps at sites a, b, and c (see Fig. 2) from Machette and Personius (1984). Morphologic age estimates are consistent with stratigraphic constraints on the age of most-recent rupture derived from offset geomorphic surfaces. General-age categories for sections of the fault zone with patterned strips are: LP, latest Pleistocene; EH, middle to early Holocene; LMH, late to middle Holocene; EHLP, early Holocene to latest Pleistocene.

similar gaps in surface rupture associated with the 1983 Borah Peak earthquake, as well as earlier Holocene events; there, gaps correlate with the proposed boundaries between major segments of the Lost River fault in Idaho.

Paleoseismic interpretations

These possible differences in the scales of late and middle Holocene surface ruptures have important implications for interpreting late Quaternary paleoseismicity along the southern Sangre de Cristo fault zone (Table 2). That is, each scale of surface rupture, if present, would probably be associated with different earthquake magnitudes. Surface ruptures less than 1 m in size confined to a single 5- to 10-km-long subsegment would be associated with earthquakes of estimated magnitudes of 5.8 to 6.2 and 6.6 to 6.8, using magnitude versus rupture-length (M-L) and magnitude versus displacement-size (M-D) regressions of Slemmons (1982), respectively. The moment-magnitude (Mo-M) relations of Hanks and Kanamori (1979) estimate magnitudes of 6.1 to 6.3 for the single-subsegment scale of rupture, using the seismic parameters of Machette (1986) in the moment calculations. A 30 to 50-km-long rupture with 1.2-m vertical displacements that extend across several primary fault segments would be associated with paleoearthquakes with magnitudes in the range of 6.8 to 7.1 (M-L), 6.7 to 6.9 (M-D), and 6.7 to 6.9 (Mo-M). More precise data on the timing, amount, and lengths of individual ruptures are required to uniquely establish the presence of the two proposed scales of earthquakes, however.

Inferred recurrence intervals and slip rates

The fault-scarp analyses do not tightly constrain the relative timing of the various scales of coseismic rupture proposed above. The cumulative displacement of the older geomorphic surfaces generally suggests broadly defined recurrence intervals of 10^4 yr between events at any one site (Table 2). This general rate is compatible with the lower part of the 10- to 50-k.y. intervals inferred by McCalpin (1982) from combined offset data and scarp morphology for the northern section of the Sangre de Cristo fault zone in Colorado. The relative frequency of discrete late Quaternary ruptures in the Taos area cannot be determined from the available data, although there have probably been at least two major ruptures, or groups of ruptures, in latest Pleistocene to Holocene time along different parts of the 50-km section of the mountain front studied.

From the available data, it is difficult to define precisely the late Quaternary slip rates of the Sangre de Cristo fault zone in the Taos area. Scarp data suggest generally low slip rates of 0.03 to 0.06 mm/yr, and certainly <1 mm/yr during late Pleistocene and Holocene time (Table 2), assuming the approximate age ranges of 130 to 200 ka for displaced deposits correlated with Bull Lake glaciations in the Sangre de Cristo Mountains (see above). These rates should be considered with caution, however, because of the absence of radiometrically dated deposits along this part of the fault zone.

PERSISTENCE OF FAULT-SCARP SEGMENTATION THROUGH PLIOCENE-QUATERNARY TIME

A second objective of the study is estimating the degree to which the geometric and rupture segmentation patterns evident in the late Quaternary persist over longer time intervals such as Pliocene and Quaternary. Therefore, selected erosional landforms and stratigraphic units along the mountain front, including triangular facets, spurs, and Pliocene basalts and benches, were quantitatively measured and analyzed to test the persistence of long-term deformation patterns along the boundary fault (see Menges, 1988, for details of this complex study).

Basal triangular facets

Height, gradient, and slope area parameters of basal triangular facets were uniformly measured from field transects and topographic maps. The facet data were grouped according to site position relative to geometric fault segments and subsegments, bedrock lithology, and the presence of dissection/aggradation on the adjacent piedmont. Major characteristics of the basal set of triangular facets appear to more closely correspond to their position relative to fault segments and subsegments than to other geologic variables and geomorphic processes (Fig. 12). For example, the facets along the relatively narrow type A zones of

TABLE 2. SUMMARY OF CHARACTERISTICS, RATES, AND PALEOSEISMICITY ASSOCIATED WITH LATE QUATERNARY RUPTURE ALONG RANGE-FRONT FAULT

1. MEAN VERTICAL DISPLACEMENTS

	Hs*	S2[†]
Most recent events		
Entire mountain front (average–all sites) (Holocene to latest Pleistocene)	2.2 m	1.2 m
Subsegments 1a, 2a, 3a (UR-CPB-DHL sites) (mid to early Holocene)	2.6 m	1.3 m
Subsegment 1c only (ER-SU sites) (late to mid Holocene)	1.7 m	0.8 m
Subsegments 3a (SCB-DHL sites) (latest Pleistocene)	3.1 m	2.0 m
	Hm[§]	S1**
Cumulative displacements of late Pleistocene surfaces (≈ Bull Lake age)		
(average–all sites)	5.6 m	3.6 m

2. ESTIMATED SLIP RATES (APPROXIMATE)

Post-late Pleistocene (≈ Bull Lake age)	0.03–0.06 mm/yr
Post-Plioocene (post Tsb basalts; 4 Ma)	0.12–0.23 mm/yr
	(120–230 m/my)

(Possible 2- to 8-fold rate decrease in late Quaternary)

3. APPROXIMATE PROBABLE RECURRENCE RATE AT GIVEN SITE

10^4 yrs (≈ 10-50 Ka)

4. RUPTURE LENGTHS

Two possible scales of rupture segmentation
   One extending along multiple segments and subsegments (≥ 30-50 km length)
   One restricted to single small subsegment (≈ 5-10 km length)

5. ESTIMATED MAGNITUDES OF PALEOSEISMICITY

	Small Rupture, Single Subsegment	Large Rupture, Multiple Segments
Regressions of Slemmons, 1982		
Magnitude-Length (M-L)	5.8-6.2	6.8-7.1
Magnitude-Displacement (M-D)	6.6-6.8	6.7-6.9
Moment-Magnitude relationships of Hanks and Kanamori, 1979 (Mo-M)	6.1-6.3	6.7-6.9

*Hs - Height of single-rupture fault scarp, or height of steepest section of composite scarp.

[†]S2 - Vertical surface displacement on single-rupture scarp or steepest section of composite scarp.

[§]Hm - Total height of composite scarp.

**S1 - Total vertical surface displacement on composite scarp.

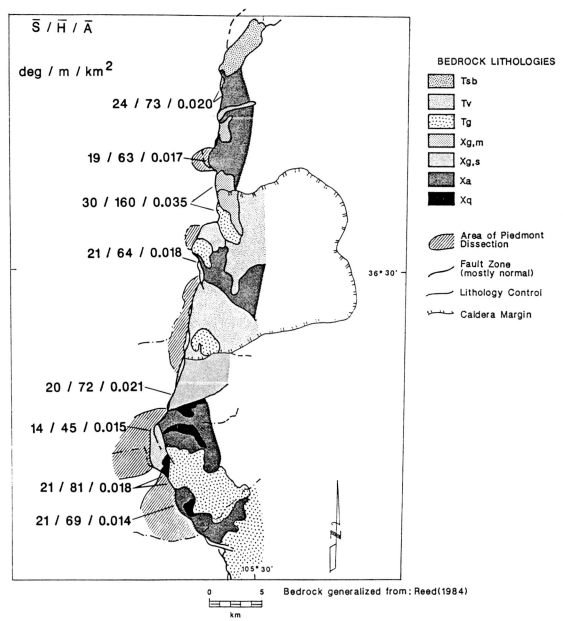

Figure 12. Map showing variations in selected morphologic characteristics of basal facets along the mountain front, relative to fault segmentation and dominant bedrock lithology. Numbers on left are means (n = 4 to 20) of three morphometric parameters of basal facets at same sites as Figure 2. Parameters, listed from left to right are: (1) site average of the mean slope angles (S, in degrees) for field profiles of selected undissected basal facets; (2) mean local relief (R, in m) of all basal facets at each site from 7½-minute topographic maps with 12.2 m (40-ft) contours; and (3) mean facet area (A, in sq km), measured with planimeter on same facets and maps as (2). Major bedrock lithologies of facets at sites are generalized from Reed (1984) and Reed and others (1983).

faulting in the central reaches of geometric subsegments display greater local relief between base and apex, greater average size and slope area, and steeper mean slope angles (≥22°) compared to facets above more complex type B rupture patterns at subsegment or segment boundaries. Facets above segment–subsegment interiors also have fewer facet benches, less developed internal drainages, and thicker colluvial mantles (Figs. 2 and 12; see Menges, 1987a, 1988). These morphologic patterns are especially pronounced on facets near the southern end of the primary fault segments defined earlier, and the largest, steepest, and least dissected facets are developed on geometric subsegments with independent fault-scarp or stratigraphic evidence (discussed below) for increased amounts and rates of surface displacements (e.g., subsegments 1c or 2d; see Figs. 2, 11, and 12). The morphologies

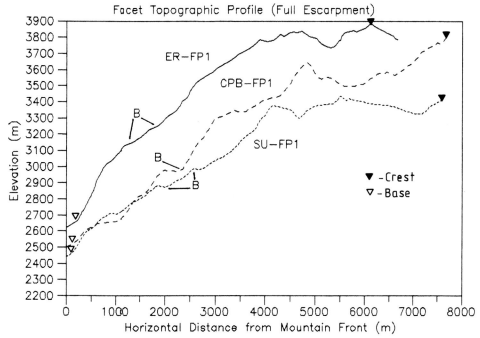

Figure 13. Three topographic profiles of the full mountain-front escarpment from 7½-minute topographic maps. Profiles begin on piedmont below base of mountain front and extend upslope along facet-spur systems to range crest. Profiles begin at three sites used in fault-scarp and facet studies that are at the northern boundary and interior of subsegment 1c (SU-FS and ER-FS, respectively; Figs. 2 and 11) and at the northern end of subsegment 2a (CPB-FS). B marks the position of mid-escarpment benches correlated with the Pliocene basalts at the north end of the range crest (discussed in text; also Figs. 4 and 14).

of facets with similar rock types likewise vary with position relative to the boundary fault, indicating the subordinate role of bedrock relative to tectonic activity in controlling the large-scale characteristics of facets (Menges, 1987a, 1988). Variations in rock type primarily affect the matrix texture and gravel size of colluvium, and the amount and pattern of bedrock exposures.

The effects of nontectonic variables do complicate the tectonically induced patterns of facet morphology at some places. For example, the average slopes of facets at the northernmost site (UR-FS; Figs. 2 and 12) are slightly steeper on felsic gneisses compared to other less-resistant rock types such as amphibolites. Also, relatively small, and in some cases, steeper facets have formed on the intensely dissected range front above the deeply incised piedmont in the south end of the study area (Fig. 12).

Parametric (ANOVA) and nonparametric (Kruskal-Wallis) one-way analyses of variance (Davis, 1986; Hayes, 1988; Wilkinson, 1988) support these qualitative observations. The total variation in the steepness, height, and area of basal facets described above (Fig. 12) was partitioned according to three grouping variables: bedrock lithology, site position on the mountain front, and piedmont dissection or aggradation. Site location is used as a proxy for the relative position of facets within the fault segmentation and rupture patterns defined from fault-trace mapping and scarp data. Variations in facet morphology among sites suggest statistically different sample subpopulations at four of eight sites located above the middle and terminal reaches of different geo-

metric segments and subsegments of the range-bounding fault. This tectonic effect is most pronounced for slope gradient, and to a lesser extent, facet-height data. Facet morphology varies less systematically, and over a smaller range, with changes in rock type, relative to the effects of site position. The bedrock influence is most pronounced in the slope-area data from facets composed of particularly resistant or nonresistant lithologies (see above; Fig. 12; Menges, 1988).

Topographic profiles on the full escarpment

Topographic profiles of 15 facet-spur systems extending from the base to the crest of the mountain-front escarpment were measured from USGS 7½-minute quadrangle maps. The profiles display morphologic variations that, like the basal facets, correlate with the specific position relative to geometric segmentation and fault-scarp rupture patterns of the boundary fault zone (Fig. 13). In general, the overall vertical profiles of the primary facet-spur system of the range front mimic the general morphologic patterns observed in the triangular facets at their base (see above). This correspondence is especially striking in morphologic characteristics such as relief and gradient, which appear closely linked to geometric and rupture segmentation on the range-bounding fault. For example, the lower part of the facet-spur profile above the interior of subsegment 1c (ER-FS, Fig. 13) is generally steeper, higher, and more convex-upward, and contains fewer and less pronounced benches, compared to profiles of the escarpment above adjacent subsegment or segment boundaries (CPB-FS and LSU-FS, Fig. 13). Similar types of variations are observed in the average gradients or sizes of basal facets at these three sites as well (Fig. 12; see above). These morphologic patterns extend vertically upward along facet-spur systems to at least the elevation of a prominent set of mid-escarpment benches that correlate with Pliocene basalt flows at the north end of the range front (see below, Fig. 14; benches (B) identified in Fig. 13).

Correlation of Pliocene benches

The long-term segmentation patterns of the range-front fault can be determined in another manner by measuring the deformation of a Pliocene surface fortuitously preserved along much of the mountain front. As noted previously, gently eastward-tilted 4.3-Ma basalt flows are locally preserved above a low-relief surface at San Pedro Mesa on the northern end of the range block (Fig. 14; labeled TsB in Figs. 2 and 4). The basalts and underlying surface are correlated along the range front to the south via a series of prominent topographic benches at upper- to mid-escarpment levels in most facet-spur systems (Fig. 13). Figure 4 depicts the positions of these benches relative to the base and the range crest of the mountain front. Points on all three reference surfaces in the figure have been projected westward approximately perpendicular to the average trend of the mountain front into a common vertical plane (using methods described in Appendix D of Menges, 1988).

The average elevation of the escarpment benches in this projection closely mimics the elevation patterns and gradients of the range crest, as well as the base of the mountain front. The latter approximates the trace of the zone of surface rupture along the range-bounding fault zone. The parallelism in the elevation of the TsB benches and the basal junction is striking along segments 1 and 2, and particularly on so subsegments 1c and 2a (Fig. 4). The elevation of the mid-escarpment bench slowly increases southward along segment 1, rises steeply above subsegment 1c, and then drops even more abruptly across the boundary between segments 1 and 2. The cumulative amount of post–4.3 Ma vertical displacement on the range-bounding fault zone can be directly estimated from the difference in elevations between the sub-basalt bench and generally correlative basalt flows in the shallow subsurface of the adjacent piedmont along the range front. These reconstructions suggest a marked southward increase in net postbasalt vertical displacement along segment 1 of 500 to 1,124 m, with 67 percent of this increase concentrated on subsegment 1c.

These analyses indicate a strong correlation among many diverse landforms in those characteristics that best reflect patterns of geometric and rupture segmentation along the range-front fault. For example, subsegment 1c contains scarps with the youngest morphologic age estimates; the steepest, largest, and least dissected set of basal facets; an unusually convex, unbenched, and steeply sloping escarpment profile; and the highest elevations of the TsB bench (Figs. 4, 11 through 13). The corre-

Figure 14. Aerial view of Pliocene basalt flows (in foreground) overlying a broad uplifted surface at the north end of the range crest (see Fig. 2a). These flows are correlated to the south with prominent topographic benches on facet-spur systems of the range front in distance (benches plotted in Figs. 4 and 13).

spondence among tectonic landform parameters at this and other parts of the range front strongly suggests that many of the more prominent segmentation patterns, including those developed at subsegment scales, have persisted over the 4-m.y. interval of deformation recorded by the TsB bench.

SUMMARY AND CONCLUSIONS

Morphometric analyses of fault scarps and bedrock landforms of the western mountain front of the Sangre de Cristo Mountains near Taos suggest several spatial and temporal patterns in coseismic rupture along the boundary fault zone. These complexities have potential significance for short- and long-term estimates of the paleoseismicity along this major rift-bounding fault zone. They may have applications to other tectonically active fault zones bounding large mountain fronts in the Basin and Range, Rio Grande rift, and southern Rocky Mountain provinces. Among the more important interpretations from this study are:

1. Variations in the pattern of fault scarps and the morphology of the base of the range front define several scales of geometric segmentation along the 50-km-long section of boundary fault zone studied in detail. These include four primary fault segments averaging 15 to 20 km in length, each composed of two to three 5- to 10-km-long subsegments. These segments and subsegments are defined by systematic variations in structural and geomorphic characteristics of the range-bounding fault zone. The main criteria, in decreasing order of importance, are fault-trace geometry (mainly the width and complexity of surface faulting), the position of the fault zone on the piedmont relative to the mountain front, and systematic changes in the altitude of the base of the mountain front that correspond to reentrants and salients in range front.

2. Morphologic analyses of fault scarps at 8 sites suggest that Holocene rupture is present along most of the range-bounding fault zone. The main exceptions are relatively degraded piedmont scarps of probable latest Pleistocene age at the northern ends of primary fault segments. Variations in the morphologic age estimates of the most recent single-rupture fault scarps suggest several scales of Holocene surface rupture. These include one or several temporally clustered, middle to early Holocene event(s) with an average 1.2-m vertical offset, which may have extended 30 to 50 km across several primary segments, and a smaller (0.8 m average offset) and younger late to middle Holocene event confined to a single subsegment 6 to 10 km long. These data suggest that surface rupture on the fault may be associated with two different sizes of earthquakes with estimated magnitudes of 6.7 to 7.1 and 5.8 to 6.3, respectively.

3. The morphology of bedrock landforms along the mountain front suggests that many of the segmentation patterns indicated by late Quaternary fault scarps have persisted over Pliocene-Quaternary time spans. Many of the major characteristics of basal triangular facets—including average size and slope steepness, the degree of internal dissection, the number and size of facet benches, and the thickness of colluvial mantles—correlate better with the position of the facet relative to fault subsegments or segments than other nontectonic variables such as bedrock lithology and piedmont dissection. Most of these morphologic properties characterize the overall topographic profile of the composite system of facets and spurs in the range-front escarpment. The morphologic characteristics of basal facets extend up to at least the level of a prominent set of mid-escarpment benches that correlate with 4.3-Ma basalt flows. Lateral projections of the probable Pliocene benches along the range front are remarkably parallel with the altitudes of both the range crest and the base of the mountain front. All three elevation surfaces generally rise abruptly to the south along the southernmost subsegments of fault segments.

Many geomorphic patterns of the mountain front may reflect large-scale variations in the structural geometry and rupture patterns of the range-front fault zone. For example, there is a general northward increase in the width and internal complexity of surface rupture along a given primary fault segment, as fault strands preferentially branch and multiply in that direction along most segments (Fig. 2). A similar along-strike asymmetry in the geometry of surface faulting occurred during the 1959 Hebgen Lake and 1983 Borah Peak earthquakes, and in both cases, coseismic rupture unilaterally migrated in the direction of splaying (Myers and Hamilton, 1964; Crone and Machette, 1984; Crone and others, 1987). Bruhn and others (1987) also interpret northward branching of fault splays on the Salt Lake segment of the Wasatch fault as evidence for probable unilateral propagation of rupture to the north from earthquakes centered at depth on the southern boundary of the segment.

By analogy the geometric asymmetry of the Sangre de Cristo fault may reflect unilateral northward propagation of coseismic rupture from earthquakes located near the southern ends of some

primary segments. In this model, a few boundary zones between geometric fault segments function as nonconservative barriers, in the terminology of Bruhn and others (1987). That is, these boundaries are mechanically strong, with high fracture toughness, and thus are especially resistant to rupture propagation. The best candidates for nonconservative barriers on the Sangre de Cristo fault zone occur near the southern terminations of fault segments marked by major discontinuities in fault pattern and range-front morphology (Figs. 2 and 4). It is proposed that most earthquakes capable of generating surface rupture would initiate at depth on these segment boundaries and propagate northward along the fault zone. Fault-scarp analysis, however, suggests that at least one large rupture event may have extended across the boundaries of some geometric segments and most subsegments (see above; Figs. 2 and 11). These segmentation boundaries did not effectively inhibit rupture propagation, and thus, they apparently behaved more as conservative boundaries (Bruhn and others, 1987) during at least this type of large earthquake.

High-angle left-oblique striations on slickensides plunge steeply to the southwest at several exposures of the range-front fault zone (Menges, unpublished data). The oblique component of slip is consistent with, but does not require, the model of unilateral propagation of earthquakes proposed above. Fault slip and rupture propagation directions are not directly comparable structural elements. Seismic and geodetic observations indicate, however, that rupture during the 1983 Borah Peak earthquake in Idaho propagated northward along the range-bounding Lost River zone in a direction generally similar to left-oblique surface displacements measured on fault scarps (Crone and Machette, 1984; Crone and others, 1987; Bruhn and others, 1987).

The lateral changes in fault-segment geometry also correlate well with along-strike variations in net post–4.3 Ma displacements estimated from the relative elevations of the TsB bench on the mountain front (Figs. 2 and 4). Both the amounts of cumulative offset and the average displacement rates of the TsB increase southward, correlative with a narrowing and decrease in geometric complexity of the fault zone, along the two northern fault segments. For example, the amount and rate of post-Pliocene vertical displacements increase from 500 to 1,124 m and 115 to 261 m/m.y. to the south along segment 1. These displacement transitions correspond to position relative to geometric and/or rupture subsegments of the range-front fault. There is only a gradual southward increase in the lateral offset of the TsB bench along the northern subsegments of any primary segment; however, variations in the geometry of the basal fault zone tend to produce changes in the morphology of adjacent bedrock facets (Figs. 2, 4, and 12). Estimated displacements typically increase abruptly to maximum values along the south-central part of the southernmost subsegment of the fault segment. Perhaps this long-term differential offset along fault segments accumulates in part from more frequent ruptures on the southern subsegments, similar to the small, isolated, late Holocene event inferred for subsegment 1c.

The vertical offset of the TsB basalt flows and benches suggests cumulative rates of post-Pliocene displacements of 115 to 261 m/m.y. on the northern part of the range-front fault. These estimates agree remarkably well with the post-Miocene uplift rates of 210 m/m.y. proposed for this part of the Sangre de Cristo Mountains by Kelley and Duncan (1986) from fission-track dating of Tertiary plutons in the range block. These rates are sufficient to generate the total relief of this part of the Sangre de Cristo Mountains since middle to late Miocene time (i.e., post–15 to 10 Ma). However, several features of the Pliocene basalts and related benches, including the presence of a low-relief erosional surface on the range block beneath the Pliocene basalt flows, and the marked discontinuity in range-front morphology associated with the mid-escarpment bench (see above), suggest that they may correlate with, or slightly pre-date, a significant lull and/or shift in fault pattern along this rift boundary.

There are also marked contrasts in the vertical displacement rates estimated from late Quaternary fault scarps and the Pliocene sub-basalt bench. Displacements of geomorphic surfaces on fault scarps along this part of the range-bounding fault suggest late Quaternary slip rates of 0.03 to 0.06 mm/yr that are 2 to 8 times lower than equivalent-unit estimates of the TsB displacement rates (0.15 to 0.25 mm/yr). The magnitude of this difference cannot easily be explained simply by uncertainties in the age calibration used to estimate the rates. It is not clear whether the apparent rate decrease reflects a real decline in tectonic activity or the large difference in the measured time intervals of the two rates (Gardner and others, 1987). The contrast in rates is probably not strictly an artifact of the sampling interval, however, as the application of the scaling function proposed by Gardner and others

(1987) to the slip rate data on the Sangre de Cristo fault only increases the magnitude of the rate decline by a factor of 4 to 6. It is possible the lower, late Pleistocene slip rates record a short-term lull in a much longer seismic cycle on the fault that is more accurately averaged by the post-Pliocene displacement rate (e.g., Pierce, 1986; Wallace, 1987). Alternatively, the late Quaternary drop in faulting rates may signal a true waning of deformation in this part of the Rio Grande rift, perhaps toward the end of a 4- to 5-m.y. interval of Pliocene-Quaternary rift extension.

ACKNOWLEDGMENTS

I would like to acknowledge partial financial support for dissertation research from the following funding sources: a Challenge Scholarship grant from the Office of Graduate Studies at the University of New Mexico; funds provided by the New Mexico Bureau of Mines and Mineral Resources; the 1986 New Mexico Geological Society Fellowship; and a 1986 Mackin grant and general grant-in-aid from the Geological Society of America. I would like to thank my dissertation advisor, S. G. Wells, and other committee members (L. McFadden, J. Callender, J. Hawley, and C. Mawer) for helpful comments and review of this part of my dissertation. I also thank T. Bullard, P. Drake, J. Wesling, and Y. Enzel for field assistance and helpful discussions of fault scarp data. Thorough reviews by M. Machette, P. Knuepfer, J. Turko, and D. Meeuwig greatly improved the original manuscript. However, I assume ultimate responsibility for all data analyses and interpretations in this chapter.

REFERENCES CITED

Andrews, D. J., and Hanks, T. C., 1985, Scarp degraded by linear diffusion; Inverse solution for age: Journal of Geophysical Research, v. 90, no. B12, p. 10193–10208.

Birkeland, P. W., 1984, Soils and geomorphology: New York and Oxford, Oxford University Press, 372 p.

Bruhn, R. L., Gibler, P. R., and Parry, W. T., 1987, Rupture characteristics of normal faults; An example from the Wasatch fault zone, *in* Coward, M. P., Dewey, J. F., and Hancock, P. L., eds., Continental extensional tectonics: Geological Society of London Special Publication 28, p. 337–353.

Bucknam, R. C., and Anderson, R. E., 1979, Estimation of fault-scarp ages from a scarp-height–slope-angle relationship: Geology, v. 7, p. 11–14.

Bull, W. B., 1984, Tectonic geomorphology: Journal of Geological Education, v. 32, p. 310–324.

Bull, W. B., and McFadden, L. D., 1977, Tectonic geomorphology north and south of the Garlock fault, California, *in* Doehring, D. D., ed., Geomorphology in arid regions: Proceedings 8th Annual Geomorphology Symposium: Binghamton, State University of New York, p. 115–138.

Colman, S. M., and Pierce, K. L., 1981, Weathering rinds on andesitic and basaltic stones as a Quaternary age indicator, western United States: U.S. Geological Survey Professional Paper 1210, 56 p.

Colman, S. M., and Watson, K., 1983, Ages estimated from a diffusion equation model for scarp degradation: Science, v. 221, p. 263–265.

Colman, S. M., McCalpin, J. P., Ostenaa, D. A., and Kirkham, R. M., 1985, Map showing upper Cenozoic rocks and deposits and Quaternary faults, Rio Grande rift, south-central Colorado: U.S. Geological Survey Miscellaneous Investigations Map I-1594, scale 1:125,000.

Crone, A. J., and Machette, M. N., 1984, Surface faulting accompanying the Borah Peak earthquake, central Idaho: Geology, v. 12, p. 664–667.

Crone, A. J., and 6 others, 1987, Surface faulting accompanying the Borah Peak earthquake and segmentation of the Lost River fault, central Idaho: Bulletin of the Seismological Society of America, v. 77, no. 3, p. 73–770.

Davis, J. C., 1986, Statistics and data analysis in geology, 2nd ed.: New York, John Wiley and Sons, 646 p.

Dethier, D. P., Harrington, C. D., and Aldrich, M. J., 1988, Late Cenozoic rates of erosion in the western Espanola Basin, New Mexico; Evidence from geologic dating of erosion surfaces: Geological Society of America Bulletin, v. 100, p. 928–937.

Dungan, M. A., and 7 others, 1984, Volcanic and sedimentary stratigraphy of the Rio Grande gorge and the late Cenozoic geologic evolution of the southern San Luis Valley, *in* Baldridge, W. S., Dickerson, P. A., Riecker, R. E., and Zidek, J., eds., 35th Annual New Mexico Geological Society Field Conference Guidebook: New Mexico Geological Society, p. 157–170.

Gardner, T. W., Jorgensen, D. W., Shuman, C., and Lemieux, C. R., 1987, Geomorphic and tectonic process rates; Effects of measured time interval: Geology, v. 15, p. 259–261.

Gile, L. H., Peterson, F., and Grossman, R., 1966, Morphological and genetic sequence of carbonate accumulation in desert soils: Soil Science, v. 101, p. 347–360.

Hacker, L., and Carleton, J. W., 1976, Soil survey of Taos County and parts of Rio Arriba and Mora Counties, New Mexico: U.S. Department of Agriculture, Soil Conservation Service and Forest Service, and U.S. Department of the Interior, Bureau of Indian Affairs and Bureau of Land Management, 220 p.

Hanks, T. C., and Kanamori, H., 1979, A moment magnitude scale: Journal of Geophysical Research, v. 84, p. 2348–2350.

Hanks, T. C., Bucknam, R. C., Lajoie, K. R., and Wallace, R. E., 1984, Modification of wave-cut and faulting-controlled landforms: Journal of Geophysical Research, v. 89, no. B7, p. 5771–5790.

Hayes, W. L., 1988, Statistics, 4th ed.: New York, Holt, Rinehart, and Winston, 1029 p.

Karas, P. A., 1987, Quaternary alluvial sequence of the upper Pecos River and a tributary, Glorietta Creek, north-central New Mexico, *in* Menges, C. M., Enzel, Y., and Harrison, B., eds., Field trip guidebook: Rocky Mountain Cell Friends of the Pleistocene, p. 51–57.

Keller, G. R., Cordell, L., Davis, G. H., Peeples, V. J., and White, G., 1984, A geophysical study of the San Luis Basin *in* Baldridge, W. S., Dickerson, P. W., Riecker, R. E., and Zidek, J., eds., 35th Annual New Mexico Geological Society Field Conference Guidebook: New Mexico Geological Society, p. 51–57.

Kelley, S. A., and Duncan, I. J., 1986, Late Cretaceous to middle Tertiary tectonic history of the northern Rio Grande rift, New Mexico: Journal of Geophysical Research, v. 91, no. B6, p. 6246–6262.

Kelson, K. I., 1986, Long-term tributary adjustments to base-level lowering, northern Rio Grande rift, New Mexico [M.S. thesis]: Albuquerque, University of New Mexico, 211 p.

Kelson, K. I., and Wells, S. G., 1987, Present-day fluvial hydrology and long-term tributary adjustments, northern New Mexico, *in* Menges, C. M., Enzel, Y., and Harrison, B., eds., Fieldtrip guidebook: Rocky Mountain Cell Friends of the Pleistocene, p. 95–109.

Knuepfer, P.L.K., and Turko, J. M., 1987, Limits to distinguishing ruptures on adjacent fault segments from scarp degradation modeling: Geological Society of America Abstracts with Programs, v. 19, p. 730.

Lambert, P. W., 1966, Notes on the late Cenozoic geology of the Taos–Questa area, New Mexico, *in* Northrop, S. A., and Read, C. B., eds., 17th New Mexico Geological Society Field Conference Guidebook: New Mexico Geological Society, p. 43–50.

Lipman, P. W., and Mehnert, H. H., 1979, The Taos Plateau volcanic field, northern Rio Grande rift, New Mexico, *in* Riecker, R. E., ed., Rio Grande rift; Tectonics and magmatism: American Geophysical Union, p. 289–311.

Lipman, P. W., Mehnert, H. H., and Naeser, C. W., 1986, Evolution of the Latir volcanic field, northern New Mexico, and its relation to the Rio Grande rift, as indicated by potassium-argon and fission-track dating: Journal of Geophysical Research, v. 91, no. B6, p. 6329–6345.

Machette, M. N., 1986, History of Quaternary offset and paleoseismicity along the La Jencia fault, central Rio Grande rift, New Mexico: Bulletin of the Seismological Society of America, v. 76, no. 1, p. 259–272.

——, 1987, Changes in long-term versus short-term slip rates in an extensional environment, *in* Crone, A. J., and Omdahl, E. M., eds., Proceedings of Conference 39; Directions in Paleoseismology: U.S. Geological Survey Open-File Report 87-673, p. 228–238.

Machette, M. N., and Personius, S. F., 1984, Map of Quaternary and Pliocene faults in the eastern part of the Aztec 1° by 2° Quadrangle and the western part of the Raton 1° by 2° Quadrangle, northern New Mexico: U.S. Geological Survey Miscellaneous Field Studies Map MF-1465-B, scale 1:250,000.

Maclean, A. G., 1985, Quaternary segmentation of the Wasatch fault zone, Utah, as studied by morphometric discriminant analyses [M.S. thesis]: Miami, Ohio University, 200 p.

Mayer, L., 1984, Dating Quaternary fault scarps formed in alluvium using morphologic parameters: Quaternary Research, v. 22, p. 300–313.

——, 1986, Tectonic geomorphology of escarpments and mountain fronts, *in* National Research Council, Active tectonics; Studies in geophysics: Washington, D.C., National Academy Press, p. 125–135.

Mayer, L., and Maclean, A., 1986, Tectonic geomorphology of the Wasatch Front, Utah, using morphologic discriminant analysis; Preliminary implica-

tions for Quaternary segmentation of the Wasatch fault zone: Geological Society of America, Abstracts with Programs, v. 18, p. 155.

McCalpin, J. P., 1982, Quaternary geology and neotectonics of the west flank of the northern Sangre de Cristo Mountains, south-central Colorado: Golden, Colorado School of Mines Quarterly, v. 77, no. 3, 97 p.

Menges, C. M., 1987a, The form and evolution of bedrock facet hillslopes along the tectonically active mountain front of the western Sangre de Cristo Mountains, northern New Mexico: Geological Society of America, Abstracts with Programs, v. 19, p. 770.

——, 1987b, Temporal and spatial segmentation of Pliocene–Quaternary fault rupture along the western Sangre de Cristo mountain front, northern New Mexico, *in* Crone, A. J., and Omdahl, E. M., eds., Proceedings of Conference 39; Directions in Paleoseismology: U.S. Geological Society Open-File Report 87-673, p. 203–222.

——, 1988, The tectonic geomorphology of mountain-front landforms in the northern Rio Grande rift near Taos, New Mexico [Ph.D. thesis]: Albuquerque, University of New Mexico, 339 p.

Menges, C. M., and Wells, S. G., 1987, Late Quaternary fault scarps, mountain front landforms, and Plio-Quaternary rupture segmentation along a range-front normal fault zone, Sangre de Cristo Mountains, New Mexico: Geological Society of America, Abstracts with Programs, v. 19, p. 770–771.

Myers, W. B., and Hamilton, W., 1964, Deformation accompanying the Hebgen Lake earthquake of August 17, 1959: U.S. Geological Survey Professional Paper 435, p. 39–98.

Nash, D. B., 1980, Morphologic dating of the degraded normal fault scarps: Journal of Geology, v. 89, p. 353–360.

——, 1984, Morphologic dating of fluvial terrace scarps and fault scarps near West Yellowstone, Montana: Geological Society of America Bulletin, v. 95, p. 1413–1424.

——, 1986, Morphologic dating and modeling degradation of fault scarps, *in* National Research Council, Active tectonics; Studies in Geophysics: Washington, D.C., National Academy Press, p. 181–194.

——, 1987, SLOPEAGE program, v. 2.1; Fenneman-Rich Geomorphic Laboratories: Cincinnati, Ohio, University of Cincinnati Department of Geology.

New Mexico Geological Society, 1982, New Mexico highway geologic map: New Mexico Geological Society in cooperation with New Mexico Bureau of Mines and Mineral Resources, scale 1:1,000,000.

Pearthree, P. A., and Calvo, S. S., 1987, The Santa Rita fault scarp; Evidence from large-magnitude earthquakes with very long recurrence intervals in the Basin and Range Province of southeastern Arizona: Bulletin of the Seismological Society of America, v. 77, p. 97–116.

Pearthree, P. A., Menges, C. M., and Mayer, L., 1983, Distribution, recurrence, and possible tectonic significance of late Quaternary faulting in Arizona: Arizona Bureau of Geology and Mineral Technology Open-File Report 83-23, 50 p.

Pearthree, P. A., Demsey, K. A., Fonseca, J., and Hecker, S., 1988, An evaluation of morphologic analysis of pluvial shoreline scarps and young fault scarps in central Nevada: Geological Society of America Abstracts with Programs, v. 20, p. 220–221.

Personius, S. F., and Machette, M. N., 1984, Quaternary and Pliocene faulting in the Taos Plateau region, northern New Mexico, *in* Baldridge, W. S., Dickerson, P. W., Riecker, R. E., and Zidek, J., eds., 35th Annual New Mexico Geological Society Field Conference Guidebook: New Mexico Geological Society, p. 83–90.

Pierce, K. L., 1986, Dating methods, *in* National Research Council, Active tectonics; Studies in Geophysics: Washington, D.C., National Academy Press, p. 195–214.

Pierce, K. L., and Colman, S. M., 1986, Effect of height and orientation (microclimate) on geomorphic degradation rates and processes, late-glacial terrace scarps in central Idaho: Geological Society of America Bulletin, v. 97, p. 869–885.

Reed, J. C., Jr., 1984, Proterozoic rocks of the Taos Range, Sangre de Cristo Mountains, New Mexico, *in* Baldridge, W. S., Dickerson, P. W., Riecker, R. E., and Zidek, J., eds., 35th New Mexico Geological Society Field Conference Guidebook: New Mexico Geological Society, p. 179–185.

Reed, J. C., Lipman, P. W., and Robertson, J. E., 1983, Geologic map of the Latir Peak and Wheeler Peak Wilderness and Columbine-Hondo Wilderness Study Area, Taos County, New Mexico: U.S. Geological Survey Miscellaneous Field Studies Map MF-1570-B, scale 1:50,000.

Schwartz, D. P., and Coppersmith, K. J., 1984, Fault behavior and characteristic earthquakes; Examples from the Wasatch and San Andreas fault zones: Journal of Geophysical Research, v. 89, no. B7, p. 5681–5698.

——, 1986, Seismic hazards; New trends in analysis using geologic data, *in* National Research Council, Active tectonics; Studies in geophysics: Washington, D.C., National Academy Press, p. 215–230.

Scott, W. E., Pierce, K. L., and Hait, N. H., Jr., 1985, Quaternary tectonic setting of the Borah Peak earthquake, central Idaho: Bulletin of the Seismological Society of America, v. 75, p. 1053–1066.

Slemmons, D. B., 1982, Determination of design earthquake magnitudes for microzonation, *in* Proceedings of the 3rd International Earthquake Microzonation Conference: v. 1, p. 119–130.

Summers, W. K., and Hargis, L. L., 1984, Hydrologic cross section through Sunshine Valley, Taos County, New Mexico, *in* Baldridge, W. S., Dickerson, P. W., Riecker, R. E., and Zidek, J., eds., 35th New Mexico Geological Society Field Conference Guidebook: New Mexico Geological Society, p. 245–248.

Upson, J. E., 1939, Physiographic subdivisions of the San Luis Valley, southern Colorado: Journal of Geology, v. 47, p. 721–736.

Wallace, R. E., 1977, Profiles and ages of fault scarps, north-central Nevada: Geological Society of America Bulletin, v. 88, p. 1267–1281.

——, 1978, Geometry and rates of change of fault-generated range fronts, north-central Nevada: U.S. Geological Survey Journal of Research, v. 6, no. 5, p. 637–650.

——, 1984, Patterns and timing of late Quaternary faulting in the Great Basin Province and relation to some regional tectonic features: Journal of Geophysical Research, v. 89, no. B7, p. 5763–5769.

——, 1987, Grouping and migration of surface faulting and variations in slip rates on faults in the Great Basin Province: Bulletin of the Seismological Society of America, v. 77, no. 3, p. 868–876.

Wesling, J. R., 1987, Glacial chronology of Winsor Creek drainage basin, Sangre de Cristo Mountains, New Mexico, *in* Menges, C. M., Enzel, Y., and Harrison, B., eds., Fieldtrip guidebook: Rocky Mountain Cell Friends of the Pleistocene, p. 177–190a.

Wesling, J. R., and McFadden, L. D., 1986, Pleistocene and Holocene glacial chronology for the glacial deposits in the southernmost Sangre de Cristo Mountains, New Mexico: Geological Society of America, Abstracts with Programs, v. 18, p. 422.

Wheeler, R. L., and Krystinik, K. B., 1987, Persistent and nonpersistent segmentation of the Wasatch fault zone, Utah: Geological Society of America, Abstracts with Programs, v. 19, p. 342.

Wilkinson, L., 1988, SYSTAT; The system for statistics, version 4 manual: Evanston, Illinois, SYSTAT, Inc., 808 p.

Winograd, I. J., 1959, Ground-water conditions and geology of Sunshine Valley and western Taos County, New Mexico: New Mexico State Engineer Technical Report 12, 70 p.

——, 1985, Commentary on hydrologic cross section through Sunshine Valley, Taos County, New Mexico: New Mexico Geology, v. 7, p. 54–55.

MANUSCRIPT ACCEPTED BY THE SOCIETY AUGUST 18, 1989

Index

[Italic page numbers indicate major references]

Typeset by WESType Publishing Services, Inc., Boulder, Colorado
Printed in U.S.A. by Malloy Lithographing, Inc., Ann Arbor, Michigan